Life is not a vessel to be drained, but a cup to be filled

Ancient Chinese Proverb

CONTENTS

CHAPTER XV

LEISURE-TIME PURSUITS IN THE SCANDINAVIAN COUNTRIES

INTRODUCTION

When B. S. Rowntree made his second social survey of York, the result of which was published in his book *Poverty and Progress*, he was struck by the inadequacy of the means provided for the satisfactory recreation of the citizens. As he had no reason to suppose that the facilities for recreation provided in York differed widely from those provided in other British cities, making due allowance for differences in their size, he thought it would be interesting to make a detailed survey of the facilities that would be needed in York to make ample provision for the satisfactory recreation of the inhabitants of that city, and it was on this restricted task that we embarked at the beginning of 1947. Early in our work, however, we realized that a much larger task was implicit in the seemingly simple one that we had set ourselves, for if the word recreation is taken in its proper sense as the activities whereby men and women re-create themselves, not only in body but also in mind and spirit, the consideration of what facilities are necessary for adequate recreation involves a study of the whole question of leisure.

It is not possible to ascertain what facilities should be provided to enable people to use their leisure happily and wisely, without first finding out just how they spend their leisure now, and why they spend it as they do. The task of finding out why people choose some activities and reject others, involves no less than a study of their philosophy of life, as well as an examination of the principal factors that affect behaviour and form character.

We found in fact that we had inadvertently embarked upon a study of the cultural and spiritual life of the nation, meaning by cultural all that has to do with education and refinement, and using the word spiritual in a broad sense to denote the higher qualities that distinguish great nations and great individuals within a nation. For such a study, upon which we should not have been so presumptuous as to embark intentionally, but from which we did not think it right to withdraw having come upon it by chance, the city of York was clearly too restricted an area. Our investigations and enquiries have accordingly been made in various parts of England and Wales, mainly in the great cities but where necessary also in small towns and in rural areas.

We may be open to the charge that we have given undue emphasis to town life. It must, however, be remembered that the vast majority of the population live under urban conditions, and, moreover, transport facilities have developed so greatly in recent years that many rural dwellers take advantage of recreational and educational facilities provided in adjacent towns. The proportion of the population who are living in regions so remote that they cannot do so is extremely small.

In making our study of contemporary life in England and Wales, we concluded that, besides the usual and obvious methods of approaching the subject, we needed some means of letting a substantial number of men and women, of all ages and social classes, speak for themselves, in the hope that, as they told their individual stories, we should build up a living picture of English life and leisure. For such a purpose as we had in mind, formal interviewing, or the use of questionnaires, would have been useless, for many of the matters about which we desired information are intensely personal, and in any case we were interested more in behaviour than in such opinions as could be elicited by answers to short, set questions. We therefore decided to build up our picture of what people are like by a system of indirect interviewing. This method consists of making the acquaintance of an individual—the excuses for doing so are immaterial—and developing the acquaintance until his or her confidence is gained and information required can be obtained in ordinary conversation, without the person concerned ever knowing that there has been an interview or that any specific information was being sought. Such a method is laborious but effective.

The bulk of the interviewing was undertaken by G. R. Lavers, but to supplement his work, and as a check on any personal bias that might be inherent in it, a substantial number of case histories were obtained for us by Professor F. Zweig, Miss Susan Garth (a free-lance journalist), Miss M. E. Walker (in Leeds) and Miss R. Raymond (in London). In addition the case histories of 12 girls who had been in a Borstal Institution were supplied to us with the permission of the Prison Commissioners, of course without their names being made known to us. Altogether we have been able to examine the case histories of 975 persons who have revealed their philosophies of life without realizing that they were doing so. Two groups of these case histories, carefully selected as being typical of the whole, are reproduced in the next chapter, 20 of them being those of persons under the age of 20 years, and 200 of all age groups above 20.

We do not of course claim that the number of persons interviewed is sufficiently large to justify us in making any statistical analysis of the information supplied. It will, however, be seen that the 220 case histories reproduced cover most sections of the community, including those often described as the upper, middle and working-classes. Although some of them were gathered in and around London, others were obtained in Plymouth, Eastbourne, Bristol, Cardiff, Sheffield, Birmingham, Leeds, Manchester, Carlisle and Newcastle, as well as some in certain small towns and rural areas that must, for obvious reasons, remain anonymous. In our view, if a substantial number of these case histories are read together, they give a reasonably accurate general impression of the philosophy of life of a majority of the people dwelling in England and Wales.

In addition to the information gathered in the way outlined above, we have made various small-scale enquiries among special groups of persons to obtain in each case an answer to some particular question. For example, when dealing with football pools in the course of our chapter on gambling, we ascertained from 498 participants in the pools how long they took to fill in their coupons. The results of these special enquiries will be found in the appropriate chapters.

As an important part of our task, we considered it neces
to choose a specimen town and to find out in
facilities are actually provided there for the use of
what use is made of them. High Wycombe, with a

of rather more than 40,000, was selected as suitable for our survey, a detailed report of which is given in Chapter XIV.

Finally, with the double object of obtaining information with which the state of affairs in England could be compared, and of ascertaining whether there were particular provisions for the use of leisure which could with advantage be copied in England, we decided to make a general survey of the use of leisure in Denmark, Norway, Sweden and Finland. The survey was made by B. S. Rowntree, who, for the purpose, visited the four countries concerned. He was accompanied by Christian Gierloff, a distinguished Norwegian economist and writer, well known in all four countries, who had arranged in advance for him to meet groups of people having intimate knowledge of the different subjects being investigated. Without this help the survey would not have been practicable in the time available. B. S. Rowntree's report on this investigation is given in Chapter XV.

At every stage of our investigations, rather than rely upon our own knowledge and understanding, we have sought the guidance of persons whose experience enabled them to speak with authority. In this way we have, sometimes formally and sometimes informally, had the advice and help of some 200 persons in widely differing walks of life, some of them eminent, some of them comparatively unknown, but all of them competent to give wise advice on some or other of the many aspects of human life which we have studied.

We have, of course, approached every facet of our subject with carefully objective minds, and our widely different personal backgrounds have helped to suppress our individual enthusiasms and prejudices, for we have been a check each upon the other.

One particular warning must be given at this point. In dealing with the problems of leisure and of behaviour, it is almost inevitable that we should concentrate on those matters which are of active contemporary interest and concern, and often means upon matters about which large sections of the either anxious or enthusiastic. Nations, like , often tend to dwell on causes of irritation and not essings, for the latter are usually taken for granted.

In England we have a great many of these unsensational blessings, won by sacrifice and effort in the past and maintained by good sense, and as a consequence of our reasonably civilized outlook. It is worth considering some of them briefly.

Few countries have such a high respect for the law, so that broadly speaking, no citizen need fear oppression, and the police go unarmed. Special enquiries have convinced us that there is virtually no corruption in English public and business life. Our law courts, those presided over by unpaid magistrates no less than the High Court itself, maintain an unsullied reputation for incorruptibility. We have freedom of speech, freedom of worship, and—as it is not the case to-day in a great many countries—freedom of association for legitimate ends.

The British rationing system has been a success and from its introduction in 1939 scarce commodities have been fairly shared without regard to wealth or birth. We were able to consult the Chief Commissioner of Metropolitan Police, for whose help we are indebted in various directions, on the subject of the Black Market, and both he and one of his senior colleagues informed us that it is of no real significance.

In connection with these "unsensational blessings" we must also remember the great tradition of voluntary work in Britain. Immediately one thinks of the magistrates, the St. John Ambulance, the Territorial Army and the voluntary workers engaged in Youth Clubs, Red Cross, the Women's Voluntary Service and countless other bodies. We met one warrant officer of the Metropolitan Police who gives five evenings a week to youth work in a poor area, and, admirable as his unselfishness is, he is only one of a vast army of voluntary workers springing from all sections of the community, and devoted to every variety of cause.

These matters, and many others like them, all portray and affect the spiritual state of the nation, and we have emphasized them here because, ordinarily, they have no "news value." Yet they are the highly satisfactory background which must be borne in mind when reading of our detailed investigations into other and sometimes less satisfactory matters.

One further point must be dealt with here. Besides the satisfactory but unsensational attributes that make up the background of English life, we have also omitted to deal with certain highly unsatisfactory tendencies, some of which are attracting public attention at the present time, because on examination their importance proves to be largely illusory, for they affect such a very small proportion of people. For example, the rise of the prison population to a point where in some prisons three men have to be incarcerated in a cell designed for one, would seem to be startling evidence of the growth of crime, but the matter is seen in better perspective when it is stated that the 20,000 persons in gaol represent less than ·05 per cent of the population. To deal in this book with matters that (however unsatisfactory in themselves) affect only such small numbers of people, would have meant enlarging to an unmanageable size a book that is already a long one. Therefore we have concerned ourselves only with those matters that are, in our judgment, of first-class importance by virtue of the number of persons whom they affect, and are consequently national issues influencing the cultural and spiritual state of the people.

CHAPTER I

SECTION I—THE CASE HISTORIES OF 200 PERSONS OVER THE AGE OF TWENTY

1

Mr. L. is a clerk in a stockbroker's office. He lives on the outskirts of a large town and travels up every day, using the last of the workmen's trains because it is cheaper than a season ticket. He is married with two children, both at his local grammar school. He saves every penny he can because he wants to give his children a good start in life. He says, 'I can't do as much for them as I'd like to, but at any rate I can see that they're put in a better position than I've ever had. If they make good, that's all the reward I want. I don't expect their thanks. It's only my duty." Mr. L. is a Methodist and attends chapel regularly. He also takes a full part in weekday activities organized by the chapel. His hobby is philately and his collection represents the major part of his savings. He says he is not afraid of inflation nor of a capital levy.

Mr. L. neither drinks nor smokes—the first on principle, the second for economy. He says he has a first-rate wife who never wastes a halfpenny and he is proud of the fact that he has never, before or after marriage, even kissed another woman. He has never been interested in games but likes gardening although he is not strong enough to do much heavy work such as digging. He has never taken part in any gambling transaction, all of which—even charity sweepstakes—he regards as sinful. He occasionally takes his wife to a theatre but regards cinemas as a waste of money.

2

Mr. R. is a retired colliery manager, aged about 70 and a bachelor. He is violently anti-socialist and ascribes all the current economic difficulties to the decrease in private enterprise. He considers that coal miners have been fairly or even generously treated in the last two generations and complains bitterly of their failure of duty in declining to send their sons into the pits.

Mr. R. likes to attend church services in the major cathedrals, but adds, "Now don't make the mistake of thinking I'm religious. I've none of that about me. I like the oratory and the music." He ascribes the failing power of the churches to the fact that "the majority of the clergy nowadays aren't gentlemen; they aren't even educated; it's all these theological colleges instead of them having to go to Oxford or Cambridge."

Although officially in retirement, Mr. R. does a good deal of "public work," of which he did not specify the nature but which concerns coal or shipping, or both. He has no time for purely personal amusement such as the theatre or cinema, but still enjoys an occasional round of golf.

He smokes and drinks in strict moderation and only bets on the major horse races. In his youth and middle age he was sexually promiscuous but he "lost interest in that sort of thing years ago. Leave it to the young fellows now."

3

Miss T. has a clerical job in a factory. Aged about 25. Trying to persuade a young artisan to marry her. It would in fact be a good match. But he wants to go to bed with her before an engagement and she fears, very reasonably, that if he does he will never come to the point. No moral issue is involved as they are both promiscuous, although coy in regard to each other.

Miss T. is not a churchgoer although she has no objection in principle. She merely says, "It's kids' stuff, but if people are so dumb as to swallow it, it's O.K. by me."

She helps keep her parents and gives a few shillings each week to a widowed sister. Fond of children.

Likes the cinema but cannot afford to go more than once a week. Likes smoking and a few drinks but cannot afford either unless her fiancé pays.

Spends 1s. od. per week on a football coupon.

4

Mr. P. is an ex-naval petty officer. Aged about 32 or 33, a bachelor. His two interests are games and women—cricket in summer, football in winter, and copulation all the year round.

He is a friendly man but has a nasty temper when roused

He gambles on football and horses, and quite enjoys an occasional evening at the greyhound races. Does not care much for the cinema but goes once or twice a month. He goes more often to music halls.

Reads the *Daily Mirror* and *News of the World*, and often reads an evening paper, but does not read books.

Surprisingly well informed about current events because he listens regularly to the news bulletin on the radio.

Gambles regularly but for small sums. Drinks in moderation and smokes a pipe.

A very self-centred man who never does anything for anybody's benefit but his own.

Not a churchgoer.

5

Mrs. Z. is the wife of a long-distance lorry driver. Aged about 40, with four sons, 19–10. Is a thin and rather acid woman with a tongue capable of lashing her husband, and a helpless wounded look (pure histrionics) capable of making him so uncomfortable that he would never look at another woman. She is very interested in money; she extracts from her husband all she can get, but also has a profitable second-hand clothes business as a side line. She is also "able to get a bit of cloth without coupons—real export quality." In fact she is a low-grade black marketeer.

She is above suspicion sexually, being of an ill-favoured and acid appearance.

She never gambles, on the grounds that she would not do so unless she knew enough to be a bookmaker.

A regular chapel-goer.

Her amusements are the cinema and gossiping with neighbours. She smokes and drinks in strict moderation.

6

Miss U. aged 21 is the younger of two daughters of an upper middle-class couple living just outside a large town. They have a medium-sized house, in about half-an-acre of garden, with a tennis court. Miss U. does not work and her whole life is devoted to the gaieties of her class—tennis parties, picnics, moonlight picnics, treasure hunts, races, theatres, cinemas, flirtations, dances and so on.

She is an innocent but quite empty-headed person. Reads one or two novels a year, the *Daily Mail*, *Women's Journal*, *Tatler*, and the headlines and film reviews of the *Sunday Times*.

She likes gossip about the young people of her class and says she is in love with a marvellous young man (who also lives on his parents' income without working), who has a fast car which he drives at night with one hand, while the other arm is around her!

She is "not interested" in any form of social or voluntary work although her mother does a good deal of it. She says "I don't see why I should bother about the working class, they're hopeless."

She goes regularly to church.

7

Mr. X. aged 28, is a salesman who hawks a patent electrical device from house to house in well-to-do neighbourhoods. He has a small salary and comission, and to do well he has to average one sale a day. As he visits sixteen or eighteen houses a day, and seldom averages more than four sales a week, it is understandable that he is depressed.

His salesman's manner is effusive and respectful but in private he is embittered and unhappy. He went straight from a minor public school in 1939 into the Army, stayed on in the Control Commission, and was finally returned to civilian life in 1948 with no qualifications of any kind.

He says he is fed up with religion, and says any religious person who had been through 1944 to 1948 in Germany would either have gone mad or cursed God.

He does a football coupon every week but has no real hope of winning although he says he clings on to the hope. Does not bet on horses or dogs.

He has been sexually promiscuous since 1940. Sees no prospect of being able to afford to marry even if he found the right girl.

Says it's all very well for the moralists to talk about what chaps like him ought to do and believe, but what chance has he had? "From school right into a bloody war that wasn't my making. Frightened to death half the time, so bored the other half that there was nothing to do but go to bed with a pretty girl. Then back to civvy street, peddling these blank machines and walking ten miles a day for fat old women to shut their doors in my face."

8

Miss M. aged about 21, comes from a poor home where a large family lives in overcrowded conditions with the father in and out of gaol. Most of Miss M's. earnings as a shop girl go towards keeping the home, such as it is, together. She is not resentful of this, only sorry that she cannot have the things she wants—mostly clothes.

Not unnaturally she is a little grubby—bites her nails instead of cutting them—has rather greasy hair and in general could do with a bath. But she is cheerful and friendly.

Is promiscuous and has been from the age of 15.

Knows nothing of religion. She might just as well be an African savage as far as knowledge of Christianity is concerned. Jesus is exactly as real to her as Guy Fawkes—she heard confusedly about both at school. She has never been inside a church, and parsons in dog-collars are just men wearing the uniform of a trade she happens not to know anything about.

A keen cinema-goer. Likes a few glasses of beer, and would be a chain smoker if she could afford it.

Doesn't gamble herself because she is fed up with "Dad" losing his money. Thinks one mug in the family is enough.

9

Mrs. W. is distrustful of her fellow humans for most of them look down on her and show it. She might be any age between 40 and 55, but says she is 39. She is enormously fat, to an extent that defies description, and though she lives in a large, well-fitted council house in a large town, she is a complete slattern. She goes about with her clothes unfastened, bare feet thrust into muddy carpet slippers, long black hair uncombed, dirty hands and dirty face. Two men live with her, to one of whom she is married, and her children are divided between them. She is now pregnant again and it is astonishing that either of the men—both decent working-class types—could copulate with such a monstrous creature.

Mrs. W. herself had her first child at the age of 17—out of wedlock. The child, a girl, in turn had her first child at the age of 17—out of wedlock. Mrs. W. says rather helplessly that she supposes any day now the second daughter, will probably come home and say she is "in trouble."

Because the neighbours openly scowl at Mrs. W. ("She lets down the neighbourhood") she seldom goes out except for shopping. She is friendly once she gets over her suspicion, and the home is clean although untidy. Mrs. W. is a good cook and a devoted though not very prudent mother. She drinks spirits heavily when she can afford them (in this *ménage à trois* there is plenty of money), and smokes heavily.

She never goes to church because, she says, when she was a kid and first "in trouble" and needed a bit of help, the church people were the first to turn their noses up at her. Now she doesn't want anything to do with them.

10

Mr. U. is an elderly Methodist minister. He is married, with a grown-up family who have left home. His congregations are a good deal smaller than he would like, and substantially smaller than they were a few years ago, but he is satisfied with their quality. He has many extra-mural activities connected with his church and he and his wife take a leading part in most of them. He has very few interests outside his work, which is in a working-class district. It is not unusual for him to devote twelve hours a day to his work, day after day, and he often feels a little hurt at the unwillingness of lay members of his church to devote an adequate amount of time to helping in the various activities.

He neither smokes nor drinks and is strongly opposed to gambling in all its forms. His marriage has been an unusually happy one, but of his four married children three have broken away from the church and he is perhaps a little disappointed in them. The fourth is a Free Church minister.

II

Mrs. D. is aged 71. Her husband is a labourer for a market gardener. There were five children, all of whom reached adult state, but one was killed at sea in the war. Mrs. D. is enormously fat, with a cheerful manner and a perpetual urge to help other people. She herself says, "In this life you ought to help a lame dog when you see one." On the other hand she herself is very independent and "doesn't want to be in anyone's debt." She is extremely talkative, and says that men don't understand that women need a good gossip. They are "shut up all day in four walls and of course they enjoy a few words with a neighbour same as men do in a pub."

Mrs. D. is a strict Baptist and doesn't remember the last time she missed going to chapel on Sunday evening. She seems to pay great attention to the sermons because she frequently quotes views from them with some such preface as "Why, only last Easter there was a gentleman preaching in chapel who said . . ."

Mrs. D. herself has never tasted alcohol, never smoked, never gambled (including raffles), and has clearly devoted herself entirely to the service of her husband, the children and the neighbours.

She has never had a holiday, except for occasional visits to married children as "The money was too small when the children were growing up, and now the money's a bit easier Mr. D. doesn't feel happy away from home." She regards herself as a very lucky woman, "I've had a good steady man, and good children. We've always had good food and good times together."

Mrs. D. has never voted, nor has her husband. Speaking of national affairs in general she says, "I don't understand them things, and I don't see how working folk ever can."

Mrs. D. reads her local paper and a woman's monthly magazine, which her daughter sends her. She listens to a few radio programmes but not to concerts nor variety shows and seldom to the news. Her favourite programmes are "Twenty Questions" and "Saturday Night Theatre."

12

Mr. P. is a labourer employed at the time of this enquiry on helping to make a hard tennis court at a private house. He and his three mates don't see why they should do this; they are all Socialists and don't think anyone should be rich enough to have his own tennis court. So they "go slow." On warm days they just sit down except when the foreman visits them. On these days they may do a couple or three hours' work—not more. On cold days they work enough to keep warm. Mr. P. is aged 23 and he likes Army life—"Plenty of grub and nothing to do." He says he is a Socialist but his only political theory is that "they" have too much money and do down the working man. He says there will be revolution before long and "then King George will have to earn his living same as I do." Mr. P. says that he is an atheist. He "isn't interested" in religion and says the "parsons are too classy to understand the working man." Mr. P. does a football pool every week and bets regularly on horses. He is a great believer in newspaper tips. He has never bet on dogs as his mates say it's no good unless you're "in the know." He is single and says he can have all the women he wants without having to keep them for the rest of his life. He likes a few pints of beer every evening—three or four—and a game of darts. About twice a week he goes to the cinema and every Saturday afternoon he watches a professional football match. He smokes about 30 cigarettes a day. Despite being a bachelor he says he can hardly make ends meet. When pressed to say where his money went he said that his weekly expenditure on beer and tobacco was about £3, football pool 3s. 0d., cinema 3s. 6d., football match 1s. 3d., bets on horses 5s. 0d., lodgings (with married sister) 25s. 0d. The rest went in P.A.Y.E., insurance, union subscriptions and small sundries.

13

Miss Y. is a waitress. She is a bouncing, cheerful girl, not very skilful as a waitress but with boundless enthusiasm and a cheerful smile. Aged about 20–21. Her home is in the North of England, but she was in the South in the A.T.S., and settled there on demobilization. Has nothing to do with her parents who are separated. She was brought up by her mother who is a drunkard. Last heard of her father in gaol for bigamy.

She is not interested in religion. Says when she was in the A.T.S. "a bloke" tried to make her go to church. She went once or twice to try it, and thought it silly.

She is promiscuous, but with discrimination. Counts on getting married some time, but is "going to be bloody careful in choosing."

Drinks occasionally, doesn't smoke. Doesn't gamble—"I work too hard for my money to throw it away."

Doesn't read much but has a great fund of common sense. Knows something of what is happening in the world because she listens twice a day to the B.B.C. news.

14

Mr. T. is proud of the fact that he is a self-made man. He is the son of a labourer with a large family, and left school at the age of 13. He started on unskilled work above ground at a coal mine and in the course of time became a fully qualified engineer with a degree from one of the northern universities as well as certain professional qualifications. He did this by study and by making a rule to profit by every experience, happy or otherwise, that came his way. He is now in the early forties, happily married to a woman to whom he says that he owes a great deal in the way of social education.

Mr. T. is a happy man for he is as fond of his work as he is of his home. His work involves occasional journeys and he does not mind this as he thinks all married couples need an occasional change from each other. He is strictly faithful to his wife, but enjoys seeing smart and well-dressed women, and says this must be an echo of man's age-old instinct as a hunter.

He smokes in moderation but does not drink at all as he dislikes the taste and effect of alcohol.

Mr. T. has a warm personality, and has many friends, who occupy a good deal of his spare time. He seldom goes to a cinema or theatre because he has no time.

He reads a good deal, a large part of his reading being technical literature. He has no interest in any form of gambling.

He has a conventional regard for the Church, and attends its services "fairly often." He has doubts about whether the supernatural parts of Christian teaching should be taken literally but "cannot imagine" himself just vanishing when he dies. He thinks there must be some other existence. He attaches great importance to the part of Christian teaching that says one should love one's neighbour, and he claims that he has tried to practise it all his life.

15

Mrs. X. is the wife of a surface worker at a coal mine. She is 50–55, with five grown-up children. She is faded, weary and bitter. She says that people who blame the miners for not getting coal ought to have tried her life—bring up five children through a depression with her husband not having two years' work in ten years.

She is particularly bitter about the Church and used very coarse but descriptive language about what she would like to do to the parsons.

Mrs. X. blames her husband in part for his long unemployment because, she says, he gave way too easily.

She has a small well-kept cottage in a Welsh valley. No garden, and of course no bathroom. She suffers terribly from varicose veins and her legs are a dreadful sight. There are no amenities in her village except a bus to the local town. She has no time for amusements. She only lives for her children.

She is a good cook and to a sympathetic listener is hospitable and kind.

16

Mrs. D. is a young housewife of 26. Her husband is an architect. They are very much in love and are anxious to get a house of their own (they are now in a furnished flat) because they want to start a family. They hope to have three children.

Mrs. D. is a very gentle person who would do anything for anyone. She has not been a regular churchgoer but was married in church and has started going occasionally. As far as can be told, her life has no vice or unpleasantness of any kind, and a church could hardly make her better!

She is a teetotaler and non-smoker. Is of course innocent sexually, and does not gamble. She likes the radio, cinema and theatre, but her main recreation is looking after her husband.

17

Mr. X. is a clerk in a Government office. Aged 39, widower, no children. Keeps aged mother and unmarried sister. He professes to be an Anglo-Catholic. Earns £8 per week. Smokes fairly heavily (30 cigarettes per day, but is trying to reduce), and drinks beer, and occasionally whisky. Does not bet.

Interested in politics but takes no active part.

Occasionally picks up a prostitute and wishes he could afford a regular mistress.

Reads several newspapers, both left- and right-wing, and is fairly well informed about current events.

Reads biographies and travel books.

Not interested in the cinema, but enjoys a good play.

Is worried about the state of the nation and would accept a measure of dictatorship if only a national leader would appear.

Oddly enough he takes days off from his work fairly frequently by taking advantage of a rule that he can be "sick" one day without a doctor's certificate and without forfeiting pay.

Was formerly a keen footballer but is now too old. Does not enjoy watching games.

Gardens to grow vegetables. Not much interested beyond utilitarian aspect.

18

Mrs. E., aged middle forties, divorced. Earns living in an office. Has two-roomed flat. She is a cinema fan and goes three or four times a week. Prefers British pictures and is critical of "sloppy love films." Reads novels, and favourite author is Sapper. Takes *Daily Express* and *Daily Mirror*, and on Sunday *News of the World* and *Sunday Graphic*. Likes radio, and favourite programmes are "Much Binding in the Marsh" and "Monday Night at Eight." Does not listen to news bulletins, nor to talks. Very keen on dancing. Drinks beer and gin, and from her conversation it appears that she is fairly often tipsy. A chain smoker.

Does not gamble as she thinks it is "a mug's game."

She admits openly the startling fact of having had four abortions. They were performed by a midwife and cost £15 each. She never lets "the gentlemen" pay for the abortion as she reckons that "if a girl is careless, it's her own look-out." Her elder daughter is now pregnant (but unmarried) and her younger daughter has recently married a man of 36 by whom she was pregnant before marriage. The elder daughter will probably have an abortion and Mrs. E. is worried about it "because it's dangerous if you haven't already had a child."

Mrs. E. likes the country and hopes to spend her holiday in the Lake District.

She was brought up as an R.C. but has not practised since her marriage and now attends no place of worship. She is intensely superstitious and says black men and lame men bring her luck.

She is a foul-mouthed person, quite uneducated, vulgar and apparently generous.

19

Mr. M. is a docker, aged 24, and single. He earns very considerable wages, sometimes as much as £12 a week, and owns a motor car (a pre-war Ford). When petrol is available his principal pastime is to drive into the country. He also uses his car for driving himself to work.

He is a keen cinema-goer and is fond of dancing and also likes to watch dirt-track races, but both of these occupations take second place to his car when he is able to run it. He smokes and drinks in moderation but is not interested at all in gambling because he regards all the main forms of gambling as swindles.

Mr. M. lives with his parents and grandparents and the three generations get on well together, although there is not much sympathy between them.

Mr. M. has no religious convictions at all, and he says that religion is for children and for the very old. Nor has he any belief in any political systems, and he takes a gloomy view of civilization, which he thinks is likely to come to an end shortly through its own inherent foolishness.

He has no wish to marry as he would have to give up his car and other pleasures if he kept a wife.

He says that his motto is "Have a good time while you can."

20

Mr. N. is a doctor. He has a busy general practice and is most conscientious although he is regarded by his patients—most of them working-class—as being rude and abrupt in his manner.

He is married with two children and is devoted to his home.

He was promiscuous before marriage, but not since.

Too busy for gambling, or for any recreation except sitting and resting. Is even too busy to read as many medical publications as he should, and says, "God help any really sick man I or any other G.P. have to treat."

Says he doesn't know whether he is an agnostic or an atheist. At any rate he knows that he doesn't believe Jesus was divine, and doesn't believe the Bible is any more true than Old Moore's Almanack.

21

Miss K. is employed in a factory. She is a heavily built, good-looking girl of about 28, with dark hair which is already showing a few signs of grey. Twice during the war she was engaged, but both her fiancés were killed, the first in the Battle of Britain and the second at sea in the last year of the war. She has not become bitter, but is largely indifferent.

She lodges with a friend who is married, and quite enjoys the home life which she gets there. On the other hand she likes going out and has no lack of young men to take her. Mostly when she goes out with men she shares the expenses as she says she is earning good money and can afford it better than they can.

She enjoys drinking, but does not drink heavily. She smokes in moderation.

She is a keen gambler, betting most days on horses through a bookmaker's runner in her shop at the factory. She likes going to the greyhounds and she does a football coupon. She says she is fully aware of the chances against her winning, but it gives her an interest in life which is otherwise lacking, and she can well afford the money she loses. She thinks that the excitement she gets "is cheap at the price."

If a man pleases her she has no objection to going to bed with him and if he pleases her very much she does her very best to persuade him to do so, but she feels that she is giving very much less of herself than she would have given to either of her dead fiancés, both of whom she remembers with great tenderness.

She is open-minded on religion, believing on balance that there must be some truth in it because so many clever people believe it. As far as her knowledge goes, she just cannot say, and it is no good asking the parsons because it is their job. She finds it very hard to believe that when she dies she vanishes completely, but she "just doesn't know."

Both her parents are still living, at a considerable distance from the place where she works, but she sees them about once a year. She also sees the mother of her second dead fiancé and is very fond of her.

Miss K. never goes to the theatre, but is a keen cinema-goer and has recently taken to going to association football matches on Saturday afternoons before going on to the greyhounds in the evenings.

22

Mr. C. comes from a good family; he went to one of the "best" schools and thence to a university. He decided to make acting his career but never had much success. He took to drink and now suffers from delirium tremens. The attacks seems to be fairly frequent and he had an attack on each of the three occasions that the investigator saw him. He is nearly destitute (he had 14s. 6d. at the first meeting) and homeless. He carries all his possessions around with him in two brown paper carriers and spends the night in one of the cheap restaurants that remain open all night.

He is intelligent and an amusing conversationalist between the attacks of his malady. His only selfconsciousness was when he apologized for the fact that "My clothes stink; I haven't had them off for a fortnight." He is otherwise clean in his person and his beard is tidy.

He formerly gambled heavily and often won. He states, probably correctly, that he is a sexual pervert and has never had any normal sexual life. His source of income is a small allowance from his father, paid monthly. He did not seek to borrow money and would clearly not do so. He is suffering as much from loneliness as from alcohol, and in the ordinary way never speaks to anyone except waitresses and barmaids.

Brought up as an R.C. but has not been an active churchgoer since he was at the university, as "Rome was charming but just didn't make sense." Still retains the illusion that one day he might have an inspiration to write a play in which he will take the lead himself.

23

Miss S. is an attractive girl in the early thirties. She is a strict Roman Catholic and is unhappy because she is in love with a married man who is separated from his wife. The man in question married very young and quite unsuitably, and his wife is quite willing to give him a divorce, but because of her religious beliefs Miss S. would not marry him even if he were the innocent party in a divorce. A bachelor of her own age, who knows about her affection for the married man, is anxious to marry her and she thinks she will accept him. Because of her religious beliefs she has always refused to become the mistress of the married man.

Miss S. comes from a well-to-do family and had an expensive education. Her main interests are domestic and she devotes much time to making her flat comfortable and attractive.

She has a secretarial job, but from the style of her living obviously has an income beyond what she earns.

She is moderately interested in theatres and cinemas and goes perhaps once a month to each. She is not particularly interested in concerts, but goes occasionally if any of her friends, male or female, want her to go with them. She would never go alone.

She reads novels extensively but not much else. Is not much interested in current affairs, but devotes part of her time to social work for her church, as she considers it her duty to do so. She tried for a time helping in a youth club, but found it was not a success as she was not really interested in the people and they realized that, and resented what they thought was her patronage of them.

Miss S. smokes and drinks in moderation.

24

Mrs. P. is the wife of a labourer. She has recently had her second child, and though she is glad to have it she is worried because she and her husband only have two rooms, and small rooms at that. She left her husband last year, saying that she would not live with him until he got a proper house, but she came back after two months because she is fond of him.

She has few interests apart from her family. On Saturdays her husband plays cricket or football, according to the season, and Mrs. P. watches him, leaving the children with her mother-in-law.

Mrs. P. likes a drink, to smoke, and to go to the cinema, but cannot afford any of them as her husband's earnings are quite small.

She is not interested in religion. She says if saying her prayers would get her a house she would say them, but "everyone knows it's all nonsense."

25

Mr. Q. is the cook in a small hotel. He is aged 30, married, but separated from his wife. There is one girl child, of whom Mr. Q. is very fond, but who lives with the wife so that it is difficult for him to see her. The separation was the result of Mr. Q. returning from the war to find that his wife had been living with another man, and he says that although he is still fond of her he will never take her back. He does not want a divorce, and he says he is finished with women and would not marry again in any circumstances.

He is not interested in religion because he says that it stands to reason that the parsons are always on the side of the bosses because if they were not they would not get any money for their churches.

He likes male company and though rather shy at first he rapidly reveals a friendly and trusting nature. He finds great difficulty in expressing his thoughts in words and says that he feels that if he had been a more educated man he might not have lost his wife. While he was away in the war he seldom wrote to her because he finds it difficult to write. He reads very little—nothing except the sporting page of a daily newspaper and a weekly paper devoted to greyhound racing.

He is keen on greyhounds and horse-racing, but does not do a football coupon. Most of his money goes on gambling and smoking. He is allowed two or three pints of beer a day at his hotel and he spends a good deal of his free time in public houses.

He is the son of a miner and has very bitter memories of the poverty and ignorance in which he grew up because his father was unemployed for a long period.

26

Miss T. is aged 24 and is a shop girl. She lives alone in lodgings, but frequently spends her week-ends with her parents who "have been married thirty years and are still in love."

Miss T. is popular with men as she is very attractive (without being particularly good-looking) and she leads an active sexual life. She is quite open on the subject and says "I don't see any harm in it. I always have one steady lover and it doesn't hurt him if I have an occasional fellow besides."

Miss T. bets on horses if she gets a good tip, but "cannot be bothered" with pools or greyhounds. She smokes heavily and drinks a good deal for a girl—mostly gin and lime. She was in the Land Army during the war and liked the life, except that it was too lonely. She is not happy as a shop girl and her superior is always rebuking her for laziness.

She is not interested in religion, and her sole knowledge of the Christian doctrine is that "at school we used to read aloud from the Bible—one verse each in turn round the class. I once went to church with my friend, but it was all bobbing up and down, and I couldn't find the place in the book."

She says her hobbies are dancing and "going round the shops."

27

Mrs. J. is a widow of about 50. Her husband was killed in a road accident in which he was to blame so that she got no compensation, though out of sympathy the owners of the bus that knocked him down gave her £500. She works as a cleaner in a hospital. Her hours are 8 a.m. to 4 p.m. six days a week and one day (not always Sunday) off. She keeps her aged mother who is senile and "rather a worry," and often keeps a son of 25 who is a ne'er-do-well and is in and out of employment. She enjoys her work at the hospital. "The nurses are ever so kind and the patients are so grateful for any little thing you can do for them." She gets home about 5 p.m., cleans the house, which the senile old lady has always disarranged and dirtied, and cooks. She does her washing on her day off.

Mrs. J. still sometimes finds time to go to chapel on Sundays. She says "It makes a nice change to see the folks and to sit quiet." She also finds time to help three German girls who have been brought to the hospital to do domestic work, to find their feet—for example, she sometimes takes them to her home on their nights off.

Mrs. J. is far from perfect—whenever she has a chance she is a heavy spirit drinker and admits that she enjoys getting tipsy—"Not drunk, you know, just happy." She smokes heavily and bets on horses almost every day, coming out "about even."

28

Mr. B. is in the catering trade. His job is to buy supplies for a large provincial café and to supervise the application of the various rationing restrictions. He receives a good wage as well as board and lodging. He is single and aged 25.

He is a Methodist and goes to chapel regularly. He devotes a good [illegible] of his leisure time to a boys' club, of which he is the unpaid leader, and he finds his work there very interesting.

Mr. B. neither smokes nor drinks nor gambles, and he is an active member of an organization which puts people in various countries in touch with each other so that they can correspond. In this way he has correspondents of both sexes in six countries and he writes to each of them at least once a month. He says that this is an interesting and stimulating way of widening his experience and knowledge of what is going on in the world, as well as giving him practice in expressing himself.

Whenever he has an opportunity he goes to concerts, plays and good films and never loses an opportunity of going to exhibitions of interest such as the Ideal Homes Exhibition, as well as to museums and picture galleries.

One of his foreign correspondents is teaching him the elements of Dutch and he hopes to visit Holland to see her.

29

Miss R. is a shorthand typist, aged 22. She lives in a Y.W.C.A. hostel and manages to be fairly comfortable and still able to send £1 a week home to her parents who are badly off.

She is a serious-minded girl, whose religion is obviously a real force in her life. In consequence she is a little cut off from most young people for she does not smoke, gamble, dance, drink, gossip, or go to the cinema. The parents were apparently members of a very strict sect and Miss R. has rather grown up smelling Satan everywhere. She really believes she has to be unhappy to be good!

This was a difficult interview because Miss R. obviously had a lurking suspicion that the investigator really wanted to seduce her!

30

Mr. O. is a retired business man now acting as a collecting agent for an insurance company. He is about 45, very hard-working and friendly. He has been separated for years from his wife and is promiscuous.

He says Christianity is a good idea but "of course it doesn't work in practice." He doesn't mind going to church occasionally, for example, to please a girl friend, but he would never bother on his own account.

Mr. O. devotes part of his leisure to a youth club and he also spends every other Sunday afternoon visiting an old sailors' home to read to the bedridden inmates and cheer them up generally.

He reads virtually nothing except a Sunday newspaper and an occasional book about travel. He likes the radio but doesn't bother about cinemas or theatres.

He enjoys a gamble but football pools don't interest him. He likes to know quickly whether he has won or lost.

31

Mr. C. is a small, round-faced man with fair hair, pink cheeks and an expression that is an odd mixture of innocence and vice.

He is sexually unusual for he is strongly and actively homosexual, but in addition indulges whenever possible in normal sexual activities. He is engaged to a girl who appeared, from the photograph he showed the investigator, to be very charming. She is trying to reform him and will not marry him until he has given up his homosexual practices, about which he has told her. He says of her, "I wouldn't marry her at all if she'd let me go to bed with her."

Mr. C. gambles in moderation on horses and football pools. He has no interest in greyhounds on the ground that they are crooked. He smokes about three ounces of tobacco a week and drinks very little because he knows that alcohol affects him to an abnormal degree.

He considers that on the whole he would like another war because he believes everyone would be afraid to use atomic weapons, and he would be better off in the Forces than he is now.

Mr. C. was an orphan (probably illegitimate, although he himself is hazy on this point, not being sure whether he "never had a father" or whether his father died when he himself was an infant). He was brought up by a grandmother who alternately prophesied that he would come to a bad end, and grossly spoilt him (thus ensuring that her prophecy would come true). He was the object at school of the homosexual attentions of elder boys and formed his own habits then.

Mr. C. is a regular churchgoer.

32

Miss V. is a spinster of 72. She was the daughter of a small tradesman who made a fair sum of money out of a sweet-and-tobacconist business. She decided early in life that her duty was to devote herself to the care of her parents, but anyhow never had any offer of marriage. Now she is alone in the world, except for a number of friends whom she visits assiduously for an hour or two in rotation, making the round about once a week.

She lives on her remaining capital and believes that at her economical rate of expenditure it is enough to last the few remaining years of her life—few because she suffers from an inoperable cancer.

Her daily routine is to rise about 8.30 a.m., breakfast off a pot of tea and some bread and margarine, tidy her bed-sitting room, gossip with her landlady for an hour, out for shopping, dinner at home, a visit to friends, followed by another simple meal and bed by 9 p.m., at the latest.

Miss V. is a Baptist. She goes to chapel at least once every Sunday, whatever the weather, and reads her Bible for half-an-hour every morning before getting up.

Miss V. has never smoked, never tasted alcohol, never been to the theatre, and only once to the cinema (in the days of silent films, which she found very bewildering).

She is very reserved and great circumlocution was necessary to get any information out of her. In spite of great loneliness and ill-health she enjoys her life and is frightened of the approach of death. She cannot afford either radio or a daily paper, but most weeks sees a Sunday paper at the house of one or other of her friends.

33

Mrs. D. is a waitress in an expensive restaurant. She conceals her age, but she has children of 24, 22 and 20, the first born out of wedlock. She was separated from her husband for some years, and eventually got evidence to divorce him. She herself is promiscuous.

She is an unattractive-looking woman, but she seems to attract a certain sort of man and to have no lack of lovers from whom she extorts gifts of clothes, jewellery, furniture for her flat, and money.

She is absolutely frank about herself because she is quite amoral and sees nothing extraordinary, let alone wrong, in her behaviour.

She was brought up as an R.C., but ceased to practise many years ago and has no religious beliefs now, nor interest in the subject.

She is fond of all kinds of gaiety—cinema, theatre and dancing.

She is a very heavy drinker, and given the chance will go on drinking whisky until she becomes incapable. Also a heavy smoker.

Is fond of her children and of her lovers (she never lets a man sleep with her *solely* because of his gifts.)

34

Mr. C., a bachelor, aged 53. Has had various jobs in different parts of the world. Is now unemployed and trying to live an upper middle-class life on a tiny income. Is pretty well unemployable as he is shy, stupid, and filled with complete confidence in his own merit.

He is mildly homosexual and this had obviously sapped his moral fibre. He may once have been quite able.

Drinks in moderation and smokes a good deal.

Is entirely indifferent to religion and says he has travelled too much and seen too much of different religions to believe there is such a thing as a true religion. Religion only means custom.

35

Mr. W. is a semi-skilled worker in a factory. He is married with one child and says his eleven years of married life have been a long honeymoon, and he grows more in love with his wife every year. He says there could never be any other woman in his life. He works hard—as much overtime as possible, and several evenings a week he works as a washer-up in a restaurant to earn more money. On nights when overtime at the factory interferes with his washing-up job, his wife deputises for him, leaving the child with a neighbour. Mr. and Mrs. W. save every penny they can and admit that, "for just working-class people, we've a nice bit put away." The aim of the saving is two-fold —to build and furnish a house of their own "one day" (at present they live in two furnished rooms), and to give their child "a good start in life." They say they do not want any other children as it would be too big an expense. Mr. W. has little time for amusements but he has an allotment which he works on Sundays, and he likes to visit a cinema occasionally, but cannot find time more than once in five or six weeks. Although in most ways very careful with his money, Mr. W. smokes a good deal—his fingers are heavily stained with nicotine and he rations himself to 20 cigarettes a day, although in addition his wife often buys him a packet of 20 as a present. He drinks very little, spending about three or four shillings a week on beer, but he "invests" 5s. od. in a football pool every week of the season. His wife also "takes a couple of lines" on his coupon (paying out of her earnings when she washes-up at the restaurant), and they always put in one line for the baby for luck. Mr. W. has been doing football pools for years, but has never had a win. He is sure, however, that one day he will succeed.

Mr. and Mrs. W. both say they have exceptionally nice neighbours, and they seem to be on good terms with everyone. They are obviously people of whom one could not even imagine that they would do a mean or unkind action.

Mr. W. attended church parades when he was in the Army—voluntary as well as compulsory ones, but in civilian life he hasn't time and in fact, outside his four years of military service, has not been to church since he was married.

36

Mrs. B. is a retired barmaid, now about 40, married to a well-to-do tradesman who is some 15 years older than she. There are no children, much to Mrs. B's. grief, although she says that her husband is glad not to have any. She is a heavy smoker (30 cigarettes at least every day) and, for a woman, a heavy spirit drinker. For some reason she dyes her hair a horrible shade of red, but she is really quite a nice woman, though naïve and a bit vulgar.

She likes music halls and cinemas. She listens a good deal to the radio (*very* loud, on the Light Programme) and is a hospitable soul who likes entertaining her friends and being entertained by them.

Very strict sexually. She says that when she was a barmaid she kept herself "very respectable." She knew her husband then, and was in love with him, but they had nothing more than a platonic friendship because Mr. B's. first wife was then alive.

A very good cook, and proud of her skill in this respect.

Although the B's. are obviously well off, Mrs. B. does all her own housework and laundry. She says that servants aren't worth the trouble, and laundries ruin the clothes that are sent to them.

Not a churchgoer. She expresses scorn of parsons, set prayers, sermons, ritual and what she calls the hypocrisy of most people who go to church.

37

Mr. F. is a working-class man of 32. He is married with no children. He is very religious and though he used to play regularly for a local cricket team, he gave up and resigned from the club when they started to play Sunday matches. He and his wife go to church regularly every Sunday and often both morning and evening.

He is very friendly, and despite his strong religious views, he is a good mixer and very popular.

He likes an occasional pint of beer and visits the public house perhaps two or three times in a fortnight. His wife also likes a glass of beer, but as they both think she ought not to go to public houses, he takes bottled beer home for her.

He is opposed to gambling on religious grounds, but does a football coupon every week because he does not regard that as gambling. He used to smoke quite heavily, but in view of the heavy increase of taxation on tobacco he has virtually given it up. He is a keen cinema-goer, but practically never goes to the theatre.

He does not read much, but about once a month takes a novel from the 2d. library. He is Labour in politics and reads the *Daily Herald* every day. A good deal of his time is spent at carpentry work in his home. He has a small workshop there and makes many articles for the house.

He helps on one night in each week at a nearby youth club which is run in connection with his church.

38

Mrs. G. is about 30, married, with one child aged one year. Her husband is a Nonconformist Minister, and her greatest interest, after the child, is helping him in his work. Mrs. G. is very devout but not to an extent likely to antagonize people who do not share her views. She naturally does not gamble or drink, but she likes an occasional cigarette (but not in public).

The G's. live in a small semi-detached house of which she does all the housework, including most of the laundry. Nevertheless she finds time for an amazing number of activities connected with her husband's church, and she also reads a good deal. She never seems to be in a hurry, but on the other hand is never idle.

Mr. G. is a very good husband and helps in the house, but when he is at home in the evenings he reads serious books, immersing himself in them entirely.

They have no time for normal recreations (quite apart from the usual limitations imposed by a young child). They do not even use their radio except to hear news bulletins and serious talks.

39

Mrs. D., aged about 40, is the wife of an agricultural labourer. There are four children aged from 1 to 12. Mr. D. is not a bad fellow when sober, but he is a heavy drinker and this absorbs much of the family income. Sometimes when Mrs. D. complains about the amount of money spent on drink Mr. D. beats her. Mrs. D. has tried to get work as a charwoman, but the poverty of the family (as shown by the ragged clothes and obvious under-nourishment of the children) has given them a bad name and nobody will employ Mrs. D.

She herself neither drinks, smokes nor gambles. She never spends money on entertainment, and the family never have a holiday. Virtually all the money that can be saved from beer goes on food with a minimum amount on second-hand clothes.

Mrs. D. does not complain. She thinks that any woman whose husband does not drink is lucky, but that for her part she must make the best of it.

Vaguely resents that the parson is fat and his children well-fed and well-clothed, but has no real hostility to the Church, only indifference.

40

Mrs. X. is a middle-class housewife, the wife of an accountant who is employed in a small firm. She is in early middle age, with two children—one girl about 14 and a boy about 10. She has no control over the children and they run pretty wild. She and her husband are happy together, and she thinks herself lucky to have so steady a man. She says she has no worries, as so many women have, lest her husband in middle age should have affairs with women younger and more attractive than her. For herself she says all her affection is given to her husband and children and she never even notices any other men.

She "supposes" she is still a member of the Church of England but takes no part in its services or activities. She thinks a woman has enough to do running a home and keeping her family without bothering her head about religion.

She is keen on entertainment—visiting friends' houses or meeting them in a public house or entertaining in her house. She doesn't bother about the cinema and is not keen on the radio. She says the children have it on so much and so loud that she gets sick of it, but she has always felt that the house is their home and they have a right to do what they like.

41

Mrs. S. is married to a professional man who is a few years younger than herself. Their respective ages are probably about 43 and 38. There are two young children, aged 6 and 2, both boys.

The S's. live in a suburb in a moderate-sized detached house which is scantily furnished, and they admit to being very hard up. This seems less due to absolute lack of money than to the fact that they both lack any ability to spend wisely. They buy expensive presents for each other, or luxuries for themselves, without first making more necessary purchases. On Mrs. S's. side this is probably due to an anxiety about keeping the affection of her comparatively young husband.

Mrs. S. does not gamble, except that she takes a few "lines" in her husband's football pool coupon, but she says that she has no real belief that she will ever win anything.

She has no time to go to church, nor much interest in religion. She used to go and doesn't really know why she has stopped except that perhaps real life is so much tougher than the sort of life parsons say you ought to lead. "Where would you be if you always turned the other cheek?"

Mrs. S. likes to go to the cinema occasionally but seldom has a chance because of the children. Her greatest regular pleasure is in tea parties with other women of her class, where they can gossip and talk about their acquaintances and their children.

Mrs. S. smokes and drinks in moderation, but would smoke a good deal more if she could afford it.

42

Mr. U., aged 56, is a clerk in a Local Government office. He is married, with two boys, one 16, the other 23. Mr. U. lives in a large working-class house of about 1900 vintage that is dark, inconvenient, and smells of dry rot. However, he loves his home.

He is a rather timid man, dominated by a large wife. He smokes in moderation, and has half-a-pint of ale each evening.

He likes the radio—mainly variety—and reads an occasional novel. For the most part, however, his reading matter is the *Daily Mail* and *Sunday Dispatch*.

He is certainly not promiscuous, being much too scared of his wife, apart from any other consideration.

He is not a churchgoer, and in this he has stood firm against his wife, resisting her attempts to make him go. He says nobody knows whether or not there is a God. As far as he can see, there is a great deal of evidence against there being a personal God, and nothing except emotion, mainly fear and hope of personal reward, to support the idea. He tries to lead a good life and that is all he thinks necessary, without trying to settle the insoluble problem of whether God exists.

43

Mr. D. is 65, a professional musician, who earns a living playing the violin in an orchestra, and who has composed a number of pieces, including a violin concerto. He has also occasionally conducted symphony concerts in the provinces, but accepts without any bitterness the fact that he is a failure both as composer and conductor. He has a deep love of music, and speaking of it he appears to grow visibly in stature, and to become suddenly years younger. Late in life—apparently about the age of 60—he married an elderly, well-to-do spinster whom he had known many years. They appear to be extremely happy, and to be grateful to each other for having overcome the loneliness of a solitary life. Mrs. D. is not at all musical. For many years Mr. D. has been an enthusiastic player of bowls and he is captain of his local club in the London suburbs. He is also extremely fond of rural life and particularly enjoys bird watching.

Mr. D. says that he has never had any need of a formal religion. He came of an artistic family—the father was a painter, the mother a writer, and his only brother a musician like himself. They never concerned themselves with anything so formal as churches. They found God in their art, and in beauty everywhere. Mr. D. does not believe in personal survival after death although he believes that a part of the human being survives in some impersonal way, and that the growth and perfection of this part depends on personal behaviour in this world. Until he married, Mr. D. attended church only on such formal occasions as weddings, but now he accompanies his wife on most Sundays because it pleases her.

Music meant so much to Mr. D. that it left no room in his life for sexual relations, and none even for innocent friendships outside the musical world or for hobbies other than bowls and nature study. He has visited a cinema only a few times in his life, and has never been a regular theatre-goer. Naturally he has never had any interest in any form of gambling.

He used to like a glass or two of sherry every day, with a bottle of wine whenever he could afford it, but Mrs. D. is a teetotaller and though she has never said anything he has somehow given up his sherry and bottle of wine. It made him uncomfortable to drink alone,

44

Mr. L. is a taxi-driver, aged 32. He is married, with three children, and is intensely devoted to his family. He says he is a supporter of the Communists, but is not a member of the party. He supports them because he says "It stands to reason that we all ought to be equal. Now there are snobs and working men. If the snobs think they're better than us, the working men will just have to show them." Mr. L. is an atheist because he believes that religion was invented by the upper classes to keep the working-class down.

Mr. L. is almost a chain smoker—he would smoke 60 or 70 cigarettes a day if he could afford it. As it is, he keeps himself down to 40 of the cheapest brands. He sometimes goes without his dinner to have more money for cigarettes. He drinks very little—not more than two or three pints of beer a week.

He does not gamble because he thinks the workers ought to stand solidly together—not try to make money out of each other. Gambling is a sure way to set working men quarrelling among themselves, and that's what the capitalists want.

Mr. L. has been married since he was 20—12 years—and in that time has had nothing to do with any woman but his wife. He was brought up in a very poor area, almost a slum, and started having sexual relations with girls when he was 15. He wants a better world for his children.

He reads the *Daily Worker* and *Daily Herald*, and is fairly well informed about current events.

45

Mr. W. is a boot repairer in a small way of business. He is a friendly man, fond of children, and with a kind word for everyone. His great hobbies are gardening and watching association football.

He smokes a good deal and likes two or three pints of beer a night. He lives alone in a small flat, being a bachelor. He says he is getting too old for women now (he is in the middle fifties) but still occasionally likes a night with a pretty girl.

He was brought up as a strict Baptist, but says the First World War, in which he fought as an infantryman from 1915 to 1918, killed his belief in Christianity. He still believes, however, that the right way to live is to be kind, help people in need, and not expect too much.

He does not gamble because, he says, he would rather earn what he needs than "win it off some chap who might let his wife and kids go short."

46

Mrs. B. is about 25 and is far gone in her first pregnancy. Despite this fact she has a full-time job in a factory because her husband does not earn enough to keep the home comfortably once he has paid the instalments on the furniture, which they are buying on the hire purchase system. She is impersonal about her child. She says she did not want it and that she conceived the very first time she and her husband "risked it" without a contraceptive. On the other hand, she says she expects she will like it all right when she has it.

One of the causes of shortage of money is her husband's gambling. He puts a few shillings on horses nearly every day and it amounts to a considerable drain on their income as he never seems to win unless its an odds-on chance. She hates gambling.

Mrs. B. cannot be bothered to go to chapel. Chapel is all right for people with plenty of time but she does her washing on Saturdays and on Sundays is so tired that after cooking the dinner and washing up she rests.

She never has time for cinemas or such like, but wishes she had. Once, about a month ago, she gave herself a treat. She fainted in the factory and was sent home but instead of going she went to the pictures and went out to tea with some friends afterwards.

47

Miss E. is the daughter of a working-class home. She is 21. The family live in very crowded conditions, the parents, three daughters and two sons, all grown up, in a two-bedroom house. The father and one son work in a foundry. There is no bathroom in the house, which has no garden, and only a narrow concrete yard to separate it from the back of the next house.

Miss E. performs a miracle in such surroundings, stepping out as clean and smart as any debutante in Mayfair (and a good deal fresher and more natural). She is engaged to an artisan in the Navy. This represents a step up in the world, and Miss E. is anxious to "keep nice" for her fiancé.

The area where Miss E. lives is a rough one. Incest is not uncommon, rape not rare, and fornication is as usual as a square meal (often more usual). Naturally Miss E. "knows all about men," but since she met her fiancé she has "given up all that."

She is trying to improve herself. She has got a pamphlet on beauty hints from a woman's magazine and is studying a comprehensive 5s. od. book on etiquette.

Miss E. smokes and drinks in moderation. Likes dancing and the cinema. Longs for a house or flat of her own and doesn't want children for a few years—"perhaps later."

48

Miss M. is a very attractive Irish girl of strikingly good looks. She is far from happy because of a love affair.

Two years ago, back in her home in Ireland on a holiday from her job as a housemaid at a hospital in England, she met a sailor. After a brief courtship they decided to get married. Difficulties arose because she was a Roman Catholic and he was a Methodist. She says, "I was a good Catholic and went to Mass every Sunday, but I did not think that his religion should make any difference to our marriage."

Miss M's. mother objected strongly to her marrying a non-Catholic and invoked the help of the local priest. The priest stopped her in the street one day when she was walking with some friends and caused her great embarrassment by calling her over and walking home with her. He cross-examined her about her life in London and her observance of the Catholic faith, and warned her that she would burn in Everlasting Hell if she gave up the Roman faith to marry a Methodist.

As she refused to promise to give up the idea of marriage, the Priest told her various sad stories of the disastrous ending of mixed marriages.

By this time the sailor had gone back to his ship but he and Miss M. exchanged daily letters. Some ten months later the sailor stopped writing and, in reply to an enquiry from Miss M., revealed that her mother had written to him asking him to give her up as if he did not do so it would estrange her from her family and make a great many people unhappy.

Miss M. gave up writing to the sailor and returned to London. She was very unhappy, took to drink and to various other forms of escape from her misery. Several times she tried to commit suicide but was stopped by a female friend.

She is still unhappy, is drinking heavily, and goes dancing every night that she is off duty in an attempt to forget her troubles. She has given up the Church and has decided she will never see her family again. She says she hates her mother more than anything in the world.

One day last week she saw her former boy friend by chance in the street. He had another girl with him and just smiled and said "Hello!"

49

Mrs. J. is aged about 55 to 60. She divorced her husband and runs a retail drapery business in the Home Counties. She has three grown-up sons, all married, but her favourite son, whom she describes as "dearer to me than all the others," was killed in the war in an air raid on Hamburg. She is intensely anti-German because "they" killed her son while he was bombing them! She is also fiercely anti-monarchy, for the principle of kingship outrages her deeply egalitarian feelings. She came from a poor working-class family but her business has succeeded so well that she is very comfortably off. She has an incurable disease which interferes with her one remaining pleasure in life—eating. She has never been in the habit of drinking and smokes very little. She says that she suffered so much from seeing "that contemptible rat of a husband of mine running after every little bit of skirt," that she has always kept away from men. Mrs. J. is profoundly contemptuous of religion. "What do those silly old parsons know about it? Can you pay the rates with prayers? I've no time for their sort of talk. I'd like to set them all to work in the mines."

Mrs. J. does not gamble. "I've had to work hard for my money and I'm not giving it to them that want to live soft."

She was formerly a keen theatre-goer, but has not been since her son's death.

She says that when the news of the son's death was known her vicar came round and tried to comfort her. "The little fool said that 'Perhaps it's all for the best, Mrs. J.', and I told him to get to hell out of it."

50

Mr. R. is an unskilled worker in Government employment. He is aged 45, married, with four children all at school. His wages are small and he has no opportunity for overtime. Because of the children his wife cannot take any paid employment.

He smokes about fifty cigarettes a week which he makes himself because they are cheaper than manufactured cigarettes. At the week-ends he allows himself a pint of beer which he usually takes as two half-pints—one on Saturday and one on Sunday. Once a week he and his wife go to the cinema and sit in the cheapest seats and he spends 1s. 0d. a week on football pools.

His whole life is dominated by an acute shortage of money and the family is only adequately fed because of the 15s. 0d. a week family allowance drawn by Mrs. R. The problem of buying clothes is almost insuperable.

He sends the children to church every Sunday, but does not bother to go himself.

51

Mrs. F. is a widow of about 70. Her husband died recently, leaving her a nice house in the suburbs of a large provincial town, and enough money to bring her in about £3 per week. She has two grown-up sons, both married. Neither of them wants her to live with them, but the younger allows her £2 a week. At present she is living alone and is desperately lonely as until her husband's death she had never in her life slept alone in a house. Her life has become quite purposeless and unless something is arranged quickly to interest and comfort her she will die. She says with bitterness, "All the boys want is to get rid of me now I'm old."

She is not a church-goer and in the 50 years between her marriage and her husband's funeral her only appearances in church were at the christenings of the two boys. She says religion is "A lot of old nonsense."

Mrs. F. is very fond of children and wishes she had had a daughter.

She neither smokes nor drinks, and has never gambled.

She suffers mildly from claustrophobia, and so never goes to cinemas or theatres.

Says the radio is a great comfort but she is so lonely she hopes she dies soon.

52

Mrs. S. is the proprietress of a clothing and haberdashery shop in a small provincial town. Her husband helps her run it and they make a very considerable income. (They told investigator that their joint income from the business was £7,500 per annum, and this may be true, as they do their own managing and buying.)

They have two children and a very nice house—well furnished, in good taste. They should be happy but have in fact a great sorrow. They are social climbers and "being in trade" cannot get into local society despite being well-to-do.

They are moderately well educated but rather empty-headed people. They read a few novels as well as right-wing newspapers, but do not concern themselves much with events except in so far as they affect their business.

They used to be Baptists, but with rising prosperity decided that they ought to belong to the Church of England because it is the national Church. They observe the forms of religion but it is doubtful whether they have any dynamic belief.

They have normal pleasures—cinema, etc.—no gambling, and are certainly not sexually promiscuous.

53

Mr. V. is a middle-aged professional man. He comes of good family and has a fine brain with a scintillating sense of humour. Yet he has "run to seed." He is enormously fat and lazy, drinks excessively, eats greedily, and is interested only in sensuous pleasures. He has a wife and four children, but after being happily married for nearly twenty years, he has turned against his wife. He says that he himself doesn't know why. She is a good woman and he respects her, but they have grown apart. He became very fond of a young working-class woman who was his mistress, but she left him and married a man of her own class. He now has a foreign mistress, the wife of a foreigner domiciled in England. He is devoted to her and says, "I've reached the age when I've got to be seduced, and she is a heaven-sent seducer."

Mr. V. bets fairly heavily on horses and cards, but considers other forms of betting vulgar. He is a fine conversationalist, and is interested in music and painting. He is a member of the Church of England, attends church every Sunday, although he says he is worried at the difference between his profession of faith and his behaviour.

54

Mr. M. is a middle-aged free-lance journalist and is fairly successful. He is married with two children, whom he finds rather trying because neither he nor his wife has much control over them. Mr. M. is a very kindly, tolerant and weak man. He was educated at an expensive school and is a dreadful snob (he gives up his seat in a bus to a "lady," but not to a working-class woman, because "that class doesn't expect it, you know").

He is not altogether indifferent to religion, but feels Christianity is hopelessly inadequate, and he hasn't the time to think out problems of religion from first principles in a scientific world, so he just shelves the whole problem. He sums it up by saying, "Is Christianity true?—No." "Is there a God?—Presumably we must assume so if we are to believe material creation as we seem to perceive it exists at all." "Is that God 'personal' in any way?—Probably not." "Anyway," he adds, "if we assume God's existence we are only begging the question, for we must then ask what sort of super-God made God?"

Not promiscuous. Gambles occasionally on horses, but not seriously. Drinks and smokes in moderation.

55

Mr. C., aged 45, is a hairdresser in an establishment with a lower middle-class clientèle. He is a friendly man with a very strong sense of humour. He accepts bets for a bookmaker and the commission he gets adds about 50 per cent to his normal earnings. He does not bet himself on horses or dogs, but does a football pool every week, normally staking 3s. 6d. He has never won. Mr. C. visits a public house every weekday evening a few minutes after opening time and normally drinks about 3 pints before he goes home. Occasionally he stays in the public house till 9 o'clock and on these evenings (about once a fortnight) he drinks about 6 or 7 pints and 3 or 4 small whiskies. On these occasions he becomes a little tipsy, but not offensively so.

Mr. C. is married, but he wishes he had remained a bachelor. He is quite fond of his wife but grudges having to spend so much of his income on his home. He takes his wife to the cinema once a week but goes for her sake as films do not interest him. He reads novels which he gets from the public library and occasionally books on travel. He is not much interested in sex as he considers that a married man just hasn't got the money to get mixed up with women and has to make up his mind to leave them alone. He smokes 20 cigarettes a day, and rather more at the week-end.

Mr. C. was brought up as a Methodist but never goes to chapel as he is "not interested" in religion which he regards as "fairy tales."

56

Miss Z. is a luxury-loving young woman in the middle twenties, who has served various terms of imprisonment. She had an impoverished but good home, but from an early age was more or less allowed to please herself. She was soon discontented with her lot and rapidly acquired a "Rolls Royce standard on a push-bicycle income," and this was her undoing. Although intelligent and capable, she was never satisfied to live within her means, and took to crime as an easy way out.

She is very plausible and likes to imagine she is giving the impression of a cultured, not to say highbrow, young woman of the world.

Miss Z. is now leading an honest life and finding it hard going. She admits, to those who know her history, that she misses the excitement and brief spells of luxury acquired by crime, "Taxis everywhere, the latest and most expensive clothes, and the best seats at all the good shows."

Hard work is a bit of a come-down, but she owns that her former way of life was of very brief duration and always ended in disaster. It is for this reason, and not from any moral sense, that she has decided that "crime doesn't pay."

She prefers the theatre to the cinema though she goes to the latter about once a week. She has no interest in gambling. Drinks and smokes in moderation.

She is not promiscuous sexually, but has had a few "affairs," and takes it for granted that all young women, especially in "high society," do so.

Religion means little to her, but she does occasionally go to a church service and, rather to her own surprise, quite enjoys it.

57

Mr. N. is an unskilled worker in a factory. Age about 35. Happily married. His wife works in the canteen at the same factory and they meet every evening after work and before they go home, and Mr. N. stands his wife two bottles of Guinness while he drinks two pints of beer. Sometimes they go out again when they have been home, had tea and washed.

Mr. N. helps his wife with the housework. They are a very devoted couple, and he doesn't like going anywhere without her.

His week's beer consumption amounts to 35 to 40 pints, her consumption of Guinness to about 20 bottles; their joint cigarette consumption to 200 per week of the cheaper kind (2s. 7d. for 20). This represents a beer and tobacco cost of over £4 per week and is only possible because Mrs. N. works. This covers their major leisure occupations, for Mr. N. plays darts, dominoes or cards during an evening in the public house, and Mrs. N. gossips.

Mr. N. is a friendly man, always anxious to help people as far as he is able.

Seldom goes to the cinema. Does not gamble except for a football pool coupon.

Not interested in religion.

58

Miss V., aged 21, is the eldest of seven children of a labourer. She is employed as a clerk in a factory and is pregnant. Her "boy" is away at sea, but has written to say he will come back and marry her. Miss V. is not the least perturbed. She was born before Mum and

Dad were married and she can't see it makes any difference anyway. She is looking forward to having lots of children. She has always been happy at home and has had lots of practice in looking after young children. Her "boy" likes large families, too.

Miss V. has never thought about religion. The question of church-going never arose at home. Everyone was too busy, and there were no "best clothes" to wear at church.

Miss V. likes a drink and a smoke and "of course" she gambles. She does a pools coupon and has a few shillings a week on horses, and she and her "boy" often go to the dogs. Sometimes too she goes with Dad.

Is surprisingly well informed about current affairs. Listens to the radio news bulletins, reads the *Daily Herald* and an evening paper. No time for reading at home (she reads in the bus and in the canteen); at home there is always too much noise and something to do—washing-up, laundry, cooking, washing the younger children or playing with them, or sewing.

59

Mrs. O. is the wife of a bus driver. She is a fat, jolly woman, with three sons of whose achievements she is immensely proud. She centres her life on her home and says there isn't a better plain cook in all England than she is herself.

She is happy, fond of her husband, and appreciates his steadiness.

She likes a drink and goes two or three times a week to the public house with her husband, and most other days has one or two bottles of Guinness at home. She does not smoke. She does not gamble but when her husband does a football pool coupon she shares it with him and they "get a bit of fun" checking the coupon. Once they won £54. They "went on the bust" with £4, put £25 in the savings bank, and sent Mr. O's. elderly mother away for a holiday with the other £25.

Mrs. O. says she is a Christian. She does not bother to go to church but she was brought up as a Christian, and is sure the Bible is true.

60

Mr. X. is a rural bus conductor, aged 32. He is married with one child. Rents a council house and is thoroughly contented with life. Keeps hens and ducks and is about to buy four goslings. Caring for these birds and working in his garden are his main hobbies. Has a retriever bitch to which he is very attached. Never goes to church because he considers that parsons are no better than anyone else, and he would respect them more if they did an honest day's work. He and his wife go to the cinema once a week but on different nights because of the child. Likes an occasional evening at the pub and a game of darts. Usually spends one evening in this way—not more because of "leaving the missus." Does a football pool coupon, but not interested in dog racing nor horse racing. Very fond of the country and stays with his present employers because he is on country runs, although wages are not good. Mr. X. does not smoke.

61

Mrs. E. is a very old lady. She is toothless and in an early stage of senescence. She says, probably truthfully, that she cannot remember her age, but she thinks it is about 80. She lives alone in a self-contained first-floor flat. The investigator met her by offering to escort her across a busy road. The crossing was near her suburban home and he carried her basket for her. She asked him to open her door as her eyes are too dim to see the keyhole clearly (a Yale lock). Her flat is stuffy and untidy but Mrs. E. says she is happy there and dreads having to give it up to go to live with a married daughter who doesn't want her and who has three "dreadful" boys. Mrs. E's. husband was a solicitor and he died in 1910, so that she has lived alone for nearly forty years. She has no radio and no labour-saving devices in her flat, except one very old gas fire. Lighting and cooking are by gas.

Mrs. E. used to read a good deal (mainly novels, judging from a large dusty bookcase), but now she only reads herself to sleep at nights with her Bible.

She still likes a glass of port or stout, and says it is her only luxury. She does not bother much about food, and on the day the investigator saw her she said, apparently truthfully, that she couldn't remember whether she had had any dinner.

Her married daughter visits her at least once a week and puts her flat tidy. Mrs. E. says the daughter scolds her because she buys food and then puts it in her larder and forgets it. But she does not worry, she has all she needs, and is not short of a few pounds.

Mrs. E. still goes to church whenever Sunday is fine. When it is wet she reads her prayer book at home. She thinks the way people nowadays treat the Sabbath is terrible.

62

Miss J. is a bus conductress, aged about 25. She is an efficient, rather reserved girl, who finds her work interesting although it is tiring. She says she has plenty of opportunity to see what people are like and on the whole she finds them pretty decent. Middle-class women are worst—often rude and always gossiping. Working-class passengers are always more polite.

Miss J. is keen on Trade Unions and as she was once a typist she does unpaid work helping the branch secretary of the Transport and General Workers' Union. She is a keen member of the Labour Party.

She was brought up as a strict chapel-goer, but when she grew up she thought the matter out for herself and decided the Bible wasn't true. Therefore she gave up chapel. She says all our best ideas come from the teaching of Jesus and he was a wise man.

Miss J. smokes in moderation and "doesn't mind" an occasional drink. Likes the cinema and always goes once a week.

Doesn't gamble in the ordinary way, but occasionally has a shilling on a horse. Can't be bothered to do a football pool.

Sees no harm in theory in sexual promiscuity, but does not practise it. If she got so carried away by a man as to want him physically she would want to marry him to make sure of keeping him.

63

Miss T. is about 55 and acts as companion to a maiden lady of over 80 who is very active and treats Miss T. as a friend. Miss T. is a staunch church-woman; whenever her employer is well enough they go together to matins and evensong every Sunday, and in addition Miss T. always attends an early Communion service. She has never gambled in her life and asked the investigator, "What *are* these football pools? We read so much about them in the papers we would so like to see one." She thinks greyhound racing "must be cruel." "I'm sure the poor dogs must be frightened." Miss T. has no relatives of her own and all her apparently warm affections are centred on her employer. "Do you know she's so good to me. She's leaving me her house in her will and a nice little income." Miss T. is a great reader, her interests being divided between novels and books of travel. She reads aloud to her employer and when a book speaks of a foreign land they always find the places mentioned in an atlas.

Miss T. likes a bottle of stout with her supper and she and her employer always have a glass of port together in the evening because "It's good for anaemia" (an apparently unnecessary precaution in Miss T.'s case).

Miss T. goes to the cinema about once a month in the afternoon, and goes two or three times a year to the theatre. She has never been to a concert but "likes the music on the B.B.C."

Following her employer's example, Miss T. sets aside 10 per cent of her income as "charity money" for deserving causes.

She says that she knows nothing about politics but always votes Conservative because her employer tells her to.

64

Mrs. Z., aged about 50, is a widow, and lived for many years in India. She is very "pukka Memsahib" and is a terrible gossip and an insufferable bore. Her tongue has a barb to it and much of her gossip is malicious.

She has to earn to supplement her pension and small private income, so she goes as a companion to "ladies of quality," or sometimes spends a season as a professional chaperone to some "young lady of good family."

Naturally Mrs. Z. has all the correct hobbies—bridge, liking for social functions, theatres, even the cinema occasionally, opera, ballet, concerts. Naturally, too, does not gamble, but expects men to bet on horses. She is not the sort of woman to suspect of sexual promiscuity—she probably does not stop talking long enough to enable a man to make improper advances!

A regular churchgoer.

65

Mr. T. is an assistant in a chemist's shop. He is about 40, married, with one child. He is qualified as a dispenser and assists a more senior man with that side of the business, but his chief job is serving at the counter, where he is in charge of five assistants of both sexes. He enjoys his work. Trade is usually brisk and there is something in the constant transactions with large numbers of small items that appeals to him.

He is happy with his wife and devoted to his child. He is absolutely faithful to his wife and says, with a twinkle in his eye, that the nearest he ever gets to being promiscuous is selling french letters to customers.

He has a semi-detached house with a good garden, and is enthusiastic about his flowers and vegetables.

As the child is young, he and his wife cannot go out much in the evening, but by saving over three or four years the money they might have spent on amusements they have saved enough to buy a television set which gives them a great deal of pleasure.

He says he is a Christian and he and his wife go to church occasionally. They used to go weekly before the child was born.

Does a football pool coupon, but "does not gamble."

66

Mrs. H. is the wife of a retired Army officer. She is aged about 50. Her husband having failed to obtain promotion was retired at the age of 50 with a pension of about £600 per annum. There are three children, aged 10, 12 and 14, and—having been accustomed to an upper middle-class standard of life—the H's. feel desperately poor. Mr. H. has tried to get a job but without success. Aged 50 and with no qualifications life is not easy for him.

Mrs. H. drinks and smokes in moderation. She has always been used to a considerable measure of gaiety—dances, cocktail parties, and official receptions of various kinds—and she misses them now she is living in a dingy house in the suburbs of a seaside town.

She is a little inclined to be querulous, and is finding it hard to adjust her standard of living.

She is not a church-goer and does not gamble.

67

Miss L. is a spinster of over 70. Upper middle-class and the youngest of a large family. Stayed at home to look after her mother and so lost chance of marrying. Devout churchwoman and is looking forward to a literal resurrection of the body. Discussed Heaven at length and has a clear view of it, including a conviction that class distinctions will survive in Heaven as people would not be happy without them. Likes a glass of dry sherry in the evenings and allows her paid companion a glass of port—"It's cheaper you know, and easier to get." Undoubtedly of complete sexual ignorance, but has avoided the sour frustration of many spinsters. Enjoys her life immensely—goes to the cinema twice a week, to concerts and the theatre once a month each. Often goes day excursions to the country and spends much time in the summer in Kew Gardens. Does not "gamble" but oddly enough she and her companion each do a football coupon, but have a rule that they must not look at the football results in the Sunday newspaper until they return from matins.

68

Mr. L. is a bus conductor, married, with no children. He is aged about 40. His wife is also in full-time employment as a typist and they share the housework including the cooking, and they pool their incomes.

He was brought up as a member of the Church of England, but now never goes to church. His main reason for no longer going is that as far as he can see people just use the church as a place where they can ease their consciences and then go off and do exactly the same as they did before. He is not an atheist and he believes in some Supreme Power that he calls fate. He thinks nobody can alter fate and therefore it is no use praying. He hardly knows what to believe.

Mr. L. is a teetotaller because he is anxious to save, and he has always found that regular drinkers are spendthrifts. He does however smoke in moderation. He never bets on dogs or horses because he thinks that he would be bound to lose. On the other hand, he does a football pool regularly because he does not miss a few shillings a week and it gives him a chance of making a large sum he could not get in any other way.

He says that his real aim in life is to make as much money as possible. He says that in his experience it is always the well-to-do people who say that money is not everything, but he has found that you cannot do anything without it. If he can save enough money or win enough on the pools, he and his wife would like to set up a shop of some kind.

69

Mrs. W. is a working-class housewife, married, and just had her first baby. She is a kindly, simple, jolly person of about 24, but she is by no means thoughtless. She believes in the aims of the Labour Party, attends meetings, studies to improve her understanding, and does elementary canvassing work. She has only found this interest since marriage as her husband is a keen Labour Party man.

Mrs. W. is a teetotaller and does not smoke. She shares her husband's football pool coupon but otherwise does not gamble.

Mrs. W. is hostile to the Church, as she says that if parsons and church- and chapel-goers practised what they preach there would be no need for political reforms. She says the Church is on the side of the over-privileged.

70

Mrs. P., wife of a labourer, aged about 45 (but could pass for 60), three grown-up children. Lives in a tiny house and says that bringing up the children was hard through the depression but life is easier now and she is proud of her family. The three children live at home and are in full-time employment. Mrs. P. does a weekly wash for five adults. The children do nothing to help in the house. Mrs. P. says, "Poor dears, they get so tired at work, I like to do everything for them."

Mrs. P. is a jolly woman who likes a glass of ale in the local. Her husband calls her the "finest woman he ever saw," and they are great friends.

Mrs. P. is a strong Tory and says that no good will come of Socialism. "There have always been gentry and always will be, and the gentry know best." In her youth Mrs. P. was in service in a peer's London house, and a faint aura of the aristocratic stays with her!

She likes an occasional visit to a cinema or music hall, but "grudges the money to go too often." Once every two or three months is enough.

Says she is "Church of England, like the King" but none of the children were christened, and she has not been to church since she was married!

71

Mrs. H. is a widow of 45, living on a small pension. She shares a small house with a female friend and came to a large town for the purpose of doing so. She finds it a very lonely place and says, "It is so difficult to make friends here, as everybody seems to be in such a hurry going after their jobs and pleasures."

She would like to get a part-time job, but though she has tried at the Labour Exchange nothing suitable has been offered to her. As a result of her difficulty in getting work, despite all the public appeals for women to return to industry, she has come to believe that the whole economic crisis is much exaggerated.

She does not read the newspapers nor listen much to the radio. As a result she has no knowledge of what is going on in the world and thinks anyway that it does not matter as the ordinary person can never know enough to be able to form any useful opinions. For the same reason she never votes in any election.

She likes reading novels, particularly murder stories, but does not read anything else.

Mrs. H. does not smoke nor drink nor gamble. For the most part she is simply indifferent. For years past she thinks she has had bad luck, but before that she had a spell of good luck when things in her life seemed to go well, so that she says she does not complain. She says that she is certainly not happy, but neither is she unhappy. She simply gets up in the morning, has her meals and eventually goes to bed again. She says that people would get on much better if they followed her example and made up their mind that they would not worry about anything or know about anything. "The main thing is to get a hold of yourself and to make the best of your life."

72

Mr. R., aged 63, a joiner. Married, with two grown-up children. Formerly a soldier in regular Army, but was invalided with tuberculosis in 1917 and spent a year in a sanatorium. Is cured, but not very strong. Visits public house every evening on leaving work and drinks two pints of beer. Sometimes returns with his wife and spends part of the evening in the public house. Smokes in moderation and would smoke more but for his "weak chest." Does his football coupon every Thursday evening and has had several small wins. Often has half-a-crown on a horse and sometimes goes to the dog races—about once every three or four weeks.

Never goes to church because he got fed up with church when he was in the Army but, in his words, "Mind you, religion's a fine thing if you don't have too much of it." Used to send his children to Sunday School to get them out of the house.

Is proud of the fact that, in 40 years of married life, he has never been unfaithful to his wife and, again in his words, "Mind you, there ain't many that can say that."

Likes "a bit of gardening," but isn't strong enough to do much. Is very proud of his work as a joiner and has a contempt for modern workmen. "Men of my age be craftsmen, but these whippersnappers today ain't got no pride. They'll never learn to do work like we do. Their heart isn't in it."

Dislikes the cinema, but takes his wife sometimes. Enjoys a good music hall "with plenty of girls," and thinks the B.B.C. Light Programme is "all right as long as you don't have too much of it." Reads the *Daily Herald* and *Reynolds News*, but never reads a book.

73

Miss K. is a typist in a Government office. Aged 32 or 33, she is the daughter of a deceased clergyman. Quite attractive herself, she is not greatly attracted to men although over the course of years she has been the mistress of three men because she liked them and just couldn't be bothered to drive them away when they were insistent.

She is well-read, interested in music, with a keen sense of humour and has a great many friends of both sexes. She is always eager to help anyone in trouble and she is a most generous and kind-hearted person.

She is fond of walking and swimming, despises dancing and likes the cinema and theatre. Music remains her main interest.

She is an agnostic, saying she has seen too much of professional

Christianity at close quarters to have anything except contempt for the Church.

Drinks too much. Does not smoke.

74

Mr. R. is a smallholder in the late fifties, who has risen to his present position by virtue of the fact that as a farm labourer he married the daughter of a moderately well-to-do farmer, and eventually inherited a sufficient share of that farmer's possessions to buy his smallholding. He is almost illiterate and all his correspondence is conducted for him by his wife. He is a very keen churchman and never misses going to church on Sundays, often going to evensong as well as matins. He is a sidesman at the church.

He is intensely superstitious and constantly looks out for omens in regard to his farming. He would not in any circumstances, for example, start any farming operation, such as harvesting, on a Friday, for that would bring bad luck. (This is a local superstition in his part of the country.)

He worries about money matters and constantly envisages ruin, although his wife says quite openly that they are doing very well.

Mr. R. does not smoke, but he likes a pint of beer at the village pub two or three times a week, and also has a few drinks whenever he goes to market.

His holding is not large enough to have much machinery, although he has an arrangement with a neighbour for borrowing certain machines, in exchange for help rendered to the neighbour with the latter's ploughing and harvest. He is suspicious, however, that the neighbour is "doing him down," and he intends to bring the arrangement to an end next year.

Mr. R. has no opportunities to gamble on horses or greyhounds, and he is too illiterate to do a football pool coupon even if he wished to. He has virtually no knowledge of current affairs and never sees a newspaper, although his wife takes the *Daily Mirror*. They have no radio as their farmhouse is not fitted with electricity, and there are no arrangements in the immediate neighbourhood for charging batteries. This could no doubt be overcome, but for the fact that Mr. R. is glad of the excuse not to have a radio.

He likes playing a game of dominoes or cards and cheats quite openly (as indeed do most of the other players at the particular village pub that Mr. R. frequents).

Mr. R. is a very kindly man, fond of children, generous on occasion but close-fisted most of the time. He is glad that he has no children because they are such an expense, but he works very hard hoping to save enough for a comfortable old age.

75

Mrs. V. is a young married woman in the early twenties, brought up by extremely strict religious parents. She married during the war at a very early age, in order to get away from home and a discipline which she resented. She went to live with disapproving in-laws, and while her husband was away on service she went to pieces completely. She was unfaithful to him and out for a good time at any price. She was eventually committed to a Borstal Institution. This pulled her up and brought her to her senses and when discharged she had really "learnt her lesson."

She and her husband were reconciled and they started out to mend their broken marriage and try to make a home together.

Mrs. V. is passionately devoted to children and it is a great grief to her that she has none, "when there are so many who don't want them." She has been told she cannot now have a child and she is bitter about this and thinks God is cruel to deny her this. Since she has had a place of her own she has proved herself a good and capable housewife, and takes a real pride in her home, which is her main interest. She is without any sense of humour and takes all her pleasures rather sadly. She likes going to the cinema, not often more than once a week, and she smokes and drinks in strict moderation, and quite often goes without smoking for weeks at a time. She does not gamble at all. She likes reading, but only of the lightest kind—magazine stories and novelettes are her principal fare.

Is not much interested in dress, and cannot afford to spend much on it as her husband's wages are on the small side—but she manages well and lives within her means.

Does not disguise the fact from herself and others that she would never have pulled herself together without her Borstal training.

76

Mr. L. is a professional man, aged 32, and was on holiday in London. His consuming interest is sex and he is promiscuous. He is married, but his wife was at home looking after their child; Mr. L. spoke of both with great affection and showed investigator their photographs. Mr. L. does a football pool "most weeks" and sometimes goes to the greyhounds—apparently about once a month. He drinks beer but not spirits, as the latter detract from his sexual power,

He smokes a pipe, but only 1 oz. of tobacco per week. He is not interested in any of the arts, nor in the theatre, but likes the cinema, and on holiday goes nearly every day. Is the son of a Methodist minister and was strictly brought up, and still goes to chapel when he "stays with the old man," but otherwise doesn't bother as "religion is a lot of punk." Is obviously very fond of both his parents and, despite his flamboyant vulgarity, has a generous disposition and a warm personality.

77

Mr. A. is aged 20, educated at one of the best-known public schools, and now working (to gain first-hand experience of industry) as a labourer in a shipyard. He is about to give up his employment in disgust at the slackness of the workers who will not give a fair day's work, and take up farming as a career. Mr. A. is very serious-minded but of a rather autocratic temperament. He is not religious but goes to church "because everyone ought to—religion is good for men."

He is shy of women, all of whom he regards as paragons of virtue. He says that as he always stands up for women if he hears men talking loosely of them, he was first teased a good deal in the shipyard, but then he noticed men gradually took his side, and now there is not much loose talk.

He sees no harm in horse or greyhound racing, and goes to the latter about twice a month. Football pools bore him but he has done one constantly while in the shipyard to have something to talk about and he won about £40 over the course of last season. He says it is fairly easy for anyone to win who does not try to gain a large prize.

Mr. A. is well read for a young man. He has flirted with the idea of joining the Communist Party, but has now given it up. He believes in nationalization, and in social security.

He is a keen cinema-goer, and seldom misses a week, although he rarely goes more than once in a week. He writes poetry (very badly judging from the specimens he showed the investigator), and is keen on amateur theatricals.

78

Mr. D., an elementary school teacher, aged 43. Married, but with no children. Is intensely interested in his work despite the discouragement of a class of nearly sixty boys in an old, gloomy building with no amenities. Mr. D. feels the inadequacy of his own education as he is constantly having to teach from books matters that he does not personally understand. He has taken a correspondence course to fill in some of the gaps in his knowledge and though this has helped, he is embarrassed to find that it has raised just as many problems as it has solved. He is an earnest Free Churchman and is obviously a man of the highest principles under whose guidance any child would develop well. He certainly does not gamble and he sometimes talks to his boys on the subject but regards this as wasted breath as the boys know that all the other teachers in the school do football pools and most of them go to the greyhounds. Seldom goes to the theatre, but goes to the cinema about once a month. Wishes he knew more about music, but enjoys some of the broadcast symphony concerts. Neither smokes nor drinks.

79

Miss B. is the daughter of a well-to-do deceased owner of a large general stores (a miniature provincial Harrods). She inherited equal shares with her two brothers. Her share is in trust, but the income makes her a well-to-do young woman. She is in love with a counter-hand in her father's stores, and was walking out with him before her father's death. The father himself "rose from nothing" and did not object.

She is a sweet girl of the "clinging" kind who must have a man to whom to cling.

Her interests are domestic and she wants four or five children when she marries.

She is a Roman Catholic but not very devout, and only goes to Mass when the priest meets her in the street and bullies her. She thinks it is "silly."

She is certainly not promiscuous. Smokes but does not drink. Does not gamble—nor even know how to.

Keen on the cinema.

80

Dr. T. is British-born, aged about 30, and with British qualifications although he is of foreign extraction. He is in general practice and is working hard to make a success of it. He is a bachelor and a widowed sister keeps house for him. He is a Roman Catholic but does not attend services. Dr. T. says he has little time for outdoor recreation. He is a keen gambler, and likes to play poker two or three evenings a week. He plays in a group of about a dozen friends, of whom roughly six play on any given evening. The winnings and losings are adjusted at the end of each evening so that the biggest loser loses £5. Dr. T. also bets on horses but not on dogs. He does a football pool most weeks "as a recreation." Of the football pool he says, "It is no harder than a crossword and there is a chance of a win."

Dr. T. drinks very little and smokes in moderation. He hasn't been to a cinema "for years," and is not interested in the theatre, except for an occasional visit with a party of friends to a musical comedy. Dr. T. says he does not consider himself a particularly good doctor, but he can usually tell if somebody is really ill, and then he gets a specialist of whatever kind is necessary. Dr. T. says he has no desire to marry. He wishes he could afford the time and money to keep a regular mistress, but as he cannot, and doesn't like casual sexual relations, he "amuses himself in other ways."

81

Mr. K. is an unskilled worker in a factory. He is married with two children. For Mr. K. the chapel is the twin centre of his life with his home. He is one of the most intensely religious men the investigator has ever met. He does a good deal of voluntary work for his chapel and occasionally goes to other chapels to preach.

He is an uneducated and extremely simple man, but the example he sets is always good.

Naturally he does not gamble nor drink. He is not promiscuous, and he smokes only in strict moderation.

He visits the sick and old, and to the best of his power helps everyone in need.

He is the sort of man who would undoubtedly help to raise the tone of a factory.

Is devoted to his family and is striving to ensure a good education for them.

82

Miss Y. is an attractive working-class girl of about 21. She comes from a poor home. Her parents constantly fought and were often drunk. She left school the day she was 14 and started earning. She ran away from home at the age of 17½ and has lived alone since then. She has resisted all the tempting offers of pimps to become a prostitute and has maintained a perfectly respectable living. She is now being courted by a young labourer. They habitually sleep together and intend to get married as soon as Miss Y. is pregnant.

By nature Miss Y. is quite intelligent, but nobody has ever helped her to develop her mind so that she has a small vocabulary, and "when on her best behaviour" talks in clichés that she has no doubt learned from the cinema.

She drinks and smokes a good deal for a girl of her age. Her favourite recreations are the cinema and speedway racing. Does not gamble. Reads the *News of the World* and an occasional paper-backed romantic novel.

No knowledge whatsoever of religion. The Sermon on the Mount is as far removed from her as Einstein's theory!

83

Mr. E. is the manager of a large suburban grocery store—one of several owned by a firm of Jewish provision merchants. Mr. E. is 40, married, with two young sons. He regards his wife with tolerance "now we are both getting on into middle age," but for years quarrelled violently with her, even to the extent of throwing plates and having them thrown at him.

Mr. E. is an agnostic whose views hardly differ from atheism. He dislikes his work and says that the more he sees of his customers the more he despises them for always trying to steal a march on each other. He also despises them as "mugs" for paying high prices for the shoddy goods he offers.

He hates his employers and says that they and his customers between them are making him anti-semitic in his outlook.

Mr. E. drinks very little—two or three pints of beer on Sundays but nothing on other days, but he smokes about thirty cigarettes a day. He thinks gambling is "a mug's game," but he fills in a football pool coupon as he doesn't miss the weekly 4s. 6d., and it might bring a big win. He has won several small amounts and was £120 up last season.

His children receive no religious teaching and Mr. E. does not wish them to do so at school.

His hobby is gardening, and he is proud of what he produces from the small garden of his suburban house. He also does all the decorating of his house, and most of the repairs.

Mr. E. was faithful to his wife through all the years of their quarrels but now wishes he hadn't been. He is now promiscuous and says that the girls in his shop who want to get on "have got to be nice to me."

84

Mr. S. is a roadsweeper. He is well over six feet tall, a pensioned N.C.O. from the regular Army, an Irishman, 58 years of age. When first seen by the investigator he was striding along the road with his hands in his pockets whistling. Behind him staggered his mate (jointly responsible with Mr. S. for a certain area of road), a bent, wizened and toothless old man of apparently great age, pushing a heavy barrow laden with all the brooms, shovels, etc., that both needed.

That first introduction to Mr. S. is really typical. He is full of blarney and charm, and probably as lazy as any man in England. His rather dull-witted mate regularly does half Mr. S's. work as well as his own.

Mr. S. is a Roman Catholic and he says that it is the only true religion, but enquiry elicits that he himself has not been to church for more than twenty years. He is married, with two grown-up children, who he says are the apple of his eye and a great success in the world, but they don't want to have anything to do with him because he drinks too much, "And when I've a drop inside me, I've a foul mouth. I know it." He spends his evenings in the public house whenever he has any money, or whenever he can get "a gentleman to treat me." Of his wife, he would say nothing, replying to every approach on the subject with an oath and the statement, "She's a fine woman." During his Army service and for a few years afterwards, Mr. S. was apparently quite promiscuous and he quoted, "I've taken my fun where I've found it," but he is now "more interested in chasers than chasing." (Note: A "chaser" is a tot of neat whisky followed by a glass of beer.) Mr. S. does a football pool every week and claims that he has won a number of small prizes amounting to "several hundred pounds." He maintained this statement over several interviews and as he seemed well provided with money it may quite likely be true. He also bets on horses, runs a football sweep every week in the season among his mates, but regards greyhounds as "too crooked."

Mr. S. smokes a clay pipe with a tobacco of incredible pungency. He is surprisingly widely read and well informed about current events. He says he's a Tory on the grounds that all politicians are thieves and rogues, and it's better to be robbed by a gentleman who'll say "Thank you" than by one of your own class.

85

Mrs. Z. is a married woman of about 37–40, working in a large charitable organization in a fairly important secretarial post. She is efficient, interested and anxious to further the work of the charity. Her husband is a doctor, and between them they are well quite off.

Mrs. Z. is not a churchwoman as she believes the Christian dogma cannot be sustained in the light of modern thought. She is, however, keenly anxious to spread the Christian ethic which she regards, on the whole, as the highest point of human vision.

Mrs. Z. says that she believes that within limits of moderation there is some value in sexual promiscuity before marriage as it develops personality and helps to ensure a wise marriage. She is however, vehemently opposed to it after marriage.

She is a keen theatre- and cinema-goer. Does not gamble ("except office sweepstakes") but doubts whether there is as much harm in gambling as moralists maintain. She thinks gambling is silly, but not nearly so grave an evil as say selfishness or nagging.

86

Mrs. A. is the wife of a stoker on the railway. She is aged about 30, and has one son, a flabby, pasty-faced boy aged 4. They live in a flat in a large block in the suburbs and Mrs. A's. mother lives with them. Both Mrs. A. and her mother-in-law work full time in a factory and the child is left every day in a day nursery. As a consequence he is tired and petulant in the evenings, just when Mrs. A. is tired out, and seldom is put to bed before 8 p.m. Mrs. A. takes a poor view of matrimony but married because the child had already been conceived. She was in the A.T.S. at the time and "didn't see any harm in having a good time with the men." Now she "hasn't time" for love-making. She gets up every day at 6 a.m. and leaves home at 7.30. She does her housework and family washing in the evenings and seldom gets to bed before 11 p.m., and often later. She never goes to the cinema but used to go three or four times a week before she was married. Never now goes to a dance and says she is "on her feet enough without dancing." She does not gamble and wishes her husband wouldn't, as he often loses half his wages at the dogs. Her only extravagance is to smoke 12 or 15 cigarettes a day. Of religion she says that she doesn't see it would do her any good "to go running off to church every Sunday."

87

Miss Z. was formerly Mrs. X. but she divorced her husband and resumed her maiden name. She is a rather dull and disillusioned woman of about 35. She divorced her husband for cruelty after he had beaten her with a dog whip in a drunken fit, and had been found by the neighbours with both hands around her throat shaking her.

Miss Z. works in a factory and is happy enough there, but is lonely in the evenings in her bed-sitting room. She is fed up with men and has enough of women all day.

She does a football pool coupon, and most days has a shilling or two on a horse.

Not interested in religion. "Went to church once too bloody often I did," she says, referring to her wedding.

Drinks two or three glasses of Guinness each night on her way home from work. Is a chain smoker.

Her world really has just come to pieces with the failure of her marriage. She mopes because there is nothing she really wants, or that really interests her except a home and a husband, and she knows she is too dull and unattractive to have a chance of a second marriage.

88

Mrs. D. is about 70, a widow, and living with her daughter and son-in-law. She is partly crippled with rheumatoid arthritis—spends most of the winter months in bed, and in summer gets about in a wheeled chair, from which she can walk about a dozen steps unaided. She is in full possession of her mental faculties and knows how each winter her daughter hopes "This may be mother's last, if it's a hard winter." The family are desperately anxious to get rid of Mrs. D. because she's a financial liability and anyhow they want the room.

She is quite capable of enjoying herself still—she reads, listens to the radio, enjoys cultivating a window box, and in particular enjoys the broadcast religious services. (Her daughter and son-in-law are regular chapel-goers.)

She is a kindly woman who likes children and animals, is in no great hurry to die and thinks it unkind that people want to hurry her on her way to save a few pounds when she gave so many of her young years to the service of the same people.

89

Mr. A. is aged 53. A professional man, he retired when his wife died a few years ago because "We had no children and I've made enough to keep me all my life." He lives in a one-roomed flat and his main interest is horse racing. He bets daily and attends all the main meetings. He complains a little of loneliness and drinks spirits heavily to overcome it. He is a nominal but not a practising Roman Catholic and he says, "When you're dead you're dead, so why worry." He is a Conservative in politics and goes to the cinema four afternoons most weeks. Keen bridge player and plays two or three times a week. Also fond of billiards. Reads the right-wing newspapers and the society periodicals (*Tatler*, etc.). Except for technical works, he says he has not read a book for years. Is worried about his health and maintains that he has a dangerous heart condition; he says, "I've spent hundreds of pounds on doctors, but they're no good. They can't find anything wrong. It's my heart and I *know*." Not interested in women, and undoubtedly misses his wife very much.

90

Mr. H. is retired from business. He is 55 and formerly owned a very profitable factory. He sold out to one of the big firms and, having no family except a wife, has decided to enjoy his remaining years of life.

He is a keen shot, a keen fisherman, and attends most of the major race meetings. He has a flair for doing things well but economically, and even his horse racing does not cost him much.

He is not interested in sex. Says he never was much interested and now he is too old anyway.

He drinks a good deal, but not to excess and smokes about 30 cigarettes a day.

Likes the cinema and theatre and often goes with his wife to one or other.

Was at one time a keen churchman, and indeed a churchwarden, but has gradually fallen off. Mainly "because the parsons are so bad and the services so dull." Has never thought much about the basic dogma of Christianity. Everybody accepted it so he did, and he supposes he still does.

91

Mr. D. is a paper-hanger, aged 57, and married. He has a small business of his own, employing several assistants, and he works with them just as one of themselves. He finds that by treating his men as equals and encouraging them and being friendly, he gets a fair day's work for a fair day's pay. He lets his men work unsupervised and they never let him down by slacking. Mrs. D. is several years older than he and besides keeping their home she runs the financial side of the business, including all the book-keeping, banking and paying out. He just has a regular amount of pocket money.

Mr. D. drinks and smokes in moderation and does a football pool coupon regularly. Last season he won £85. He does not bet on greyhounds or on horses.

His father was a gardener and Mr. D. has retained a great interest in gardens and he spends much of his spare time in his own. His special interest is in roses and he likes experimenting to produce new varieties.

Mr. D. has no time for reading and hardly ever goes to the cinema, which he does not particularly like. He is keen on the theatre, but does not go very often, largely because it is difficult for a man living in the suburbs to get to the best theatres after a day's work.

Mr. D. is not a churchman, but he accepts the principles of Christianity and says that the trouble with church people is that they keep religion for Sunday. He tries to bring religion into his everyday affairs by helping the community and giving encouragement to everyone.

92

Mr. H. is a milkman, aged about 45, married, but with no children. He is very cheerful and friendly and puts himself out to help his customers. He is happily married and saves all he can. His wife is the daughter of a small tradesman and being the only child she inherited "a nice bit of money" on the death of her parents. Part of this Mr. H. and his wife have invested and part they have set aside for pleasure, which has taken the form of holidays abroad. So far they have been abroad twice, once to Switzerland and once to Italy, and there is enough money for them to go at least two or three times more.

Mr. H. takes an interest in current affairs but does not believe that the man in the street ever really knows what is happening because one cannot trust what one reads in the newspapers or hears on the radio, and so there is no source of really reliable information.

He reads books from his local public library, mostly those dealing with foreign countries. He is not much interested in novels because, he says, in his job he sees quite enough real people.

Mr. H. smokes in strict moderation and hardly drinks at all. He does not gamble because he is sure he would lose. He sees no harm in gambling in moderation but knows a lot of people who gamble to excess, always hoping to regain earlier losses. He thinks that attitude is foolish.

He and his wife are happily married and are obviously devoted to each other, and there is no reason to doubt Mr. H. when he says that he never even thinks of any woman besides his wife. Most of their evenings are spent at home but they go to the cinema occasionally—perhaps once in two or three months. They do not care much for the radio, but think that they might buy a television set later, but not until television has improved technically.

They are a little worried because Mr. H's. elderly mother is a widow living alone, and is rapidly getting past the stage when she can do so. They very much hope they will be able to find a home where she can be looked after, as they do not want her to live with them. Mr. H. thinks that it is all right for old people to live with their children when they are really fond of each other, but in cases like his, where they have drifted apart without ever quarrelling, it is asking for trouble because the old person always knows that he or she is not wanted and the young person grudges the burden and the expense.

Mr. H. does not call himself a religious man and he never bothers to go to church, but he thinks it important that people should act decently towards those whom they meet because otherwise the world would be an impossible place.

93

Mr. M. is an elderly pensioner from the Navy, where he never rose above able seaman. He supplements his pension by running what he calls a market garden, although it is on a very small scale. However, he seems to make a living mainly by selling direct to upper middle-class houses at full retail prices.

He is a lonely man, whose wife deserted him some years ago, probably because he spent too much of his earnings on beer and horses. Now he keeps a dog for company and says "A four-legged bitch is better company than a two-legged one." He is a fairly heavy drinker, never having less than five pints a day. He smokes in moderation. He used to gamble heavily, but now does not back horses or dogs at all, and gambles only on his football coupon.

He is a keen sportsman and acts as unpaid groundsman for a cricket and football club, never missing attendance at their games. He is sociable and a good darts and dominoes player.

Reads little but has an odd store of knowledge and a rich stock of experience of the world.

Too old now to bother about women, but used to be promiscuous.

Not a church-goer. Says, "The parsons have a bloody fine job. I don't blame them. They've got a good racket and make the most of it."

94

Mr. J. is the owner of a small business. He is aged about 45 and married, with one child. He is a keen business man and success in building up his business means more to him than anything in the world, certainly more than his family for whom he has conventional regard but no more.

He is sexually promiscuous, but only with prostitutes. He would not get "mixed up" with a respectable woman as in his experience it leads to too many complications. He says, "If you pay a prostitute there you are with no complications. And if you take presents and things into account, a prostitute is cheaper in the long run."

Mr. J. does not gamble as it is a mug's game. He has few relaxations—plays golf occasionally, likes an occasional game of chess, enjoys a music hall, is bored by the cinema. Drinks and smokes in strict moderation.

Thinks church-going is no use as "You're no different when you come home from what you were before. The parsons mostly couldn't earn an honest living if they tried."

95

Mr. S. is aged 82 and he lives with his son and daughter-in-law and their three children, the eldest of whom is 7. The family are very hard up as Mr. S. has only his old age pension, while his son is a labourer. The daughter-in-law is not a very good housekeeper and though the children are always clean, they have very irregular meals about which Mr. S. grumbles a little.

The young couple are fond of the old man and kind to him, and he in turn is devoted to his eldest grandchild, although the two younger ones, aged 2 years and 6 months, are a great trial to him because of their noise.

Mr. S. is a little worried that he has to live with his son as he says there is not really room for him and the only way he can be fitted in is for the eldest child to sleep in his room (and share his bed) and for the other two children to sleep in their parents' room.

Despite his age Mr. S. has retained all his faculties and he is happier at the present moment than he has been for a long time, as he has got new spectacles under the new National Health Service Act, and can read again with some comfort. For two or three years past he has found reading extremely difficult, but in view of the expense he did nothing about getting new spectacles. He reads the paper eagerly every day and is a great reader of novels, particularly classical novels of adventure (such as those by Conrad and R. L. Stevenson).

Mr. S. does not consider himself very religious, although he goes to church on Sundays whenever it is fine.

He was not brought up to go to church, but started going soon after he was married as his wife was a great churchwoman, and he kept the habit up all through his married life and has continued it now he is a widower.

The family have a radio set but Mr. S. does not hear much of it except on special occasions because they do not switch it on through the day so as to save electricity and he goes to bed soon after half-past seven in the evenings.

He likes a pint of two of beer when he can get it, but because of the cost he does not reckon to go to the public house more than about once a month, usually on a Sunday evening, when he will sit for a couple of hours over two pints. He enjoys the company and the talk and watching a darts match or game of dominoes, and goes home feeling he has had "a real evening out."

He does not go out much in bad weather, but in the summer finds great pleasure in taking his eldest grandchild for a stroll in the nearby park where they watch tennis, and sometimes cricket, and where Mr. S. often sits on a seat in the warm weather while the child plays nearby on the grass.

Mr. S's. smoking, like his drinking, is strictly limited by the cost, but he enjoys an occasional pipe. He cannot afford more than an ounce of tobacco every two or three weeks, so he saves his pipes up for special occasions.

Mr. S. has a constant fear that his son may one day be unable to keep him in the house should he become helpless or should any more grandchildren be born. If he had to leave, he would try to get a place in an old people's home, of which he has read in the papers, where he thinks he might still be fairly happy, but he says that if he had to go to the workhouse he would die in a matter of days.

96

Miss R. is a barmaid in a small hotel. She "lives in," although her family live in the neighbourhood. Her father was a first violin in a well-known orchestra until he injured a hand in the First World War. He subsequently took employment in an office and on leaving school at the age of 14 Miss R. worked for two years in the same office. She disliked this, and being an enterprising girl she eventually left. She has had a variety of jobs—stable "lad," shop girl, traveller in toys, and others. She looks years older than her age and has been in the habit of passing as 22 or 23. She finds hotel work quite interesting but intensely dislikes the atmosphere of the staff room where she says that nearly all the talk is of sex and betting. Miss R. does not drink, but she smokes a good deal. She is bitterly opposed to sexual promiscuity and despises anyone who indulges in it. She is very keen on dancing, enjoys going to the cinema, but now rarely has time to go, and reads more than the average—mostly novels but occasionally books of travel. Miss R. says that she profoundly believes the Christian doctrine to be true, but she does not go regularly to church although she used to do so. Her reason for not going is that she doesn't think much of the average parson.

She is sorry that in her present work she cannot keep a dog, as this is the first time in her life that she has been without one.

She is very devoted to her parents, and to her brothers and sister.

She particularly enjoys visiting the latter (who is married) as she "enjoys a good girlish gossip."

Before she went to the hotel, Miss R. was inclined to Communism (of an idealistic form), but now she says, "Men are so beastly I don't care what happens to them," so she says she is now a Tory.

97

Mrs. R. is about 30, an attractive but rather hard-faced blonde. She is married to a man who is always about to make a lot of money but somehow never does, although he is in regular employment. In consequence of her husband's low earning power, Mrs. R. works full time in a factory. She rises at 5 a.m. on each day from Monday to Friday, does an hour's hurried housework, leaves home at 6.30 a.m., and gets back about 5.30 p.m. On Saturdays she does the family washing and on Sundays cleans the house. She grumbles a moderate amount, particularly about the early hour at which she has to get up, but quite enjoys factory work as it is companionable without responsibility. She has a daughter of 6 who is given breakfast and sent to school by her husband and whom Mrs. R. hardly sees, except at week-ends. Mrs. R. is bitter about her husband's gambling on horses, and she says he sometimes loses her earnings as well as his own. She doesn't mind him doing a football coupon as it is harmless and is very glad he is not attracted by greyhound racing. Mrs. R. and her child are neatly dressed. The investigator saw the child sitting on the pavement waiting for her parents outside a public house where Mr. and Mrs. R. have a few drinks together every Saturday evening. It was then 9.30 p.m. Despite the worries about money and gambling, Mrs. R. is devoted to her husband, and they seem an affectionate couple.

Mrs. R. has absolutely no religious beliefs and thinks that going to church or not is just like going to a cinema or not, "It's a matter of what suits you." Mrs. R. adds that personally she hasn't got time for either, and any free time she has got, she'd sooner sit in the pub with a bit of company and have a glass of stout.

She looks forward to her annual holiday as the greatest treat of the year, but even then is unable to rest or go away as she has the house to look after. Nevertheless she always manages two or three day trips by coach to the seaside.

98

Mr. F. is a labourer, 68 years of age, but still in regular employment. He is short and heavily built. Very uncompromising in his ways, slow of speech and obstinate in his views. He dislikes modern innovations and is a born Conservative. He is kindly and is quite strikingly and unusually courteous to women (for example, he gives them his seat in a bus). He lives with a sister as his wife died many years ago, and he has no children. He likes a pint of beer whenever he can afford it and smokes a very pungent and unpleasant tobacco incessantly in a pipe that bubbles and stinks.

He has a pleasant twinkle in his eye and a good, although slow, sense of humour. He is a regular chapel-goer and reads his Bible regularly, apparently on most days. He reads nothing else, and has no radio, so national events simply don't exist for him. He works in his garden on Saturdays and summer evenings, and is proud of his flowers and vegetables.

It is difficult to imagine Mr. F. as a young man, but it is impossible to believe that he has ever done a mean action.

99

Miss P. is a very emotional young woman of about 30. She is a university graduate and is employed in a large store. She is very much in love with a married man, who works a considerable distance away, and whom she consequently does not normally see, although they occasionally spend a week-end together, but is inclined to think that she will marry a young bachelor who is very much in love with her. She also spends week-ends with the young bachelor, although she says that she does not really approve of sexual promiscuity and always despises herself for practising it.

She is very highly cultured and paints with considerable skill. At one time she had wanted to become an artist, but her parents dissuaded her. She was brought up very strictly as a Nonconformist and her parents are still strict Nonconformists who would be horrified if they knew anything of her mode of life. Although she was made to attend church, she never really had any religious faith though she regards Christianity as a great ideal. She is fond both of the cinema and of the theatre and goes frequently to each, she is a keen dancer, and goes to a classical concert about twice a month.

Her parents are fairly well off and she has a large allowance from her father which enables her to keep a motor car of her own.

She is almost a chain smoker and drinks fairly heavily, mostly spirits. She says that her nerves are so sensitive that she needs alcohol to dull them and she consequently drinks whisky at any hour of the day, including the morning, if she is feeling "nervy."

100

Mr. P., aged 54, is a cutter in a firm of tailors. He is an intelligent man, suave on the surface but secretly embittered. Is married, with three children. His work is constantly bringing him into contact with the "upper classes" and as far as he can see most of them are pretty much like the working classes except that they were born to well-to-do parents. He says that if he were young he would join the Communist Party because he believes that with all their faults the Communists really do work for an eventual classless society.

Mr. P. used to go to church but gave up going because "it was the same old clap-trap. Most of the parsons only think about a living."

Mr. P. does a football pool coupon because "it gives me just a chance of getting away from this slavery," but does not gamble otherwise.

Mr. P. is devoted to his home which includes his aged mother and his wife's aged father. Mr. P. calls them "lovely old people," and is obviously glad to house them though his father-in-law is bedridden.

Smokes a little but has never been a drinking man because he preferred to spend money on his home and education for the children.

101

Miss R. is a 22-year-old prostitute, who frequents expensive bars. Without make-up she is unnoticeable, but with it on people stop and stare. She is well known to barmen and the local police.

All day long she is either drunk or drugged. At night she is alive and alert. "A short life and a happy one," she said, "I don't want to grow old. I'm having a wonderful time now. It might last another ten years. I don't care if I die then."

She is always hard up. She can't hold money twenty-four hours. Debt collectors and writs follow her throughout her many changes of home. She doesn't want too many people to find out where she lives—only those she wants to see.

Her suitcases and clothes are littered throughout a number of boarding houses. When she can't pay her rent landladies keep her clothes, evict her and wait until she can pay before they release her clothes.

She doesn't care, "They can keep her things if they want them." She can always get some more, and there's always another landlady somewhere else. Her legion of men friends 'phone for her from one place to another. She is extremely popular.

Some of her admirers are cultured, well-educated men. Miss R. makes them laugh with her fund of funny stories. She has a big following of men aged from 22 to over 60. Many of them are content to sit alongside her in the bars. The younger men like dancing with her. She likes company—men's and women's. She enjoys going to bed with some of the men—with others it's a job that has to be done to get some money. She loves buying clothes and jewellery. Many of her friends sell their clothes to her when they are in a desperate plight for money.

She's having a good time. She's not worried about anything. She reads a lot of magazines before going to sleep when she is alone.

102

Mrs. G. is the wife of a soldier serving overseas. She is about 45 and has three children and the only home they have been able to find is a small barn which has now been divided into a two-roomed wooden hut. A small kitchen has been built on. There is no sanitation, no water, not even a drain.

Mrs. G. is not unhappy. She is fond of her children, turns them and herself out "spick-and-span" and does a good job under appalling conditions.

She is an awful gossip, this being her one joy in life, and when she starts talking she is intolerable.

Besides being a gossip, she is unattractive physically, so there can be no question of her sexual virtue.

She has no radio, goes occasionally to the cinema, likes a drink at the public house occasionally and smokes a good deal.

Sends her children to church but says she has "grown out of such things."

103

Miss O. is a manicurist in a man's shop. Aged about 25–30, plump and quite attractive. Is expected to make herself pleasant to customers. The shop has an exclusive clientèle and Miss N. receives many strictly dishonourable proposals. She goes off occasionally for a week-end or a night with one or other of the younger or more important customers. She thinks nothing of it; it is a normal part of making herself pleasant and she enjoys it.

Miss N. lives with an elderly widowed mother and is her main support. She hopes to marry but would only marry a man who would let her mother live with them. "The poor old thing hasn't got many years. I'm not going to shorten them by leaving her,"

Miss N. is intelligent and amusing. Quite well read. Gambles on horses "for fun."

Is fond of old people and has a regular visiting list of more than a dozen to each of whom she devotes an evening every five or six weeks.

Keen on cinema and theatre. Not on dancing.

Drinks a good deal and smokes in moderation.

Not interested in religion.

104

Mrs. R. is the wife of a successful professional man. She is about 50–55 and worried about her husband's health as he is overworking so grossly that his doctor has warned him that he is endangering his life. Mrs. R. has no control over him and he takes no notice of her appeals that he should rest more.

There are six children, the youngest 15, and the three eldest are married.

Mrs. R. says her life has been happy on the whole but her husband has been so wrapped up in work that she has often been lonely. She is rather shy and most of her pleasures are solitary—the cinema, concerts and art exhibitions are chief among them.

She does a certain amount of voluntary work with youth organizations but all on the administrative side. She is too shy to work with young people. She also does administrative work (unpaid) at the headquarters of a national charity.

Mrs. R. does not gamble and her sex life is undoubtedly irreproachable. She drinks and smokes in moderation.

Her attitude to religion is neutral. She goes to church to set an example but gets nothing out of it.

105

Mr. S. is the vicar of a large industrial parish. He is 54, married, with two grown-up children. He worked for many years as a labourer in a foundry, but was always very religious. At the age of 35 he became a licensed lay reader, and at 45 he entered a theological college and eventually took holy orders. He has remained in close touch with working-class thought. His theology is very simple and unsophisticated. He is still a fundamentalist and believes that scientific discovery will one day prove Darwinism to be false and Genesis true.

He works immensely hard going into the homes of people in his parish, non-churchgoers as well as churchgoers. Although a wealthy parishioner offered him a car he goes everywhere on foot on principle, and he says that his boots have to be soled every fortnight.

He neither smokes nor drinks, and has no time for amusements nor even for reading. His whole life is simple devotion to the spiritual needs of his parish. He says he has no better attendances at church than most other parsons, but this does not worry him as he says the churchgoers don't need him.

He says he has never been interested in sex, and attributes this primarily to the excessive sweating when he worked in a foundry.

106

Mrs. T., aged 37–40, is a doctor by profession although she no longer practises. Her husband is a professional man and there are four children. Mrs. T. is rather a stupid woman and she can scarcely have inspired much confidence as a doctor.

She is not greatly interested in anything outside her home, and the doings of friends of equal social standing and their children. She dislikes so intensely having to do her own housework, or part of it, that she talks of the "foolishness of the working-class, sending their children into factories instead of into service."

She is a member of the Church of England, and attends church every Sunday.

She drinks and smokes in moderation, but does not gamble.

Her present sexual habits are undoubtedly irreproachable (in any case she isn't attractive enough to tempt even the most ardent male!), but there is no clue to her pre-marital habits. She simply would not say.

107

Mr. F. is a clerk in the early fifties, married, and with three children. He is a very mild little man with an agreeable but rather domineering wife, of whom he stands in considerable awe. His wife's mother lives with them and she is a senile old lady well on in the eighties. She has reached the stage where she is really rather objectionable in her habits. When her daughter married Mr. F. she was sure that she had "married beneath her," and was in consequence systematically offensive to Mr. F. for a number of years. It would not be surprising therefore if Mr. F. now resented her presence. In fact, he does not do so, and treats her with great patience and good humour.

He is devoted to his children, but is a weak disciplinarian and tends to spoil them.

He is intensely devoted to his home and spends nearly all his spare time there. He likes a glass of beer at home in the evenings but never goes to a public house. His main extravagance is smoking. He formerly smoked 50 cigarettes a day, but their high cost has forced him to reduce this to 20.

He never gambles, for he says that a gambler can never win.

He is a keen gardener, growing both vegetables and flowers.

He is an agnostic and maintains that the whole question of the existence or purpose of God is something too difficult for man to consider. He does not exclude the possibility of God's existence and indeed considers it probable, but thinks that human limitations are such that no progress towards an understanding of God can ever be made with man's limited intellect. He definitely disbelieves in the divinity of Jesus, though he says that he imagines that the existence of Jesus was an historical fact. Much of the gospel stories, however, he says must be legends written by the supporters of Jesus.

Mr. F. is a keen supporter of a local association football team and he never misses their matches at home and often manages to travel with them to see their away matches. He seldom goes to the theatre, but goes to the cinema about three or four times a month.

He says that he has never borrowed money in his life, never refused help to anyone if he was in a position to give it, and has never looked at any woman except his wife since he was married. He thinks that people do not need a formal religion to tell them what is right or what is wrong and that an agnostic or even an atheist has got just as much chance in the next world as any churchman.

108

Mr. D. is aged 27, but looks less. He is very handsome, dark, with wavy hair, and is vain about his appearance. He is a waiter and is unmarried, living as a lodger with a married sister. He works long hours and his leisure is divided between watching football or cricket according to the season, drinking in a public house, and making love to any attractive girl he meets. He was a fighter pilot in the Battle of Britain. Of his leisure pursuits the principal is watching football, and he is such a keen supporter of a certain professional team that if they are beaten unexpectedly, "It makes me miserable for the week-end. I don't even want to drink."

Mr. D. does a weekly football coupon but otherwise does not gamble; his normal stake is 7s. 6d. He drinks moderately but regularly, but on the whole uses the public house as a place where he can talk about the star professional sportsmen he admires, and sometimes even meet them. He never reads a book but reads the *Daily*

Express and the *Star* on weekdays and the *News of the World* on Sundays. His sister doesn't mind him taking his girl-friends to bed in his lodgings and he says, "It's only natural. Why not? The girls enjoy it as much as I do. Mind you, I wouldn't have a prostitute. It's no good unless you both enjoy it."

Mr. D. has no interest in religion. He says, "Where does it get you? Nobody really believes all the nonsense they read out in church. The parsons just do it to earn their living. I bet my sister's Alsatian has got more soul than most of the church people, and as for chapel, they're a lot of —— hypocrites."

109

Mr. O., aged 42, is the son of a country rector. He himself went to a good public school and has a degree from Cambridge. He married early in life and is separated from his wife who will not agree to a divorce. Mr. O. is so "fed up" with the life led by his father's class that he has taken a series of jobs as cellar-man in big public houses (itself a skilled occupation). He drinks a good deal (14 or 15 pints a day regularly, but from usage they have little effect), and smokes heavily. He pours acid contempt on other hotel servants in his present job who gamble, and he alternates between weeks of puritanism in a sexual sense and brief intervals of licence, including homosexualism.

Mr. O. is a keen cinema-goer, mostly in the afternoons, and he is an implacable enemy of all forms of organized religion. He is extremely fond of children and of animals, and both seem to trust him and be grateful for his notice.

110

Mr. F. is a bus driver, aged about 35–40, married, with one child, to whom he is greatly attached.

Is not promiscuous sexually as he says he has a nice home and all the money he has he likes to spend on it.

Does not bet on horses but does a football pool coupon regularly which he says is not gambling. He gets a bit of fun and excitement out of it, and if he wins a bit, as he has a few times, the money goes straight into his child's savings account. Would like to win a big prize for the child's sake, but as for himself he is absolutely happy.

Drinks occasionally and smokes in moderation. Makes his own cigarettes.

Never goes to church. When asked why not, first said, "Not interested," then added, "And blimey, just look at the —— parsons."

111

Mrs. M. is the wife of a stockbroker. She is aged about 40 with a very ample figure, and an enormous appetite—particularly for sweet things. She was married at the age of 18 and has two children, aged 16 and 12, both boys. She is devoted to her husband and sons. She has no religious faith—"Not an atheist, you know; I just don't bother. I like the boys to go to church because they ought to know their way around the church services. They look such fools if they don't and if they ever *have* to go to church." Mrs. M. bets on horses if she gets a tip, and she and her husband "invest" 7s. 6d. each week on a football pool. She is not interested in greyhounds. She smokes in moderation and "adores the flicks" (i.e., the cinema), going regularly two or three afternoons a week. She belongs to a bridge club and plays several times a week. She drinks because it is socially necessary, but doesn't care much for most alcoholic drink. She is a strong Tory and hates the Labour Government, which she blames for every ill, including her indigestion. ("It's all this starchy food 'they' give me.")

112

Mr. F. is a night watchman aged 64 and married. He works only four nights a week and receives 15s. 6d. for twelve hours. He has had many jobs before ending up in his present one and sums up his experience of life by saying that it contains "ups and downs, but not on the whole too bad."

He was brought up as a member of the Church of England, but now never goes to church. As far as he can see, religion does not make a man any worse but he is equally doubtful whether it makes him any better. It certainly does not seem to make men any happier and Mr. F. believes that religious people on the whole enjoy life less than the irreligious and seem to be more gloomy. Nevertheless, Mr. F. sometimes prays when he is lying awake in bed. He thinks that in bed is the right place to think about religion, as during the day people have too many other things to think about. He has a completely open mind on the possibility of an after life.

Mr. F. says that the trouble with the world is that what people say and what they do are very different. People can manage kind words and nice phrases, but what is in their heart is very different. Mr. F. says that in his view greed is the greatest scourge of mankind.

Mr. F. sometimes reads the newspapers, not regularly, and never a book. He says he has not sufficient education to read much. His main hobbies are a smoke and a pint of beer.

113

Mrs. R. is the wife of a country solicitor, with two children. She is 41 or 42 and her main interest is in the little daily happenings to her friends, and in gossip about them. She smokes and drinks in moderation, goes to church once a month or so, and leads a completely empty, harmless but useless life. She has no interest in world affairs, no interest indeed beyond the narrow circle of her own acquaintance and class. Every event in the world only has significance to her in so far as it directly affects her and those of her family, whom she considers a part of herself.

She is of course not promiscuous, does not gamble, does nothing vicious.

114

Mr. O. is aged 28, an assistant at a men's outfitters. He is good-looking, patient and friendly. Married, with one child and very much attached to his home.

Does not like his job but receives good pay for it, and is not specially qualified for anything else.

Does not drink but smokes in moderation. Does a football pool coupon but does not otherwise gamble, "except perhaps for five bob on the Derby once a year."

Is very much in love with his wife and feels sure he will never want anything to do with another woman. Was occasionally promiscuous before marriage.

Has tried church-going to please his wife, but can't see anything in it. He leads precisely the same life whether he goes or not; he isn't impressed by the sermons, and the set prayers don't seem to him to mean anything—for example, it seems nonsense to pray for "Our Sovereign Lord King George, our gracious Queen Elizabeth, Mary the Queen Mother, the Princess Elizabeth, the Duke of Edinburgh, and all the Royal Family."

115

Mr. N. is an accountant, aged 30 and unmarried. He is very keen on his job and is still studying in the evenings to take certain professional examinations.

He is keen on crossword puzzles and does that in *The Times* almost every day. It gives him a feeling of satisfaction when he solves a puzzle and he is certain that only intelligent people can do them. Sometimes, however, he feels too tired after working and studying to be able to tackle them.

He is theoretically a member of the Church of England, but in practice prefers going to the cinema on Sundays rather than to church. He thinks that most people do not practise what they preach and this is true in politics as well as religion. He says that he personally is an individualist.

He is a heavy smoker and though he drinks very little (seldom more than half a pint of beer a day and often not even that), he is very short of money. Often to keep up his expenditure on cigarettes he has to economise on food and even go without his midday meal. With a job such as his, an ambitious man must be well dressed and this too is a very heavy drain on his income.

He does not bet on horses or dogs because he knows he would have no chance of winning any substantial sum, but he does a football pool coupon regularly as he says that he sees that is the one way he might get a really large sum of money.

He would like to marry but would not marry unless his wife had some money, as he could not possibly keep her. If he did marry he would certainly want children and that too is a heavy expense.

He does not feel lonely, both because he is so busy and because he has a good many friends. He wishes that he had more spare time, as he would like to read a good deal more than he does. His favourite books are biographies and memoirs.

116

Mrs. S., aged about 55, is the wife of an artisan with a good, steady wage packet. She has one child—grown up and happily married. She considers herself to be lucky because her man has never been unemployed for more than a couple of weeks and has always been considerate and kind. For herself, she has always tried to put his views before her own on the grounds that as wage-earner, and as the male, he has a better idea than her about everything.

Of course she has always been faithful to him, and she imagines that every now and then he has had another woman, "Just as men do; it's natural to them and nothing for a wife to fash (i.e., worry) herself about."

She likes a glass of beer, but does not smoke. She does not gamble but always pays half her husband's 3s. 6d. weekly stake on the football pool coupon on the understanding that any winnings are half-and-half.

Thinks church is all right for those who have nowhere else to turn but she has always been able to look after herself.

117

Miss W., aged 20, is the daughter of upper middle-class parents who have made great efforts to give her the best education possible. She has been to one of the most expensive schools, followed by eighteen months at a finishing school in Switzerland. She has formed expensive tastes and expensive friendships and, having made gigantic sacrifices to pay for the education, the parents simply cannot afford to keep the finished product! Therefore Miss W. is disgruntled. She wants a life of idleness and luxury, with horses to ride, balls, expensive clothes, parties, etc. After all, as she says, that is what she has been taught to consider normal. Now there is even some talk that she might have to get a job. She is disgusted.

Though spoilt, she is really quite a nice girl. Drinks and smokes in moderation. Likes all forms of gaiety and has been taught to have something of the viewpoint of an eighteenth-century aristocrat.

Goes regularly to church.

Naturally does not gamble.

Probably not promiscuous, but investigator not quite certain she is telling the truth on this point. May have had one or two "adventures."

118

Miss X., aged 28, is trying to make a career as a sculptress. She has had one or two trivial pieces accepted for exhibition and is just beginning to make her way. She is desperately keen on her work, to which she devotes the large majority of her waking hours.

She is a warm personality, and quite charming. She says, probably truthfully, that she has had several offers of marriage but is determined not to marry until she has made a real success of her work or until it is proved a failure.

She neither drinks nor smokes except on special occasions, but is occasionally promiscuous sexually as she cannot see that it does any harm.

She has no time for amusements such as the cinema but goes occasionally to dances and enjoys long country walks.

Says she is not religious in a church-going sort of way, but that in her search for beauty in her work she is expressing her religion.

119

Mrs. R. is in the late thirties. Her husband is a well-to-do professional man. Their income is probably in the range £1,500–£2,000, but they are in constant financial difficulties because most of their friends have either larger incomes or smaller families, and the R's. try to live at the same standard. There are six children, ranging from 15 years to 6 months. Mrs. R. and her husband are both very fond of children and would like any number they could afford, but they have decided that they must not have any more. The last one was a "mistake."

She is well dressed and friendly. Not very well educated and her voice is affected. She probably married "above her." She is devoted both to her husband and to her children but unhesitatingly puts her husband first at all times, and says this is the essential condition of a happy home. She would never think of any man except her husband but she knows that he is sometimes unfaithful to her, and she accepts this as natural. She is proud of the fact that basically nobody matters to him except her.

She is very worried by their shortage of money and regularly does a football pool in the hope of making a substantial sum for a stake that is insignificant in her total spending plan. She does not back greyhounds because the odds are too small, but bets on horses if she gets a tip from someone she trusts.

She goes to church occasionally. She hardly knows why she does, but she thinks that Christianity really corresponds with the good life she would like for herself and her family. But she does not believe in the "supernatural parts." Her children have been taught the well-known prayers and they go fairly regularly to church. Not to Sunday School, where they might be taught things that Mrs. R. does not think are true. "Church is different. It's passive. You can take it in or not, as you like."

120

Mr. T. is 37. He is a professional man, separated from his wife, who will not give him a divorce because she is a Roman Catholic. He is in love with a girl of 30, who returns his affections and they want to marry. As they cannot, and as they cannot live together openly because of her family, she has become his mistress and they spend as much time together as they can.

Mr. T. is fairly well off and he lives in a very comfortable flat. He smokes heavily and at times drinks heavily, although for the most part he drinks in moderation.

He is interested in music and ballet and the theatre, but not much in the cinema.

He gambles fairly heavily because he says he is bored. He maintains that for the most part his gambling is successful as he endeavours never to bet without some inside information,

He has two children by his first wife but never sees them and does not wish to. He says that they were the beginning of his estrangement from her, because after they were born she diverted all her affection to them.

Mr. T. is widely read but does not read much now except novels and books relating to artistic subjects, in which he is interested.

In politics he is a left-wing intellectual, but would never take any active part in political work.

121

Mr. W. is recently retired from the Indian Civil Service. He reached pensionable age just before the transfer of power to the two Dominions and is now living on his savings and pension. He finds it hard to adapt himself to English life, and cannot understand democratic ways. He deplores the lack of servants, the high taxation, the fact that people of his own class have given up dressing for dinner, and what he calls "All this mollycoddling of the working-class." He prophesies the greatest possible disasters. He "doesn't bother much about going to church," but would go if he lived in the country "to set an example." He is nominally Church of England. He has no objection in principle to gambling but has no desire to do so in England except when he attends any of the major race meetings. He doesn't see why people shouldn't gamble if they want to, and indeed thinks it a good thing to provide any means of "taking their minds off all this Socialism." He is happily married and has been faithful to his wife for all the thirty-odd years of their married life. Mr. W. smokes in moderation and never drinks before evening. Then he likes a fair quantity of whisky—about a quarter of a bottle each evening—but he finds it difficult to obtain and more expensive than he can readily afford.

He has no real hobbies; he reads a bit, mainly novels, rides occasionally, plays golf and tennis a little, and is very bored. He says he feels "out of it," and thinks it "a damn shame that the Socialists gave up India."

122

Mrs. Y., aged 45–50, is the wife of a fairly successful professional man. They live on the South Coast and are childless. Mrs. Y's. interests are entirely social and sporting. On a fine morning she plays a round of golf, or meets her friends for coffee. She lunches out, plays bridge or golf most afternoons, and is always dressed for dinner by the time her husband returns from the city, ready to give him a cocktail before he dresses. They often dine out or have friends to dinner. They are both expert bridge players but play for small stakes being only a few pounds up or down at the end of a month.

Mrs. Y. reads all the fashionable novels, the society papers, and the *News of the World*. Apart from bridge, she does not gamble. Smokes and drinks very heavily. The Y's. spend over £15 a month on tobacco and about £20 a month on alcohol.

Mr. Y. is a fourth husband, and was his wife's lover before he married her after a double divorce.

Mr. and Mrs. Y. are fairly frequent attenders at church, but appear to have no dynamic beliefs, thinking rather that going to church is the right example to set the working class.

Mrs. Y. is superstitious to a quite unusual degree.

123

Mr. N. is a bank clerk aged about 50. A very steady sort of man. Married, with three children. Says he has always been a very careful saver, and as his wife never wastes a penny, they have been able to buy for investment two houses besides that in which they live. Each child has sufficient money spent on it for special coaching to enable it to win a scholarship, so that the children have been educated almost without cost.

Mr. Y. has a garden and an allotment. He uses the garden for recreation—has a croquet set, a swing for the children, flower beds and fruit trees. Most of the garden is cultivated by his wife. He works hard on the allotment, sells the surplus produce and makes enough to cover all outgoings on garden and allotment, so that his vegetables are free, and he has a few pounds a year in hand which he is careful to declare in his income tax return.

Does not gamble. Is an agnostic (and can explain why). Does not drink or smoke. Grudges money for cinemas and theatres, but goes occasionally to please his wife.

The family's one extravagance is a fortnight's annual holiday, for which they usually go to Guernsey.

124

Mr. R. is 72, and is a railway pensioner who supplements his pension by growing vegetables and fruit, and selling them. He has been happily married for 48 years and he and his wife regret only that they had no children. He is a regular chapel-goer, a teetotaller and non-smoker. He has a rather malicious tongue and appears to delight in telling endless stories about neighbours and acquaintances, often rather unkind stories. He says openly that the customers for his vegetables call him a skinflint, and he admits that he takes a pleasure in out-smarting them.

He reads a daily newspaper but nothing else. He never goes to any place of entertainment, but he and his wife listen to the radio almost every evening, usually to the Light Programme.

There can be no doubt that his sexual life has been irreproachable. Mr. R. clearly has faith and hope, but the charity is not so certain!

125

Miss T. is about 22, the daughter of upper middle-class parents. She has trained as a shorthand-typist and works intermittently, although her parents prefer her not to.

She is a very attractive blonde, but obviously quite innocent, young for her years and naïvely distressed because she has noticed that men find her attractive. She says that the way some of them stare at her is "beastly."

She reads a good many novels but not much besides and is rather empty-headed. She is fond of rather simple gaiety and is secretary of the local Young Conservatives Association, although she is not interested in politics and belongs solely for social reasons.

She smokes and drinks in strict moderation. Is keen on dancing, the cinema, tennis, and the radio (Light Programme).

She goes to church because her parents go and she has always been brought up to go.

126

Mr. J. is a retired professional man, who gave up his professional life at a very early age to manage a medium-sized estate he had inherited. He is married but childless. He has taken a great deal of trouble to learn about estate management, and judging by his own account, he is making a considerable success of running his.

He is fond of his wife but is glad to get away alone occasionally for a few days, to enjoy the company of his male friends.

Mr. J. is a fairly heavy drinker, mainly of spirits and wines, and is a very heavy smoker. He likes company and all forms of entertainment except the cinema, which he finds too unrealistic. He quite enjoys gambling, particularly playing cards and dice. Is willing to "make one" of a party attending horse or greyhound racing, but never bets off-the-course. He is regular in attendance at church when living at home, but otherwise never goes. He does not bother himself about religion at all, and is content to lead the conventional life of his class.

He was formerly a Liberal in politics but has now become a Tory, partly because he believes that it is a waste of time to support the Liberal Party, and partly because the Tories are more likely than any other Party to look after his interests.

127

Mr. K. is a labourer, aged about 53 or 54. His married daughter and her husband live with them. The daughter is dying of cancer. Fortunately there are no grandchildren.

Mr. K. is bitter and blasphemous, and curses God and the Church on account of his daughter. He says it is killing him to see her slowly dying in agony.

He drinks a good deal of beer. Less now because he tries to save to buy extra nourishment for the daughter, but even so he never has less than 2 or 3 pints a day. He is a heavy pipe smoker.

He gambles as a matter of course. All his mates do. Why not? He might win.

He married at the age of 20 and since then has not had anything to do with any other woman. He says that most decent working-class men are the same. In the working-class only a few blackguards go after other women once they are married.

Has a garden and was once proud of it, but does not bother now.

128

Miss N. is a manual worker, is engaged to an artisan, and feels fairly happy. She is about 25–30 and lives alone in a bed-sitting-room. She has been promiscuous, but has given up sex since she became seriously engaged.

She "couldn't care less" about religion, and says, "What has God done for me? I didn't ask to be born. Mum died of T.B., Dad was a drunkard, and when I joined the W.A.A.F. in 1943 I found I had congenital syphilis that had to be treated."

Miss N. likes the cinema and dances to any music that isn't too "classy." She wants to marry and settle down but doesn't want children.

She smokes a good deal, drinks in strict moderation, and gambles as a way of getting out of the near-poverty that oppresses her. Naturally she loses steadily on balance despite occasional wins.

129

Mrs. B., aged about 40, is a bus conductress, and works on the bus her husband drives. She grumbles about the hardness of the work, but really likes it and would not change. She and her husband are happy together. They go fifty-fifty with the household expenses and with everything else. They go into a public house every evening when they are off duty and stand each other a drink, or sometimes two drinks (i.e. four each altogether).

Mrs. B. smokes a good deal. She has little time for cinemas, etc., because off duty she does housework and washing.

There are no children and they want none.

Mrs. B. is not interested in religion. She says when the bus brings people home from church on Sunday they don't look any different to her, and she hears them gossiping about one another just as spitefully as usual.

130

Mr. B. is a courageous man of 75 who is still earning a weekly wage in a wireless factory. He has been with his firm for 21 years and among men of his own status has an immense reputation.

Mr. B. is actually rather a tired and slow old gentleman, but his failures of timekeeping are overlooked because of his influence on young workers, who understand "Old Dad" must often be late.

He has been happily married since 1898, and his wife is still as courageous as he although she is almost entirely bedridden.

Mr. B. used to be a regular chapel-goer but he gradually dropped off until now he only goes on the anniversary celebrations of his own chapel. For the rest, he and his wife still accept the same simple doctrines in which they grew up, and still say their prayers together each night.

He has always "liked a few pints" and still does. He smokes in moderation but does not gamble.

131

Miss F. is a middle-aged spinster who earns her living as a companion. She has rather a trivial outlook on life. Her horizon is bounded by games of patience and bezique, hot-water bottles, taking the dog for a walk, fetching cushions, reading old-fashioned novels aloud, and all the similar tasks of a middle-aged companion.

She neither smokes nor drinks, goes to church every Sunday, gets no closer to gambling than raffles at bazaars, and is of such forbidding exterior it is inconceivable that anyone can ever have wished to seduce her, so her virtue is undoubted.

She enjoys a good gossip about her acquaintances and likes a spice of malice to add flavour to the gossip, but there is no harm in her—only an abysmal emptiness of life.

Miss F. being constantly on duty with her "friend" (i.e., employer), has no time for leisure pursuits. She likes the cinema and concerts, and enjoys the latter on the radio. But all her amusements are subject to the condition that her employer wants them because otherwise Miss F. cannot have them. Nevertheless there is genuine affection between the two women.

132

Mr. P. is a labourer. About 45, married, with two children—18 and 14. He admits that he can hardly write, and finds considerable difficulty in reading, yet he runs a young people's organization attached to his church, and arranges programmes of lectures, concerts, Bible readings, dances, and so on. The secretarial work in this connection is done under his direction by one or other of his children.

Mr. P's. life has twin centres—his home and his church. His children are outstandingly good-mannered, and cheerful, and have been taught to attend church twice every Sunday, as Mr. P. does.

Neither Mr. P. himself nor his children are "goody-goody," and they enjoy a good laugh with anyone, but they spread a strong atmosphere of true goodness.

Mr. P. is opposed to gambling on religious grounds, but he likes a drink and visits the public house two or three times a week—always taking a bottle or two of ale home to his wife. He smokes a good deal, 15 to 20 cigarettes a day, and finds he simply cannot stop.

He is keen on the radio, particularly serious talks as long as they are in simple language. He likes popular concerts (not dance music), but usually finds concerts of classical music are too long and dull.

He doesn't have much time for cinema- or theatre-going, but about once a fortnight he takes his wife to a cinema or to the local theatre.

133

Mrs. E. is an upper middle-class woman of about 50–55 who is married to a chartered accountant. There have been two (or possibly three) previous husbands. One died, and one (or two) divorced Mrs. E. Her explanations of previous matrimony are difficult to follow.

She has an adopted child who she says was an orphan, but who bears a suspicious resemblance to her.

Mrs. E. is a hard woman and gives the impression of being ruthless. Her husband looks crushed.

She is a keen bridge player and two or three afternoons a week plays at friends' houses or invites them to hers. They play for moderate stakes,

Is a keen gambler on horses, and rather oddly, on football pools. (Oddly because she is a snob and thinks professional football vulgar.)

She drinks a great deal for a woman and after two or three drinks gets a fierce gleam in her eye—a rather frightening woman.

Plays golf two or three times a week, including every Sunday. Not interested in religion.

Quite well read.

134

Mr. M. is aged 42, a foreman in a factory, and a member of the Communist Party. He is highly intelligent, well read and with a good sense of humour. He is absolutely convinced that Communism is the right path for human development, and equally certain that it will eventually embrace the whole world. He would give his life without hesitation for its furtherance.

He does not drink because he believes working men should keep their brains alive, not dull them with alcohol. He smokes occasionally.

He is of course an atheist. He is not married and when he became a member of the Communist Party twelve years ago he gave up sexual promiscuity because he wanted nothing to divert him from his work for the Party.

He never "wastes time" on theatres and cinemas, and only listens to serious broadcasts.

135

Mrs. F. is a widow, probably about 50, or perhaps less, who was married to a man 30 years older than herself, to whom she had previously been housekeeper.

She now lives alone in part of the large house she inherited from her husband and lets the other part, which provides her main source of income.

She is a rather uncommunicative and unattractive-looking woman who has a kind heart. She is lonely, but too shy to make friends.

She never misses a chance to do small kindly acts for neighbours, but as soon as they are done she scuttles away again to her lonely dwelling.

Mrs. F. listens a great deal to the radio, works in her garden, reads the *Daily Express* and an occasional novel. She neither drinks nor smokes, and does not gamble although she occasionally does a football pool coupon.

She says she "supposes" she is Church of England. She used to go regularly but has "somehow given up going." Very likely she is just too shy to be seen by so many people.

136

Mrs. G. is about 30 and is in the later stages of a first pregnancy. Her husband is a labourer and they live in two rooms, sharing a kitchen and bathroom. They are very hard up because they are charged an excessive rent but are afraid to seek a reduction from the Rent Tribunal as the landlord houses them at considerable inconvenience to himself, and could probably prove he needs the rooms and they fear that then they would be homeless.

Mrs. G. is not enthusiastic about her baby. She wishes now she had had an abortion. She says, "Folks that talk about the country wanting children ought to try it on £5 a week in two rooms."

She is not religious and is slightly hostile to the Church, which on the whole she thinks is an institution for helping the "haves" against the "have nots."

She takes a poor view of sex and says, "Blimey, that's all a man's after the whole time," but this may be a temporary phase due to pregnancy.

Likes a drink and a smoke, but cannot afford either. Cannot even afford a cinema, in fact, "We're bloody well broke."

If Mrs. G. can find a day nursery to take her child when it is a few months old she will seek work in a factory, "to get some money and have a bit of fun."

137

Mrs. E. is a retired working-class prostitute. Aged about 50–55, she is still willing to come out of her retirement to oblige a friend, but she is so bloated and repulsive it is inconceivable that she should often be troubled. She lives in the same house as her husband, a plumber, but has not spoken to him for ten years or more. He cooks his own meals and she hers, but every Friday evening he gives her 35s. 0d. She lives rent free; gas is from a shilling-in-the-slot meter and she puts a couple of shillings in each week and her husband pays the rest. Her daughter and son-in-law also live in the house and Mrs. E. cooks for them. They are both working and both give her something so that she is quite well off.

Mrs. E. is a very friendly soul and she seems to be lonely. She has made many attempts to "make it up" with her husband but he takes no notice. She has one grandson, who also lives in the house and is mostly cared for by Mrs. E., who is very fond of him.

Mrs. E. smokes heavily—as many cigarettes as she can get—but hardly ever drinks now although when she was "working" she used to find her men in public houses.

She occasionally bets on horses but does not gamble in other ways except for sometimes "taking a line" in her son-in-law's football pool coupon.

She is a keen cinema-goer—twice a week regularly—and takes her grandson (aged 3).

138

Miss A. is a shopgirl probably aged about 28 (she says 21). Her real Christian name is Muriel, but she calls herself "Christina" because it is more romantic. She is an empty-headed creature whose mind has been fed with too many films and too many cheap novelettes. She sets up to be a "femme fatale" and does the best her dumpy figure will allow to develop a "slinking" walk like her favourite film star.

She is really a warm-hearted and friendly girl. She is sexually promiscuous.

Apart from her novelettes her only reading is the *Daily Mirror* and the *News of the World*. Her passion is the cinema and she goes three or four times each week. When there is a big film première in London she always joins the crowds to watch the film stars arrive.

She drinks in moderation, smokes heavily and gambles from time to time, when she gets a tip about a horse.

She was brought up as a Roman Catholic and still goes to church occasionally.

139

Mrs. F. is the wife of a man working abroad at a place where she cannot join him. She is about 32–35, fairly intelligent but full of patriotic and imperialistic clichés. (Not quite as bad as "the white man's burden," but nearly.)

She lives with her mother and occupies her time in rather intermittent voluntary work. She has had two or three paid posts in the last three or four years but has been dismissed from each on account of absenteeism.

She is occasionally promiscuous. She does not believe for one moment that her husband is faithful to her and she sees no reason why she should be to him.

Does not gamble except for a football pool coupon.

Is a heavy smoker but only an occasional drinker.

Quite well read. Few real hobbies except housework. Rather lazy and spends a good deal of time doing nothing.

140

Mr. P. is an undertaker. Off duty he is a merry, talkative little man of about 60, who enjoys telling an endless series of whimsical stories about funerals, corpses and coffins!

Asked whether he believed in life after death he said, "How should I know? I've put hundreds of dead 'uns into their coffins but none of them yet told me they were still alive." His general outlook is fatalistic and though he goes to church himself he says, "People expect an undertaker to go to church," and he clearly does not take the services very seriously.

His wife is about his age but looks withered and oppressed, as though her husband's talk of corpses had worn her down. There are no children.

He does not gamble and has few amusements except his garden, which is his main recreation. He is a great lover of flowers and birds, and when the birds ate most of the cherries in his garden he said, "That saves me the trouble of picking them." He is a natural, simple philosopher with a merry heart and a kind nature.

141

Mr. P. is a retired professional man. He is a bachelor, now quite elderly, and he lives in a small but extremely comfortable flat and spends a good part of each day in his club. He is a friendly rather garrulous man, whose conversation is divided between reminiscences of thirty or forty years ago, and gloomy estimates of how fast the Socialist Government is ruining the country.

Mr. P. has nostalgic longings for the days when "the commonn people" were kept in their place and when the "better classes" could lead a more elegant and gracious life than he finds possible to-day.

Yet Mr. P. is a good man, a sincere churchman with a kindly and even generous nature. He has taken a full part in the pleasures of his class and, though he is now too old, was a particularly keen horseman.

Having few interests remaining in which he can take an active part, Mr. P. has become something of a gourmet, an attitude which in present circumstances gives him the opportunity for many enjoyable grumbles. He drinks and smokes in moderation. Except for newspapers he reads very little, and keeps himself fit by a daily walk.

142

Mr. L. is a fitter in a shipyard, a stout and uncompromising little man with an ailing wife whom he calls a "silly, whimpering woman." The L's. lost two grown-up sons in the war and Mrs. L. broke under the blow, which has merely made Mr. L. bitter and tough.

Mr. L. is a regular chapel-goer, though his wife lost faith at the death of the sons. Mr. L's. religion is not of the submissive sort, and he clearly although unconsciously regards his continuance of chapel-going as a defiance of the Almighty. As though he were saying, "Do your worst!"

He is a man of habit. To work by 6.30 a.m. bus; home 5 p.m.; high tea; wash and read the paper; an hour's walk, alone; half-an-hour at the public house; home and bed at 9.30 p.m. Saturdays he gets home at 1 p.m. to dinner and in the afternoon watches football or cricket according to season.

Believes the woman's place in at home, and never takes Mrs. L out.

Has a great contempt for anyone who "wastes his money" on women or gambling.

A man who does most of the right deeds for the wrong reason.—very little human warmth.

143

Mrs. O. is a working-class housewife of about 45. She has one son and one daughter. The O's. own their house which was bought in pre-war days out of money Mrs. O. inherited from a father who had a small shop. Mr. O. is in good employment, the boy is in the R.A.F., and the girl has just won a scholarship to a high school, so the family feel they are in clover.

The whole family are very strict chapel-goers of the particular kind who regard themselves as "God's elect" and their fellow men as almost certainly damned. They complain of the "stand-offishness" of their neighbours and this complacency of the O's. is probably the reason.

Mrs. O. does not drink or smoke, but Mr. O. smokes in moderation and has a glass of beer occasionally—"perhaps once in six weeks." Naturally Mrs. O. does not gamble and her sex life is no doubt irreproachable. She enjoys listening to the radio and going once or twice a month to the cinema.

Mrs. O's. bedridden mother lives with them and Mrs. O. made the rather surprisingly callous remark, "I hope she hurries up and dies. We want the room."

144

Miss R., aged about 20 or rather more, is engaged and shortly to be married. She comes from a bad home—drunken parents, large family and a good deal of privation when dinner money is spent on beer and horses. Nevertheless, Miss R. is clean and well turned out. She is looking forward to a home of her own but will start married life in two rooms of her mother-in-law's house. Of her future mother-in-law, Miss R. says, "She is more of a mother to me than my Mum has ever been."

Miss R. smokes a good deal and likes a drink occasionally. She says she cannot remember a time when she did not drink. She remembers that when she was a very little girl she was given beer to keep her quiet when she cried because she was hungry.

She lives in a poor neighbourhood and all her friends are promiscuous sexually. Apparently it is normal to start sexual intercourse about the age of 16. Miss R. is quite frank. She had her first sexual experiences at 15 which is "a bit younger than most."

Her fiancé is of a better class and when she is married she says she will "live up to him." She "won't drag him down."

No knowledge of, nor interest in, religion.

145

Mr. S. is a full-time paid Trade Union official in a position of substantial, but not national, responsibility. He is aged about 50 and is very left wing; although not a member of the Communist Party, he is in full sympathy with it. He is an atheist and has brought up his three children to the same view. He gives an impression of great energy and appears to be highly efficient in his work. He smokes in moderation but says he hardly ever drinks. He used to be a heavy drinker spending so much that his family lacked necessities—but he gave it up when he fell under Communist influence as he saw in alcohol merely one of the ways the bosses keep the workers poor and weak.

He seldom has time for recreation and has not been to a cinema or theatre "for years." In his spare time he studies, reading books on politics, economics and history, all for the purpose of better understanding and helping "in the class struggle." He takes an active part in politics, speaking at Labour meetings and canvassing for that Party.

He used at one time to be sexually promiscuous, especially when drunk, but now has no time for sex as he finds his work and studies more interesting.

146

Mrs. A. is an elderly widow, probably in the late sixties. Her deceased husband was a farmer but on his death Mrs. A., who had been brought up in a large town, moved back there. She is worried because her income (which in 1938 was adequate for her needs and even for a few luxuries) is so reduced in value that she has to supplement it by spending her capital. She had three children all of whom are dead. She lives alone in a large airy flat, furnished with heavy old furniture which it is one of her main occupations to polish. As a result her sitting-room is spotless but not very cosy. She has a radio, reads both right-wing and left-wing papers and periodicals and takes an intense interest in current events. She is a strong Tory but is glad that the tendency in legislation is to care for the under-privileged. She tells many stories of what she, as a prosperous farmer's wife, saw of poverty among agricultural labourers a few decades ago.

Mrs. A. enjoys doing a football pool coupon, and out of the football season she does an occasional crossword puzzle (in competitions for which prizes are offered). She has no illusion about her chance of winning either, but she says that in her solitary life it is something to think about for the intervening days until the results are known.

Although Mrs. A. does not smoke (a habit she considers "unladylike") she likes Guinness (and allows herself one bottle each evening), and she keeps brandy in her flat "for emergencies."

Despite being very conscious of being alone, Mrs. A. does not seem lonely. She has a generous and friendly nature, has a considerable number of correspondents, and spends much time knitting and sewing for people worse off than herself. Her great worry is the diminution of her capital, and she is determined to die before she becomes too poor to maintain her present standard of living.

She is a regular churchgoer with what seems to be an absolute faith in the doctrine of the Church of England.

147

Mr. R. is a bachelor of about 40, running an export-import business with his brother. They are obviously fairly prosperous and Mr. R. has plenty of money to spend. His tastes are fairly frugal, although he is very generous and entertains his friends in a way that is almost lavish.

He is shy with women and though he has been engaged once or twice, the women concerned have broken it off, probably being repelled by a shyness which they mistook for coldness. He has very little experience of sex and is certainly not promiscuous.

He works extremely hard at his business, often to a point where he is mentally and physically exhausted and has comparatively little time for recreation. He is very keen on the theatre but not much interested in the cinema or in music and he never listens to the radio.

He is widely read and as he has an exceptionally good memory his conversation, which is always on a serious note, is well furnished with facts stored away during his reading.

He is rather right of centre in politics but finds it impossible to subscribe to the beliefs of the Conservative Party. Indeed there is no party which really reflects his views and he therefore takes no active part in politics.

He thinks that it is his duty to do a certain amount of voluntary social work and makes an effort to do so from time to time. He is not successful, however, partly because he is really too busy to devote an adequate amount of time regularly to any undertaking and partly because people are repelled by his rather humourless outlook.

He does not gamble, although he sees no particular objection on principle to it, because he finds the interest, risk and excitement that he wants in his business. He adds that anyhow if he had plenty of time to spare there are a number of things he would do before he turned to gambling.

148

Miss T. is a school teacher, aged about 30. Comes from a lower middle-class home and obtained education by scholarships. States she is an atheist but appears to be an agnostic. Miss T. has rather coarse features, but is attractive—a good example of what the French call *une jolie laide.* Never received any religious instruction at home, and home life appears to have been shallow and rather sordid.

Admits that she is sexually promiscuous and sees no reason why she should not be. She states that she "goes to bed with any man who pleases her." She is a keen theatre- and cinema-goer, averaging at least one theatre a month (preferably straight plays) and two cinemas a week. Does not gamble. Dislikes country life and not interested in any outdoor activity. Dislikes children and the teaching profession and thinks it is time that she chose a husband.

She is a rather boring and stupid person to talk to, for her conversation runs on the smart restaurants she has visited, the hotels she stays at, and the clothes she wants. Negligible sense of humour. She has, from what she says, been influenced a good deal by the cinema, but her mind runs fairly consistently on sex.

149

Mr. J. is about 60, and is in full-time employment in a factory. He is married, without children, and is one of the most grumpy, unfriendly men imaginable. He is always grumbling and his principal theme is how much better everything was in his youth, and how glad he is that he won't live long because everything is going to be so much worse in the future.

He says himself that he has no friends. "I've always been independent, and kept myself to myself. If you have a lot of friends it means a lot of expense. I don't want to go to other people's houses, and I don't want them in mine."

Mr. J. does not drink but he smokes a pipe, although he strictly rations himself to four pipes a day.

He does not gamble. In forty years of matrimony neither he nor his wife has been away for a holiday. He has never missed a day's work from sickness or voluntary absence, and has never been late. Says he has never accepted anything from anyone and doesn't encourage idleness by giving anything away.

Glad he has no children because he doesn't like them when they are small, and when they are grown up they don't want their parents.

A regular chapel-goer.

150

Miss N., aged about 50–55, makes a good job of being a spinster. She admits she would like to have married, but the men whom she loved didn't ask her, and those who did ask her she didn't even like.

So she lives on a small private income and devotes herself to minor deeds of kindness. She hasn't the ability to take up any important form of public work, but she looks after children for harassed mothers, takes under-nourished children into her home and feeds them up, collects goods and sends parcels to Germany, and performs countless similar deeds.

Is a great idealist and is naturally a pacifist.

She reads widely but not very wisely, e.g., recently, thinking she ought to know something of economics, she bought and studied the first text book on the subject that she saw. It happened to be a text book of Marxist economics! She is thoroughly muddle-headed on most subjects.

Never goes to church and almost splutters with fury whenever she sees a parson. She says they should spend more time helping people and less mumbling prayers to a God who apparently doesn't listen.

Doesn't worry much about entertainment. Hasn't even a radio. Says she gets more pleasure out of spending 3s. 6d. on something for a child than if she spent it on a cinema seat for herself.

Often a foolish woman in her speech but absolutely unselfish and a fine character.

151

Mrs. X. is the wife of the vicar of a large urban church in a middle-class district. She is about 55–60, very much occupied with church affairs, and entertaining a good deal in the vicarage, for the living is a good one and Mrs. X. has a moderate private income.

Mrs. X. drinks an occasional glass of sherry but does not smoke. ("Some people are so prejudiced that I think it better not to.")

Although she is an energetic organizer of raffles for charities, Mrs. X. does not gamble in any harmful way.

She is charming, but so wrapped up in her church work that the larger non-ecclesiastical world has almost ceased to have any reality for her. She seems to have very little idea what life is like in the majority of homes and she has no inkling of how to help young people. She lifts up her hands in an almost theatrical way and says, "I really don't know what young people are coming to. It was so different in my day."

Both Mrs. X. and the vicar are great sticklers for ritual and ceremony (e.g., women entering his church with bare heads are asked to leave!). They spend a lot of money on robes and on decorations for the church (altar cloths, banners for processions, flowers, etc.).

152

Mr. F. is a business man who is separated from his wife and is living with a much younger woman (he is about 50), whom he introduces as his wife.

He is said to be very clever at the more devious ways of the law.

Smokes and drinks a good deal—probably rather excessively, although he seems none the worse for it.

Likes domesticity and settles down in the evenings to play double-handed patience, or dominoes, or sometimes chess with his spurious wife. Goes occasionally to the theatre or cinema, but mainly to please his "wife."

Gambles a good deal, mainly on horses.

Not the least interest in religion and rather looks down on religious people as "superstitious mugs."

153

Mr. B. is managing director of a firm engaged in heavy industry. He is a religious man, in early middle age, and he is keenly interested in any movement likely to lead to a religious revival. He regards the normal methods of the Church as being out of date, but has so far found no acceptable alternative.

Mr. B. gives a good deal of his spare time to the boys' club movement.

He is happily married and his wife shares his interests.

He is a keen bridge player, likes to ride and to play golf, usually goes to the cinema once a week and to the theatre about once a month. He regards greyhound racing and football pools as a waste of time and money, and sees no antidote to them except to teach young people, through club life, to seek worth-while ways of spending leisure.

Mr. B. works very hard himself and believes work is more important than any other personal activity because, if it is well done, it is a contribution to the well-being of the whole community, and not just a selfish satisfaction. Mr. B. says that when he drives to his office on Saturdays, and sees his employees (who work a five-day week) lounging about the streets waiting for the pubs to open, his heart aches with a desire to help them to find a healthier outlook. He adds, "I'm as keen as anyone on a drink at the right time, and pubs can be useful places, but my God! what an outlook, just to hang about after breakfast on Saturday until opening time!"

154

Mr. K. is a professional man living in the provinces. He is about 50, is married, with children of 19, 14 and 6, and is the senior partner of a remunerative family business. He is devoted to his home and is a bit of a trial to his two elder children because he tries to lead their lives too much for them. He is a keen gardener, an excellent chess player, and helps to run his local rugby football club in which he was a keen player in his younger years.

He is unfortunately almost entirely devoid of a sense of humour, and realizing this always has a lurking suspicion that people are laughing at him for being pompous (and quite often they are!).

A fairly regular churchman, he admits to being rather doubtful about the Church's theological dogma. He is, however, so kindly by nature and so incapable of doing anything "shady" that he would follow the Christian ethic even if the organized Churches vanished.

He is a staunch Tory and feels genuinely that it would be "better for the working class" if the Labour movement had never arisen.

He is fond of the social life led by his circle—amateur theatricals once a year, cocktail parties two or three times a month, dances, treasure hunts, tennis parties, and so on. In all this he takes a full and often a leading part.

He drinks and smokes in moderation, has never gambled, and says that he has never had any sexual experiences outside matrimony.

155

Mr. F. is a clerk in the docks of one of the major ports. He is a keen worker, interested in his job and in everything to do with the traffic in the docks. He is very hearty in his manner—perhaps to a rather tiring degree. He is aged about 40, married, with two children. He is very devoted to his family, and though he is on Christian name terms with a score of young women he would never be unfaithful to his wife.

He is an enthusiastic gardener and works every week-end, wet or fine, when there is anything to do to bring his garden as near to perfection as is humanly possible.

He is not a church-goer and says he sees no need to be. Right and wrong are clear to him and he tries always to choose right.

He takes his wife out whenever they can conveniently get a sitter-in, and they go to dances and the cinema, or when they are hard up, sometimes just for a walk or a bus ride.

He does a football pool coupon most weeks but otherwise does not gamble.

156

Mrs. N. is a working-class housewife of about 45. She has three sons. Her husband always gives her his wage packet intact. She allows him £1 for beer and tobacco, another 10s. 0d. for five dinners in his works canteen, and 5s. 0d. for fares. She is left with "less than £4 10s. 0d." for all household expenses, and that includes 10s. 0d. family allowances. They live in a council house and Mrs. N. says that her whole life is "scraping and pinching to make do." She can afford no recreations for herself—no smoking or drinking, although Mr. N. sometimes brings her a bottle of beer from the public house.

She cannot afford to go to the cinema except as a very rare treat, and as for going to church she says she spends "enough time on my knees scrubbing floors without kneeling on Sundays." She adds, "Anyway, what good does it do?"

She likes listening to the radio and her greatest joy is sometimes during the daytime, when everyone is out, to make a cup of tea and sit down and listen to Women's Hour.

157

Miss X. is a middle-aged school teacher in a girls' high school. She is tall and rather stout, but active and a keen disciplinarian. She is not really interested in her work but feels she dare not give up a job with a pension. She is well read and is a keen follower of current affairs. Her interests are divided between music and politics, and she feels frustrated.

She smokes and drinks, both normally in moderation, but on occasion heavily. She says that in her youth she had a few "adventures" with men, but that any thought of sex is one of the ideas that a school teacher has to sacrifice.

She is a rather unconvinced member of the Church of England. She goes to church as a matter of form but makes so many mental reservations she hardly feels that in private she can call herself a Christian at all.

She is keen on the theatre, on opera, and on the cinema. She never listens to the radio.

Hers is a pretty colourless life. Her desire for security has made her afraid to do any of the things she would otherwise like to do.

158

Mr. E. is an officer in the Armed Forces. He is 32, a bachelor, and a very friendly rather stupid man. Quite promiscuous sexually. Gambles a good deal, particularly with cards (mainly poker, vingt-et-un and bridge). This gambling is mostly for fairly small stakes, but Mr. E. says he has lost as much as £25 at a sitting at poker.

Is keen on horse-riding, swimming, fencing and shooting. Has no intention of marrying unless he finds a woman with a net income of at least £750 per annum. Says he lives very comfortably now and isn't going to reduce his standard of living voluntarily.

Keen on the theatre (musical comedies in particular) and cinema.

Does not read much—newspapers and an occasional novel.

Doesn't worry about religion. Goes to church to set an example, but doesn't listen much to the service.

159

Mr. Q. is a retired labourer, aged about 70–75. A bachelor, he lives alone in a small cottage in the country and devotes himself to his garden. He appears to be very feeble but maintains he is quite well and strong enough to live alone for another ten years. He knows that the only alternative is the workhouse and that when lonely old men are taken there they usually die in a couple of weeks. He has seen this several times in the last few years in the case of old friends. He is conscious that of his band of cronies only he remains.

In his youth was interested in politics.

His main recreation is to sit in the village public house and drink a pint or two. He also gets satisfaction from his clay pipe, in which he smokes a horrible-smelling tobacco.

He says that in his day he was as fond as anyone of going to bed with a pretty girl, but for many years now he has been too old. Similarly he used to back horses but now he knows nothing about them.

He doesn't go to church. When he lived and worked in town he could never see that God or the parsons were any good to the working man. Now he is old and alone he still sees no reason to run after them. Church is all right for people with money.

160

Miss C. is a very prim spinster of about 45 or 50. She is intensely religious and belongs to an evangelical movement. She carries their pamphlets in her bag and gives them to anyone to whom she talks.

She is a kindly, gentle soul, but rather timid because she says people speak so roughly to her when she talks to them of God.

She is in part-time work as a cook-housekeeper (four days a week for a man who is away from home for the other three), and is happy in her work. She has a small inheritance which supplements her wages and enables her to live frugally but happily.

She is a keen gardener with apparently a good deal of skill in flower-growing.

She is almost uneducated, seems to read no newspapers except the religious press, and virtually no books except religious books. She thus has a grotesquely unbalanced view of the world. She sometimes listens to the radio but does not care much for it.

The theatre and cinema she calls "the devil's works." Naturally alcohol and tobacco come under the same suspicion of infernal origin.

161

Mr. P. is dying of cancer. He is aged 65 or so, but manages to walk about although he is in great pain. He is not greatly disturbed at his approaching end and bears pain with wonderful fortitude. He is a retired carpenter, and a very strong Christian believer. He is a little sanctimonious, but his religion is a real force in his life. He is almost illiterate and his very ignorance has protected him from all the blasts the modern world directs against organized religion.

He neither drinks nor smokes, and frowns on theatres and cinemas. Says that in his life he has seen gambling ruin more men than drink.

Narrow-minded undoubtedly, but if there's a Heaven, he will probably go there!

162

Mrs. B. is a widow of about 55–60. She is in full-time employment as caterer-cook at a small industrial canteen. She earns a good living and is able to save the whole of a small pension as well as part of her wages towards the time when she cannot work. She is a simple woman with no enemies, no close friends and few relatives. She is not unhappy, having a small comfortable flat and enjoying her work.

She does not drink or gamble but smokes occasionally.

She listens a good deal to the radio and goes occasionally to the cinema. She reads novels from the 2d. library and reads the *News of the World.*

She says she is better fed now that she has ever been in her life and her wages are bigger than her husband ever earned. He died some years ago and she speaks of him quite impersonally.

Went to chapel as a girl but has not been for years. When asked why not replied, "Well, people used to go years ago. It's different now. I don't see I'm any worse for it."

163

Mr. V. is a professional musician in a dance band. Aged 35–40. Very keen on his job and genuinely convinced that "swing" is a real musical discovery. Is not much interested in anything except music. Has composed a few dance tunes but so far with no great success, although two have been published. Is saving hard to have his own dance band.

He lives with a woman—almost any woman as long as she is young and passionate and is willing to pay her share of living expenses. He changes women every few months. His women are only incidental to him. He regards them as little more than part of the furnishings of his flat.

He has no time for cinemas and theatres, but when he can manage it he likes a day off for a long country walk—alone. He walks as much as 20 or 25 miles in a day. Aimlessly and always thinking about music. He dreams that he might one day write a symphony in swing rhythm.

Never thinks of religion.

Vain and egocentric, but a real artist with perhaps a touch of genius.

164

Mrs. K. is a farmer's wife. Aged about 50. The farm is a small one and the buildings are dirty and untidy, for the farmer tries to work it with only the help of his family. They are however fairly prosperous.

Mrs. K. works immensely hard. She does all her housework and washing, milks the cows, keeps the hens and pigs, feeds the calves and does all the paper work of the farm, for her husband is illiterate. It is quite normal for her to work a 100-hour week and more at busy periods when she helps in the harvest field.

Her life is bed-and-work. She adores her two children, both almost men, and is on good terms with her husband.

Is too busy for sex, entertainment or gambling.

Goes to chapel about once a month and has one day off a year, the chapel outing to the seaside by motor coach.

Mrs. K. has never ridden in a train, and never spent a night away from home.

165

Mr. S. is a skilled craftsman. He is a bachelor, aged 28, and his main interests are dirt-track racing and women. He follows one of the well-known dirt-track racing teams and hardly ever misses one of their matches. He is quite promiscuous sexually, and says he has a circle of girl friends to whom he gives equal attention.

He is not the least bit interested in religion and says that he has never been to church in his life except for certain compulsory services he had to attend in the Army. He could not make anything of them and after listening with some curiosity to the first couple of such services he gave up paying any attention.

He does not spend much on his dirt-track racing, but his girl friends cost him a good deal of money, and most of the rest, after he has paid for his lodgings, goes on tobacco and beer.

He is a supporter of the Labour Government and thinks it is a good thing that the clever Labour leaders are willing to take over the running of the country. He does not think there is any point in the ordinary man thinking about politics because he can never know enough to understand what he is talking about.

Mr. S. does not mind going to the cinema with one of his girl friends if she wants to be taken, but he is not interested in films and he has only been to a theatre two or three times in his life.

Mr. S. regards the greyhounds as crooked. He thinks horse-racing is all right if you have sufficiently good "inside information," but for the ordinary person "it's a mug's game," for, he says, "it stands to reason that the bookmaker must win." He does a football coupon each week, not particularly expecting to win but because he does not miss the 3s. 0d., and somebody has to win.

When he was in the services he used to enjoy playing outdoor games. It was pretty well the first time in his life that he had had the opportunity, except for kicking a ball about in the street. He thinks that every child ought to be taught to play properly. Now that he is demobilized he has no chance, and anyway he thinks he is getting too old.

Mr. S's. parents are still alive, but he has nothing much to do with them, although he supposes that he would help them if they were in trouble. As far as he knows they never did much for him. He does not trouble to keep them informed of his address when he changes his lodgings, but they know where he works and could get hold of him there if they needed him.

166

Mr. A. lives alone in a wooden hut. He was brought up in a well-to-do family and had a grammar school education. Drink and women, mainly the former, brought him to his present position as a casual labourer. He has a small allowance from his family, lives mainly on beer and does not work more than about one month in three. When not working it is quite usual for him to spend every minute of opening time in a public house (i.e., eight hours a day), and at these times he is never quite sober.

Quite promiscuous but does not worry about women during his drunken spells.

No interest in religion and is one of the most foul-mouthed and blasphemous persons investigator has ever heard.

No interest in such entertainments as the cinema, theatre or radio. Reads the *News of the World* and nothing else.

167

Mrs. Y. is the wife of the vicar of a very poor living in a lower middle-class area. The Y's. are desperately poor, even to the point of not having enough to eat, but they manage to put aside some money to relieve the distress of people even poorer than themselves.

Mrs. Y. is a fine woman, about 60, with a manner which is both gentle and authoritarian. She does a tremendous amount of parish visiting, particularly among people who don't come to church. She says she spends more time teaching young mothers how to look after babies (she had seven of her own, now all grown up) than she does doing anything else.

The Y's. have little faith in organized church activities (socials, etc.) as they only reach a small proportion of the parish. They try with the help of a few devoted laymen to take part in all the secular activities of the parish. Mrs. Y. lectures to the Red Cross, Mr. Y. is a Rotarian, Mrs. Y. is a leading figure in the Girl Guides; they jointly run a youth club with no visible religion in it. Mr. Y. has persuaded his curate to stand for the borough council.

Naturally Mrs. Y. has no time for hobbies. She reads a little, listens sometimes to the radio, sews and knits. A real life of service. With a nice touch of humour Mrs. Y. says, "Philip (her husband) is such a poor preacher he would drive anyone away from church, so we have to get hold of people wherever we can."

168

Mr. C. owns a small business. He is 28, married, with two children, and is very ambitious to make a real success of the business. He is extremely Tory in his views, although he is of working-class origin, as he says his business is hampered by controls and trade unionism (he has 20 employees). He is devoted to his children, but rather takes his wife as a matter of course, and is quite proud of the fact that women run after him. He says he is faithful to his wife, but adds, "or as near to faithful as matters," and in fact he is probably promiscuous.

He smokes and drinks in moderation and gambles on horses and football, saying that he sees no harm in doing so because it is on a small scale for his amusement.

He is a keen cricketer but plays no games in the winter, preferring to watch professional football.

Goes occasionally to chapel and accepts the Christian doctrine without questioning it because he says he has too many other things to think about.

169

Miss L. is a typist. She is about 28 or 30, gay and full of energy.

Sexually promiscuous, she has one lover at a time, and is faithful to him while her affection lasts—normally about six months.

A heavy drinker and smoker.

Despite these traits she is a conscientious girl who works hard and has a highly developed sense of responsibility.

She is fond of parties, dances, cinemas and theatres, but is also well read and intelligent in her conversation.

Gives up one evening a week to a girls' club in a London slum where she teaches slum girls personal hygiene and dress-making.

Is quite irreligious, but has thought the problem out and knows why. Says that if she believed in God she would not lead a wild life, but as she is convinced that no religion has divine sanction she pleases herself.

170

Mrs. J. is an artificial blonde. She is a hard-faced female who sells vegetables and fruit from a barrow. Has several times been prosecuted for such frauds as short weight, prices above maximum allowed by law, foreign goods marked British.

Her husband left her some years ago and she does not know if he is alive or dead. She is now probably about 40 although she pretends to be much less. Is quite promiscuous.

She gambles on horses if she gets a good tip—not otherwise.

She is naturally not interested in religion.

Besides men and drink she has few amusements. For a woman, is a very heavy drinker.

171

Miss R. is a copy-typist in a large office. She is 21 or so, and lives in a bed-sitting-room. She finds it difficult to make both ends meet but is happy because she is free, because she has plenty of boy friends and plenty of entertainment. She is quite promiscuous and sees no harm in it. Indeed, she doesn't see why people make so much fuss about it; it just seems natural.

She is most of all interested in "boys," then in clothes, then in dancing and cinemas. She hopes to marry one day and settle down, but not for a long time.

She reads a daily paper and an evening paper, and always the *News of the World*. She doesn't bother about radio except sometimes the Light Programme.

She doesn't gamble usually, but sometimes in the office they put up 1s. 0d. each and back a horse just for fun.

Not a churchgoer. She thought the very idea funny. "Me—like all the stuffy people in their best clothes? That's a good one. Fat lot of difference it seems to make to them anyway. No, not me."

172

Mrs. R. is the wife of a professional man 11 years younger than herself. There are four children of the marriage and, despite a shortage of money, Mrs. R. is very happy. Her husband seems less so, and the only real contact between them is the children whom both of them spoil. Mrs. R. is a doctor by profession, although she has not practised since her marriage. She is a Roman Catholic but not a particularly devout one and "seldom has time to go to church."

She smokes and drinks in moderation but gambles to a considerable extent on horses and football pools "in order to make money for the children's education." Naturally she loses.

She has never had sexual relations with any man except her husband and deplores the sexual habits of most of her friends. She has an excellent sense of humour and on the question of sex she adds, "I suppose there's a bit of envy in my disapproval. No one has ever asked me to go to bed with him."

Her hobby is her family. Not only does she cook, clean the house, make most of the children's clothes, and so on, but she teaches the children subjects that they do not learn at the local council school that they attend.

She never goes to the cinema but goes to a matinée of the theatre once every three or four months—usually to opera.

173

Mr. Q. is a retired professional man. He is a bachelor, aged about 60 or rather less, but his activities are restricted by a permanently damaged heart. He is moderately well off and lives comfortably in a service flat.

He reads a good many books, mainly works of travel and biography. He reads right-wing newspapers and the society weeklies. Although he lives in London he is very fond of the country and he used to hunt regularly and was a keen shot and fisherman. Even now, and in defiance of his doctor, he has an annual ski-ing holiday of three weeks abroad. He says that he keeps to the simple ski-runs and risks damaging his heart.

He is a regular church-goer and a keen rather high churchman. He will not eat meat on Fridays and in Lent gives up smoking and drinking. At other times both smokes and drinks in moderation. Keen on cinema and theatre. Bets regularly on horses.

174

Mr. K. is the vicar of a remote country parish, more than 150 miles from London and 12 from the nearest big town. He was formerly a schoolmaster, and is intensely fond of young people, to whom he devotes much of his time in his parish. He is theologically rusty and a bit muddled, but is thoroughly happy in his work because his parishioners only want "the regular services and simple homely sermons." His congregations are very small—only half what they were 20 years ago when he took the living. "They are not drifting away so much as just dying, and the young people don't replace them. They'll come to a dance or a social, but not to church. I expect they know what's best for them and they're good young folk—straight and decent. We're too old, that's what it is."

Mr. K. is married, but is childless. He says he has always had young people around him and so hasn't missed children of his own.

He says, with a smile, "In politics I'm a reactionary old sinner—I believe in God and the King, and they go together."

Mr. K's. main hobby is fishing. He does not gamble "because people expect a parson not to, but I don't see much harm if it's in moderation."

175

Mr. A. is a customs clerk, aged 35, married, with two children. He is an extremely kindly man, but is garrulous and his conversation is very superficial. He is interested in his work and talks a good deal about it. Almost all his leisure is devoted to his children and to doing various jobs in his house, which he owns, to improve it. He smokes fairly heavily but cannot afford to drink. Does not gamble, although he did a football pool coupon for years until he became convinced that he would never win. Never goes to church and never thinks about religion. He says that he likes to help people in small ways but that "it stands to reason you can't really put yourself out for people except your own family." Likes the society of women, particularly those from 18 to the early twenties, but has no money to spend on them so that they remain casual acquaintances. Mr. A. is undoubtedly faithful to his wife and equally certainly wishes he wasn't!

176

Mr. S. is in the clerical department of a factory. He is about 46, married, with one son, of whom he is very fond. He is happy with his wife and wants no other woman.

He is fond of a glass of beer and drinks a couple of pints every evening before going home. He meets a few old friends and they sit in a corner of the public house for an hour and gossip. He then usually settles down at home for the evening with a book or newspaper and, usually, the radio. Sometimes however he takes his wife to the cinema or music hall for a change. On Saturday afternoons in the winter he likes to watch a football match.

His wife and son go to church on most Sundays, but he never goes. He likes to settle down and have a good rest. He tries to lead a decent life and doesn't see how he could behave differently even if he did go to church. As far as he knows he never does anyone any harm.

177

Mrs. J., a middle-class housewife, exceedingly fat, very friendly and aged about 50. Her main interest in life is food and she is disturbed because she cannot find a black market butcher. "Mind you, we don't do badly. Had a lovely beefsteak on the side this week, but I mean we don't get it regular. I mean, we've got to eat so many eggs I shall start clucking. Lucky to get the eggs I suppose, but I mean, it's meat I need." Is apparently not interested in sex, nor in drink. Does not smoke but likes betting on the main horse races and accompanies husband to dog tracks once a week. "Been doing it for years, but I've never seen a race. I stay in the restaurant and hubby bets for both of us. Doesn't do badly out of it." Keenly interested in people and is shocked that most people are so unfriendly. "It does you good to have a chat." Has no discernible cultural interests and does not seem to read. Likes the radio (Light Programme). Brought up as a Baptist but never goes to church. She says, "Religion's all my eye."

178

Mr. G. is a railway porter, aged 28, with a contempt for all well-to-do passengers, which conflicts with a respect for all those who give a good tip. He says he is a Socialist and thinks Socialists ought to join with the Communists and "stop the people with money robbing the workers." On the other hand he seems to know nothing at all about Communism, although he says he has "been to a few meetings."

He says he is an atheist, but he cannot remember that anyone has ever explained the Christian religion to him. He was brought up in a "scattered home" where he thinks they used to be taught some prayers but he doesn't remember. He remembers reading from the Bible at school but it didn't mean anything. He has seen lots of pictures of Jesus at different times, usually in a long white robe, and thinks the pictures are rather silly.

He gambles on pools, horses and dogs, and with cards (playing gin rummy and solo). Sometimes he wins, but mostly he loses. He likes a few pints, but hardly ever gets drunk, not more than two or three times a year. He smokes, and when he has money likes 20 Woodbines a day. Is not married but usually lives with a woman. When they get fed up with each other they part. He expects the woman to earn, as he finds it hard enough to keep himself without keeping her.

179

Mr. L., a well-to-do man, aged 47. Keen amateur yachtsman and owns a light plane which he pilots himself. Is a motor mechanic (services own plane) and has a workshop where, as a hobby, he carries out a variety of light engineering jobs. Brought up as a strict Churchman but is now an agnostic. Ceased to go to church and lost his faith during 1914–18 war. Gambles fairly heavily on horses and sometimes on greyhounds. Smokes continuously and drinks very heavily—sometimes a whole bottle of whisky at one sitting. Intensely keen on good music (favourite composers are Bach and Haydn) and interested in town planning. Is a staunch Conservative on grounds that he is fairly well-to-do and it pays him to support the "Haves" against the "Have nots." Has been married within last few years to a woman over 20 years younger than he is. Was sexually promiscuous from age of 17 to time of marriage, but gave no indication of present habits in this direction. Has no sporting activities but enjoys watching county cricket.

180

Mr. G. is a working-class man of about 35. He has a "white collar" occupation, but all his friends are labourers and he does not put on airs of false superiority. He is married, with two young children, to whom he is much attached, and he and his wife seem very happy.

He spends a good deal of his time in his local public house, where he plays cards and darts and sometimes dominoes. He goes there four or sometimes even five nights a week, and probably stays an hour and a half. At the week-end in summer, when the children can be left outside the public house, his wife sometimes accompanies him.

Mr. G. is a steady gambler and bets on horses every day throughout the flat-racing and steeple-chasing seasons. He follows form and though on balance he admits that he loses, he says that the net loss is trifling and is well worth the entertainment he has. He also does a football pool coupon regularly but does not bet on greyhounds because he says they are not honest.

He occasionally plays cricket in the summer, but is not very keen on it. He used to play football every Saturday in the winter, but considers that he is now too old.

He does not read books except for an occasional novel, but reads one of the daily newspapers and listens a great deal to the radio, mostly to the Light Programme, but sometimes to serious talks.

He is very genial and friendly and is obviously popular in his circle.

He never goes to the theatre, which does not interest him, but he goes occasionally to the cinema, perhaps once a fortnight, and about as frequently he stays at home in the evening to look after his children so that his wife can go to the cinema.

Mr. G. was brought up as a Nonconformist but does not now attend church or chapel. He gave up doing so because it did not seem to make any difference whether he went or not, and it was inconvenient to go, and the services were very dreary.

181

Mr. S., aged 50–55, is the proprietor of a provincial taxi business. He runs five cars, all rather old and dirty, and sometimes he himself drives one. He is a very heavy drinker; it is not at all unusual for him to drink 12 or 15 pints in a day, and his business suffers both because he neglects his office and because money that ought to be spent on the upkeep of his cars is spent on his beer and cigarettes. As he is also a heavy smoker, it is fair to estimate that his beer and tobacco bill for the month cannot be less than £25.

He is married, but though he and his wife live together, they are not on good terms. Mr. S. is promiscuous.

He backs horses on most days of the week but does not do a football pool coupon.

He occasionally goes to race meetings, and once or twice a month to the cinema.

Religion does not enter his life in any way. He is quite a friendly man but is completely materialistic on a low plane.

182

Mr. E., aged about 45, is a commissionaire. At one time he was in the regular Army, but the duration of his engagement having come to an end, he was demobilized after the war. Before he joined the Army he was a waiter and his object in taking up his present job was to get evening work as a waiter, but he finds this is hard to do as the hours do not fit. He admits, however, that he enjoys getting home in the evening, settling by the fire and not having to go out again, so that he is no longer looking very hard for an evening job.

Mr. E. is married, with one child, and his wife rather grumbles at the small money he brings home. She says either that he will have to earn more or she will have to go out to work.

Mr. E. is a very keen supporter of greyhound racing and if he could afford it would go every night. He goes once a week, but also has a few bets on races at stadia other than that which he attends.

He also bets regularly on horses—normally spending three or four shillings a day, sometimes being up at the end of the week, and sometimes down. He does a football pool coupon regularly, enjoys an evening two or three times a month playing cards with money stakes, and is indeed willing to gamble at any time in any way.

He has a very quick brain, is intelligent with an excellent sense of humour. He is quite well-read and travelled widely during his Army service.

He reads the papers, listens to serious broadcasts as well as the Light Programme and has a good knowledge of what is going on in the world.

He smokes fairly heavily and goes to one or more public houses on his way home every evening, never having less than three or four pints.

He says that he is quite fond of his wife as they are used to each other, but he is no less fond of a pretty girl than he used to be when he was younger.

In politics he is a strong Conservative, as he says the working-class have neither the brains nor the education to run the country.

Mr. E. is sceptical about religion and his remark about it was, "Nowadays people are educated and know better than that."

183

Mrs. H. is a widow of 68. She is a strong-minded woman who is really rather remarkable because despite her age she is acting as manageress of a large haberdashery store with twelve girls and three men under her. She works very long hours for she does all the paper work relating to rationing and coupons, as well as actively supervising the shop and doing a good deal of the buying. She says, probably truthfully, that she always works a 70-hour week and often longer.

She is happy in her work and enjoys her rare leisure. She is fond of a drink, smokes in moderation, finds time to bet on horses three or four times a week and she mothers the girls working under her.

She says that all her life she has been strict on sexual morals, and in her long business career considers that by her advice she has "saved scores of girls from going wrong."

She likes a good sentimental novel (it must be well written—no trash), and an occasional biography. She is too busy for cinemas or theatres, and seldom listens to the radio.

Mrs. H. is not a churchwoman as in her experience churchgoers are no better than anyone else and are often worse. She doesn't worry about abstract theories; she knows what a good, straight life is, and she tries to live one.

184

Mr. N. is a labourer, aged 28, very well built and attractive in a hard-faced sort of way. He complains that women won't leave him alone, and it is probably true. He drinks a good deal, smokes moderately, and says that his two hobbies are playing darts and copulating (he uses another word).

He was brought up as a regular chapel-goer and still goes once or twice a month, saying that he supposes it is a habit. He gambles regularly on horses, never on greyhounds because he believes it to be corrupt, and occasionally on football pools if he can be bothered to fill in the coupons. He thinks that "they" ought to make the pool coupons easier to fill in.

He goes two or three nights a week to the cinema when he has "a girl in tow," but otherwise prefers to spend his evenings in a public house. He is a bachelor and has no intention of "buying a cow" (i.e., marrying).

185

Mrs. H. is an extremely well-to-do woman of about 50, who is separated from her husband, whom she is just divorcing. She has no affection for the husband, but on the other hand she has no hostile feelings. She is glad to be rid of him and intends to make him an allowance "of enough to live on quietly like a gentleman," as she feels she is largely to blame for the failure of their marriage. She says her husband was passionate while she found that sex did not interest her.

She lives out of England for several months of each year partly because of servant difficulties and partly because "life here isn't worth living" with rationing and shortages. Mrs. H. is very shrewd and well informed. She hates Socialism and democracy because they interfere with her comfort. It is an intelligently controlled hatred based on solid information not on prejudice. (For example, while she resents the shortage of meat she points out that it is mainly because of the deliberate decision to see that the poorer sections of the community get a fair share at a subsidized price.)

Her main hobbies are riding, sailing and bridge. She has her own small yacht. Mrs. H. is keen on the theatre but "hardly ever bothers" with the cinema.

She does not worry about religion and thinks it is morbid to do so. She goes to church because she thinks the Anglican Church has a good effect in holding "the right people" together. There were no children of the marriage and she desired none.

Mrs. H. has several friends who own race horses, and she often attends race meetings with them. She then bets as a matter of course, but does not otherwise gamble in England. Abroad she is fond of playing roulette (but considers the French variation—boule—a swindle as the odds are unfair), and will play baccarat on social occasions.

186

Mr. D., aged about 45, used to manage a boot shop for one of the large manufacturers. Now he has a small boot shop of his own and is doing so well that he thinks of opening a branch.

He is hard-working and he describes his aim as "trying to give the public better value and more courtesy than any other shop."

He has a rigid code of business ethics and would not indulge in sharp practice or sell inferior goods on any account.

He is married, with one child. He and his wife get on well enough but they don't really care much for each other. Mr. D. is faithful to his wife when at home ("It pays to be respectable—customers like it.")

He is not interested in religion because he says he has always been too busy to study it, but he goes to church occasionally because it fits in with the picture of himself he is trying to build up.

He does everything in moderation—smoking, drinking, seeking amusements. But he does not gamble. He says, "I work hard for my brass, and I'd be right daft to give it to a chap who does nowt to earn it."

187

Mrs. U. is the wife of a labourer who has semi-acute T.B. and cannot work. They live on his insurance money plus her capital. (She was the daughter of a publican and inherited some money a couple of years ago.)

There are two daughters—one at school and the other recently started work. The elder girl is "a bit wild," and worries Mrs. U.

Mrs. U. does not complain. She is bright, makes her husband comfortable and keeps up his hopes of recovery. She is planning to take a full-time job herself as soon as her husband is a bit stronger and can look after himself at home.

She is not a religious woman. Used to go to chapel but just drifted away. Says a quiet prayer occasionally but thinks it is silly really as prayers are never answered.

Has no time for amusements, but fond of radio. Reads *Daily Mirror* and *News of the World*.

Does not smoke or drink. No gambling.

188

Mrs. F. is a working-class housewife with three boys, aged 14, 12 and 2. She is probably in the early forties herself. Her husband's earnings are small and she has great difficulty in making ends meet. Before the birth of her youngest child she went out every week for a day's washing and now she tries to take in washing. This is difficult, however, because she has no facilities as the F's. share a house, having the upstairs rooms with a common entrance, and backyard.

Her whole life is a continual round of work. She gets up at 6 a.m. on every weekday and is never idle—even when she is sitting down in the evenings she sews and mends.

She considers herself lucky to have a good steady husband who doesn't drink, and whose only extravagance is smoking in which she encourages him because she thinks he deserves a bit of luxury. During the war he was abroad for nearly five years without a break, and Mrs. F. had to bring up the boys alone. She is devoted to her children, but worried about the eldest boy, who is lazy, dirty, a liar and always after the girls. She ascribes this to the lack of his father's influence in the war.

Mrs. F. herself is a most frugal woman. She neither drinks nor smokes, nor gambles. She used to go once a week to a matinée at the cinema but now does not do so—partly to save the cost and partly because she cannot easily leave her youngest child.

She never goes to church and says—probably truly enough—that she really hasn't got time to do so. She adds that in any case she hasn't got any clothes fit to be seen in at church, as people are so quick to notice if anyone is shabby.

189

Mr. H. is the son of a publican. He is aged 22 and helps in his father's business, which he hopes to inherit. He gambles heavily on horses every day, loses usually, and has twice been in trouble for passing dud cheques. He drinks a good deal—probably not less than 10 or 12 pints a day because although he drinks slowly he is hardly ever without a glass during opening hours. He smokes heavily and considers himself rather a Don Juan.

He has no discernible interests except gambling, women, and drink. He hates exercise and goes everywhere in a small car.

Takes his girl friends to dances if they wish, but only if there is a bar at the dance. Sometimes goes to the cinema in the afternoon to sleep off the beer he has consumed between 10 a.m. and 2 p.m.

A nasty bit of work.

190

Miss B. is a shop assistant in a large store. She is aged 20 and although not at all good-looking she is attractive in a youthful way.

She lives in the suburbs with her parents (the father is a labourer) and four sisters. The family are apparently very devoted to each other, and the whole of Miss B's. leisure is devoted to home interests. Two of the sisters are very young (6 and 2½) and Miss B. enjoys looking after them.

She is a merry and a happy person who has never come across any evil in her life and hardly believes it exists.

She smokes occasionally in a rather self-conscious way, but does not drink. Her father does a football pool coupon regularly and she takes six "lines" in the penny-points pool. She gets great fun out of checking the results but her plans for what she would do with a big prize are vague. Her first idea is "Have a girl to help Mum," and she has various other projects of the same nature.

Miss B. likes listening to the radio but would like to listen sometimes to "better-class music," but the rest of the family prefer variety and music hall programmes, so she has to give way.

She goes two or three times a month to the cinema, and used to go regularly to a girls' club, but considers she is now too old. She has never learned to dance because having all sisters she has never known many boys.

Nobody in the family goes to church, so it has never occurred to Miss B. to go. She is vague on the entire subject of religion, having "done Bible reading" at school but never having received any religious instruction. Neither she nor any of her sisters have been baptized, but when she marries she will want "a white wedding" and to be married "properly" in church.

191

Mrs. M. is a rather faded woman of about 60. She has four grown-up children (three of them still living at home), and her husband, aged 65, has recently retired from work. Partly because of the retirement, and partly because of some losses through speculation, Mr. M's. income has been very sharply reduced. Having been used to an upper middle-class life with three servants, the M's. are now almost in penury. The grown-up children cannot help much as two are undergraduates, one is unfit to work through war wounds, and the fourth is married. The M's. live in a large house (three floors, basement and attics), and a good many of the rooms are never used. Mr. M. is rather crushed by his misfortunes and Mrs. M. does all the work, including cooking and laundry. She does not complain but the effort seems quite clearly to be killing her.

She is not a church- or chapel-goer, although she went regularly until quite recently. She will not give any reason for stopping but it appears to be the result of some unkindness on the part of prominent members of the congregation (possibly over the M's. financial losses).

Mrs. M. is devoted to her husband and children, and is strikingly gentle and kind with her husband. She is obviously lonely and misses the large numbers of friends they used to have, and from whom they have withdrawn themselves to avoid either slights or patronage.

Mrs. M. has virtually no recreations because she never stops work. She tries to listen to the radio occasionally but is usually too busy, and if she sits down for long without concentrating on sewing she falls asleep. She neither smokes nor drinks.

She is a well-read woman but now does not read at all. Her life is "bed and work."

192

Mr. S. is a middle-aged business man. He is prosperous, but being unhappily married is not very content with life. He is clearly a man of high ability and a good sense of humour.

Is an agnostic but has a considerable regard for the Church and says he wishes he could believe its doctrines, but cannot honestly pretend to do so.

He is a heavy smoker, but drinks very little because he finds that even a small amount of alcohol fuddles him.

Is strongly opposed on principle to sexual promiscuity and says that since the failure of his marriage he has placed all thoughts of sex out of his mind, preferring to use his energies in other ways.

Does not gamble except for the two or three occasions in most years that he attends one or other of the principal race meetings.

Reads widely, this being his main hobby, but is also a keen theatre-goer. Is much interested in photography and has a room fitted as a dark-room.

193

Mr. F. is a successful barrister. He is between 50 and 60 and married not many years ago after remaining a bachelor until well into his forties. He is extremely interested in his profession and devotes himself to it with great energy. His wife is an enormous help to him and they are very happy.

He lives an extremely regular life—attends church every Sunday, but will not commit himself as to whether or not he believes the doctrine, keeps excellent wines in his comfortable house, and enjoys them in strict moderation, has a good stock of cigars which he says are "very respectable," and does everything methodically and in moderation.

He is not much interested in politics, but supports the Tory Party. He considers that as a prosperous and successful man he has duties to the community so he subscribes to many charities and he, and to an even greater extent his wife, devote time to various kinds of voluntary social work.

He is not much interested in the cinema, but likes the theatre and sees most of the successful plays put on in London. He is not at all interested in music, which bores him horribly, but he occasionally goes to a concert with his wife, who is keen.

He does not gamble because he thinks it is stupid to imagine that one can do so successfully over any considerable period of time.

194

Mr. B., aged 42, is the cook in a small and cheap restaurant. He is enormous in bulk and genial in disposition. He states, presumably correctly, that 20 years ago he was an amateur international footballer and he is still a keen follower of the game. He is happily married, with one child. He has been worried lately by two or three anonymous letters alleging that his wife is unfaithful. He does not believe them, and says, "If I could find the —— who sends them I'd bash his —— face in." Mr. B. does a football coupon every week and thinks football pools are a fine thing. They give an interest to millions of people who lead dull lives. He never bets on greyhounds because "they are a swindle". Likes going to horse races and "doesn't mind an occasional flutter." Doesn't go to church because he "isn't interested in religion." His philosophy is, "If you lead a clean life you haven't got anything to worry about." He has very little spare time but he enjoys watching football matches, to which he takes his wife and son. He is "fond of a pint," and takes Mrs. B. to the public house every Sunday evening. He calls at the public house on his way home each evening and has one pint—"Never more." Hasn't been to the cinema for years but likes his wife to go in the afternoons because it prevents her from being lonely. Wishes he was young enough to give up cooking and go to the mines. He considers the miners have let the country down.

Mr. B. does not smoke and his sexual life is clearly irreproachable.

195

Mr. T., aged about 22, is a clerk in a Local Government office. He is the son of a factory worker and feels he has "gone up in the world." He is walking out and saving up to get married. In the meantime he is content to wait for his love-making as he has always been taught at home that extra-marital sex is shameful.

Home influence has been very strong on Mr. T., but he has broken away from it in one respect. His parents are very religious and he was brought up as a strict chapel-goer. He gave it up in the Army, and his period of national service so changed his views that he now refuses to go to chapel at all.

He is an active member of the Labour Party. Reads the *Daily Herald* and various left-wing periodicals (*New Statesman*, *Tribune*, etc.). Hasn't the education or experience to separate fact from propaganda in his reading, and he accepts everything he reads as true.

Likes the cinema but has no outdoor pastimes, and does not dance, which is a disappointment to his "young lady."

Smokes and occasionally has a glass of beer. Does a football pool coupon but otherwise does not gamble.

196

Mrs. K. is a shop girl. She is short and plump and very vivacious, and is married to a waiter in one of the large hotels.

She is very independent and told her husband before they were married that she was not just going to be his "squaw," but would lead her own life and have her own friends, male and female. She is blatantly promiscuous and says that her husband does not mind.

She is very extravagant and fond of luxury and most of her earnings go on clothes and on going out to meals at expensive restaurants with female friends.

She is very keen on the cinema but thinks that the theatre is dull, except for musical comedies.

She does not gamble because she says she has to work hard to earn her money and she would only gamble if she knew she were going to win.

She smokes and drinks, but not to excess.

She dislikes housework intensely and does as little as is possible. She is determined not to have any children, because she says that if she did she would not be able to work, and life shut up with what she calls "a squalling brat" would be intolerable.

Mrs. K. was brought up as a Roman Catholic but has not been to church for years.

She is very fond of dancing but will not go to the cheaper dance places as she considers the people who do so are vulgar. As a result she can only dance when one of her male friends is willing to take her to one of the comparatively expensive restaurants or hotels.

197

Mrs. L. is the wife of a professional man. She is in the early forties and has one child. She spoils the child, which has quite the first place in her affections. She regards her husband as a very worthy but rather stodgy man and most of the real interest that she has apart from her child is centred in her dog and her friends.

Her greatest entertainment is to meet a group of female friends and exchange gossip about their various acquaintances and families. She is very houseproud, but is lucky enough to have a hard-working servant who does all the heavy housework.

Mrs. L. reads nothing except light novels and though she is fond of the theatre and the cinema she always chooses the lightest plays and films. She is keen on the radio, particularly the variety programmes.

It never occurs to her to wonder whether or not she is religious, but she goes to church occasionally because she always has and because "everyone" in her little world does. She smokes and drinks in moderation, although her husband grumbles a little because he thinks she smokes too much—a dozen or 15 cigarettes a day.

Most days she goes out in the morning for morning coffee at one of the restaurants where her friends gather, and she says that she "adores cocktail parties."

She wonders why her husband does not make much progress in his profession and says, "I am sure I help him all I can." Her method of helping him is to get to know people who she thinks might be useful to him and their wives, but her tedious prattle probably does her husband a good deal of harm.

198

Mr. A. is aged 35 and single. He is a labourer who lives in the cheapest kind of hostel. No means are provided in the hostel for keeping clothes and other personal property, and there is so much thieving that Mr. A. finds it simpler not to have any belongings. Most of his income goes in gambling, food and tobacco. In the week before the investigator met him he had lost 50 per cent of his net wages on the greyhounds and for the last couple of days of the week had to go without food. He spends nearly one-fifth of his net wages every week on tobacco and about a quarter on drink. His food costs him well under one-fifth.

He feels that he cannot go on in his present living conditions and would like to find lodgings in a private house. He would then be prepared to alter his whole spending pattern and pay between one-third and a half of his net wages for board and lodging. The greatest difficulty in the way of him finding lodgings is that he is so shabby that no decent landlady would take him in.

He used to be a keen supporter of the football pools and last season won £30. He does not now do a coupon because there would be little likelihood of letters reaching him regularly in the conditions in the hostel.

Mr. A. was brought up as a Roman Catholic but he no longer believes in Christianity and it is some years since he was last at church. He says that it is impossible for a man to know what is right in regard to religion as so many of the churches have different views and contradict each other.

Mr. A. recognizes and is rather ashamed of his present somewhat degraded condition and says that he realizes that it is entirely his fault as he is a good workman, earning quite a good wage.

He would like to marry, but thinks it unlikely that any decent girl would look at him, the more so because it is so long since he had anything to do with decent girls that he has forgotten the way to talk to them. Occasionally he picks up a prostitute in Hyde Park but cannot often afford to do so. When he has money he goes to the cinema twice a week and whenever he can he reads the newspapers, either buying them or sometimes going to the public library. He reads nothing else.

He says that his greatest need is somebody to help him to overcome his weaknesses. He thinks that if somebody could do so for a few weeks he would have no difficulty, with their help, in reforming and becoming a decent citizen.

199

Mr. B. is a professional man, aged about 52 or 53. He is unable to work much as a few years ago he had T.B. and though cured is only allowed to work about half time. Is married happily, with four children.

He is a very conventional man, undoubtedly faithful to his wife, kind and rather lacking in personality.

He does not gamble. Had to give up smoking because of the T.B., but drinks in moderation.

Goes occasionally to the cinema but his favourite recreation is playing bridge. He is an expert player, and plays several nights each week for small stakes.

He gives the impression, probably justly, of being a mean man. It is doubtful whether he has ever done a wrong action in his life; it is quite certain he has never done a generous one. Absolutely honest and reliable but would not go a hair's breadth out of his way to help anyone.

A regular churchgoer.

200

Mr. Q. is the janitor of a block of office buildings. He is over 60 and finds the work almost too much for him. He is a pensioner from the Army and has a flat in the basement where he lives with his wife. There are three grown-up children, all married.

Mr. Q. has few interests because he is too tired to go out at the end of the day. He occasionally goes to the cinema. He acts as a bookmaker's runner for the substantial number of office workers in the building. He gets a percentage of the stakes and, over the course of years, has saved "hundreds of pounds" for his old age from this one source. He always saves the money he "earns" this way. He is "not such a mug" as to gamble himself but he does a football pool coupon because everyone has a fair chance.

Mr. Q. likes the radio, Light Programme, and is happy in his home. His horizon is darkened by a dread about where he and his wife will live when he is too old to work.

He smokes heavily and likes a pint or two of beer, especially at week-ends.

SECTION II—THE CASE HISTORIES OF 20 PERSONS UNDER THE AGE OF TWENTY

1

Mr. P. is a pageboy aged 16½ at a provincial hotel. He lives with his parents and only works in the hotel by day. He is allowed 7s. 6d. a week pocket money, which he finds insufficient, but was lucky recently in winning £8 in a football pool. He spent a good deal of it and got drunk for the first time in his life. He did not think much of the experience of getting drunk, but reckons he will do so often again. His father has borrowed 15s. od. of his winnings and lost it on the greyhounds, but he is determined to get the money back from his father. His mother also borrowed 5s. od. for some unspecified purpose and he does not think there is much chance of getting it back.

One of his own particular interests is whippet racing and he has two dogs of his own which often win prizes.

He is not much interested in girls, but thinks the "young lady who serves in the American bar" is "very nice."

As far as he can remember has never been to church in his life, and has no idea what goes on there. Has always been taught that the Church is on the side of the bosses and is therefore the natural enemy of the working-class. His father is a Communist and does not hold with his son being a page in an hotel, but he finds that people are very kind to him and he likes the work. His main complaint against his work is that he does not finish until 8 p.m., and it is then too late for him to go to the cinema, as his mother insists on his going straight home from the hotel. He likes the cinema, particularly musical comedy films. He thinks he will stay in his present job until he has been called-up for military service, but does not know what he will do then.

He does not think he has read a book since he left school, but still reads the comic paper *Beano*, and also reads the *News of the World* on Sundays. Not interested in any youth organization and thinks the Scouts are silly.

2

Miss X. is an intelligent capable girl, nearly 20 years old. Her home was a good one but she was spoilt as a child. She had a very good education, but her social ambitions led her to gratify them by irregular means and finally earned her a Borstal sentence. From this she emerged with the feeling that she had benefited by the experience, and a determination not to repeat it.

She does appreciate that it is possible to make a success of life and enjoy it without having recourse to crime. She is not afraid of hard work especially as she finds it "keeps me out of mischief." Her sexual relationships have been calculated and deliberate and confined to men who are in a position to be useful. She assumes that all modern girls have such relationships, but she despises those who have not been successful in avoiding maternity.

She is attractive, lively and interested in all manner of things, and her pleasures are nicely balanced between grave and gay.

She takes social questions seriously and likes to be well informed on current topics. She dresses well, and spends a good deal on expensive clothes. She is fond of dancing, theatres, and goes two or three times a week to the cinema. Smokes at least 20 cigarettes a day, and at times drinks more than she should. Is a gambler by nature, but experience has taught her caution.

Miss X. really hankers after a home life, with a husband and family of her own, but not below a certain social level. She has quite a well-developed sense of humour and although she has quite a good opinion of her achievements does now and again enjoy a laugh against herself.

3

Miss D. is 18 years of age and has been a member of a local youth centre since she was 14. She has had a good secondary school education and has one sister older than herself.

From quite an early age she has been interested in dancing, and during the war gave entertainments for local charities and collected a good deal of money for them. She is a first-class tap dancer and goes to hospitals to give an hour's entertainment to the inmates from time to time.

Miss D. is a shorthand typist with a local firm during the day and is not interested in dancing professionally. She attends the centre regularly and is a member of the Musical Appreciation Group. Is very interested in drawing and painting and has done quite well in both groups.

She is extremely careful of her appearance and is well spoken and well mannered, entirely unspoilt, and very popular with members of the opposite sex and is encouraged by her parents to take them home.

Miss D. enjoys her Keep Fit group once a week. She does not smoke or drink, and so far does not appear to be interested in politics.

4

Mr. H. is a clerical worker, aged 19, shabbily dressed, but intelligent. He works in a gramophone shop for 40 hours a week with Saturdays free for £3, but he makes some extras on errands and other jobs. His parents live in Bristol and he stays in London but not always in the same place. When he has money he stays at an hotel for £2 a week, when not, somewhere else. He spends 5s. 0d. a day on cigarettes and his hands are heavily stained with nicotine. By the middle of the week he is often "broke" and has to go without food. To-day he has only had breakfast, tea with toast, to last him the whole day. Does he prefer a smoke to food? "I don't know, but lots of times I have gone without food for a smoke, but never without a smoke for food." He learned to smoke in Bristol during the blitz when he was 13.

He likes a pint of beer in a pub, because he likes the atmosphere there and the company, but he can do without drink. He has no friends of his own age, preferring the company of older men.

He doesn't care for gambling. Goes twice or three times a week to the pictures but not to dances because he is not suitably dressed. His pet hobby is reading, mostly fiction.

He belongs to the Church of England and used to go to church frequently in his childhood for the Sunday services, but now he only goes rarely.

He likes serious music, especially Handel, Tschaikovsky and Mozart.

Wouldn't he be better off if he learnt a trade? "I learnt a trade, I went to a trade school for secretarial work and learnt shorthand and typing, but I have given it up because it was too boring, so now I can't either type or do shorthand. But an ordinary labourer couldn't do what I do and I wouldn't care for digging or shovelling, not because it is heavy work, but because it doesn't suit me."

He has three brothers and one sister, with the exception of one, all younger than he is. When he can, he sends them a few shillings to help out. His father is a lorry driver. From time to time he pays them a visit, although the return fare from London is 30s. 0d.

He has no ambition in life. He just wants to carry on as he is doing now.

5

Mr. D. is a young soldier, about 18½, recently called up for military service and still receiving his initial training. He comes from a lower middle-class home—his father being a manager of a small shop. He has obviously been carefully brought up, but without being pampered. He has never previously been separated from his home and he feels a little lonely, but he makes friends readily and has found several recruits whom he likes. He has been in the habit for a couple of years (despite the licensing laws) of going out twice a week with his father to a public house, and drinking two or three bottles of light ale. In consequence, now that he is on his own he behaves reasonably—neither drinking to show that he is grown up, nor going to the other extreme. He smokes a good deal—about 25 cigarettes a day—and wishes he could send some to his father, as they are easy to obtain in his canteen but hard in the part of London where his home is situated. Mr. D. has a sweetheart at home, and says he is not interested in other girls. He writes three times a week to the sweetheart (as well as every day to his mother), and she answers every letter on the day she receives it.

Mr. D. was brought up as a Baptist, but for some years he has been going to Anglican Churches, and now that he is in the Army he goes every Sunday. He enjoys the Anglican service and intends to ask his Army chaplain how he can be confirmed.

Mr. D. is a shop assistant in private life and although there is no doubt that he is fully literate he never reads anything except his letters and football coupons. He does not even read a newspaper for the football results because he either copies them from the B.B.C. broadcast or gets a friend to do so for him.

He is an enthusiastic cinema-goer and goes two or three times each week, choosing adventure films for preference.

6

Miss F. is aged 19, a copy typist in a big office. She lives with her parents and grandparents. She is a regular chapel-goer and takes part in many of the extra-mural activities organized by her chapel. The home is a happy one and her grandparents in particular do all they can to "spoil" Miss F.

She is walking out "seriously" with a young man who is away in the Army so that she only sees him at rare intervals. She will have nothing to do with any other men.

She is saving up for her bottom drawer, but finds it hard to resist buying anything attractive that she sees in the shops, so to protect herself she has a rule that she never carries more than 5s. 0d. in her purse.

Her greatest hobby is knitting, to which she devotes hours every day. She knits socks, scarves, pullovers, cardigans, gloves and mittens as well as baby clothes.

She is keen on the cinema and on the theatre, but goes seldom to either on account of the cost. She smokes occasionally but "practically never" has a drink. She does not gamble.

She is looking forward eagerly to the still undetermined day when she will marry her "boy" but is worried a little because she has never been taught to cook and has little knowledge of running a house. She thinks it would have been better if her mother had made her do more housework.

7

Mr. P. is 17 years of age and has been a member of the local youth club since he was 14 years old. He is a difficult lad—easily led and not given to accepting discipline of any kind easily. When he keeps himself to himself he is manageable and quite a different lad, but for most of the time he is a member of a "gang" and fires the bullets that other people make.

Periodically he is suspended for a fortnight to cool him down, and on several occasions he has been threatened with total suspension. He was put on probation at quite an early age, but has managed to keep away from the courts since attending the centre. Mr. P. is given to using bad language and annoying the members of the opposite sex in stupid ways.

He is a baker by trade and strangely enough does well at his work and is liked both by his employer and the men he works with. He has become a member of the wrestling club and the master is taking him in hand generally and he shows signs of improving. He is also a member of the discussion group and is responding quite well.

He smokes and drinks and fills in his football coupon each week. Mr. P. is communistic in outlook and is not interested in any form of religion.

8

Miss C. is a cashier in a restaurant. She is an attractive girl of nearly 20 and likes her work because there is plenty to do and there are always a lot of men about—both customers and staff. She has a keen sense of humour and a friendly nature. She is promiscuous sexually and at present is having an affair with one of the male staff—a married man double her age. He takes the affair seriously and wants to leave his wife and set up house with Miss C. She says he is "silly" to be so serious about her. She has no intention of settling down with a man 20 years older than herself.

Miss C. smokes and drinks in moderation. She started smoking because everybody else seemed to and at first she disliked it. Now she says she cannot do without her 10 cigarettes a day. Does not really mind whether she drinks or not.

She is a keen supporter of one of the best-known motor-cycle speedway teams and tries to arrange her evening off so as to attend their home matches. She enjoys any form of entertainment and her various male friends take her to greyhound racing, the cinema, a *palais de danse* and occasionally to a musical comedy or music hall.

Miss C. grew up in a respectable working-class family and says that her father was "steady" but that her mother had a hard time to make both ends meet. Miss C. had no religious instruction other than Bible reading at school but about the age of 15 she took to going occasionally with a girl friend to chapel. Does not now remember why she started but it was quite a good place for meeting boys. Gave up going as soon as she got her first serious boy friend.

9

Mr. D. is 18. He is expecting from day to day to be called up for National Service. He left school over two years ago, and after trying two jobs as office boy took an open-air unskilled job. He is rather unhappy at home because of a domineering mother, but he looks forward to National Service as a way out.

He has been brought up as a Baptist but says that, "speaking for himself," he sees nothing in all the chapel-going. As for Christianity, he thinks it would be all right if people believed in it.

He has started to smoke within the last twelve months, and has also learned to drink light ale.

He is much attracted to local girls but is certainly too inexperienced yet to have been promiscuous.

He is a keen cinema-goer, has never been to a theatre, and always when at home switches on the B.B.C. Light Programme, whether he is listening or not.

10

Miss K. is a counter clerk at the post office. She is about 19 or 20, lives at home with her parents and four other children. Shares a room (and bed) with two younger sisters. She is resentful of parental authority and wants to leave home and live in a bed-sitting room on her own but is too scared of her mother to do so. It might mean a final break with the family and she doesn't want that. At the same time she is fed up with sharing a bed and having to be in at 9.30 p.m.

She is very interested in boys but apparently still in an innocent way, although if she left home her interest would probably soon cease to be innocent. She says she will not marry for a long time as she wants to have years and years of fun first.

Miss K. is a keen cinema fan. She goes two or three times a week, and never misses joining the crowd outside a film première to see the stars arrive.

She is not interested in religion.

Reads the *Daily Mirror* and *News of the World* as well as women's magazines and paper-backed novelettes.

Drinks when "out with a boy," and smokes in moderation.

Does not gamble because she says that post office employees caught gambling are subject to immediate dismissal. Whether or not this is true, Miss K. believes it and has given up taking a few lines in "Dad's" football coupon.

11

Miss M. is 19 and works in a paper mill. Quite pretty and rather vain. Lives with her parents and brother and is fond of her home.

Has had various sexual experiences with boys who were walking out with her and sees no great harm. Thinks it would be wrong if she were married. Hopes to be married within two or three years and have several children. Thinks that making a home is the only real career for a woman.

Learnt little about housekeeping at home as her mother always says it is easier for her to cook herself than teach Miss M. how to do so, so Miss M. took an evening course in homecraft (cooking, cleaning, baby-minding, etc.) at an L.C.C. evening school.

Sometimes "sits in" with neighbours' children in evenings to let the neighbours go out together.

Fond of dancing, the cinema, and boys. Reads a women's weekly and a few novels. Drinks and smokes occasionally. Shares in her father's football pool coupon.

Brought up to go to church but has given up now as she says, "It's silly. Nobody really believes all that nonsense."

12

Mr. D. is just over 18 years of age and is waiting to be called up for National Service. His father has a flourishing retail business and he has been working in the shop for the last 18 months. Mr. D. is rather lazy and unreliable, and is dreading the Army, where he thinks the discipline will be unpleasant. He is a "mother's darling," and she often protects him when some escapade has particularly annoyed the father.

Mr. D. smokes to a moderate extent and drinks if he is at a party but not otherwise.

He is a keen saxophone player and plays frequently in a dance band run by a friend of Mr. D's. elder brother. He is also keen on dancing and divides his free evenings between the dance band, dancing and the cinema.

He is a little shy with girls and has not passed the stage of wanting to be promiscuous without actually daring to be.

Does not gamble as his father has always prohibited it and Mr. D. has therefore come to believe that "it's a mug's game."

Mr. D's. father and mother occasionally go to church on Sunday evening and at one time Mr. D. used to go with them, but he gave it up because the services bored him. He went to Sunday School as a boy but never paid much attention.

13

Miss C. is 18, a junior typist in an office. She lives some distance from her work, and leaves home every morning at 7.15 to catch a train due in London soon after 8 a.m. From then until her office opens at 9 a.m. she wanders around the dress shops. Her twin passions are clothes and boys. The former she used to indulge by buying the clothing coupons from as many of her relatives and friends as could be induced to part with any, and she also used to buy some on the black market. She is paid £4 10s. 0d. a week; her fares (workmen's rates) are 7s. 6d. a week; income tax is 7s. 0d. or 8s. 0d. After paying insurance contributions and giving her mother 15s. 0d. for her keep she still has close on £3 per week pocket money. She smokes heavily (20 or 25 cigarettes a day), spends a certain amount on make-up, 5s. 0d. on the cinema and virtually all the rest on clothes. Her only reading matter is one weekly magazine for adolescent girls and the *News of the World* on Sundays. To an enquiry whether she belonged to a youth club, or would like to do so, she replied, "No kids' games for me, thank you."

Miss C. was christened but has never been confirmed. She says that, as far as she knows, she has *never* been to a service in a church or chapel since she was christened. She knits baby clothes in the train for a small niece but says she is never going to have any children, as "When girls start having kids they don't have any more fun." She likes to have plenty of boys around her, but "doesn't let them go too far."

Miss C. likes light ale and port-and-lemon, when a boy friend takes her into a pub. Most of her boy friends take her to pubs. She doesn't like boys who are "stuck-up little stiff shirts."

14

Miss Z. is a junior clerk, aged 19, living at home with her parents and just beginning to find her feet in the world. "Her best friend" is still a girl, but she also has her first "boy."

There can be no doubt of her sexual innocence.

She has an exceptionally nice nature—kind and gentle. and has been very well brought up. She goes to chapel most Sundays, does not gamble nor drink, but has recently started to smoke.

Her hobbies are knitting, sewing, cycling and playing tennis. She likes the radio and goes to the cinema once a week, or occasionally twice. She thinks "every girl ought to be able to dance" so she is taking lessons, and "so far likes it very much."

She thinks a great deal about the possibility of one day getting married. Her own mother was married at 19. Miss Z. has learnt a good deal about cooking and housework.

Inexperienced, but likely to make a good wife for some lucky man.

15

Mr. U. is 19 and is unfit for military service although he plays both cricket and football. He is learning the hotel trade. His parents are quite well-to-do but he is learning "from the bottom up" and at the time of the interview was acting as washer-up.

He is a pleasant youth—a mixture of ambition and dreams. He has recently had his first sexual experiences with a maid in the hotel who came into his room at night when he was asleep. He is grateful to her and not in the least shocked. He sees no harm in sexual intercourse.

Drinks very little and does not smoke. Likes dancing, films (especially "musicals" of the American type) and variety theatres. Also likes country walks, preferably alone.

Doesn't read much—a daily paper and perhaps half-a-dozen books a year, but when he does read a book it is a "good one," either biography or politics or travel.

16

Miss O. is a shop assistant, aged 19. The shop is a branch of a multiple provision merchant catering for working-class people. Miss O. is the second of seven children, all the others being boys except the youngest—a girl of 6—who shares Miss O's. bed.

She is unhappy at home as money is always short and there is no peace. A year ago Miss O. met a young airman, who has now been demobilized, and they are engaged and will marry as soon as they have saved enough to buy furniture and other household requisites. Miss O. is "sick of kids" and hopes not to have any children of her own.

Miss O. never goes to church because nobody in her family ever does. She was not christened as a child and as far as she knows has never been to church.

Miss O. does not drink as she has been "fed up" all through childhood with her parents, both of whom are heavy drinkers. She has often had to go without food because they had bought drink instead. On the other hand she smokes heavily for a girl.

She does not gamble, as she prefers to save her money, and before she started courting she preferred to spend her money on clothes.

She goes regularly twice a week to the cinema.

17

Mr. R. is a young clerk, aged 19, whose home is in the West Country and who has been given a job "with very good prospects" in a large town. He has been there for seven months and is desperately lonely. He has been brought up in a very happy home and has for both his parents an affection of almost exaggerated intensity. The family apparently have never made friends outside the very close circle of near relatives and Mr. R. has had virtually no friends outside his own home. He has never belonged to any youth organization and has never been in contact with any religious body. Both parents are agnostic and though Mr. R. was christened he has not been confirmed, and the only time he can remember going to church was one Christmas Day when he was about seven years of age when his grandmother took him to matins. Religious instruction at school made no impression on him at all.

Mr. R. has never smoked, never tasted alcohol, never gambled. His father does them all in moderation and Mr. R. feels vaguely that he will start one day.

Besides Mr. R. and his parents, the others in the family are a brother and a maternal grandmother. Mr. R. has never been out with a girl, and "except at Christmas parties," has hardly even spoken to one.

His main interest is in association football, although he has never played himself as his parents "did not want him to mix with the boys who played football as they were very common." He is therefore a watcher of football rather than a player, and this is his main relaxation.

He is a frequent visitor to cinemas but more because of loneliness than for any other reason. He enjoys the darkness of a cinema because people cannot look at him.

He is very observant and has a great desire to overcome his shyness. At present his life must be agony outside office hours, but he has already been sharp enough to notice that although few people are as shy as he, a great many of his contemporaries are equally lonely and lost, and that the public house and the flirtations to which they have recourse, do not solve their problems.

Mr. R. says he intends to try going to concerts (he is quite ignorant of all art), museums and the National Gallery to see if he can find anything to make life worth while.

18

Miss F. is aged 17 and is employed in a solicitor's office. She works the telephone switchboard, runs errands, looks after the post and sometimes helps with the typing. She is reasonably contented with her work which she regards as a necessary evil for the period of time that must pass before she marries.

She is not happy at home because there are four other girls, all younger than she, and her father earns only a small wage. In their overcrowded home she has to share her bed with two sisters and put up with all their noise and with the way they borrow her handkerchiefs, mess up her lipstick and powder, and generally tease her.

Miss F. has a great desire to "make the best of" herself and to marry someone who can give her a "nice" home. She is fond of children and hopes to have two of her own. She thinks it is unfair on the children to have more than two as it reduces their material prospects.

She is keen on "boys" but is wary in her dealings with them. She says it damages a girl's chances to be thought "cheap," and she doesn't want to have to marry somebody she might not care much for just because he had made her pregnant. She sees nothing wrong in sexual promiscuity but thinks it is a foolish habit for a girl.

Once a week Miss F. goes dancing and once to the cinema. In the winter she takes a course at a recreational institute. Last winter it was a needlework course and the previous year cookery.

Smokes and drinks "at a party" but not otherwise,

Not interested in religion,

An active member of a Young Socialist organization affiliated to the Labour League of Youth.

19

Mr. Y. is 17 and works in a regional office of a nationalized industry. He is a secondary school boy and very proud of having a "white collar" job as his father is a labourer.

He is a nice lad though at a rather difficult age when he feels the urge to experiment in all sorts of ways without having the experience to tell good from bad. He was glad to talk with an experienced adult as he felt he could not talk to his parents.

A fortnight before meeting the investigator he had gone for a country walk with a girl older than himself, and after a little kissing and cuddling she had seduced him. As he knew nothing at all about sex he was puzzled and frightened as well as delighted. He had not dared to seek his parents' advice as he believed that as they had not told him about sex it must be shameful.

Mr. Y. has started going into public houses but he realizes the danger, and says he will never let alcohol become a habit. He also smokes in a self-conscious way.

He plays no games but goes for long cycle rides, usually by himself. A keen cinema-goer—twice a week or sometimes more.

Never misses a Sunday at chapel.

20

Mr. Z. is 18 years of age and attends the local youth centre. He is simple and dull mentally, and has always attended a Special school. During the daytime he acts as a barrow boy or helps with a light horse and van delivery. He has been on probation for stealing on two occasions.

He lives with his mother in a block of flats which were erected under a slum clearance scheme. He is one of a large family and most of the children are of dull mentality.

At the youth centre young Mr. Z. is a member of the junior discussion group, woodwork and singing groups. He is very interested in football and is in the third team by way of encouragement.

About two years ago a member's bicycle was suddenly missed whilst he was in the centre, and three days later Mr. Z. was seen by the police riding it. On making further enquiries it was found there were four missing cycles in the block of flats and when the case came up it was felt that the mother had knowledge of the thefts. The lad was put on probation on condition that he attended the youth centre each evening.

Since that time Mr. Z. has improved considerably in discipline and personal appearance, and has a more reasonable and settled outlook on life. He smokes, drinks and gambles whenever possible and can be seen playing pitch and toss on the pavement outside the flats during the week-ends. Mr. Z. is improving in spite of great odds and poor and difficult home conditions.

CHAPTER II

COMMERCIALIZED GAMBLING

Having shown in the foregoing pages what is the prevalent attitude to life of a large proportion, indeed probably a large majority, of the people in the areas which our investigations covered, and which we have no reason to suppose are in any way exceptional, we turn now to examine in detail ways in which some people spend their leisure time. In this chapter we deal with the question of gambling.

Resolution number 44 of the Lambeth Conference of 1948 "draws attention to the grave moral and social evils that have arisen in many lands through the prevalence of gambling," whilst in his book, *English Social History*, G. M. Trevelyan says (page 571): "Gambling now perhaps does more harm than drink." These two statements are a sober indication of the gravity of the matter.

What constitutes gambling?

There is no better definition of gambling than that given by the late J. A. Hobson when he says,[1] "Gambling is the determination of the ownership of property by appeal to chance. By chance is here implied the resultant of a play of natural forces that cannot be controlled or calculated by those who appeal to it." A tendency to gamble has long been discernible in man. Even at the Crucifixion the soldiers thought it natural to cast lots to determine which of them should have Jesus' robe, and many simple operations which are technically gambling, such as small privately run sweepstakes on the Derby, although undesirable on a strict assessment, are generally regarded as being fairly harmless. We are not concerned in this chapter with such minor activities, but with the large-scale gambling that is promoted as a business.

[1] *The Ethics of Gambling*, by J. A. Hobson, p. 1.

This commercialized gambling is a comparatively new phenomenon. Save for certain conditions, such as the relatively restricted purchasing power of the middle-class to-day (1950), or the great hardships arising from the trade depression between the wars, the general situation in this century has been that a larger and larger number of people have enjoyed a steadily rising standard of living, while, at the same time, their normal period of leisure has increased by ten or more hours a week. In an article in *The Economist* of the 29th March, 1947, it was stated that "the margin of working-class incomes available for free spending was multiplied eight times over between the two world wars." This situation has been exploited by a class of persons who, on a large scale, have provided facilities for gambling as a means of filling some of the extra hours of leisure and of transferring a proportion of the augmented wages from the pockets of the workers into their own.

The volume of gambling

It is convenient at this point to consider whether it is possible to form any useful estimate of the volume of gambling in Britain and of the number of persons who gamble.

The volume of gambling would be best indicated by the total annual turnover of the main sections of the industry. Such a figure would of course not give the *cost* of the gambling industry to the community—that is a matter to which we refer later. Various figures have been published from time to time purporting to represent the industry's annual turnover, and we do not question that they have been based on the best calculations that their respective authors have been able to make. Yet the complexities of the subject are so great, and the unknown factors about which it is necessary to guess are so numerous, that we have not always felt able to accept the published figures as even approximately accurate. Of recent years, however, an independent statistical organization, Research Services Ltd., working on behalf of the Hulton Press, have made a large-scale social investigation into various matters including gambling.[1] The conclusions to which they

[1] In the course of this book we quote from Research Services' investigations on various occasions. We should like to record here our thanks to Research Services Ltd., its Director, Dr. Mark Abrams, and to the Hulton Press for permission to do so.

came have been used by an anti-gambling organization, the Churches' Committee on Gambling, as the basis of various calculations, including the following table, showing for the years 1947, 1948 and 1949, the turnover of the principal forms of gambling:

	1947	1948	1949
	£ million	£ million	£ million
Horse-racing	400	350	450
Greyhound-racing	300	210	200
Pools	70	69	67
Other forms (including fun fairs)	25	21	18
Total	795	650	735

As a basis of comparison *The Economist*, in the article of the 29th March, 1947, from which we have already quoted, estimated that in the year 1938–9 the turnover of the gambling industry was £381 million. Although this figure was not computed on such accurately determined facts as those given in the table above, and may have erred somewhat on the low side, it provides a useful indication of the growth of commercialized gambling in the last twelve years.

From the figures quoted in the foregoing table it appears that gambling on greyhound racing has suffered a sharp decline in the last two or three years, although it is still at a much higher level than before the war, whereas gambling on horse-racing and pools have, broadly speaking, maintained their positions. Those who are occupied in the promotion of greyhound racing usually attribute the decline to the betting tax instituted in 1948, and which does not apply to horse racing. Since, however, the tax applies to football pools which have remained fairly steady, this explanation, although it may be a contributory factor, does not by itself seem an adequate one. We believe that the decline in greyhound racing since 1947 mainly indicates that the thriftless element of the population has spent the ready money it acquired through war gratuities and wartime savings. The same effect would naturally not be apparent in the totals for horse racing and pools, which are made up mainly of a great multiplicity of small amounts, spent not infrequently in amounts of one or two shillings at a time. Greyhound racing, with its easily accessible stadia, is the medium *par excellence* for spending spare cash in substantial amounts. Furthermore, as supporters of greyhound racing become short of money, the cost of transport to and from the stadium and the price of admission act as deterrents. "Off-the course" betting on horses is a cheaper amusement than "going to the dogs," and this no doubt contributes to the popularity of that form of gambling at a time when betting on greyhound racing has declined.

How many people gamble?

To see the matter in perspective, however, it is necessary to have some idea about how many persons have contributed to the annual turnover that we have been discussing.

Because of the prevalence of illegal betting, to which we make reference below, it is impossible to make any reliable estimate of the number of persons who bet on horses. It is, however, a habit with a substantial proportion of men of all classes, and with a much smaller proportion of women. There is such interest in obtaining the results of races as early as possible, that evening newspapers print the results in the stop-press, and successive editions are hawked by newsvendors with such cries as, "Winner of the 4 o'clock," or "All the winners."

As long ago as 1923 a Select Committee of the House of Commons reported, "Indeed it is stated that there is scarcely a works in the country employing more than 20 workmen where one is not a bookmaker's agent, and this Your Committee believe to be near the truth."

Towards the other end of the social scale the interest is not much less intense, as is shown by the installation in many clubs in the West End of London of special "ticker-tape" news machines that, except for a few cricket scores, normally relay nothing except information about racing and betting.

More exact information is available about the number of persons who bet on greyhound races, because, first, the numbers who attend these races can be fairly accurately determined, second, only an insignificant number of persons attend greyhound races without betting, and third, "off the course" betting on greyhounds, although by no means a rarity, is not the common occurrence that it is in the case of horse races.

In their statistical examination of betting habits, Research Services ascertained that 90·5 per cent of men and 96·9 per cent of women *never* attend greyhound races. The percentages of the population over the age of 16 who attend them, and the frequency of their attendances, were found to be:

	% of Population	
	Men	Women
Twice a week	0·9	0·2
Once a week	1·8	0·3
Once a fortnight	0·7	0·1
Once a month	1·3	0·3
Less than once a month ..	4·8	2·2

On this basis, and making some allowance for the small, but not negligible, number of persons who bet "off-the-course," we deduce that approximately 50,000,000 bets are made each year on greyhound races.

The number of persons taking part each week in football pools has also been determined by Research Services with considerable accuracy. In the first quarter of 1949, the latest period for which information is available, the number of participants over the age of 21 averaged 11,250,000 weekly. Further details about the sex and ages of these persons, and about the amounts that they stake, are given on page 136.

Illegal (i.e., "street") betting

So far in this chapter we have been concerned with aspects of the gambling industry that are perfectly legal, however undesirable they may be. There is, in addition, a vast and complex network of illegal gambling transactions, and it is these that we next consider.

Ready-money betting, although legal on race courses, is illegal anywhere else, so that persons whose financial position is such that they cannot readily obtain credit, and that means virtually the whole of the working-class and a fair proportion of the lower middle-class, must either refrain from betting altogether, because they cannot bet legally, or they must resort to illegal betting for ready money.

Illegal betting is almost entirely restricted to working and lower middle-class areas, but it is prevalent there. In such areas there is a widespread belief that there is no harm in such betting, and a feeling that the law should be amended to legalize it. The present prohibition is laid down in the Street Betting Act, 1899, and the penalties under that Act are a fine of £10 for a first offence, of £20 for a second, and of £30 or three months' imprisonment for the third and each subsequent offence. Because of the grading of the penalties, it is a frequent practice for illegal bookmakers to hire as assistants only those men who have not previously been convicted, and indeed it is even a recognized practice for a man not previously convicted to be hired to take the place of a really guilty party if the appearance of the police makes arrest seem imminent. Such substitutes are known by the slang name of "Jockeys" and, if arrested, their fines are paid for them by the bookmaker and they are given a fee.

There seems to be no doubt that the penalties under the Street Betting Act are no real deterrent to-day, and this is at least partly due to the great decline in the value of money since the Act was passed in 1899. To become a deterrent, the financial penalties would have to be very much heavier, but even more effective would be an amendment to the Act making it possible to proceed against the principal (i.e., the bookmaker, who stays quietly in the background), instead of merely against his agent, who is the hireling who accepts the money and betting slips.

When discussing the matter with the Superintendent of one Metropolitan Police District (an area with a working-class population of approximately 750,000) we were told that at least 100 illegal bookmakers were known to the police in his area, some with as many as a dozen touts to act as go-betweens, and to give warning of the approach of the police. Another Metropolitan Police Superintendent spoke to us of the frequency with which children act as intermediaries between their parents and the street bookmakers, a lesson they are not likely to forget.

We saw something for ourselves of the activities of the street bookmakers when we drove around a poor working-class district of London with yet a third Superintendent of the Metropolitan Police. As the police car came in sight, knots of men in street after street broke up and ran, like sparrows scattering at the approach of a cat. They were the street bookmakers, busy in a way, and to an extent, probably not remotely imagined by the large majority of citizens.

Horse racing

Before going on to consider some of the moral, psychological and economic problems arising from the development of the gambling industry, it is convenient here to discuss briefly each of the main media for large-scale gambling.

Horse racing, the first gambling medium we consider, is by no means a harmful or undesirable activity in itself. Divorced from serious gambling (and small bets made as part of a day's outing *by people actually present at a race meeting* can hardly be so considered), it provides legitimate recreation in the open air. Apart from serious gamblers, people attend races so infrequently that it does not become habit-forming for the normal person. Horse racing also has obvious value in relation to horse breeding. In this connection it is worth quoting Lord Astor, who wrote,[1] "The race course discovers which horses possess certain desirable qualities. To me it occupies the same place as the flower show does to the grower of roses. It is the competitive testing ground for theories and methods of breeding . . . I never bet on my own or anyone else's horses, and have never recommended anyone else to do so. I have always felt that gambling was not sport—that it tended to spoil the true spirit of sport."

Unfortunately, however, an immense number of persons, women as well as men, regard horse racing neither as an

[1] In a letter to *The Times* on 4th May, 1926.

opportunity for a day's outing nor as a sport, but simply as a medium for betting. Whether such betting is conducted legally on credit, or illegally in cash, depends mainly on the social status of the individual gambler. We have evidence that gambling on horses is prevalent in rural as well as urban areas, and is so widespread and frequent that it has developed its own vocabulary and is accepted by its devotees as a normal part of the national life. For example, the enquiry, "What have you done to-day?" often does not receive an answer such as "Cut the grass and put in the late spuds," but rather "Moonshine for the 2.30, and doubled it with Delusion for the 4 o'clock." Just as there are still millions of individual citizens who do not smoke, there are millions who do not bet on horses, but the prevalence of gambling on horses is such that it is quite possible that non-smokers are not much rarer than non-gamblers.

Although most bets on horses are for small amounts, a favourite one being "a shilling each way," which signifies a total bet of 2s. od., the aggregate of an individual's bets over a week or a month may be such as to impose real hardship on him and his family. To illustrate this, and various other aspects of betting on horses, we give the following illustrations from our case histories:

(*a*) Mr. X. is married, with two children. He earns £6 a week and is £175 in debt to a bookmaker from whom he obtained credit by making false statements about his true position. He is paying the bookmaker £3 a week and his wife, in consequence, has had to take work as a charwoman. Mr. X. still bets on horses several times a week, but now on a ready-money basis.

(*b*) Mr. Y. is a jobbing gardener. He also acts as tout for an illegal bookmaker and earns £5 or £6 commission in a normal week. He says he has recently had a run of bad luck, and for the last two or three months has lost more each week by gambling himself than he has earned in commission.

(*c*) Mr. W. is employed as a labourer in a foundry. He was met by an acquaintance at noon in a bus and asked, "Hullo, having a day off?" He replied, "No. The foreman always lets me out for an hour in the morning to get the money on" (i.e., to "arrange the bets").

(*d*) Miss Y. is aged 65, the receptionist in an hotel. She bets on two or three horses on most days of the year that there is racing. She says she does it "for a bit of fun and to give an interest to life." Occasionally she wins, but she often loses £5 or £6 a month.

(*e*) Mr. Z. is a professional man of about 50. He bets whenever he gets a good tip—usually two or three times a week. Claims to win over a long period, but has had "ghastly luck lately—£50 down in the last month."

(*f*) Mrs. G. is the wife of a professional man. A few years ago somebody gave her a good tip for the Derby. She risked £5 and won at 66 to 1. She took her family for a holiday abroad on the winnings. She had never previously bet but now does so regularly. She does not tell her husband, but she spends about 15s. 0d. a week of the housekeeping money on horses. Her milkman acts as a bookmaker's tout and puts on her bets.

(*g*) Mrs. H. is a charwoman aged about 50. She is a widow. She bets regularly on horses and she keeps a fair-sized notebook in her handbag with records of all her betting transactions.

(*h*) Mr. K. is a professional man, retired and very bored. Bets every day there are horse races. He says he has "nothing better to do."

(*i*) Mr. L. is a local government clerk. He used to bet regularly, but lost so much money that his home was in danger of breaking up. He is fond of his wife and decided in his own words, "to make a bit instead of being a mug." He nows acts as an illegal bookmaker on a small scale. He claims to make £10 or £15 a week profit, with no serious risk to himself, for if large bets are placed with him he covers himself by a corresponding bet with a bookmaker in a bigger way of business.

(*j*) Mr. S. is a farm labourer. He is well thought of by his employer and is industrious. Three or four times in most weeks he takes a short time off to ride on his motor-bike to a small town nearby, where an illegal bookmaker sits in a public house collecting bets. The employer accepts this situation and sometimes asks Mr. S. to place bets for him.

Greyhound racing

Greyhound racing differs basically from horse racing in two respects. First, it is never free, as horse racing can be, from betting, and second, the volume of "off-the-course" betting is small in proportion to that "on-the-course." The normal greyhound racing meeting lasts for approximately two-and-a-half hours, in the course of which there are eight races. The actual races last for a total of under five minutes, and the remaining 145 minutes are devoted to betting. In that fact lies the justification for the view, often expressed, that greyhound racing tracks are nothing more than vast open-air gaming places.

There are approximately 150 licensed tracks in Great Britain, on each of which racing is allowed on 104 days in the year. We do not wish here to describe the rather shoddy scene at a greyhound racing meeting, although we have attended meetings to see for ourselves what goes on, for our description would be so unfavourable that we might appear to be prejudiced. We know of no better description than that by Charles Dimont, published in *The New Statesman* of the 30th November, 1946, which we accordingly reproduce in the Appendix on page 465.[1]

One special development of greyhound racing deserves mention, more because of its potentialities than because of its present significance. In 1934, when Parliament laid down the conditions under which such racing might take place, the rather peculiar exception was made that greyhound racing might take place at any time without licence, and merely after the promoters had notified the police of their intention of holding a meeting, provided such unlicensed racing did not take place more than eight days in any year on one site. While this precludes the building of unlicensed stadia, at great cost both for the buildings and the totalisators, it has resulted in the production of mobile outfits, which enable greyhound racing to take place anywhere where there is a field of suitable size. Furthermore, the condition about the number of days on one site is observed if the outfit is moved from one field to the next. Attendances at such meetings are at present small, often no more than 100 or 150 persons, and the betting is usually with bookmakers. There is no means of knowing how many of these mobile outfits exist, but we have ascertained that in 1947 notices were given to the police of the intentions of various promoters to hold upwards of 5,000 meetings in England and Wales.

[1] We are indebted to the Editor of *The New Statesman* and to Mr. Dimont for permission to reproduce his article.

Football pools

Football pools have certain unique features, of which the two most striking are, first, that a great many of those who take part in them do not consider them to be gambling at all, and, second, that in the most popular pools a small stake can, and not infrequently does, win really large sums. It is something of a sensation for a horse to win a race at odds of 100 to 1, while odds on greyhounds are invariably quite short, but it happens sufficiently often for the credulous to think it normal that in a football pool a prize of £10,000 is paid for 1d. (i.e., odds of 2,400,000 to 1), while wins at even longer odds occur at intervals in each season.

The rigid moralist may at this point lift up his hands and say, "Ah, the naughtiness of avaricious man!" And there is no denying that avarice is a vice that exercises a deleterious influence on moral fibre. If the majority of persons taking part in football pools were actuated by avarice they would stand condemned on moral grounds. There is, however, another side to the question. Although the tendency for at least half-a-century has been to provide a steadily increasing measure of social security, and although it is probably true to say that poverty through sheer lack of means has been so reduced that it now afflicts only a very small proportion of the population, yet large sections of the population live under a constant sense of frustration due to lack of means. Quite often their reasons for wanting money are entirely reasonable and proper, such as a desire for a better chance in life for their children, or to provide modest comfort, in pleasant surroundings, for aged parents or in their own old age, or simply for capital to run a little business. In the case of some 90% of the population, these financial problems cannot be solved by thrift alone. It is therefore quite understandable that they should seek, through the football pools, money they could never obtain by thrift. It is as though they said to one another, "Look here! We can't all be satisfied. Indeed very few of us can, but if we each put up a small amount per week, a few of us—and we realize how few—can win a really large sum and the rest of us won't miss our contributions." Although, naturally, men and women speaking of football pools hardly ever speak in those precise terms, our interviewing work has convinced us that that idea is present in the minds of a large number, perhaps a majority, of those who compete. It would be pharisaical for any who are not themselves living and bringing up a family on a small income to condemn too strongly on moral grounds those who, frustrated by lack of money, and realizing the utter impossibility of getting it through hard work, seek it through the pools. Persons gambling on the pools may be gullible and foolish, for they seldom understand the odds against them, but it cannot in our view be maintained that their actions are seriously discreditable.

A further feature that differentiates the pools from other forms of gambling, is that the forecasts can be made in the home, and virtually the whole of the gambler's part of the transaction completed there at his leisure. This gives rise to features which the anti-gambling organizations particularly condemn, and to other related features which those who condone football pools, whether or not they compete in them themselves, consider to be advantageous. On the one hand it is claimed that the introduction of football pools into the home and the discussions, anticipations and excitement to which this gives rise, have a bad influence on the children, predisposing them to be gamblers almost from their infancy. It is frequently said, in support of this view, that the greater part of one evening a week is devoted to filling in the football coupons, and the family assemble to take part in it. The supporters of the pools, on the other hand, sometimes make the same assertion about the family, and then claim that, at a time when it is commonly believed that family life is breaking down, the pools provide a new unifying influence.

The belief that most persons who participate in football pools spend one evening a week in filling in their coupons did not seem to be borne out by the information we gathered from our case histories, and we therefore determined to test it.

We accordingly made special enquiries from 498 persons, almost all of them either of the working- or lower middle-class, who fill in football coupons frequently (though not necessarily every week), and we asked them how long they devoted to filling in their coupon in an average week. 373 of them gave answers varying from ten minutes to half-an-hour, 101 said that they took times varying from over half-an-hour up to an hour, and only 24 of them took more than an hour. This seems to us for practical purposes to dispose of the claim that pools are a unifying influence in family life, and it also limits the amount that they can be held to be a harmful influence on the children. Nevertheless, the fact remains that children who see their parents fill in a pools coupon, however quickly, and see them check the forecasts with the results at the end of the week, are preparing themselves subconsciously for the time when they too will be old enough to gamble on football pools. In so far as the pools are harmful, the children are exposed to their harmful influence.

As in all forms of gambling, the pools demand a high level of credulity from those taking part, for even though they realize the odds are heavily against them, very few competitors have any notion how heavily. A single example will suffice. In one of the pools (although it is not one in which the big prizes are won) it is necessary to pick three draws out of a list of perhaps 52 matches. It is probably safe to say that in an average week 8 of the 52 matches will result in draws. To a person who "follows form" it does not appear in advance that he should have much difficulty in picking out three draws, but the fact that he overlooks is that he is picking a *special group* of three games, and that from 52 matches it is possible to make 22,100 of such groups. If—as sometimes happens—there are only 3 draws in the 52 matches only one special group out of 22,100 alternatives is correct, and the odds against a correct forecast are 22,099 to 1. Every additional draw in the 52 matches decreases the odds against a correct forecast substantially because it rapidly increases the number of alternative correct solutions. But even if there are 8 draws, as is about average, the odds against a successful forecast are still 394 to 1.

Another fact that has impressed us is that a study of expert forecasts printed in newspapers reveals that the experts, following form, are wrong as often as they are right. Over four successive weeks the experts of two papers—one a national weekly and one a national daily—obtained the following percentage of correct forecasts of all the matches in the English League:

Weekly	44%	57%	64%	48%
Daily	37%	55%	57%	50%

These forecasts are based on a highly skilled appraisal of form, and of the various matters that affect form, and yet on that basis the experts can only forecast approximately half the matches correctly, and that half includes the matches that are omitted from the coupons as being "too easy." Bearing in mind that the number of persons filling in football coupons is so large that to win a big prize a coupon must in practice normally be either absolutely correct, or at most contain only one error, it follows that form which will not give a forecast averaging more than about 50% accuracy is of little help. Indeed the very existence of the printed forecasts of experts is proof of this statement, for if by relying on form sports writers could win football pools they would probably prefer gambling as a career to journalism. We can only conclude that skill enters to a negligible extent into football pools, which are, in our view, almost a pure gamble.

Mention was made above of the fact that small stakes could win large prizes, and it was argued by inference that the contribution to the pools by the majority of those taking part was a small item in the family budget. The statistical survey by Research Services Ltd. for the Hulton Press, from which we have already quoted in this chapter, contained an enquiry from those persons who said they filled in football pool coupons about the size of their stake (or "investment"). The enquiry, made in the first quarter of 1948, was repeated a year later. In each year the average stake, for 9,830,000 participants in 1948, and for 11,250,000 participants in 1949, amounted to 3s. 2d. a week. The following table shows the proportions of men and women of various income groups who took part in football pools in the first quarter of 1949 and their average weekly stakes.

On the basis of these figures, and having regard to the contemporary levels of wages and salaries, it can hardly be

	Men			Women			Men and Women together		
	% participating	Av. stake		% participating	Av. stake		% participating	Av. stake	
		s.	d.		s.	d.		s.	d.
Upper middle-class	22·5	7	7	8·6	2	1	15·1	6	0
Middle-class ..	34·5	4	6	14·4	2	0	23·7	3	8
Lower middle-class ..	42·8	4	0	17·0	2	0	28·9	3	4
Working-class ..	53·3	3	7	20·3	2	0	3 ·3	3	1
All classes together ..	49·5	3	10	18·8	2	0	33·1	3	2

maintained that football pools are contributing appreciably to the secondary poverty (i.e., poverty due to the unwise spending of means adequate in themselves) which Professor F. Zweig showed in his book, *Labour, Life and Poverty*, often arose from gambling in general,[1] and of which we gave some specific instances on page 129 in relation to horse racing.

The attitude of individual persons to football pools was shown by our case histories, of which the following are examples:

(*a*) Mr. A., a professional man, fills in a football coupon every week, spending 2s. 0d. He does not even bother to check the coupon when the results are known, as the pool promoters will inform him if he has won. He says he does not miss the 2s. 0d. and it is worth taking the chance, however small the likelihood of success.

(*b*) Mr. B., a retired man of the middle-class. Spends 3s. 6d. per week on his football pool. He says, "It's worth the money for the fun, and you never know, you might be lucky one day—after all, I only spend the price of a packet of cigarettes a week."

(*c*) Mr. and Mrs. C., a working-class couple, fill in a joint coupon, spending 1s. 6d. a week each. They take about 35 minutes to fill it in, and on Saturday evenings they check it together. They always

[1] *Labour, Life and Poverty* by F. Zweig, published by Gollancz, p. 22.

hope for a big win, but never expect it, so they are not disappointed when they lose. They reckon the entertainment plus the chance of a win are worth the money.

(*d*) Mrs. D. is a well-to-do widow. She was introduced to football pools by her companion, and now finds they have added a new interest to her life. Spends 5s. od. a week.

(*e*) Mr. E. is a labourer. He spends 2s. 6d. a week on football pools, which give him an interest and the chance of a large win. His aim is to win enough to buy two houses, as at present he and his wife, two married sons, their wives and two children, and two unmarried adult daughters all live in Mr. E's. five-roomed house, and Mr. E. says, "I can tell you, Mister, there ain't much peace."

(*f*) Mr. F. is an artisan, married, with a young child. Spends 3s. od. a week on football pools. Does not regard it as an amusement, but as his only hope of winning a large sum of money. Would like to buy a house (at present lives with Mr. F's. parents) and ensure a good education for the child.

In sharp distinction from greyhound racing, which, despite vigorous efforts by its organizers and authorities to ensure its integrity, is regarded, as our case histories showed, with a great deal of suspicion by the man-in-the-street, there is absolute and undoubtedly justifiable confidence that all the major football pools, which between them handle a very high proportion of the total football pool betting, are honestly conducted. The pool promoters normally take 5 per cent net commission, and a further amount, determined by their own accountants, for expenses. The betting tax now in force[1] is also deducted, and the amount distributed in prizes is normally somewhat less than 60 per cent of the gross amount staked. From the point of view of the pool promoters, the football pool industry is an entrepreneur's paradise, for their equipment is comparatively simple, their risks are nil, and their profits certain and substantial.

Since such a vast number of persons of nearly all classes of the community take part in football pools, and see no harm in them, it is certain that it would be a practical impossibility to abolish them. This does not mean, however, that no reforms are possible. It might, for example, be well worth giving consideration to a reform along the lines of the Scandinavian

[1] At present (May, 1950) 30 per cent of winnings.

football pools,[1] which are publicly-controlled monopolies, the profits of which are devoted to desirable social purposes. Such a system would not only make the profits of pools available for worth-while social purposes, but would eradicate the advertizing and canvassing which are undesirable features of the present system. In other words, there would be football pools for everybody who wanted to participate, but nobody would be urged or persuaded to do so as is now the case. The transference of football pools to public ownership would be more difficult in England than was the setting up *ab initio* of a similar system in Scandinavia, because the question of compensation would arise. If the present proprietors were to be compensated at the market price, the pools would be extremely expensive to purchase. On the other hand, the proprietors have no costly capital equipment, and they have rendered no useful social service. They have merely enjoyed a rich and certain harvest for a number of years in return for the provision of simple, and comparatively harmless, facilities for gambling. We believe that the community has at least as great a moral right to take over those facilities at cost price as the present proprietors have to continue their exploitation.

If a scheme of public ownership of the pools were prepared, many persons no doubt would have scruples about whether the State would be justified in owning and profiting from a gambling medium. For better or for worse, however, that question has already been decided, for, by imposing a tax of 30% on winnings, the State has already become a beneficiary. Indeed in some ways the situation is analagous to that which existed in Carlisle before the State acquired the ownership there of the breweries and public houses.[2] Drinking in public houses, although perfectly legal, had assumed such proportions as seriously to reduce the output in certain munition factories that were vital to the war effort. It was impracticable to abolish it and, therefore, for purposes of control a system of public ownership was instituted with considerable social advantages to the community and, purely incidentally, with profit to the Exchequer. Without pushing the analogy too far

[1] See page 415 *et seq.*, where we give the results of certain enquiries into leisure time pursuits made by B. S. Rowntree in the Scandinavian countries.

[2] We discuss the Carlisle scheme in detail in Chapter III.

it seems reasonable to suppose that a method found suitable to deal in Carlisle with the problem of drink might well prove suitable in principle, though with a quite different organization in detail, to deal with the problem of football pools.

"Fixed odds" football coupons

A new development of betting on football occurred at the beginning of the 1949–50 season, when the practice of betting on football matches at fixed odds (i.e., a simple transaction with a bookmaker analogous to backing a horse) rapidly grew in favour as a result of the adaptation to it of the technique of pool betting. Persons wishing to bet on "fixed odds" football coupons receive from the bookmaker of their choice a weekly coupon that is similar to a pool coupon. The difference is that instead of all the sums staked going into a pool to provide profits and expenses for the promoter, tax for the Treasury, and winnings for a few lucky individuals, every individual makes a separate bet with the promoter, who pays fixed and advertised odds on every successful forecast.

The odds offered on the fixed odds coupons vary greatly according to the status and resources of the promoter, but they are seldom closely related to the real mathematical chance of success. For example one of the more generous bookmakers offers 35 to 1 against the forecasting of 3 draws in a list of 56 matches. The mathematical odds against a correct forecast in an average week are more than ten times as great! Similarly although the same bookmaker offers 400 to 1 against a client correctly forecasting the result of 7 matches, the actual odds against a correct forecast are 2,186 to 1.

Gambling machines

Probably the most widespread of the remaining forms of betting is that on machines in amusement arcades. These machines are frequently known as pin tables, because a popular form of them consists in guiding metal balls through pegs, or pins, set in a glass-covered table as obstacles to the free run of the balls. In fact, however, they take many forms, quite a frequent one being a crane operated by a handle and with a claw at the end that can (with luck) be made to seize prizes lying inside the glass lid of the machine.

There is no way of knowing how much money is taken in these machines. The Churches' Committee on Gambling and *The Economist* agree at putting it at £10 million per annum, a staggering sum when it is remembered that most of the machines are operated by inserting one penny. It is certain that the gross profits are large, for in many of the great cities arcades furnished with these machines are situated in streets where rentals are very high.

The arcades are patronized, for the most part, by young people, both adolescents and young adults. A survey conducted in both urban and rural areas by the Lancashire Standing Conference of Voluntary Youth Organizations in 1946 into the gambling habits of young people of both sexes, showed that the percentage of their sample of 1,404 young people attending amusement arcades was:[1]

Ages	Attended	
	Occasionally	Regularly
	%	%
11–14	0	32
15–18	6	31
19–21	2	27
All (11–21)	3	31

We do not quote these figures as being applicable to every part of the country, and further surveys in other parts would doubtless give substantially different results—for example, rural areas and small towns have no amusement arcades. Nevertheless, the figures give a disconcerting picture of the situation in one part of England, which there is no reason to suppose is exceptional. The picture is all the more disconcerting when it is remembered that, from its very nature, the Lancashire Standing Conference of Voluntary Youth Organ-

[1] Quoted by kind permission of the Community Council of Lancashire from their pamphlet "Gambling among Young People."

izations was only able to make its enquiry among young people who were members of its constituent organizations. The large numbers of young people who "don't belong to anything," and whose standards are certainly not likely to be higher than those with definite attachments to worth-while organizations, were not included in the survey.

The situation with regard to the existence of these machines is anomalous, for they are illegal, yet in most parts of the country they are tolerated by the police because of the very small value of the prizes. The amusement arcades are, however, closely watched by the police, and the introduction of machines on which the gambling was other than trivial would result in immediate intervention. This tolerant attitude is obviously approved by the majority of citizens, for protests against it are extremely rare, although retailers with a high reputation can scarcely relish amusement arcades as neighbours. Nevertheless, it seems to us that the tolerance is a mistake, for the arcades are tawdry and sordid, and even apart from the actual gambling, their atmosphere is by no means that to which a prudent nation would desire a substantial proportion of its young people to be exposed.

Sweepstakes

As in other forms of gambling, the amount of money spent on sweepstakes of various sorts, including raffles, is a matter of conjecture. In comparison with the really large amounts that represent the turnover of the greyhound and horse-racing industries, the amount spent on sweepstakes is small. *The Economist*, in an article dated 29th March 1947, put it at £4 million, and it is probably safe to assume that this estimate indicates the order of magnitude of the total involved. If certain stringent conditions are observed, it is possible to organize among groups of private persons sweepstakes that are legal. The large majority of the sweepstakes that are a common feature of contemporary English life nevertheless contravene the Betting and Lotteries Act of 1934, and are therefore illegal. Those that are trivial are, however, generally tolerated by the police, especially when they are for a charitable purpose. Few people condemn sweepstakes and raffles unconditionally, although the anti-gambling organizations do so as a matter of principle. The present arrangement seems to us to be a sensible one, and we feel that there are many reforms more urgent than the enforcement of the law that would prohibit raffles at church bazaars, garden parties and similar gatherings.

State Lottery

One form of sweepstake—the State Lottery—is a very different matter. We mention it here because there are influences at work that seek to persuade the Government to reintroduce it into British life. Few people realize now that in the eighteenth century there was a State Lottery in Britain. A Select Committee appointed by Parliament in 1808 to enquire into the whole question reported unanimously against the continuance of the lottery, attributing many evil consequences to its existence. It was largely as a result of this report that Parliament later abolished the State Lottery. The Royal Commission of 1932 reconsidered the matter, but formed an opinion similar to that of the Select Committee. Quite apart from the views of the Committee and the Commission, we have found no evidence of a general desire at the present for a State Lottery. To adopt one would deliberately create a large, and now non-existent, demand for a new form of gambling at a time when the volume of gambling should already give rise to great anxiety. It would be a retrograde and unfortunate step.

Newspaper competitions

Some newspapers, particularly some of those published on Sundays, run for their readers competitions in which the element of skill is almost negligible and that of chance is correspondingly great. But because it is possible to maintain that some degree of skill is needed as well as a great amount of luck, these competitions are legal, for a gambling enterprise, to infringe the laws relating to lotteries, must be dependent entirely on chance.

There are two main forms of these competitions:

(*a*) Fashion competitions. In these a number, usually nine, of pictures of women's clothes are shown and competitors are asked to choose six in order of merit. The competition is judged by a person, usually described anonymously as "A fashion expert," who awards the prize to the competitor making the selection that the judge deems best. At first sight this form of competition seems to be a legitimate test of skill. That it is in truth almost entirely a gamble is shown by the fact that the odds against selecting a group of six out of a group of nine and of arranging these six in a special order (i.e., the order the judge deems "best") are 60,479 to 1! Obviously with such odds the element of skill is slight indeed! The prize offered usually varies, according to the paper, from £500 to £1,000. The entrance fee is small, a typical charge being four tries for threepence or two for three-halfpence. Even so, given the vast circulations of some of the Sunday newspapers, and the gullibility of a great many of their readers, it seems reasonable to suppose that the entrance fees at least cover all the outgoings in respect of the competition, and may even show some profit for the proprietors of the paper, quite apart from the fact that not a few people buy the paper simply on account of the fashion competition.

(*b*) Crossword puzzles. Some newspapers, again particularly those published on Sundays, have contrived to turn crossword puzzles, which are normally a perfectly harmless and an interesting way of spending leisure time, into what can only be called a gambling device. In crossword puzzle competitions of the kind to which we refer, a puzzle is published that is easy of solution, and to make doubly sure that it is within the capabilities of the average reader, nearly one-half of the solution is often printed with the puzzle. There is, however, only one correct solution, and the puzzle is so arranged that in a number of cases it will be absolutely impossible to tell which of two or more alternative words to insert in the puzzle. If the possible combinations of the alternative words are allowed for, the total number of variations is very great. For example, in a puzzle of the kind that we are here considering and which was published in a Sunday newspaper, there are 49,152 alternative solutions. Only one of them is correct and there is no means, other than pure chance, of determining which it is. Entrance fees for these crossword puzzle competitions are normally 3d. or 6d., and the prize varies, the normal maximum being £1,000.

The Stock Exchange

When dealing comprehensively with gambling, the question of gambling on the Stock Exchange always arises—less, we believe, because there is in fact a serious volume of gambling there, than because its operations are seldom understood by the man in the street, who imagines the Exchange to be a place where wealthy speculators gamble with the full approval and protection of the law, and to the detriment of the community. Such a picture is of course fantastic. Since the greater part of industry and commerce has to be financed by comparatively small sums contributed by a comparatively large number of people through the device of joint stock companies, a market is essential where their respective partial ownership of those companies (i.e., their shares) can be bought and sold. The Stock Exchange is as essential, and as respectable, an institution as any other market, but like many other institutions it can on occasion be abused.

There are two principal opportunities for gambling on the Stock Exchange, those provided by the systems known as Contangos and Options.[1] In the Stock Exchange buying and selling transactions are settled on "account days" at intervals of two or three weeks. The Contango system allows a buyer to postpone settlement until the account day after that on which he would normally have settled his account. At any time in the interim either party can cancel the transaction and pay or receive the difference between the agreed price for theshares and the actual price on the day of cancellation. Such a system is obviously capable of being used as an instrument for gambling to an extent that might seriously derange legitimate transactions by creating artificial demands for shares.

The system of Options is equally open to abuse. It enables a person, by payment of a moderate premium, to buy the right to purchase shares at an agreed price on a future date. It is also possible under the system, known as a "put option,"

[1] With Mr. F. W. McPherson's permission we have used his pamphlet *The Stock Exchange—A Market for Enterprise* as our source of information about the possibilities of gambling on the Stock Exchange.

to buy the right to sell at a future date at an agreed price. Used properly, and with skill and discretion, the system of Options can be a valuable method of insurance against future commitments. But it can equally be used as a medium for gambling by the irresponsible or the ignorant.

During the war years, and for some time afterwards, both Contangos and Options were forbidden on the Stock Exchange, but they have now been reallowed. To assess whether the balance of advantage lies in allowing or prohibiting them would require an intricate knowledge of the Stock Exchange not likely to be possessed by laymen. There is a Council of the Stock Exchange to whom the matter can safely be left. The system of accounting days, without Contangos, does of course itself make a certain amount of gambling possible, but the consequent convenience and economy of labour far outweigh the disadvantages.

Why do people gamble?

That then is broadly the picture of the gambling habits of the British people, for whose desire to gamble a great industry now caters. Faced with such an enormous volume of gambling we are bound to seek to answer the question, "Is gambling wrong, and if so, on what grounds—ethical or economic, or both?" But before this question can be profitably considered, it is necessary to try to determine why people gamble.

We neither of us claim to be exceptionally virtuous. We have both knocked about the world a lot, and think we can claim that we are not narrow-minded. Yet we have no desire to gamble; the time G.R.L. spent on his experimental football pool coupons during our investigations he found extremely dull and tiresome; when we went to the greyhound-racing tracks one of us put a few shillings on the totalisator to see the routine of betting, but neither of us felt the slightest desire to plunge wildly; neither of us can be bothered to follow up the tips frequently given to G.R.L. by an acquaintance of his, although the man from whom he buys his evening paper is a bookmaker's runner, and would be delighted to place bets for us. And the same is true of most of our friends; they can't be bothered to gamble. In that statement we believe there is a clue to why people do gamble.

It is often said that people gamble because in a highly industrialized society their lives are dull and lack adventure. This superficially reasonable statement breaks down however when we remember the extremely high incidence of gambling amongst those classes of the community whose lives are neither dull nor lacking in adventure. For example, in his book, *Men in the Pits*, Professor F. Zweig speaks, in Chapter 23, of the phenomenally high incidence of gambling among coal-miners. He gives one example of a postman delivering football pool coupons at 90 houses out of a group of 93, and he tells a story of miners in public houses so determined to gamble that in the absence of any other medium they bet on the raindrops running down the window pane. Soldiers and sailors too are certainly not less prone to gamble than the majority of private citizens. It seems therefore that the idea that people gamble because their lives lack adventure or because their work is uninteresting is not sound.

No doubt some people gamble from cupidity. Many others gamble because of the clever advertising by members of the gambling industry, and because of the indirect advertising which arises from the vast amount of space devoted by most newspapers to forecasts and results of sporting events, and to such items of news as the winning of large sums in a football pool. A few people probably gamble because of the example of others—couples, or parties, going to the "dogs" together for an evening's outing, and so on. But though there is something in each of these reasons, we do not believe that they can account for the enormous amount of gambling that we have shown exists to-day.

When we referred earlier in this chapter to the great increase which has taken place during this century in the margin of working-class incomes available for free spending, and to the great reduction in working hours, and stated that the gambling industry had exploited that situation, we ought perhaps to have added, in order to give a complete picture, that the exploitation had only been possible because society in general had failed to provide worth-while ways for people to spend their new leisure and their new earnings. Not only has society failed to provide worth-while leisure-time facilities, but it has also failed to ensure that individuals are fitted, by a broad process of what is now called "further education," to create interests for themselves. As a consequence, persons untrained to do anything more difficult than to read the names of the winners in the stop-press of the evening paper, or to pass half a crown through the window of a totalisator, have turned in large numbers to gambling, *faute-de-mieux*.

Is gambling wrong?

Now the ground is clear for us to consider whether or not it is wrong for people to gamble. This question appears to us to have two distinct sides, the ethical and the economic. The ethical side, with which we intend to deal first, likewise has two facets, namely those absolute principles of human behaviour that are true for all civilized human societies at all times, and certain principles that are distinctively Christian in a broad sense and would not necessarily apply in any community where Christian principles were not respected.

The purely ethical judgment has been brilliantly expounded by J. A. Hobson in his essay, "The Ethics of Gambling," and we have drawn freely on that source. In Hobson's view, with which we agree, the essential ethical harm of gambling lies in the implicit abandonment of reason. The gambling man is an ignorant and unreasonable man, for he either neglects to inform himself about the nature of the odds against him as do, for example, the credulous people who believe that they have any significant chance of winning a large prize in a lottery or football pool, or, knowing the odds, he deliberately makes himself believe that the figures do not mean precisely what they say.

Thus gambling, being based on what Hobson calls "the organized rejection of reason," is a rejection and betrayal of the long and painful progress of man from his primitive animal state. For the individual, no less than for the community, civilization consists of and is measured by a capacity for rational control, and in Hobson's words, by "a slow gradual imperfect taming of animal instincts which make for emotional anarchy."

A civilized man must be able to trust in the orderly process whereby a foreseeable effect consistently follows a given known cause whose effect has been observed under the same conditions on previous occasions. When a man decides to back a horse the known cause (that he hands over a sum of money to a bookmaker, or promises to do so) will have a foreseeable effect, namely, that he will irretrievably lose his money unless a certain improbable event occurs, the exact degree of improbability being expressed mathematically by the odds. But a man betting does not expect the reasonable effect to follow the cause; he expects the improbable to happen as a matter of course, and intellectually he projects himself into a fairyland of superstition, where miracles are the order of the day.

Among gamblers a belief in systems is widespread. Frequently systems are mathematical in nature, and wherever they are used they imply an inhibition of the reasoning faculty, for they are based on the utterly unjustifiable assumption that a series of separate occurrences are so connected that each is affected by the preceding occurrences of the series. The same unjustifiable assumption is made by the equally widespread circle of persons, more usually women than men, who back horses or greyhounds for reasons far removed from the animals' probable capacities to win their races—for such reasons as the animals' names, facial expressions or even colours.

In short the first ethical objection to gambling is that it is a formidable enemy of the intellectual order on which civilization is based.

The second ethical objection relates not so much to the act of gambling as to the reason for it. Gambling is unethical because it is an attempt to obtain property without effort, whereas the true ethical basis for the acquisition of property is effort followed by satisfaction.[1]

Before going on to consider the Christian objections to gambling, we ought here to assess how far the ethical objections indicated above could reasonably be expected to be a deterrent

[1] We do not wish to devote space here to a reiteration of the ethical argument on which this statement is based. It is clearly set out in "The Ethics of Gambling," by J. A. Hobson, on pp. 3 *et seq.* of *Betting and Gambling*, an anthology edited by B. S. Rowntree and published by Macmillan.

to those who wish to gamble. If we were dealing with a nation of educated and cultured men we should expect them to recognize the ethical issues to which we have referred, and in so far as they disregarded them we could say that their conduct was wrong, either wilfully, or through deliberate disregard of the issues involved. Therefore at this stage we have shown sound reasons why none of the educated and thoughtful sections of the community should gamble, and in this condemnation, for the part of the community referred to, we must include the football pools, which we earlier described with more tolerance than we accorded to other major forms of gambling.

But at this point in our national development the "educated and thoughtful sections of the community" are still not only a minority, but even a small minority of the whole. To talk to the majority of people of the ethical supremacy of reason, or to tell them, in a world undermined by selfishness, that almost the only ethically valid way of acquiring property is first to render some service for it, is to talk a language which is simply beyond the comprehension of the majority of citizens.

When we deal with the attitude of religiously minded people to gambling the situation is simpler, but the validity of our argument is restricted to those persons who are either practising members of one of the Christian Churches or, although outside the Churches, are what the Americans call "good citizens" (i.e., persons filled with a sense of duty towards their fellow men and a desire to promote their well-being). For these two groups it would be wrong to gamble, for gambling involves an attempt to obtain money from some unknown person without giving anything in exchange, and disregarding the fact that this may in certain cases cause real privation to the person from whom the money is taken and perhaps to his family.[1]

On moral grounds gambling is clearly wrong when subjected to a test indicated by the late Archbishop Temple.[2] The Archbishop laid down that an activity was intrinsically wrong

[1] Although we believe this doctrine to be universally true as far as commercialized gambling is concerned, we agree with the widely held view that it has to be applied in social life with some flexibility. For instance, there is a great deal of difference between betting on greyhounds and playing a friendly game of bridge for small stakes, or a game of golf "for the ball."

[2] We take the idea of applying this test from *The Wrong of It*, by Canon Peter Green, M.A.

if it issued from a bad state of mind, if it exemplified a bad principle and if it had bad consequences. Gambling stands condemned on all three counts, for it issues from a desire to profit by the misfortunes of others, it outrages the principle that material benefits should be distributed according to merit and not by chance, and it leads to many evil consequences, fraud and poverty being among the more frequent.

We turn now from the moral to the economic aspect of gambling, although to some extent it is unrealistic to divorce the economic aspect of any question from the moral aspect, for a nation is unwise that takes any action on grounds of economic expediency if that action infringes moral principles. On the other hand where there is no moral objection to a certain course, but no particular moral reason why it should be followed, economic reasons can then legitimately determine whether or not the course of action should be taken.

In the case of gambling the economic question really is whether the nation is paying too high a price, in money and resources, for the services of a gigantic amusement industry.

The net money charge of the gambling industry to the nation is comparatively low, and represents the share of the gross expenditure by the public that is retained by the persons organizing and running the industry, plus the capital expenditure on the industry. There is no means of making an accurate assessment of the net charge, but there are good reasons for believing that it may be about 9 per cent of the gross turnover.[1] If this is so, the direct net money charge of the gambling industry would be less than 1 per cent of the current annual total of personal incomes.

This comparatively low net charge on the national income for gambling does not, however, by any means adequately measure the adverse effects of gambling on the national economy. It is now widely realized that one of the most urgent questions facing Britain is to make possible an increase in the capital resources of the country through saving. The amount of money lost for this purpose in gambling is not merely the comparatively small figure represented by the net charge on

[1] Our calculation of 9 per cent is close to that given in *The Economist* of 29th March, 1947, p. 446, where, on an estimated gross charge for 1946–47 of £582 million, the net cost was estimated as £55 million.

the national income, but the much larger figure representing the money that is circulating between the gambling sections of the community, now in this man's pocket, and now in that one's, but never doing a useful job. In saying this, we do not of course suggest that if the gambling industry vanished suddenly all the money now spent on gambling would be saved. A great deal of it would no doubt be spent in other ways, but a proportion would be saved, and that proportion, even if it were as low as a fifth or a sixth, could have important beneficial effects on the national economy.

Even this, however, is not all of the case against gambling on economic grounds, for the main forms of gambling involve the use of material resources to a substantial degree. We have in mind such examples as:

(*a*) Transport by road and rail for a large but unknown number of persons, involving the use of coal, electric power and liquid fuels, as well as the services of transport workers, including the maintenance staffs and cleaners of vehicles. Some 50,000,000 persons are carried to and from greyhound-racing tracks alone in the course of a year.

(*b*) The use of paper for football-pool coupons and envelopes (probably more than 400,000,000 of each in the course of each season), greyhound-racing programmes (commonly used in booklet form to constitute also "tickets" of admission), and for all the other purposes of an enormous business.

(*c*) The existence of a special sporting press. We have traced 16 papers devoted to horse racing, greyhound racing and football-pool forecasts, of which 2 are dailies, 13 are weeklies, and 1 is published twice a week. Some of these papers are of considerable size; for example, a copy of the *Greyhound Express and Coursing News* which is before us as we write has 24 pages.

(*d*) The resources of the General Post Office, involving postmen, counter clerks, telegraphists and telephonists. Some twelve or thirteen million football-pool coupons each week are posted and delivered, and over eleven million of them are returned again through the post after postal orders have been inserted, while bookmakers make heavy demands on the telephone system, for even those in a modest way of business frequently have 20 telephone lines, while others have as many as 100.

(*e*) The wastage of manpower. It is impossible to estimate accurately how many persons are employed by the gambling industry. We have, however, made a rough calculation and have come to the conclusion that the number of persons so employed is equivalent to the full-time labour of not less than 300,000 persons nor more than 400,000. The exact figure is immaterial, for even if the right answer were not appreciably greater than the low limit we have indicated, it would mean that the gambling industry is employing almost as many people as the cotton weaving industry, and twice as many as the total strength of the Royal Navy.

The list we have just given of the indirect ways that the nation's true bill for gambling is swollen is not exhaustive, but it serves to make our point. There is, however, one further matter to which we may suitably refer here, though it is also a moral question and not purely economic. For several decades past, under Liberal, Conservative and Labour governments, the tendency has been for wealth to be distributed more and more according to need, and less and less according to the chances of birth, or to the power of individuals to accumulate it at the expense of others. When the main tendency of at least two generations has been to take from the comparatively few well-to-do, for the benefit of the many, it is odd that the great growth of gambling exactly reverses the process, for money spent on betting, largely by people of slender means, tends to enrich no one except the few promoters and organizers and a mere handful of winners.

In considering the economic effects of gambling, regard must, of course, be had to the direct effects of gambling on production. Broadly speaking there are two opposite schools of thought. One holds that gambling, being a perfectly legal recreation, is a positive aid to production. The other view is that gambling increases absenteeism, decreases the tempo of work because men's thoughts are elsewhere and, in words used by Sir Austen Chamberlain in 1919, "At a time when the one lesson you have to teach everybody is that there is no salvation except in work, you teach them to expect salvation by luck,"

Probably there is a good deal to be said in favour of both these views. The moralist and the educated citizen all too seldom understand the emptiness of the lives of many hundreds of thousands of workers in some industries. The five-day week is an accomplished fact in many industries, yet for large numbers of men the new leisure is often a void and they have "nothing to do." In the course of our investigations, G.R.L. visited the South Wales coalfield, and the shipbuilding area of the Tyne. In each he found the same story which could be repeated in varying degrees from most parts of industrial and urban Britain. Small inconvenient houses, for the most part without gardens; scarcely any facilities for spending leisure in worth-while ways; ugliness in the streets, and the country not easily accessible. In a word, "Nothing to do until the pubs open." In our view it would be an act of considerable unkindness, as well as a psychological blunder on the industrial side, to deprive people in such circumstances of their recreation of gambling, without first seeing that they are provided with means of employing their leisure, not only more profitably, but with greater satisfaction to themselves.

But the opposite view is also, no doubt, valid in many cases and cannot be neglected. We have come across a few individuals, and have heard of others who say, "Work's a mug's game. Gambling is the way to spend your time." Short of this extreme view there must be a large number of persons, probably a perceptible proportion of the total labour force, for whom gambling constitutes a more important interest than work and home life. Obviously such a view is wrong economically, and by every canon of citizenship, but it is difficult to see what can be done about it. It is no good saying "Naughty," nor is it any good prohibiting all gambling by law, because it would then simply be pursued illegally. The only practical action for society is to take more active steps to encourage people to spend their leisure rationally and enjoyably and to provide the means for them to do so.

Betting tax

No account of the economics of gambling would be complete without consideration of the case for a general betting tax. We do not share the extreme view that such a tax is wrong because it gives formal recognition to the business of gambling. Gambling is admittedly in a rather peculiar position in that debts incurred in gambling cannot be recovered at law, but nevertheless unless gambling were legal in its main forms it would not be indulged in. Furthermore, by a series of Acts of Parliament, such as that concerning the licensing of greyhound-racing tracks, and by a series of administrative actions of Ministers, such as the agreement with the football pool industry about the restriction of its use of paper, ample legal recognition has been given to the industry by the community.

There is perhaps a little, but probably only a very little, in the idea that when there is some activity that the community might subsequently wish to abolish or restrict, it is unwise to give the Treasury a "vested interest" in it by making it a source of national revenue. We do not believe for a moment that a department so vitally interested in national saving and economic prosperity as the Treasury would ever be likely to encourage gambling for financial, or indeed for any other reasons.

The only valid test in deciding for or against the desirability of a betting tax is whether it will decrease gambling. There can be no certainty on this point, but the reactions of some sections of the gambling industry, and subsequently of a good many persons who gamble, to the limited tax introduced in 1948 seemed to show both alarm and annoyance. The heavy taxation on alcoholic drink has undoubtedly been a contributory cause of the decline in excessive drinking, and it is probably legitimate to anticipate a parallel movement in gambling if a heavy tax were imposed.

A tax heavy enough to have any appreciable effect on the volume of gambling would introduce a number of new factors into the situation, and whatever the advantages it would need extremely careful consideration. For example, the primary purpose of taxation is the raising of revenue, not the furtherance of social reform. Yet there is the precedent of purchase tax for imposing a heavy tax in order to make persons refrain from an activity which is not in the national interest, and it may well be that if a nation is entitled to protect its economic position by a purchase tax, it is equally entitled to protect both its economy and its moral fibre by a heavy betting tax.

If betting transactions were made liable to a heavy tax it is hard to see that the Gaming Act, whereby the payment of gambling debts can be avoided, could remain in force. It would be illogical to tax what is in effect a contract between two persons and still deny the right of either of those persons to legal enforcement of the contract. It is difficult to say whether any real harm would follow the repeal of the Gaming Act. As we have already pointed out, gambling is perfectly legal, and it seems rather far-fetched to believe that it would become more respectable or more prevalent simply because persons could no longer safely default on their gambling debts.

A more serious objection might be the need to license bookmakers. It is hard to see how a tax of serious proportions could be enforced unless bookmakers were licensed and illegal bookmakers energetically repressed. To do the latter effectively it might be necessary to legalize ready-money betting on the premises of licensed bookmakers, for so long as it is legal to gamble, it is clearly wrong to differentiate between the comparatively well-to-do, who can get credit, and the poorer sections of the community, who cannot. There seems no reason to suppose that licensed bookmakers as a class would be less ready to co-operate with the Inland Revenue authorities, and act as unpaid tax collectors in return for being allowed to operate and make a profit, than is the case with licensed victuallers. Moreover, the licensed bookmakers would have a direct interest in suppressing all betting which was not done through them. Certainly there would be little hope of making a betting tax work unless the bookmakers did co-operate.

With such co-operation it should be a fairly easy matter to tax winnings on gambling transactions, and winnings are undoubtedly the point in the whole transaction of gambling most sensitive to taxation, because the bookmaker, who is in physical possession of the money, has to pay it out, and has no incentive (short of the dangerous course of conspiring with a client to defraud the Crown) to pay a smaller sum in tax than is due.

When a tax on winnings is discussed it is always necessary to consider whether, if winnings were taxed, losing bets should be subject to some rebate of taxation. The losings represent the bookmakers' expenses, his profit, which would be taxed as his income, and the winnings of successful clients, which would also be taxed. It would therefore appear at first sight that some rebate should be allowed on sums lost. But we do not agree with this view. A man who bets and loses has bought entertainment and the chance of gain. If he wins he has entertainment and the chance of gain before the event, and material gain after the event plus the return of his stakes.

It is the increment of satisfaction (i.e., the material gain) that the State might wish to tax, and just as it would be wrong in a tax on winnings to tax the man's stake, which would be returned to him with his winnings, so also we see no reason for allowing him any rebate of taxation on what he loses.

Our views on the betting tax thus amount to this: that we doubt whether the tax first imposed in 1948 has had as great an effect on the volume of gambling as is sometimes stated, but we believe that it would be possible to devise and administer a tax that would be a sharp deterrent. Such a tax, in our view, would have to be levied on winnings, and the percentage of the winnings deducted as tax would logically increase with the magnitude of the winnings. We accept the view that this proposal would involve the licensing of bookmakers, and probably the authorizing of ready-money betting on specially licensed premises.

A betting tax will never solve the gambling problem, but it might be a useful auxiliary.

SUMMARY

As the result of the great increases over the last half-century of real wages and hours of leisure, coupled with a failure on the part of the community to provide worth-while means of spending leisure, an enormous gambling industry has grown up, which exploits the situation for the benefit of a comparatively small number of organizers. We believe that over the course of this century the volume of gambling has grown from small proportions in 1900 to an annual turnover which we are inclined to put at about £750 million. Gambling on this scale probably involves a net direct charge on the national income of about £65 million, plus at least as much again for services and materials used by the industry, plus an unknown, but large, amount representing the goods that might have been produced by the gambling industry's labour force (which may well be equivalent to over 300,000 persons working full time) had they been productively employed. In addition the industry has a strongly deleterious effect on saving, and so on the creation of capital.

The two most objectional forms of gambling seem to us to be greyhound racing and "off-the-course" betting on horses. The harm done by football pools is often exaggerated and, without thinking for one moment that they would be among the leisure time amusements of a highly civilized and cultured nation, we would put them together with most "on-the-course" betting on horses among the less objectionable forms of gambling.

To the question, "Why do people gamble?" we reply that there are various contributory reasons, but that the main one is that the community has not yet provided the means for the cultural training which will lead people to realize the fact that there are ways of spending leisure which give greater satisfaction than gambling.

On the moral plane there are unanswerable reasons why nobody should gamble who is a Christian, or who has a well-developed cultural background. We recognize that these two groups together constitute only a small minority of the nation (at the most one-quarter and probably less) and for those who are neither Christian nor intellectually awakened we can find no ethical reason that they would consider relevant to their lives and outlook why they should not gamble. On the economic plane there are clear indications that the nation cannot afford gambling on its present scale, but we have noted the great emptiness that already exists in the lives of many, and we believe it would be a psychological, and therefore an economic, error entirely to remove gambling from their lives, even if that were possible, until measures have been taken to enrich their lives intellectually and spiritually. This is particularly true of persons living in urban areas and working under conditions, all too prevalent in modern industry and commerce, that tend to reduce them to the level of automata.

CHAPTER III

DRINK

BEFORE embarking on our examination of the problem of drink as a factor affecting contemporary English life, we should perhaps make our own position clear. We are neither of us teetotallers, although one of us (B.S.R.) is by inclination and practice virtually so. It follows that we are neither of us prohibitionists. We feel, therefore, that we can claim with some confidence that we approach the matter with objective and undistorted minds.

Drunkenness

A common error in considering the drink problem is to imagine that it is synonymous with that of drunkenness. If that were so, there would indeed be grounds for substantial satisfaction, for the number of convictions for drunkenness in England and Wales fell from 183,514 in 1913, and 44,954 in 1938, to 28,600 in 1948.[1] Although the figures for 1948 were considerably above the lowest previously recorded (16,901 in 1945), a nation in which the convictions for drunkenness are equivalent to approximately 0·7 per cent of the population must be considered tolerably sober. Allowance has of course to be made for the fact that neither convictions nor even prosecutions for drunkenness truly represent the incidence of that condition. It is safe to say that only quite a small proportion of persons obviously drunk in public are prosecuted. However, we do not intend to deal with drunkenness in this chapter, because even after multiplying the figures of known cases several times to allow for the unrecorded cases, it is still happily a rare condition.

[1] *Annual Abstracts of Statistics*, 1937–47 and 1938–48, compiled by the Central Statistical Office and published by H.M. Stationery Office.

The problem of drink arises, in fact, from the behaviour of the regular but moderate drinker, whether he takes his whisky and soda in his drawing-room or his pint of mild at the "local."

Level of consumption and cost

In 1948, 29 million bulk barrels of beer were consumed in the United Kingdom, compared with 25 million in 1938.[1] Consumption of spirits in 1948 was 9 million proof gallons, compared with 10 million in 1938. In addition, 11 million gallons of wine were imported in the year ending 31st March, 1949. The total personal expenditure on alcoholic beverages in 1948 was £762 million, compared with £285 million in 1938. If the level of taxation in 1938 had been the same as in 1948, the total personal expenditure in 1938 would have been approximately £580 million.[2] At the level of expenditure in 1948, the nation was spending:

(*a*) one-quarter more on alcohol than the total spent on rent, rates and water charges;

(*b*) more than five and a half times as much on alcohol as on books of all kinds, and on newspapers and magazines;

(*c*) seven shillings on alcohol for every £1 spent on food;

(*d*) more than twenty times as much on alcohol as the total net savings in the post office savings bank, the trustee savings banks and by the purchase of National Savings certificates.

But the true cost of the drink habit does not appear only in figures such as those we have just quoted. There is still a heavy cost in the effects of drinking on individual lives. In the course of our investigations we have come across many cases, in widely differing classes of the community, where heavy drinking has caused hardship and even poverty. As examples of this, we quote five typical cases:

(*a*) Mrs. S. is an elderly working-class housewife. She and her husband are happy together, but he is a consistently heavy drinker, spending six or seven shillings every evening on beer, although he never gets drunk. As Mr. S. also smokes fairly heavily, he does not give his wife enough for the rent, rates, food and other household expenses. She has therefore taken a full-time job in a factory, leaving

[1] *Annual Abstract of Statistics*, 1938–48.

[2] We have not overlooked the fact that a large proportion of the money spent on alcohol returns to the Exchequer as taxation, and we deal with that aspect on page 194.

home at 7 a.m. each day, doing her housework in the evenings, and the washing on Sundays.

(*b*) Mr. P. is a clerk with a salary of over £500 per annum. He is a heavy whisky drinker and in an endeavour to keep the home together his wife has sold everything of value that could be spared, including a good deal of the furniture. She has tried having lodgers, but they will not stay as Mr. P. often becomes very truculent, without being drunk in any legal sense. Mrs. P. is fond of her husband, but is trying to make up her mind to leave him, as she feels he is beyond her help.

(*c*) Mr. H. is a clerk who once occupied a good position. He was, however, a heavy spirit drinker. Not only did he drink the greater part of his earnings, he also embezzled money to buy more drink, and served a prison sentence. His wife was loyal to him, but when he came out of prison he began to drink again and she left him. He now lives with another man's wife, and when they are particularly short of money she also works.

(*d*) Mr. D. is a labourer, but he has a cultured voice, is widely travelled and, when drunk, boasts of being a university man. He has drinking spells, during which he will go for some weeks without being really sober. Besides his wages, he admits having an allowance from somebody connected with him in the past. He says that he "was married once upon a time," but that his wife left him and took the children with her.

(*e*) Mr. R. earns about £700 a year, but spends heavily on drink, so that his wife and child, aged 2, are short of the necessities of life. Their home is sparsely furnished (for example, they only possess three chairs altogether), and they are in debt to various tradesmen. Although their debts total only a few pounds, Mrs. R. cannot pay them, and Mr. R. will not. Mrs. R. has no regular housekeeping money. She tries to get a few shillings out of Mr. R. each morning, and he usually gives her a small sum and tells her to make do. She is very lonely, as she has nobody to talk to all day, and Mr. R. is usually in a very surly stage of intoxication when he gets home. Mrs. R. is in constant dread of another pregnancy.

Leaving aside for the moment the moral consequences and the physiological effects of heavy drinking, it is clear from the facts and figures we have given that the problem of drink is one of grave magnitude. This becomes even more certain if we consider two other economic aspects of the matter, namely, the manpower occupied in the industry, and some of the raw materials used by it.

Manpower

Without a complicated piece of research it would be impossible to get accurate figures relating to manpower for, as in most industries, a good many people are either indirectly employed or are only part-time or seasonal workers, such, for instance, as agricultural workers growing barley, and hop-pickers. Nevertheless it is possible to arrive at a figure, of which we can say with a good deal of confidence that it is an under-estimate rather than an over-estimate, of the number of persons in direct full-time employment. According to the *Monthly Digest of Statistics* for January 1949, the number of persons directly employed in the drink industry in the United Kingdom in November 1948 (excluding the distribution and retailing of drink) was 130,800, of whom 94,500 were men and 36,300 women. In 1948 there were 73,384 licensed premises, including hotels, in England and Wales with "on" licences, and 22,025 additional establishments with "off" licences. In Scotland, in the same year, there were 3,776 public houses, 1,594 licensed inns and hotels, and 2,081 additional "off" licences. In the same year, there were 18,370 registered clubs in England and Wales, and 834 in Scotland. If we make the cautious assumptions that on the average:

(*a*) each of the premises with an "on" licence requires the full-time work of two and one-half persons;

(*b*) each "off" licence (not held in connection with an "on" licence) requires the full-time work of one-fifth of one person;

(*c*) each registered club requires, for the ordering, custody, accounting and sale of alcoholic liquor, the full-time work of one-half of one person;

we can deduce that the retail liquor trade gives full-time employment to the equivalent of at least 210,000 persons.

Thus, without allowing at all for the persons engaged in the wholesale distribution of alcoholic liquor (of whose numbers we can form no reliable estimate though they must amount at least to several thousands), it appears that the labour force directly employed in the industry is not less than 340,000 persons, which is approximately 50 per cent more than the total number of workers in all sections of the gas, water and electricity supply industries.

Grain and sugar

In the matter of raw materials for the industry, the two most important commodities used by brewers and distillers are barley—approximately 900,000 tons per year—and sugar, 65,750 tons for the year ending September 1948. Of this vast quantity of barley, some 10 per cent may be deducted as the amount used in the distillation of whisky sold abroad for scarce currencies, and therefore, from the economic point of view, a valuable export. The remaining 810,000 tons is still about half of our total crop of barley, which was estimated at 1,619,000 tons in 1947. According to J. W. Robertson Scott, if these 810,000 tons were devoted entirely to animal feeding, from 100,000 to 125,000 tons of extra pork, and 1,000,000,000 extra eggs, would be available for human consumption.[1] Without concerning ourselves with the exact accuracy of this estimate, we give the figures as indicating the general measure and nature of the foodstuffs the country is losing.

Our picture of the drink industry up to this point is therefore that of an industry involving total personal expenditure of about £760 million per annum, employing at least 340,000 persons full time, as well as many further thousands indirectly and part time, and using in the preparation of alcoholic beverages primary foodstuffs that, if used for animal feeding, would produce useful amounts of human food.

The true purpose of any industry is to produce goods or provide services which are of benefit to mankind, having regard of course to the interests of the community as a whole, as well as to those of the individual. Our next step must be to examine the arrangements for consuming the products of the drink industry, and the first three questions to consider are, "Who drink alcoholic beverages?" "What do they drink?" and "Where?" Later we shall also have to try to answer the questions "Why?" and "With what result?"

[1] Extract from a speech in Manchester in October 1947.

Drinking habits

Detailed information about drinking habits were obtained by Research Services Ltd., in the course of the Hulton Readership Survey, from which we have permission to quote. The survey was confined to persons over the age of 16, and was conducted on a statistical basis which expert statisticians regard as affording information which is representative of the population as a whole. The proportion of these who drink alcoholic beverages, and their drinking habits, are summarized in the two following tables:

Those who drink	%
Beer only	19·3
Spirits only	1·9
Wine only	4·6
Beer and spirits	6·2
Beer and wine	3·1
Spirits and wine	8·0
Beer, spirits and wine	25·3
No alcoholic liquor	31·6

Frequency of drinking	Beer	Spirits	Wine
	%	%	%
Every day	8·7	1·5	0·7
More than once a week but not daily	12·1	3·3	1·7
Once a week	11·5	4·8	2·8
Less than once a week ..	21·9	31·9	36·0
Never	45·8	58·5	58·8

These two tables show the drinking pattern of the community as a whole fairly clearly. Nearly one-third (31·6 per cent) of persons over 16 never take alcoholic drink at all, and if the numbers of "occasional" drinkers (i.e., those who drink less often than once a week) is added to those who do not drink at all, we can see what proportion of the community are "regulars,"[1] namely:

32·3 per cent are regular beer drinkers.
9·6 per cent are regular spirit drinkers.
5·2 per cent are regular wine drinkers.

The real core of the drinking community are, however, those who drink every day, namely:

8·7 per cent who drink beer every day.
1·5 per cent who drink spirits every day.
0·7 per cent who drink wine every day.[2]

If the drinking habits of the two sexes are considered separately, the fact emerges that, as might be expected, the percentage of women who never drink alcoholic liquors (40·1 per cent) is almost twice as high as the corresponding figure for men (21·5 per cent). Again, as might be expected, the largest percentages of men who never take alcohol is found in the youngest age group (16–24)[3] but, rather unexpectedly, more women in the age group 45 and over (46·4 per cent) say that they do not drink alcoholic beverages than is the case in the age group 16–24 (44·0 per cent). The largest percentage of both men and women who drink are in the age group 25–34.

Where do people drink?

We turn now to consider the question, "Where do people drink?" The answer is threefold. First, in their own homes or in the homes of others. Second, in registered clubs. Third, in licensed premises, including hotels.

Liquor for drinking at home is purchased at an establishment holding an "off" licence,[4] that is to say either at a

[1] "Regular" here means once a week or more often.

[2] There will be some overlapping here, particularly in beer and spirit drinking, as the habit of drinking neat spirits washed down with beer is fairly common in some parts of the country, and, at any rate in the North, this habit is given the descriptive name of "chasers."

[3] It is illegal to serve a person under 18 with alcoholic liquor on licensed premises, or to buy alcoholic liquor for such a person, but in practice it is often impossible to judge a young person's age (particularly a girl's) to a year or two, and most young people of 17, and perhaps even 16, can get beer and other drinks easily enough if they wish.

[4] Licences for the sale of liquor are of two kinds—those for the sale of alcoholic beverages to be consumed on or off the premises. They are commonly referred to as "on" and "off" licences. "On" licences are further divided into "full" licences (i.e., for sale of all alcoholic beverages) and "beer" licences, and still further into "six day" and "seven day" licences. A "six day" house cannot open on Sunday.

licensed hotel or public house (for every "on" licence automatically includes an "off" licence), a grocer or a chemist. Registered clubs, with which we deal below, are also authorized to make "off" sales to members. Although the fact is not widely realized, it is not unusual for chemists to hold an "off" licence, although in many cases their sales are restricted to medicated wines, to which we refer later. The sales of intoxicants by grocers under an "off" licence undoubtedly leads to home drinking by many persons who would not think it "respectable" to visit even the off-sales counter of a public house. It is virtually impossible to estimate how much liquor is sold for consumption at home—the very fact that an "on" licence includes an "off" licence prevents any calculation at all. One can only say that the total amount is obviously large, or there would not be so many shops, and departments of grocers' shops, maintained expressly for the purpose of "off" sales.

Registered clubs

Registered clubs, the second of the three sets of places where people drink, present considerable difficulties in describing the drink problem, because the law that regulates them is itself unsatisfactory. As stated above, in 1948 (the latest year for which figures are available) there were 18,370 registered clubs in England and Wales, and they varied from eminently respectable social and political clubs, including the most famous clubs in the country, to places existing solely as drinking establishments, sometimes in sordid surroundings. It is impossible to say how many persons were active members of the 18,370 registered clubs, but it is probably safe to say that they totalled more than a million.

For the establishment of a registered club, it is only necessary for the Clerk to the Justices of the Petty Sessions to be notified of the club's existence, and registration is then automatic on payment of a fee of 5s. and the supply of information as to the title, addess, rules and membership of the club. Membership must not be less than 25. A Court of Summary Jurisdiction can strike a club off the register for various forms of misconduct, but the same proprietor can register another club in premises adjoining those of the first club, with another name but the same membership, immediately after having been struck off.

It would be wrong to give the impression that the majority of clubs are anything except desirable institutions, performing a thoroughly useful function, but some are little more than drinking houses that contrive to be exempt from the regulations applied by statute to licensed premises. Recommendations for dealing with the situation were made by the Royal Commission on Licensing, 1929–31, and were to the effect that:

(*a*) Applications for the registration of clubs should be considered by magistrates specially appointed from among the local Justices of the Peace.

(*b*) Registrations should be for only one year, after which the magistrates would consider applications for renewal for another year.

(*c*) Persons affected (such as the police, or residents in premises close to the club buildings) should have the right to object to the registration.

(*d*) There should be a carefully guarded right of entry by the police.

(*e*) Licensed premises should be disqualified for five years from registration as clubs after the licence ceased.

(*f*) Clubs should not supply liquor for "off" consumption.

(*g*) Hours for the supply of liquor should conform to those for licensed premises in the same area.

(*h*) No person under the age of 18 should be a member of a registered club.

Of these recommendations only (*g*), relating to the hours of supply of liquor, has been implemented. It is difficult, however, to enforce even this regulation in clubs run by ill-disposed persons, since the police have no right of entry into registered clubs without a search warrant, that can only be granted by Justices before whom information of some malpractice has been sworn on oath. Evidence of the difficulty of enforcing the law was obtained by G.R.L. who, in the course of our investigations, visited, as a guest, three clubs in the West End of London of the type that are run for profit, and saw drinks being served in each, an hour after the permitted hours. As far as the other recommendations are concerned, it is hard to understand why most of them have not been adopted, particularly the first three and the last, which seem so highly desirable. We do not however believe it is wise—even in so good a cause—to give the police the right of entry into private premises, but there would seem to be no reason why police officers with reasonable grounds for suspecting malpractices in any club should not be able to obtain from a Justice of the Peace a warrant specifically authorizing entry. This would be a relaxation of the present system, to the extent that previous evidence on oath of a specific malpractice would not be necessary.

One particular kind of registered club is now assuming some importance, namely, the holiday camp. Bars in these camps are allowed only because the camps are registered as clubs, and visitors to them have to pay a trifling fee for membership. In connection with our investigations, G.R.L. spent five days in one of the best known, of the holiday camps, and it is therefore from personal observation that we say that, although the bars in the camp visited were run with absolute propriety and strict regard for the law, we doubt whether the provision of large and ornate bars (two in the camp in question) is desirable in the presence of so large a number of adolescents and children. Because the premises are a "club," young people are deprived of the safeguards that they enjoy in regard to public houses.

Medicated wines

Medicated wines, which are extensively sold by chemists with "off" licences, and to a lesser extent by other holders of "off" licences, were the subject of particular comment by the Select Committee of the House of Commons reporting on patent medicines in August 1914. The Committee reported, "In addition to the various classes of patent and proprietary medicines, our attention has also been forcibly called to the advertisement and sale of medicated wines, and weighty opinions have been quoted to us regarding their mischievous effects. The trade in these wines is a very extensive one." It is significant that since 1913 both *The Lancet* and the *British*

Medical Journal have refused to accept advertisements for these wines.

Many people undoubtedly believe that medicated wines have some mysterious power of "doing you good." In our case histories these wines were mentioned on a number of occasions, usually by middle-class women, and a typical comment was that of a bank clerk's wife who said, "A bottle of —— is the finest thing out as a pick-me-up. I always have it when I'm run down."

On another occasion a male teacher in a secondary school said to us. "I've been taking——tonic wine every winter for years, and I never have a cold. It builds up your resistance and helps the appetite. I have two glasses every evening and so does my wife. We both believe it has saved us pounds and pounds in doctors' bills."

The danger in the sale of these much-advertised wines is that persons believe they are taking a tonic and a food, whereas they are drinking wine with an alcoholic content that may on occasions be as high as 17 per cent by volume, and that, in the words of *The Lancet* of 24th November 1906, "possesses no food value whatever. Meat and malt wine is in fact a farce."

In his evidence before the Royal Commission on Licensing, 1929–31, the Rev. Courtenay C. Weeks, M.R.C.S., L.R.C.P. (who had many years' experience in medical practice before taking Holy Orders), said that, looking back over his practice, some of the most tragic cases of alcoholism were those of people whose drunkenness was due to drinking medicated wines. Later in his evidence, speaking of cases in inebriate homes, he said, "Again and again, and yet again, parents, friends, husbands have told us that the alcohol habit which led to such disaster was primarily due to the use of medicated wines."

Under the Labelling of Food Order, No. 2169 (1946), the labels of medicated wines must indicate the approximate percentage of added ingredients on which the claim is based that the preparation has tonic, restorative or medicinal properties. But this seems to us to give little security to the layman who is exposed to the full blast of advertisements for tonic wines, and we feel that the public has every right to demand statutory protection against advertisements that might cause people to take the first and important steps towards excessive drinking, under the delusion that they were consuming a valuable and innocent tonic.

Licensed premises

We come now to the question of premises licensed for the sale of liquor for consumption on the premises. They are of four kinds—hotels, public houses, restaurants and bars, the last being a comparatively new type of drinking place. We do not intend to deal with the sale of alcoholic liquor in restaurants for consumption with meals, nor in hotels for sale to residents. Our interest is in places where people "go in for a drink," and in the people themselves who visit them. Before discussing these, however, we want to make a rough estimate of the number of people who enter public houses in the course of a week. As the basis for our calculation we take the estimate arrived at for the city of York in 1935.[1] It was estimated then (on the basis of an actual count of the number of persons entering a proportion of the public houses during a given week) that in that city of 100,000 persons there were about 180,000 visits to public houses every week. If the drinking habits of the citizens of York are approximately those of the nation as a whole, and there seems to be no reason why they should not be, this would represent nearly 80,000,000 visits a week, with the population of England and Wales at its 1949 level, if its drinking habits were still those of 1935. We know, however, that since 1935 the consumption of beer has increased by more than one-quarter, and we therefore conclude that many more than 80,000,000 visits are now paid to public houses in England and Wales every week. We have no means of knowing how many individual persons pay these visits, but it must be a high proportion, quite possibly a majority, of the 33,500,000 persons who are over the age of 16.

Bars and public houses as centres of social life

We turn now to a consideration of bars and public houses, and the part they play in the lives of those who frequent them.

[1] *Poverty and Progress*, by B. S. Rowntree, p. 355.

As they undoubtedly have an important influence on the characters and opinions of a considerable proportion of the population, we thought it necessary to obtain first-hand information on an adequate scale. To obtain this information one of us (G.R.L.) visited a substantial number of bars and public houses in different parts of the country, in both urban and rural areas. Our views are based on what he observed and on conversations that he had with customers, licensees and employees in the various premises visited.

Bars

We deal first with American bars, often known simply as "bars" or "lounge bars." These exist for the most part only in towns of some importance, where at least a section of the local inhabitants are leisured and well-to-do. Bars of this kind are often run in conjunction with hotels or restaurants. In American bars catering for the "best class" of trade, it is usual for only wines and spirits (including cocktails) to be sold. Beer is not served, but soft drinks are available although very seldom asked for, except to mix with alcoholic drinks as, for instance, gin and ginger beer. In bars in industrial areas, however, bottled beer is quite frequently served, and everywhere in bars that seek to attract a less exclusive clientèle bottled and sometimes draught beers are served.

A good deal of attention is usually paid to the decoration of bars, both as regards the fittings and furniture, which tend in the most exclusive bars to be expensive, and in the cheaper to be flashy.

It is generally held that bars are more respectable, and socially more select, than public houses. They are therefore frequented, for the most part, by people who would not normally go into a public house, except perhaps their own rural or suburban "local," and, in the case of the cheaper bars, by young people anxious "to see life and have a good time." The better bars are patronized almost exclusively by the upper middle-class and, in the provinces, by some of the local business men. Each bar normally has its core of regular customers, and it is by no means unusual for a few of the "regulars" to visit their favourite bar twice a day on five days a week. Other customers, who might be considered "regulars," pay two or three visits a fortnight, year after year.

Both men and women are to be found in near y all bars, although usually there is a preponderance of men. Nevertheless, in the more sophisticated parts of the country it is quite common to find women in pairs or threes "dropping in for a drink" in exactly the same way as men do. It is unusual for a woman—except for a small minority who are definitely hoping to be "picked up"—to enter a bar alone, unless she has arranged to meet somebody there.

The function of a bar is to provide for those who like to "drop in" somewhere for a drink. It exists solely to sell alcohol and there is no question of any social contacts between its customers unless they already know each other. It is as completely impersonal as a chemist's shop. That is not to say that one cannot strike up an acquaintance with a stranger in a bar; it is often possible to do so, but with no greater ease than would be experienced in making the same person's acquaintance in, say, a queue or railway carriage.

Since most of the conversation in bars is between persons who are already acquainted, it follows that it ranges over a wide variety of subjects, and that much of it is purely personal. The following are a few typical examples of conversations that were overheard:

(*a*) A group of two men and two women were discussing a holiday two of them were shortly to take abroad. One of the men was explaining a "foolproof" system for obtaining a larger amount of foreign currency than was allowed.

(*b*) Two men, just returned from watching a cricket match between England and Australia, were discussing the play.

(*c*) A man with his wife and married daughter were discussing the daughter's forthcoming divorce, and marriage to a man with whom she was already living.

(*d*) A group of four men were discussing exports of agricultural machinery, and how one of them—apparently a manufacturer—was held up by inadequate supplies of steel.

(*e*) Two middle-aged women were talking about a female acquaintance of theirs who had taken a very young man as a lover.

(*f*) A group of three men and one woman were discussing the bets they had made at a race meeting they had attended a day or two earlier. They also talked about the prospects of various horses at forthcoming race meetings.

(*g*) A man, apparently a mining engineer or consultant, was explaining to two other men details of a visit he had recently paid to a coal mine in the Staffordshire coalfield.

Perhaps the only surprising fact about the subjects of conversation in bars is the number of times business matters are discussed. The head barman of one of the best-known bars in London told G.R.L. that a great deal of business is done in the best bars, especially by the regular customers.

It is only rarely that any customer in a bar shows by his behaviour that he has drunk too much. The barman in one bar in London said, "The only trouble we have is when young fellows in the twenties spend the afternoons drinking in the clubs and then come in here at 5.30 when we open for the evening."[1]

Some bars, including a few that cater for a "good-class trade," are occasionally used by prostitutes as places to seek customers, but this is not often the case.

The prices charged in bars are high, for example, a large whisky and soda seldom costs less than 5s., and often costs 7s. or even 8s., and in addition to these high prices the barmen expect tips, though tipping is noticeably less frequent and less generous in industrial areas than in London. As a result the personal expenditure of individuals in bars is often extravagant. This can be illustrated by a few actual cases:

(*a*) A man regularly visits a certain bar twice every day, on five days a week. At midday he has two large gins with angostura bitters. In the evening he has two large whiskies and soda. Including tips, his weekly expenditure in this bar is £7.

(*b*) A man entered a bar alone and said to the barman (who evidently knew him as a regular customer), "I have to go to a very dull concert. Will you anaesthetize me?" He drank four large cocktails in 35 minutes at a total cost of 32s. including tips. His face became slightly flushed, but he showed no other reaction to this large dose of alcohol.

(*c*) A middle-aged man sat in a bar with a youngish but tough-

[1] The clubs referred to are registered clubs run for profit (see page 167). They should observe the same hours for sale of drink as licensed premises, but in some of them drink is sold illegally out of the permitted hours.

poorer working-class districts. Football pools are discussed surprisingly little, except on Saturday evenings and Sundays. Politics are scarcely ever mentioned, and are discouraged by most publicans since an exchange of political opinions is thought to lead to some customers becoming offended. Items from the newspapers are often talked about, particularly those of a sensational nature, and there is exchange of rather doubtful stories among a certain type of customers, although the majority hold themselves aloof from this. Sport of every kind is discussed, quite apart from any question of betting, and items of personal scandal about mutual acquaintances seem to be much appreciated both by men and women. In public houses with a particular neighbourhood connection, such as a village "local," there is always plenty of talk about purely local matters, such, for instance, as whether it is too early to plant the potatoes, or whether So-and-so is not getting so feeble that he will soon have to go to the workhouse, or whether one man or another is the better wicket-keeper for the village cricket team. The subjects of conversation in public houses do nevertheless have one thing in common. They are almost invariably trivial, although for the most part harmlessly so.

As was stated on page 174, the atmosphere of a public house is principally determined by its location and the type of persons from among whom, in consequence, it draws its customers, but whether a public house is a happy or friendly place, or the reverse, depends also largely on the publican and his assistants. It is strange that there should be so many morose publicans—only a minority, of course, but an appreciable minority. This state of affairs may merely be a result of the "seller's market" that existed for some nine years in the retailing of liquor, and which came to an end in 1949. The happiest public house is often where the publican's family assist him, in place of a paid bar staff. A publican's children are often pressed into this service at an early age, and in our investigations we came across:

(*a*) A schoolgirl of 15½ serving in an urban public house, doing her homework in the intervals of serving, with her school books propped up against the shelf on which stood bottles of spirits, wines and beer.

(*b*) A youth of 16 working full time in the bar of an urban public house.

(*c*) A boy of 15 serving in a rural public house.

All three were the children of the publican. The first two appeared to regard the work with considerable distaste, but the third was obviously enjoying himself.

Besides being places of relaxation and sociability, a proportion of public houses provide facilities for groups of people to meet for specific purposes. As Lord Beveridge has pointed out in his recent work, *Voluntary Action and the State*, some of the great Friendly Societies originated in groups of persons meeting in public houses. It is still quite usual for public houses to run slate clubs which share out at Christmas, and in some there are small provident clubs, although this is unusual since the introduction of comprehensive legislation for social security. In rural areas the village pub often shares with the village hall the position of social centre for the community, and it is the meeting place of such bodies as the committee of the village cricket team.

There is thus a good deal that is useful and even admirable in the best type of public house, but the fact remains that they exist for the sole purpose of retailing alcoholic liquor, and scarcely anybody enters them who does not wish to take alcohol in small or large quantities. The amount spent by individuals varies so greatly that the quotation of specific cases might be misleading. A regular and fairly heavy beer drinker can spend a substantial sum in the course of the week. One "shopkeeper" encountered during our investigations left most of the shopkeeping to his wife, and spent almost all the hours from opening to closing time, both morning and evening, in his favourite public house. His expenditure amounted to about 15s. a day, and a heavy beer drinker can spend this amount easily enough. On the other hand, we encountered a man of about 25 and his fiancée who spend every evening in the same public house as the shopkeeper, drinking only two half-pints of beer each in two or three hours, at a total cost of about 2s. 4d. Without making an extremely detailed and costly study of individual spending habits, it is not safe to say more than that of persons using public houses a minority, that may even be an appreciable minority, spend on drink money that they ought to spend on necessities for themselves or their families, and that an even larger number of persons spend on drink what appears to be an undue proportion of the money left to them after paying for strict necessities.

Place of licensed premises in national life

Our next task is to try to assess what place each of the various kinds of licensed premises that we have described above fills in our national life. The two extreme views are first that of the most fervid temperance reformers, to whom all licensed premises are anathema, and second that of persons (often themselves financially interested parties) who advance the view that public houses are "poor men's clubs," and are indeed almost community centres. We believe that neither of these views is true of licensed houses as a whole.

We conclude that on the whole bars are undesirable places, particularly those where only the strongest forms of alcoholic liquors are sold. Although the practice of drinking an apéritif before a meal (even a strong cocktail) is probably held by most people to be comparatively harmless, bars certainly encourage the "apéritif" to take the form of several highly concentrated drinks. Bars also offer a strong inducement to people to form the habit of "dropping in" for the sole purpose of taking alcohol in considerable quantity.

As far as public houses are concerned, we feel that we cannot state our conclusions about their desirability or otherwise better than by quoting from an earlier work written by one of us.[1] In that work it is stated:

> Public houses provide facilities for people to meet for recreation and social intercourse under conditions chosen and created by themselves. They are enjoyed and taken advantage of by many thousands of people, young and old, of both sexes, every week and would be greatly missed if they were closed.
>
> The 'atmosphere' or 'tone' of public houses, where people mix together so freely, tends to be that of the majority, and any young fellow or girl who makes a habit of frequenting them comes under its influence. If, previously, their ideals were higher than those generally

[1] *Poverty and Progress*, by B. S. Rowntree, p. 366.

held in the public house, its influence upon them will probably be bad. On the other hand, if a misanthrope frequented a public house, he might be persuaded by what he saw and heard around him that the world was a kindlier place than he imagined. On the whole, however, I cannot but think that thoughtful parents, even if they are not teetotallers, and place no teetotal embargo on their elder children, would not like to see them making a habit of spending their evenings in the public house. How often, too, one has heard the expression, when men's names were being considered for responsible posts, 'I am not very keen on that fellow—he spends too much time in the public house."

In giving this view we do not however overlook the fact that some public houses are genuine centres of communal life in the areas that they serve. But they are only a minority of the whole, and are found mainly in rural areas.

Improved public houses

For some decades past, signs have not been wanting that brewers realize that the amenities of their public houses should be improved. In most cases their reforms have been restricted to the building of "better" public houses, offering comfort and good taste in the furnishings and decorations. Indeed brewers have sometimes surrendered two or more licences to build one new house, and have then built one so palatial that its drinking space is greater than the total of that of the houses of which the licences were surrendered.

One effect of the "better" public house is that it gives a greater appearance of respectability, so that persons often become regular customers who would never visit a normal public house. This is particularly true of women. The provision of these houses, therefore, represents good business for the brewer, as well as, no doubt, being a sincere attempt to achieve a higher all-round standard in the interest of his customers, actual and potential.

Cultural attractions in public houses

Some brewers have gone further and have introduced definitely cultural attractions into their houses. By far the most important work in this field is being done by the Committee for Verse and Prose Recitation, more often referred to simply as "Poetry in Pubs," which has a section known as "The Taverners" for performing plays in public houses.

"Poetry in Pubs" began in June 1937, and the first performance by The Taverners was in February 1938. The enterprise is financed by a group of brewers and there is a full-time paid organizer. The poetry readers and actors give their services free.

During the poetry readings, the audience sit at small tables with their drinks, and do not preserve the complete silence that a reader would expect in a drawing-room. He has to accept the movement of members of the audience to the bar when they want to refill their glasses, or the movement of a waiter, and perhaps the ringing of the cash registers. Nevertheless, there is a good deal of evidence that the poetry readings—which range from Milton and Shakespeare to light satirical verse—provide a cultural interest for a limited number of people to whom it would never come in any other way.

Naturally performances of plays by The Taverners are more popular than the poetry readings. They are performed in a large room, virtually without scenery or properties, but in full costume with make-up. The audience sit at small tables, and the actors often have to pass through the audience to make their entrances and exits. The service of drinks continues during the performance.

Although a large proportion of the audiences have never seen a stage play of any kind, they have a natural appreciation of plays of the highest calibre. The Taverners' claim that this is so is borne out by examining the list of plays that they have performed and the authors. The latter include Chekhov, Sheridan, Shaw, St. John Ervine, Galsworthy and Shakespeare. In the view of Henry McCarthy, the organizer of The Taverners, this strong preference for good plays is evidence of the existence of an inherited national culture, and points to a higher standard of true, as opposed to formal, education than is usually believed to be general.

A copy of the full programme of poetry readings and plays for two typical months is given in Appendix II, page 469. Substantial as the work is for a small group, it makes little impact on the country as a whole, although it is capable of expansion, and before the recent war separate groups of Taverners were working in various provincial centres as well as the parent group in and around London.

Another cultural contribution of some importance is the series of concerts started by a large firm of Sheffield brewers in September 1944, and continued ever since, although somewhat irregularly and often at considerable intervals. They have been given the name of Tavern Concerts, but despite the similarity of the names, they are not in any way connected with the activities of The Taverners.

Concerts in public houses are of course frequent enough, and all too often centre round rather objectionable "music hall" turns. The distinct quality of the Tavern Concerts is that they are of classical music, performed by some of the most famous soloists of the day. The performers have included Mark Hambourg, Leon Goossens, Louis Kentner, Cyril Smith, Nina Milkina, Moiseiwitsch and Solomon.

The one-hundredth concert in the series took place in April 1948, and Gordon Nicholson, the organizer of the concerts, informed us that up to that time approximately 35,000 persons had been present at the concerts.

The experience of the Tavern Concerts coincides with that of The Taverners, that public-house audiences have a natural taste for artistic work of the highest quality, if it is made available in familiar surroundings. The programme played by Solomon at the one-hundredth concert is given in Appendix III, page 472.

The Tavern Concerts are of course vastly more expensive than, say, a poetry reading, or even a play by The Taverners, because the performers are not merely professionals, but professionals of the first rank, whose fees for the concerts are no doubt commensurate with their reputations. Not only does this mean that concerts can only take place at considerable intervals, but it results also in music lovers who are not normally customers of a public house taking the opportunity of hearing a star performer "on the cheap." The brewers thus provide for a wider audience than their own customers, and they also get some advantage in prestige and advertisement.

Disinterested management of the liquor trade

In the foregoing pages we have described some of the principal efforts of the liquor trade to improve the material standard of licensed premises, and to raise their tone. We turn now to consider two efforts by bodies outside the trade to deal with the same problem. The first of these is the State Management District of Carlisle, and the other the Glasgow Public House Trust.

During the First World War there was so much heavy drinking in Carlisle that production was hampered in the large neighbouring munition factories. The situation had become so serious that, with the approval of Parliament, the Government purchased all the breweries and public houses, and most of the hotels, both in Carlisle and in a considerable area around the city. Since that time the whole of the liquor trade in the area has been conducted on behalf of the Home Secretary by a Manager, who is a permanent civil servant. The profits are paid into the Exchequer.

We discuss later in this chapter whether the principle of State ownership of the liquor trade is desirable or not. At this point we are concerned only to describe the system as it is.[1] To gather first-hand information B.S.R. paid a brief visit to Carlisle, and saw some of the public houses, and G.R.L. paid two special visits in 1946 and 1948, staying several days on each occasion and examining every aspect of the problem. Although he was given every assistance by Mr. W. A. Goddard, the present Manager for the area, he spent most of his time wandering around alone finding out, as a normal citizen, what the public houses and their staffs were like, and how satisfied, or otherwise, customers seemed to be.

The first striking fact about the public houses is that, although the number of them has been reduced from 126 to 54, nobody has to walk far to get a drink.[2] Public houses are only

[1] There is a second State Management Area in Scotland, but it is in a thinly populated area and we have followed the normal practice of regarding Carlisle as the "working model" of State Management.

[2] When the State Management scheme first started there were 129 licences of all kinds. They were reduced almost immediately to 83, and by degrees to the present number of 57. In addition there are now two occasional licences for Auction Markets. Of the 57 two are held by hotels and one by a restaurant in private ownership.

half as numerous per thousand of the population as in the overwhelming majority of urban areas. In Carlisle the density is approximately 1 to every 1,100 of the population. The average for England and Wales as a whole in 1948 (the latest year for which figures are available) was 1 to 592.[1] In two towns in which we have made special studies the corresponding figures were 1 to 576 in York in 1938, and 1 to 527 in High Wycombe in 1950.

Even so, in a walk of not more than half a mile down the main street of Carlisle, G.R.L. noted that there were five public houses, whilst there seemed to be a liberal number in the other streets, and in the residential areas.[2] This would suggest that, quite apart from any question of the relative merits of State and private management, the number of public houses in most towns must be grossly in excess of the real needs.

Structurally, the public houses in Carlisle are of two distinct types, namely, those that were originally purchased from the brewers and those that have been designed and built under State Management. The first type cannot as a rule be improved structurally beyond a certain point. The rooms in these houses tend to be uncomfortably large (probably as a result of removing internal subdivisions that originally existed), and the high standard of furnishing and decoration does not entirely make up for an absence of "cosiness."

The newer houses, specifically built for State Management, are however structurally excellent. The rooms are well laid out, well proportioned, adequate in size but not too big, and with an outstandingly high level of furnishing and equipment.

The staff of all the houses are civil servants, and their remuneration depends in no respect on the amount of liquor sold. The managers receive a commission on sales of food, but a system formerly in force whereby they also received a commission on sales of soft drinks is being allowed to lapse as new managers are appointed. The staff wear white coats, a form of dress that has long been thought best for the country's

[1] *Annual Abstract of Statistics*, 1938–48.

[2] It was explained by the District Manager that a certain new housing estate in Carlisle lacked a public house, which would be built as soon as conditions permitted, and would have been built earlier in normal circumstances.

smartest and most fashionable bars, and which seems equally suitable in a public house, and they are polite and efficient. When time permits, they are as ready for a chat with a customer as any normal publican, and if an experienced beer drinker landed by parachute in Carlisle without knowing where he was, it is unlikely that he would realize that he was buying a State pint from a civil servant.

It is often suggested by opponents of the system of State Management that harsh rules are enforced in the public houses of Carlisle, and G.R.L. during his visits particularly examined this aspect of the matter. The allegations are usually threefold, namely, that nobody is allowed to drink standing up, and that neither games nor singing are allowed. We do not wish to devote much space to refuting these suggestions, but as a result of our enquiries on the spot, we can say that the statements are incorrect. Customers are asked, by means of printed notices, to sit down; in the new and most comfortable houses they mostly do so; in the older houses a good many customers, sometimes as many as a half, stand. Games are not forbidden; dominoes and cards are played regularly; several of the newer houses have excellent bowling greens, and the Home Secretary has ruled that darts are to be provided wherever a demand exists and space can be found. As far as singing is concerned, we know that it is not forbidden, because G.R.L. was present in one of the public houses on a Saturday evening at a sing-song lasting over an hour.

As is the case with all monopolies, the State Management system in Carlisle has an inherent danger, viz., that the customer's wishes may not be adequately consulted. Although the District Manager has a consultative council, we doubt whether the average "pub-goer" in Carlisle has a proper chance of making his voice heard. We do not suggest or believe that there are at present grievances needing redress, nor that the present Manager is anything other than a capable, reasonable and thoughtful official. Nevertheless, disregard of the "little man" is so grave a danger in monopoly that we believe there ought to be a democratically elected Consumers' Council in Carlisle to assist the District Manager.

Neither of us is a connoisseur of beer and, though G.R.L.

drank various half-pints of it in Carlisle, he can only say that it tasted to him very much like any other beer. He made enquiries of customers with whom he got into conversation at several public houses, and found that the majority of men he consulted had either never tasted any other brew, or had done so only rarely or long ago, so that they had no standard of judgment. Men recently demobilized mostly indicated that it was "all right." Nobody was enthusiastic; nobody was definitely condemnatory. Proprietary brands of spirits, and of bottled beers and stouts, are also on sale in the State public houses.

Soft drinks are on sale in all the public houses, just as they are in nearly every house in other areas under private ownership, and some of the houses have notices offering tea or coffee. The availability of tea or coffee was found by G.R.L. to be a polite fiction in the two houses in which he specifically asked for it, but in fairness it should be added that he asked late in the evening, at a busy period.

Hot meals are available in a small number of the houses, and G.R.L. had an excellent and cheap dinner at one house, including, on this occasion, a cup of tea. Most of the other houses have pies for sale and occasionally sandwiches, but the quality of those tried was poor.

Glasgow Public House Trust

We have no personal experience of the public houses maintained by the Glasgow Public House Trust, and we have not thought it necessary to make a special journey to Glasgow to see them. The Trust maintains 18 licensed houses, two actually in Glasgow and the remainder in six Scottish counties. It does not own its own brewery, and Trust houses compete for custom with those run by private enterprise for profit. Profits distributed by the Trust are limited to 5 per cent, less income tax. Surplus profits are spent by the Trustees on projects which are of public benefit, and in particular on providing counter-attractions to public houses. As we write the latest object to which surplus profits have been devoted is the provision, in conjunction with the Glasgow Corporation, of a Social Centre in one of Glasgow's housing estates, in which former slum dwellers have been rehoused. The Trust donated £2,500 towards the cost of this Centre.

Nature and effect of alcohol

We must turn now from details about the places where people drink, to consider what are the nature and effect of alcohol, and why people drink alcoholic liquor. Taking first the question, "What is alcohol?" we accept the modern medical view that alcohol is a narcotic drug—the exact opposite of the stimulant which it was long imagined to be, and as it is still frequently but inaccurately described. We likewise accept the medical view that the physiological effect of alcohol is first to produce a feeling of well-being and friendliness, and then to affect those parts of the brain that, in an evolutionary sense, are of latest development, and the action of which most obviously differentiates human from brute behaviour. It follows that the consequential effect of alcohol is to lead people to speech and actions that show a recession from the individual's highest and best standards. The drug is habit-forming and it is all too obvious, without the pronouncements of either doctors or social students, that once the habit of heavy drinking is formed it can only be broken by skilled treatment, or by extraordinary strength of mind and unusual moral courage.

If we ask why people drink alcoholic liquors, we find that there are two main reasons, and that most regular drinkers are influenced by both. First, people value the effect of the drug, or become so accustomed to it that they cannot easily do without it. Second, places where alcoholic drink is sold are open, and offer warmth, light and at least the opportunity of companionship in the evenings at a time when, for the large majority of citizens, these are not available in other places of assembly.

A large majority of the persons who enjoy the effect of the drug are moderate drinkers. But even the man who contents himself with a pint or two of mild beer appreciates the slight glow of well-being that he feels, whilst many who are worried, unhappy or lonely value the anaesthetic effect of stronger potions. It is in our view safe to say that nearly all regular drinkers are attracted primarily by the sequence, "Drink—

exhilaration—more drinks—anaesthesia." The precise point in the sequence at which any individual stops is determined by his taste, pocket, and other circumstances. The truism is often forgotten that nobody would drink alcoholic liquors (most of which taste nasty to most people until they become used to them) unless they contained alcohol.

We deal later in this chapter with the second reason for drinking. For the moment we wish to turn to another matter, and to ask, "Why do people *start* drinking, where do the muddled ideas come from that enable people to disguise from themselves the true nature of their devotion to the narcotic drug, what influences people to continue a course of action they find so harmful to their pocket, and in not a few cases to their prospects and to their health?" There is little doubt that, in most cases, the heavy advertising by the liquor trade supplies the answer to all these questions.

Advertising by the liquor trade

Without a large and costly investigation it would be impossible to ascertain how much the trade spends on advertising. In preparing his evidence for the Royal Commission on Licensing, 1929–31, Viscount Astor made the necessary investigation, and in his evidence before the Commission he was able to show that in 1928 the trade spent over £2 million on various kinds of advertising. That estimate was made, however, before the institution in the 1930's of a large-scale and sustained advertising campaign by the brewers, so that the present figure would no doubt be very much higher than that calculated by Lord Astor. The exact figure is in any case immaterial. The fact is that a vast sum, measured in millions of pounds, is spent annually in advertising by the liquor trade, and that sum would not be spent unless it were a profitable investment, leading to proportionately increased sales of alcoholic liquors, either at the time of advertising or in the future, or both.

Even twenty years ago brewers were becoming aware of their common interest in advertising beer in general, as opposed to any particular brand, as is shown by the following extracts from their trade press:

(*a*) We feel that it is as certain as that day follows night that collective publicity will be adopted by the brewing trade; it is only a matter of time. And when we have it, brewers will wonder however they came to disregard and leave unexploited so magnificent an opportunity of creating public opinion in favour of the commodity they produce. (*Brewers' Journal*, 1924.)

(*b*) We must have sufficient faith to keep on advertising. . . . A continual and never-ceasing pressure and persuasion is essential not only to preserve old and regular customers, but to capture the younger generation growing up. (*Brewers' Guardian*, June 1928.)

(*c*) Every pleasing beer advertisement has a certain psychological and propaganda value. It helps to maintain a favourable atmosphere about beer which serves the interests of the Trade. (Article in the *Brewers' Guardian*, 1929.)

A general campaign of advertising by brewers was in fact launched in 1933 when the late Sir Edgar Sanders was Director of the Brewers' Society. He expounded the principles of the campaign in a speech intended for a trade audience (and therefore entirely frank), but the contents of which were revealed by the Rt. Hon. Isaac Foot, into whose hands a copy of the speech fell. One of the most striking passages of Sir Edgar's address ran, "We want to get the beer-drinking habit instilled into thousands, almost millions, of young men who do not at present know the taste of beer. These young men, if they start with what beer they can afford to-day, as they grow up, will afford better beers to the greater advantage of the brewing industry."

That the campaign to prove, in its own words, that "Beer is best" was a financial success for the brewers is shown by the fact that from 1935 to 1948 the consumption of beer rose by 26 per cent—from 23 million to 29 million barrels per annum.

Further proof of the success of the advertisement campaign is provided by our case histories. Time after time persons interviewed have described their reasons for drinking in phrases used widely in advertisements as the following examples show:

(*a*) Mrs. A. is an elderly widow employed as a charwoman in a large London office and supplementing her earnings by taking in laundry. Her recreation is visiting her favourite public house in the evenings, and it is because she spends so much there that she has to work so hard. Her normal drink is a famous brand of stout of which she drinks four or five bottles almost every evening. She says it does her good and that without it she would not have the strength to work so hard.

(*b*) Dr. B. is a general practitioner with a large urban practice composed of working-class and lower-middle-class patients. He says that for many years he has been advising patients who need to be built up physically to have a bottle of a well-known stout every day and he is sure it has a strengthening effect. He states that he himself always has a bottle of the same stout with his midday meal and he adds, "It's worth the price for the psychological value alone, and I'm sure the stuff itself does a man good."

(*c*) Mr. C. is a shopkeeper. He is a friendly man and spends a good deal of time in public houses although he is a rather fastidious and by no means heavy drinker. He never drinks beer and describes most spirits as "muck." His regular tipple is a certain brand of whisky which he says he chooses because it is mellow and properly matured. To support his opinion, Mr. C. frequently quotes an advertisement for this whisky which emphasises its age.

(*d*) Mrs. D. is an upper-middle-class housewife. She is a most friendly woman and entertains extensively. A large cocktail cabinet stands in the drawing-room of her London flat and among the other spirits and liqueurs with which it is stocked there is always one particular brand of gin. Mrs. D. says, "I always have ——'s gin—I think it's the basis of nearly every good cocktail," This remark is in fact a close paraphrase of one of the advertising slogans used for the particular brand of gin.

(*e*) Mr. E. aged 22 or 23, plays football every Saturday afternoon in winter. It is his main recreation. Before each game he drinks two half-pints of beer and he says he does it as part of his training. Opposite his house, and on the tube station from which he travels each weekday, are large posters which show a strikingly handsome man dressed as a footballer, with a large crowd of spectators in the background. The poster advertises beer.

The situation about advertisements by various sections of the drink trade amounts in fact to this: The essential ingredient of all alcoholic liquors is alcohol; the trade has had a great measure of success in increasing the sale of those liquors by advertisement, and this success has included purchase by an unknown, but certainly a very large, number of persons who would not otherwise have become consumers of alcoholic liquors at all. In other words, for the private profit of interested persons the public is being persuaded by advertisements to consume what may truthfully be termed a narcotic and habit-forming drug. In our view the community would be wise to protect itself against such advertisements by putting statutory restrictions upon them. There is already on the Statute Book a law which, with only minor alterations, could serve as a model for a Bill dealing with advertisement of alcoholic drinks. It is the Moneylenders Act, 1927. If a new Bill were drafted on the lines of that Act, advertisements by brewers and distillers would not be prohibited, but would be restricted to particulars of the name and address of the manufacturer, wholesaler or retailer of the product concerned, the name of the product or the name and address of licensed premises.

Twice unsuccessful attempts have been made in Parliament to have legislation enacted on these lines. The first occasion was in the House of Commons in 1931; the second was in the House of Lords in 1935. If such a measure could be enacted, no single person who wanted to drink alcohol would have his liberty interfered with in any way. The only effect would be to protect those who did not want to drink, or wanted to drink only in moderation, from being persuaded by clever propaganda to drink more than they really wanted, for the benefit of men whose interest it is to sell the greatest possible amount of a toxic substance.

The question of advertisements of the drink trade does, however, raise a wider issue, for it brings us face to face with the fact that in the manufacture and sale of alcoholic liquor there is at present a basic conflict of interests between private enterprise and public well-being.

The case for public control

While things remain as they are now, brewers, distillers and publicans, quite naturally, use every legitimate endeavour to increase their sales. But to increase the sale of alcoholic liquor is opposed to the public interest. Is the drink trade one that should be left to private ownership, or should it be subject to some form of control that removes all private profit, and therefore removes all incentive to increase sales? We have no doubt it should be so controlled.

We are not prepared at present to advocate any one particular form of public control because we believe that careful research is needed to determine the form which this should take. Broadly speaking, the alternative possibilities are:

(*a*) Full nationalization of brewing, distilling and retailing.

(*b*) Nationalization of brewing and distilling, but with retailing left in the hands of private individuals under licence, and with advertisements controlled by statute.

(*c*) Public control of either production or retailing, or both, but with the control vested in a Corporation or Trust, free from Government control.

(*d*) Control by the Local Government authorities.

(*e*) Control by regional corporations, such as those charged with planning and building new towns.

On the whole we feel that alternatives (*d*) and (*e*) would be unwise. In the case of control by the Local Government authorities there would always be the danger, particularly in the smaller towns and rural areas, of the sale of drink being encouraged in order to give relief to the rates. Our objection to method (*e*) is simply that conducting the drink trade is in itself so large and specialized a business that we doubt if it could be efficiently performed except by an *ad hoc* body.

We think that there is room for experiment on the lines of public control of production, by the State or otherwise, leaving retailing to private individuals under licence, as it is at present. In this way it is possible that the measure of public control that appears essential would be achieved, but consumers would be protected against the impact of a State monopoly, and publicans, who can do very little in the way of "pushing" sales, would be able to retain the individual character of their houses. If such a system were adopted, the density of public houses per thousand of the population would have to be carefully considered. As we pointed out above, Carlisle gets on very well with about half as many public houses per thousand of the population as there are in other towns.

Need for cafés of a new type

We stated above that the drinking of alcoholic liquors is encouraged by the fact that public houses are open when most other places of assembly are closed. We have been impressed by the widespread demand that this situation should be changed, and that establishments should be opened where men and women, young and old, can meet and sit in the evening, without having to buy alcoholic liquor. This proposal has been made to one or other of us in places as far apart as the Rhondda Valley and Newcastle-on-Tyne, and by a bishop, senior and junior civil servants, representatives of both management and labour in industry, housewives, shop girls, and men in academic life. In fact it is certain that there is a widespread demand for such places.

Naturally, different people have different ideas of just what is wanted, nor indeed would one standard pattern of establishment meet the needs of all districts and classes. Broadly, however, the type of place required resembles the Continental café. In some there might be music, in others not. They would be small and numerous rather than large and few in number, and they would be comfortable but unpretentious. There would be non-alcoholic drinks, hot and cold, light snacks would be served, and in some cafés full-scale meals. There would be newspapers, perhaps games, and above all a cheerful and friendly staff. The question of whether such cafés should be licensed for the sale of light beer only might be a matter for experiment. In any case we would not recommend a spirit or wine licence. It would be essential that the cafés should be open every evening including Sundays and that they should not close earlier than the licensed premises in the same area.

We do not minimize the difficulties of such a scheme. A completely new tradition of service to the public would have to be created to replace the widely current idea that the customer in a café is merely a body to be served and ejected as quickly as possible, so that he can be replaced by another body. The customers too would have to develop a new tradition of a leisured approach to a café, in place of the contemporary habit of fidgeting until served, eating and drinking fast, and departing. There would be enormous financial difficulties, too, especially in those cafés where the Catering Wages Act applied, but the financial difficulties might be overcome, not inappropriately, by subsidizing such cafés out of the profits of a publicly controlled liquor trade. The certain facts are that the demand exists, and that it would be in the public interest to satisfy it.

New soft drinks wanted

If such cafés were established, a powerful contribution to their success would be the provision of more palatable non-alcoholic drinks than there are now, and indeed the provision of such drinks would be a considerable public benefit even without the cafés. Soft drinks that can be drunk by adults with full enjoyment are rare in England. There are certainly a few good varieties of unfermented apple juice, but they are not generally available, and there is no equivalent of the Continental *sirops-de-fruit* or of the unfermented grape juice that are available in many wine-growing countries. We understand that, under Government auspices, research is proceeding into the production of good soft drinks, and this is greatly to be welcomed.

Education about alcohol

A striking fact about the drink problem in England to-day is the ignorance of the ordinary citizen, not only about the problem in its national aspect, but also in its purely personal application. The trade, through its propaganda, and the cinema, by so often representing drinking as part of the kind of life many of the audiences would like to live, have a virtual monopoly in educating the public about drink. There is little objective teaching, and instruction about the nature and effects of alcohol is only given in a small proportion of schools. An enquiry made by the British Temperance League in 1945–6 suggested that frequent instruction was given in less than one-sixth of all day schools, while in more than two-thirds instruction about this matter was never given at all. Without vouching for the accuracy of the figures, which we have not personally checked, we imagine that they give a pretty fair indication of the situation. That this should be so seems to us to be clearly a failure of the education system. We believe that factual education about the whole alcohol problem should be given in every school. Temperance workers, particularly those connected with churches, should also be more active in making their special appeal in Sunday schools, youth clubs, and in centres of adult education.

Although later in this book we deal at length with the cinema, and briefly with broadcasting, we feel that we must say here that the British Board of Film Censors and the British Broadcasting Corporation could help a good deal more than they do in educating young people to understand the true nature of alcoholic liquor. Without suggesting that either films or radio should undertake positive measures of education, it would be a considerable gain if films were prohibited from giving their present prominence to drink and drinking-places, and if joking references to the subject were forbidden on the radio.

Taxation of the liquor trade

Earlier in this chapter we made a brief reference, in a footnote, to the question of taxation of the liquor trade, and we now wish to consider the matter further. In the financial year 1947–8, taxation of alcoholic liquor amounted to £376 million. Many people point out the importance of this sum to the Exchequer, and draw a doleful picture of a Chancellor who would not know where to turn for money if revenue from the taxation of liquor were much reduced or abolished altogether. In considering this question three considerations must be borne in mind. First, the money has to be raised from some source and the Chancellor has to select a means of raising the sum required which will not injure the community. High taxation of alcoholic drink may not be popular either with the trade or with consumers of drink, but it will limit the amount of drink sold, and that would be an advantage to the Chancellor, because a high level of consumption involves the country in a heavy financial loss, both through reduced efficiency in industry and commerce, and through the increased costs of police forces, prisons, hospitals, and so on. Second, if we can imagine a reduction in the consumption of alcoholic liquor so great that the total yield from taxation became insignificant, the whole taxation structure of the country would be affected by the consequential changes. The country would become richer because the goods and services now used by the liquor trade would be available for productive purposes. Third, it is a function of good government to put principle before expediency in taxation, as in all other fields of governmental activity. If the large-scale consumption of alcoholic liquor is opposed to the national interest, it would be a bad government indeed that maintained that consumption by encouraging or countenancing propaganda, merely for the purpose of raising revenue.

Suitability of British licensing laws

There is only one further matter that we wish to discuss, and that only briefly. It is whether the licensing laws in En land could be improved so far as they affect the times at which strong drink can be sold, which are much more restricted than in certain countries overseas. The answer to the question really depends on whether the aim of the licensing laws should be primarily to limit the consumption of alcohol by the sheer force of the law, or whether it is a recognition that the legitimate practice of consuming alcohol is liable to abuse by a minority of persons. In our view, the latter is the correct attitude. In saying this we do not overlook the fact that a large reduction in the consumption of alcohol in this country is highly desirable, and even urgently necessary. But social reform cannot go much ahead of public opinion. The folly of trying to do too much too fast, even from the best of motives, was illustrated in the experiment of total prohibition in the United States.

If this is so the British system of permitted hours seems admirable in principle, and better than the more repressive laws in other countries. The hours during which sales of alcoholic drink may take place in Britain are now eight in each weekday and five on Sunday, with the condition that there must be a break of at least two and a half hours in the afternoon. For some curious reason, licensed premises in London are allowed an extra hour each weekday. When public opinion has been educated to accept a further alteration of licensing hours, there is plenty of scope for reduction of the permitted hours without involving any change of the principle. London's extra hour is an obvious target for temperance reformers, and it would not be easy to prove that there is any valid social reason for "on-sales" in the middle of the day from Mondays to Fridays, except for the service of drinks with meals.

SUMMARY

There is still a grave drink problem in Britain. It does not manifest itself in excessive drunkenness, but in the high total consumption of a large number of mainly moderate drinkers. The result is twofold. On the national side, resources and labour are diverted to the drink industry to an extent that is unreasonable, especially at a time when Britain has become a poor nation, short of capital equipment for industry, and needing a high level of exports, not only to maintain her standard of living, but to extricate her from her present economic dependence on America. On the personal side, the proportion of individual incomes spent on drink is so high as to lessen savings, the material well-being of many families is imperilled, and an unknown, but certainly large, number of individuals fail to achieve the success in life that might have been theirs had they been more temperate.

There is statistical evidence of drinking by young people of both sexes to an extent that, by ensuring that a new generation of drinkers is growing up, offers little hope of an automatic reduction in the consumption of alcoholic liquors in the next few decades.

The heavy increase in the consumption of beer since the beginning of the brewers' advertisement campaign in 1933 emphasizes the degree to which advertising creates the demand for liquor. As a heavy and increasing demand is opposed to the public interest, we feel strongly that advertisements by producers, wholesalers and retailers of beers, wines and spirits should be restricted by statute. We believe that the need for this reform is extremely urgent. The restriction of advertising by the trade would protect the public, without interfering in any way with the liberty of those who, of their own accord, wish to drink.

In attempting to assess the part played by licensed premises in national life, we have been greatly struck by the impossibility of treating them as a homogeneous whole. As a general rule we believe bars to be objectionable places. They have no social value and are designed for the purpose of persuading people to consume comparatively large quantities of alcohol. At the other end of the scale, rural and semi-rural public houses are often valuable centres of communal life. Urban public houses vary enormously. Many are sordid, some are vicious, others make a useful contribution to the life of the neighbourhood they serve.

It is impossible to overlook the sharp conflict of interests between the trade and the community. On the one hand the trade naturally wishes to sell as much as possible of its products to as many customers as possible. On the other hand, the national interest is to restrict the consumption of alcohol. This being so, we are forced to the view that the liquor trade is not one that should be run by private individuals for profit. We have not formed a definite opinion about which alternative form of public control is preferable, and we would like to see more experiments made in this connection. In particular we would like to see a trial of a system whereby brewing and distilling were under public control (either of the State or of a Public Trust), leaving retailing to individual licensees.

The necessity of introducing new measures for the control of public houses should not divert attention from registered clubs. No doubt the situation regarding them would be improved if the unfulfilled recommendations of the Royal Commission on Licensing, 1929–31, were implemented, although we do not believe that the police should be given power to enter clubs without first obtaining a magistrate's warrant.

In considering reforms that are desirable in connection with places where alcoholic liquor is retailed, we have become aware of a widespread demand in the country for an entirely new sort of establishment—a place where comfort, warmth, light and companionship are the main attractions and alcohol has no, or virtually no, place. We recommend strongly that experiments should be carried out with cafés that conform roughly to the Continental pattern, where a customer can sit, talk, read the papers, look at the other customers, and perhaps listen to music. If it proved possible to establish such cafés, they would doubtless need subsidies, and the most suitable source for funds appears to us to be from the profits of a publicly controlled liquor trade.

Whether such cafés can be established or not, there is a demand for more attractive soft drinks, such as those sold in many European countries.

Finally we believe that much more attention should be paid to factual education about the nature and effects of alcohol. Although for the most part this should be given in schools, it might also usefully be given less formally in places where adult education is carried on, and by means of lectures in youth clubs and other suitable gatherings. We do not believe we are bigoted, but it seems to us that, at present, adolescents and young adults are left too much without guidance, with the result that the trade reaps a rich harvest, for which the nation pays the bill in the forms of lost production, reduced efficiency, impaired health, and avoidable unhappiness in individual and family life, to say nothing of the expense of police supervision, the cost of prosecutions, and the maintenance in prison of the unhappy persons, not inconsiderable in numbers, who but for alcohol would never have fallen foul of the law.

CHAPTER IV

SMOKING

WE had not originally intended to write anything in this book about the habit of smoking, but we have been so greatly impressed by the widespread addiction to it and the harmful effects which it produces on the lives of many individuals and families, that we feel we must make some reference to the subject.

In 1948 the total consumption of tobacco in Great Britain amounted to 214 million pounds,[1] and this represented an increase of approximately 17 per cent on the amount consumed in 1937. The total personal expenditure on tobacco in England and Wales in 1948 amounted to £772 million. This means that in 1948 the nation spent:

(*a*) Considerably more than twice on much on tobacco as on fuel and light.

(*b*) More than four times as much on tobacco as on all forms of entertainment.

(*c*) Slightly over 17s. 6d. on tobacco for every £1 on clothing.

Rather more than 80 per cent of the expenditure on tobacco returns to the Exchequer in taxation. But since a large proportion of the tobacco has to be bought in the U.S.A. for dollars, the Chancellor of the Exchequer, far from being pleased at the high yield of the tax, described it in a recent Budget speech as "unfortunate."

Large as the consumption of tobacco is, it reflects the moderate consumption of a great number of persons rather than heavy smoking by a minority of the population. When making the surveys described in the last two chapters, Research Services Ltd. enquired into the smoking habits of the persons

[1] *Annual Abstract of Statistics*, 1938–48.

interviewed. It appears that 81·1 per cent of the men and 41·6 per cent of the women over the age of 16 are smokers. At the time of the survey there were 36 million persons over the age of 16 in Britain and the total consumption of tobacco in 1948 was 214 mill on pounds, as stated above. Thus the average smoker consumes almost exactly 10 pounds of tobacco a year—a little less than half an ounce a day. Half an ounce of tobacco is equivalent to 12 or 13 cigarettes. In actual fact men tend on the average to smoke more, and women less than this number. Information obtained by Professor Zweig when preparing his book, *Labour, Life and Poverty*, and the facts given in our case histories, suggest that when they can get them and can afford them, a majority of the men who smoke like to have about 20 cigarettes per day.

Regarded, however, from the personal standpoint, smoking is a luxury which gives much pleasure and which is probably innocuous if indulged in moderately, but medical evidence points to the fact that heavy smoking is injurious to health.[1]

Seen from the national viewpoint, a substantial amount of real wealth is literally going up in smoke every year. This is all the more serious at a time when our chance of balancing our dollar account with the United States, from which so much of our tobacco comes, is remote in any foreseeable future. At the present moment, when we are the recipients of remarkably generous gifts from the United States to enable us to recover our economic equilibrium, we can only sustain our smoking habit by using part of the Marshall Aid grants for the purchase of Virginia tobacco. Although our behaviour in this respect is rather unpleasantly reminiscent of the genteel beggar who tells a hard-luck story about a starving family, and then, having been given half a crown, steps into the nearest public house, it is hard to see what else we could do. For it is certain that the

[1] An interesting article by Roger William Riis, which appeared in the *Reader's Digest* for February 1950, and which we quote by permission, ended with the words:

"A word of personal testimony. When I began research for this article, I was smoking forty cigarettes a day. As I got into the subject, I found that number dropping. As I finish the article, I am smoking ten a day. I'd like to smoke more, but my investigation of the subject has convinced me that smoking is dangerous and, worse—stupid. Finally, I enjoy my ten cigarettes ever so much more than I did the forty!

"To me, it all adds up to this: Smoking is a very pleasant, very foolish habit. Most people can indulge in it with no apparent damage. Eight cigarettes a day, apparently, harm no normal person. No one should indulge in smoking as much as he wants to. Everyone should smoke less, if only for the reason that one enjoys it more."

smoking habit has so strong a grip on many of those who indulge in it that, if no American tobacco were imported and the supply of cigarettes were greatly reduced, industrial production would undoubtedly be lowered.

Time after time we have come across cases in our investigations, where men and women admit that they cannot do without tobacco, and we quote the following as typical examples:

(*a*) Typist in late twenties. Earns £5 a week, with great difficulty has cut down consumption of cigarettes to 20 a day. Cannot afford so many and goes without necessities to buy cigarettes. If she stops smoking becomes extremely dejected, and experiences acute trembling of hands.

(*b*) Artisan in factory. Aged 35. Smokes 20 cigarettes a day. Cannot afford so many because he is married with two children, but cannot do without. Has tried several times to give up smoking, but becomes so irritable that home life is impossible and his wife begs him to start smoking again.

(*c*) A solicitor. Aged 38, married, with two children. Not in practice on his own account and salary quite small. Smokes 40 cigarettes a day. Sends children to an elementary school. If he neither smoked nor drank he would send them to a private school where he believes they would have a better education. He says he can give up drink at any time, but not smoking.

(*d*) An agricultural labourer. Wages £4 14s., plus a cottage. Smokes continually if he can get enough cigarettes. He would like 50 a day, but has to content himself with 20 or 30. Even though he makes them himself, for economy, it is a heavy drain on his income. He visits the public house on Saturdays and Sundays, but does not spend more than 5s. a week on beer, yet his tobacco costs him nearly 25s. a week. His wife has to take in laundry work in order to earn money to provide clothes for the children.

(*e*) A middle-class housewife. Her husband works "in the city" and has quite a reasonable income. She used to smoke about 50 cigarettes a day but with difficulty has cut the number down to 25. She considers 25 the absolute minimum on which she can manage, and even so, says that she still suffers from a craving for more. She keeps as many of her daily 25 as she can for the evening, so that she shall not be irritable when her husband is at home.

(*f*) A clerk, aged 21. He spends 5s. per day on cigarettes. By the middle of many weeks he is so short of money that his breakfast of tea and toast is his only meal of the day. He says, "Lots of times I have gone without food for a smoke, but never without a smoke for food."

Two facts seem certain about smoking. First that in the nation's economic interest it is desirable that the consumption of tobacco should be substantially less than it is at present. Second that although some people have given up smoking and many thousands of others no doubt could do so, it is nevertheless true that a majority, perhaps a large majority, of regular smokers, have become so dependent on smoking that they cannot do without tobacco except for a short time. It follows that a reduction in the total amount of smoking can best be obtained by concentrating on those who do not smoke, particularly on the young, and persuading them to continue their abstinence.

CHAPTER V

SEXUAL PROMISCUITY

In the whole field of human relationships there is probably no subject about which it is harder to get reliable information than about sexual promiscuity. And this is still true notwithstanding the fact that in recent decades many people have become more willing to discuss the matter, for there are very likely as many who exaggerate out of bravado as there are who conceal sexually promiscuous activities. The further difficulty arises that it is impossible authoritatively to compare the present with the past, for if reliable information about the present is sparse, that about the past is practically non-existent. It is commonplace nowadays to assume that sexual promiscuity is infinitely more widespread than formerly and this may very well be true, but it is not capable of proof and much of the apparent increase may be due to the greater frankness with which the subject is now approached.

In the case histories printed in Chapter I we have given a good deal of information about the sexual habits of individuals. In collecting the views about sex expressed in the 220 case histories printed, and in the 755 others which have not been printed but which have been taken into account in forming our views, and from which extracts printed in this chapter have been taken, special care was taken to test the truth of the statements made by the persons interviewed, for it was felt that they were more likely to be untruthful on the subject of sex than on any other. Any doubtful cases were rejected and we feel confident of the accuracy of our information as far as it goes.

In the matter of sexual promiscuity we have noticed considerable regional differences. In the first place, as might be expected, it is less prevalent in rural areas than in large towns, for the anonymity of town dwellers protects individuals from the condemnation and scorn of their neighbours in a way that is unknown in the country. This is not to say that sexual promiscuity is unknown, or even rare, in the country; it is less open, opportunities are less and therefore on the whole it is less frequent.

In some areas there is an almost Puritan degree of condemnation of sexual promiscuity, and in such places we believe that public opinion is strong enough to make it an infrequent practice. Such areas are not always rural; for example, in a visit to the coal-mining area of the Rhondda Valley we were informed in various villages, by persons representing every section of the community, that in that area great emphasis was placed on sexual morality and that it was the most important single factor by which the community assessed the behaviour of individuals. In England and Wales as a whole, however, this is certainly not the case.

Acts of sexual promiscuity fall normally under two headings, and it is convenient in this chapter to consider them under those headings, namely, as acts of specific association or as prostitution. By specific association we mean the action of two specific individuals who have sexual intercourse and who, whatever their motive, at that time each desired to have intercourse exclusively with the other. In prostitution on the other hand, not only is the intercourse granted in exchange for money, but the person receiving the money is indifferent within broad limits to the identity, nature and personality of the person paying the money, and is indeed usually willing to accept intercourse with a rapid succession of different persons provided each can pay the desired sum.

Specific association

Although, as we have pointed out, direct evidence on which to base an estimate of the amount of sexual promiscuity other than prostitution is extremely difficult to obtain, some startling facts bearing on the subject are given in the Registrar General's Statistical Review of England and Wales for the years 1938 and 1939. In that review it is shown that nearly 30 per cent of all first-born children are conceived out of wedlock. Nearly one-third of them (i.e., broadly speaking, one in ten of all first-born children) are born illegitimate, but over two-thirds of the mothers who have conceived their first-born children out of wedlock legitimize them by marrying before the birth of the child. If the number of marriages contracted in these circumstances is related to the total number of marriages, it appears that in 1939, the latest year for which figures are available, one bride in every six was pregnant on her wedding day. As the intervening years have largely been a time of war and disruption, it is unlikely that the situation has improved since 1939 and it may well have worsened. When it is realized that sexual irregularities actually resulting in the birth of children must be a very small proportion of the total number of cases of illicit sexual intercourse, the facts quoted provide a measure of the magnitude of the problem we are considering in this chapter.

Cases of specific association may be classified under three headings, with which we propose to deal in turn:

(*a*) *Long-term associations*. These occur when two persons who either do not wish to marry, or more often are unable to do so because one is already married, accept each other as respectively lover and mistress, and in that relationship remain faithful to each other. As the term "unmarried wife" has been accepted in certain Government departments to describe women living openly and permanently with men to whom they are not married, and as Parliament has voted public money for the support of some such "unmarried wives" (e.g., marriage allowances when they are living with men in the armed forces), we do not include them in our consideration of persons indulging in sexual promiscuity, for, whatever the moral and legal positions, they have—largely through the necessity of providing for them during the war—gained recognition of their status amounting to a degree of respectability. In compiling our case histories a substantial number of long-term associations came to our notice of which the following can serve as examples:

(i) Mr. X. is married but separated from his wife. He holds a much respected professional position and though his wife would like a divorce Mr. X. refuses to have one as he fears it would harm his position in the world. For over five years he has been the lover of Miss Y., a highly educated and wealthy young woman who is infatuated by him. Mr. X. is completely self-centred and refuses to give up his association with Miss Y. (which is known to her parents and disapproved of by them), and is impervious to pleas that he is wrecking her prospects and—since she is neurotic—her health. Miss Y. has left home and has taken a flat near to Mr. X's. residence, and he visits her there at somewhat infrequent intervals. He refuses to be seen with her in public.

(ii) Mrs. Q. is a Roman Catholic, unhappily married to a man a good deal older than herself. She has accepted financial help and advice for years from a man to whom she was engaged before she met Mr. Q., and about a year ago he became her lover. Mrs. Q. does not care much for her lover but if she stopped sexual intercourse with him she is afraid he might go away and she needs his help.

(iii) Miss P. has a small flat which she shares with a female friend. She is in full-time employment but finds it difficult to make both ends meet. She is in love with a man who has no interest in her and she is unhappy. Two years ago she met another man, Mr. W., who would like to marry her but for whom she has no feeling beyond a mild liking. As Mr. W. is obviously very unhappy Miss P. allows him to sleep with her at the flat one or two nights a week. Asked whether her female friend did not object to this arrangement she replied, "Oh no. She quite often has one or other of her own boy friends in for the night."

(*b*) *Casual pick-ups.* Our investigations have shown us that there is a good deal of sexual promiscuity between people who become casually acquainted, spend a few hours together, and then either never meet again or greet each other indifferently almost as strangers. Sometimes, but by no means always, these "adventures" are begun under the influence of alcohol. Many persons who indulge in them do so only rarely and after long periods of continence. To others they are a frequent and almost normal activity. The habit of "picking up" is not confined to the poorer classes of the community, indeed, one young professional man bemoaning his lack of success said, "For a good pick-up you really need either a flat or a car, and I haven't got either." Often there is considerable disparity in the social classes to which "picker" and "picked" belong, but it would be wrong to imagine that the male is always the pacemaker—quite often the woman takes the initiative.

"Pick-ups" occur almost anywhere that people congregate, such as streets, public houses, restaurants, cinemas and trains. Our records include the following cases:

(i) Miss W., middle-class, aged about 30, travelled alone in a railway compartment with a grey-haired man who was rather distinguished-looking. They started a conversation and rapidly became friendly. On reaching the terminus (about 9 p.m.), instead of going to their respective homes they went first to a restaurant and then to the man's office in the West End of London, where they had sexual intercourse. They left the office at 1 a.m. and, in Miss W.'s words, "Parted good friends."

(ii) Miss X., aged about 25, and a female friend went into a public house for a drink, which they bought at the counter and carried to a table. After about fifteen minutes, during which they had several times caught the eye of two young men standing at the bar, the latter joined them at the table. After a few more drinks, Miss X. went off with one of the men. They went to several public houses and eventually to a cheap hotel, where the management is used to couples arriving without luggage. They spent the night together in the hotel.

(*c*) *Sexual promiscuity within a circle of friends.* It happens not infrequently that persons addicted to sexual promiscuity will practise it within a circle of friends similarly addicted, not going outside that circle but not being faithful to any particular individual within it. It seems likely that this is mainly restricted to young unmarried persons, although one case came to our notice where the "circle" consisted of seven married couples who were quite frankly promiscuous among themselves.

Effect of bad housing

Before going on to deal with prostitution, we wish to refer briefly to the degrading effect of bad housing on sexual morality. On a number of occasions in our case histories, young people who had grown up in areas where housing standards are very low referred to the fact that as a matter of course they, and their acquaintances similarly placed, had become sexually promiscuous at a very early age, quite often when 15 years old, and sometimes even earlier. An experienced officer of the Metropolitan Police, who acted as our guide on a tour of one area of London where housing conditions are very bad, confirmed the accuracy of what we had been told.

The subject of housing is outside the scope of this book, but where people live in slum-like conditions, as many hundreds of thousands of persons still do, normal decency is almost unattainable. In such areas young people who have never had a chance of learning to respect themselves or others, will inevitably become promiscuous almost immediately the physical urge develops.

Prostitution

Prostitution is a subject about which it is extremely easy to get inaccurate information and correspondingly difficult to arrive at the truth. Through the kindness of the Chief Commissioner we were able to get valuable information from the Metropolitan Police. To supplement it, and to obtain a picture from a rather less official viewpoint, we obtained the help of Miss Susan Garth, a free-lance journalist who had already made a special study of prostitution and had made the acquaintance of many prostitutes and had gained their confidence.

Prostitution by itself is not an offence against the law. Women can, however, be charged with soliciting and causing annoyance to a person or persons, with obstruction, or with using insulting words or behaviour. A number of convictions under one or more of these headings are necessary before a woman can be classified in the police court charge sheet as a common prostitute. The maximum legal penalty for the offences with which prostitutes can be charged in connection with their activities as such is a fine of £2, and this is not sufficient to act in any way as a deterrent. Prostitutes regard their periodical fines as merely part of their out-of-pocket expenses, and the Metropolitan Police told us that some women have been fined as many as 150 times.

There are probably few towns of any considerable size without some prostitutes but usually the proportion is higher in the great cities. In some towns, such as seaports and garrison towns, the proportion of prostitutes to the total population is abnormally high, while in others, such as the principal cathedral cities, it is abnormally low. In the big cities there is often a recognized area where prostitutes walk the streets in search of customers and this area is frequently close to the main railway stations. In the small towns, where "street-walkers" would be unduly conspicuous, prostitutes often sit in public houses and make their contacts there.

Prostitution is usually thought of as a feature of night life but, at any rate in big cities, it flourishes also by day, and indeed Miss Garth's enquiries elicited the fact that some of the better-class prostitutes do their most remunerative business between 11 a.m. and 6 p.m.

Although most persons letting flats and rooms, even in dubious neighbourhoods, immediately turn out any tenants if they find that they are prostitutes, there is a small class of landlords who let premises at exorbitant rents to women who they know perfectly well will use them for the practice of prostitution. It is an offence against the law for a man to live directly on the immoral earnings of women but landlords whose rent comes from that source commit no offence.

From the facts provided by the police and from Miss Garth's researches, we estimate that in London, where the incidence of prostitution is probably higher than anywhere else in Britain, there are some 10,000 prostitutes of whom 2,000 trade in the West End. Their prices vary from about £5 for a session of some 20 minutes, in the expensive areas, down to quite small sums in poor districts. Most of the women are between 18 and 40 years of age, but in exceptional cases prostitutes continue their trade to a much greater age. Miss Garth told us of one prostitute whose convictions date back "for the past 40 years" so that she cannot be much less than sixty. According to the police the incomes of successful prostitutes "seldom fall below £20 a day when they are 'working'" (i.e., carrying on their trade), and it must be remembered that they pay no income tax. French prostitutes, who provide a strong contingent in the West End of London, often "work" diligently and save hard to reach some target figure, sometimes in the region of £12,000, which they not infrequently want as a dowry for marriage after their return to France.

Even if, in every town, prostitutes were as numerous proportionately as they are in London, which is almost certainly not the case, the total number in Britain would be quite small, perhaps 60,000 or 70,000, but their importance far transcends their numbers. In London alone it is probably not an exaggeration to say that, in times of reasonable prosperity, the 10,000 or so prostitutes have intercourse in exchange for money with upwards of 250,000 men every week. This formidable total is the real measure of the great evil that prostitution represents. Lest it should be thought that we exaggerate, we think it worth quoting a statement made to us by a Chief Inspector of the Metropolitan Police. When searching a prostitute's room in connection with a certain charge, he found a box containing 37 gross of rubber contraceptives. The woman explained that she purchased them in bulk for economy and added that she used them at the rate of a gross a week.

The whole outlook of prostitutes and the circumstances of their lives are so remote from the understanding of thoughtful and respectable citizens that we think it worth giving the following information about three women typical of different classes of prostitutes:

(*a*) Mrs. R. is 20 years of age. She married at the age of 17 and has a child who is living with her mother. She is no longer supported by her husband although she sees him occasionally and they are quite friendly. She became a prostitute at the age of 18 and is in the highest class of her trade. She pays £10 a week for a room near her beat, to which she conducts her customers, but she herself lives in another district in a bed-sitting room. She keeps the two sides of her existence, "work" and home, quite distinct. Of her trade she says, "It's all right. You can earn good money, and spend it fast, too. I'm not doing any harm to anyone. There's nothing wrong in it. We've got to live." Nevertheless she doesn't want her mother to find out what she is doing as "she wouldn't like it very much." Mrs. R. complains that competition is getting too keen as "there's a lot of girls coming on the streets now." Mrs. R. is not interested in religion or politics and she says that her "ambition" is to save up enough for "a nice holiday abroad." She "likes reading," but her only reading matter is American comics and women's magazines.

(*b*) Mrs. H. is a middle-class prostitute in a big city. She is 29 and lives apart from her husband because he cannot earn enough to keep her in comfort. He would like her to return to him and is willing to overlook her present mode of life but she says that she prefers her freedom. She has two sons who live with her sister and she is anxious to earn enough to give them a good education and also hopes to save enough to live comfortably in her old age. Most of her evening customers are men in their twenties, rather flashy and affected, the sort who frequent dog tracks and public houses. She reckons to have four or five of these customers a night at a charge of £2 or £3 each. She claims also to have a day-time clientèle of well-to-do professional men, and though this may be partly true, she probably exaggerates a good deal when talking of her "gentlemen customers." She lives in a bed-sitting room at a cost of £3 a week but cannot take her customers there. She has no "business" premises and if her customers cannot take her to their rooms or flats she takes them into a park near her beat. Having no place indoors to take them, Mrs. H's. trade is heavily affected by bad weather. She sees nothing wrong in her way of life and maintains that she does good to her customers. She says, "I'm better than a Harley Street specialist for them, and I cost less."

(*c*) Mrs. D. is a working-class prostitute in a small town. She sits in the corner of the saloon bar of an otherwise quite respectable public house and waits for men to get into conversation with her. She is coarse and unattractive in appearance, aged 45 at the least. She still lives, on and off, with her husband, who provides for her even when they are apart, and she has two grown-up children. She takes her customers home with her quite openly, but does not trouble to "work" more than three or four nights a week. She says, very likely truthfully, that she is just as anxious for company as she is to make money. She says her neighbours are "standoffish" with her because of her trade, but she herself sees no harm in it. Her son won't have anything to do with her "since he married a stuck-up piece of goods," but her daughter lives with her and often has her male friends in for the night, but she is "young and silly" and "won't take money from them."

We do not wish to prolong our discussion of this unpleasant subject, but we should not adequately fulfil our task if we failed to point out that the men who comprise the customers of the prostitutes are by no means only the young and foolish. Many apparently staid and respectable citizens are among them and the sight of such men prowling in search of some favoured prostitute seems to us to be an even greater degradation of human dignity than the peregrinations of the prostitutes themselves.

Perversion

It is almost impossible to get valid evidence about the incidence of homosexualism and other forms of sexual perversion because some of them, such as sodomy, are forbidden by law, and when detected are punished by imprisonment. Sometimes homosexual practices are commercialized, and are then the equivalent of prostitution. More often they are indulged in by acquaintances for their mutual satisfaction. All persons with whom we have discussed the matter, including the police, agree that there is a good deal of homosexuality, but neither they nor we can estimate its real extent. It is only necessary to see a few of the unfortunate persons who have become addicted to it to realize how demoralizing and degenerating an influence it is.

The Armed Forces

We have no doubt that the civilian heads of the Armed Forces, and senior officers in general, both at the ministries and commanding in the field, are as fully aware of the evils of sexual promiscuity as any other thoughtful citizens. They are, however, primarily concerned with maintaining the full physical effectiveness of those under them, and for this reason are sometimes tempted to take the view that all is comparatively well provided officers and men are not incapacitated by venereal disease. To maintain physical health the practice was started some years before the recent war of making free issues of rubber contraceptives (which are at least a partial protection against venereal disease) to any officers and men who asked for them when going on leave, whether such leave was for a few hours only or for a longer period. Where this system was adopted it had a substantial effect in reducing venereal disease, but to make it effective the issues of the contraceptives had to be made in such a way that there was no suggestion that sexual promiscuity was morally reprehensible. Any condemnation would have scared away a proportion of the applicants and would thus have defeated the object. We feel that despite the reduction of venereal disease that was achieved in normal times, this system is open to the gravest objections on moral grounds, for it must appear as a full condonation by the authorities of sexual promiscuity and is indeed a positive encouragement of it. As the contraceptives are paid for out of public funds, it is strange that it has not been more seriously challenged.

We certainly do not wish to be alarmist, but the high figures of venereal disease in the British military forces serving overseas are evidence that in matters of sexual morality something is gravely wrong in the Army, and we know of no reason for thinking that, with similar temptations, sailors and airmen would be more continent than soldiers. In *The Spectator* of 8th August 1947, Lord Moran, in an article entitled "V.D. and Conscription," gave the following figures showing the incidence of venereal disease among British army personnel serving overseas, stating that the figures were accepted by the Army Medical Department of the War Office:

Serving in Japan	22·8	per cent
Serving in Germany	18·5	,,
Serving in Austria and Italy	16·8	,,
Serving in Burma and Malaya	14·1	,,

Although it may well be that since that date a substantial reduction has been obtained, even if they were halved, the figures would still be evidence of grave moral evil, for it is certain that only a fraction of men who indulge in sexual promiscuity contract a disease. The full gravity of this matter only becomes apparent when it is remembered that the military forces overseas are not now composed of seasoned troops but largely of National Service men—mere youths of 19 who may be forming habits that they will bring back to civilian life.

What harm does it do?

As we stated earlier, it is almost impossible to give an authoritative opinion about whether sexual promiscuity is more widespread than it used to be, or whether the appearance that it is so is due to a reduced desire for concealment. We are however on safe ground if we say that, whatever change may or may not have taken place in the amount of sexual promiscuity, there has been a considerable change in the point of view of many, possibly of the majority, of people about whether or not it is wrong. Formerly even people who were promiscuous recognized that society had definite fixed standards, and that their personal behaviour in outraging those standards was wrong in an absolute sense. With the decay of absolute standards, following on the decline in religious belief, of which we have much to say later in the book, people have tended to say of sexual promiscuity, "What after all is the harm?" Some people, an important group but a minority, will no doubt continue to be restrained from sexual promiscuity by religious beliefs. For those who have none, or whose beliefs are not sufficiently strong to be reflected in their conduct; it is not difficult to find purely secular and social reasons why sexual promiscuity can still categorically be condemned as wrong. In our view this condemnation falls under three headings:

(*a*) It is usually grossly selfish. It is the supreme example of the pursuit of personal pleasure without concern for the effect on others. This is obvious in cases such as promiscuity leading to illegitimate births, or abortions, or to the spread of diseases. It is equally true, although less obvious, in other cases; for example, it often forces one of the partners to be deceitful at home and sets up barriers in family life. Furthermore, it not infrequently involves the exploitation of the personality of one of the individuals concerned for the satisfaction of the other.

(*b*) In the large majority of cases it is a purely animal satisfaction without the psychological or spiritual element that is the quintessence of sexual union as ideally practised. Any glorification of the purely animal part of man inevitably lowers his ideals and weakens his character.

(*c*) It is an obsessional activity, the desire for which grows with indulgence, so that it can, and in many cases does, end by becoming a consuming interest to the satisfaction of which are sacrificed energy, time, money and thought that should have been harnessed to constructive purposes.

A future problem

One aspect of the problem of sexual promiscuity is likely to become even more acute in the future, and strangely enough as a direct result of one of the benefits conferred on mankind by medical science. There can be no doubt that at present the fear of venereal disease is a strong factor in making many persons either refrain from sexual promiscuity or indulge in it less frequently than they otherwise would. There is, however, a widespread belief that science, largely through the discovery of the sulphonamide and similar drugs and of penicillin, is on the verge of conquering the venereal diseases so that even the worst of them would become quite trivial. If this belief should be fulfilled, the community will be faced with a much more serious problem, and there is little sign at the moment that people will be prepared to face the moral issues involved. Abstention due to fear may be less worthy than abstention due to self-discipline, but it is at least better than indulgence through lack of fear. Naturally everyone hopes earnestly that science will overcome the horrible venereal diseases, but as the possibility becomes gradually translated into probability, and then into certainty, a prudent nation would also remember that a restraining force was being removed and that in consequence the moral issue would become more vitally urgent.

Aims for the future

Quite apart from the question as to whether sexual promiscuity is more widespread now than it used to be, to which we have already said there is no decisive answer, we can safely say that it is a great deal more prevalent than is desirable if the quality of life in Britain is to be that of a great and vigorous nation. Sexual excesses are both a symptom of national weakness and a powerful secondary cause of it. As in so many other fields of activity, the best hope for the future would appear to be to concentrate on the young people who have not yet contracted bad habits. Efforts to prevent them from doing so might well take three forms:

(*a*) A reduction of the powerful encouragements of sexual promiscuity that are now offered to young people in a variety of ways. For example:

(i) There is eroticism in certain newspapers.

(ii) Sex is often treated by adults as a subject for a

sniggering type of jest, and adolescents absorb an unhealthy attitude to it.

(iii) Films, and to a lesser extent plays, sometimes have undesirable scenes. A single scene can do widespread harm.

(iv) Contraceptives of different kinds are offered openly for sale, and are displayed in the windows of even reputable chemists. They are sometimes advertised, *inter alia*, in publicly owned transport vehicles, and though the advertisements are discreet, being restricted to the trade name of the article without any description, they help to build up sales, for otherwise money would not be spent on them.

(*b*) People are usually more idealistic in adolescence, and for some years afterwards, than they are at any other time of their lives. Considerable advantages might accrue from an advertising campaign, on the lines of the Ministry of Health's campaign against venereal disease. The campaign would be conducted on hoardings, in the press, by means of pamphlets and perhaps by such means as broadcast talks and discussion groups. The aim of the campaign would not be to give factual education about sex; this, as we suggest below, should be given in other ways. The aim would be to appeal to and reinforce the idealism of young people, with the object of making them feel that illicit sexual relations, whether with prostitutes or otherwise, are unworthy of them. We showed in Chapter III the substantial effect on the material plane of the brewers' advertising campaign in favour of beer. Although what we have in mind would be much more difficult, we nevertheless believe that a well-conducted campaign in favour of chastity could also be successful, and might be a powerful factor in improving the nation's moral fibre. But if such a campaign were undertaken, it could not be successful if planned parsimoniously. The brewers were successful because their advertising was highly efficient; a campaign for chastity could not be run on the cheap.

(*c*) Factual education. Sex is still surrounded for many adolescents by an atmosphere of mystery and stealth. Factual education would help to create a healthy understanding and to put the whole subject into a proper perspective. In many ways well-informed parents are the ideal persons to give factual education, but unfortunately many of them lack the combination of qualities necessary for the purpose, and many others shirk the duty. In the circumstances schools, youth clubs and, when they are established, county colleges seem to be the places where that education can best be given, of which the dual aims will be to prevent "experimenting through curiosity," and the forming through ignorance of bad habits that cannot subsequently be eradicated.

It may be thought that the foregoing proposals are an uninspired way of dealing with the situation, but they are practical measures, and it is reasonable to expect that, if they were persisted in over a period of time, they would make a substantial contribution to the reduction of sexual promiscuity. But for a fundamental cure we must look elsewhere, to a revival of the nation's spiritual life, and to a consequent rejection of the selfishness and hedonism that are the basic attributes of those who are promiscuous. In Chapter XIII we discuss the chances of such a spiritual revival.

CHAPTER VI

HOW HONEST IS BRITAIN?

For generations past the British people have enjoyed a world-wide reputation for honesty, so great that, before the days of Exchange Control, an unknown Englishman's cheque would be accepted in almost any great city in the world. The idea of English integrity has been so high that it has even found expression in some foreign languages, such as the *mot anglais* of the French, to denote a promise that would not in any circumstances be broken.

In consequence of the long years of unquestioned integrity, the British have come to think of themselves as an absolutely honest nation, and to a very large extent that idea still prevails.

When considering the subjects we should deal with in this book, we thought that there would be no need for us to deal with the question of honesty, because, except for a small criminal class, we believed that people in Britain were honest. We were advised, however, not to take that fact as true without enquiring further about it, and the results of our enquiries are set out in this chapter.

It is stated in the *Annual Abstract of Statistics* that the indictable offences known by the police to have been committed in England and Wales rose from 266,265 in 1937, to 415,010 in 1944, to 498,576 in 1947, and to 522,684 in 1948. Apart from a drop of about 1 per cent from 1945 to 1946, there has been a steady rise in every year covered by the latest edition of the *Annual Abstract of Statistics*, 1938–48.

Although some of the offences are comparatively minor in nature, it is alarming to reflect that on the average one citizen in every 83 in England and Wales committed an indictable offence in 1948. Even worse is the high incidence of young persons among those guilty of these offences. Of all persons against whom indictable offences were proved in the courts in 1948, 34·3 per cent were under the age of 17 years, and a further 11·6 per cent were between 17 and 21.

Our main concern has, however, been with what may be potentially a much more serious matter, namely, with those actions of ostensibly honest citizens that give evidence of a recession from the high standards of the past and seem to be caused by an acceptance of lower moral standards than hitherto.

Our enquiry resolved itself into two separate parts: (1) Is the standard of honesty in business higher, lower, or the same as it was? (2) What is the standard of honesty in private lives?

Honesty in business

To make our assessment of the level of honesty in business to-day we consulted a banker, two industrialists with widely different interests, and an accountant—all of them eminent persons in their particular fields of activity. All four of them were in agreement that the standard of honesty in business is extremely high. We think it worth quoting the accountant, whose main views are broadly shared by the other persons consulted:

"Taking the country as a whole, the standard of honesty in business in Great Britain is higher than in any foreign country of which I have personal experience. In high financial circles in London the standard is extremely high. On the whole, perhaps, the standard of honesty in business is higher in the South than in the North. In London and other southern cities a tremendous amount of business is done purely on the basis of a gentleman's agreement, but in the big industrial cities of the Midlands and North there is some evidence of the idea that sharp practice in business is legitimate and even clever, provided it does not go outside the limits of the law."

We also consulted the Bribery and Secret Commissions Prevention League, of which the aims are obvious from its name, and which makes a constant and detailed study of its subject. We were informed that there is no corruption in British commercial life, and that there is the same high standard of commercial honesty as before the war. Our informant added that civil servants, and the professional classes in general, are still quite incorruptible.

Personal integrity

Our next concern was to ascertain how honest people are in their private lives and to do this we made two separate enquiries:

(*a*) From persons who in the course of business come into contact with large numbers of persons from different classes of the community.

(*b*) From individuals about their own habits.

Neither of these enquiries was on a large scale, but the information obtained showed so consistently that there is a great amount of petty dishonesty that we decided no useful purpose would be served by multiplying our enquiries. It is possible, however, that there may be local variations, both for better and for worse, in the situation we describe below. As we have made no enquiries on this subject in Wales, our remarks should be taken to apply only to England, where we gathered our information in small towns and rural areas as well as in large towns.

Before giving the results of our enquiries, we must point out that the frankness with which individuals described their own petty dishonesty startled us, until we realized that the persons making the admissions fell into two classes—those who did not consider that they were dishonest, and those who thought that their dishonesty was rather clever and therefore creditable. The widespread existence of these two attitudes of mind, the complacent and the "smart," seems to us in itself to be a significant fact.

Views of knowledgeable persons about public honesty

Once we had explained to the persons whom we consulted that we were not dealing with the sort of dishonesty that ordinarily lands people in the police court, but with the strict degree of honesty that might be expected from a nation whose moral fibre is really sound, none of them would go so far as to say that people in general are strictly honest. The following are a selection from the views expressed to us, and the facts related:

(*a*) The manageress of a seaside hotel catering for upper middle-class people told us that in her hotel, where there are 100 beds in about 70 rooms, she has lost over 10,000 coat-hangers in 15 years. At present prices she can no longer afford to provide coat-hangers.

(*b*) The man in charge of a medium-sized provincial Y.M.C.A. branch told us that he regularly has to renew the electric light bulbs three times each week in the wash-places and water-closets, as they are stolen.

(*c*) The managing director of a firm running a number of restaurants for middle-class and upper middle-class people related how his firm had fitted up the ladies' cloakroom of a restaurant with tasteful decorations, which included a piece of lace worth £5 under the glass top of a dressing-table. The lace vanished the first day the ladies' room was open, and even the curtains were stolen in due course.

(*d*) A man with more than 35 years' experience of work in educational settlements and clubs for working-class youths said that he had a poor opinion of the standard of contemporary honesty, particularly among children. "People nowadays see no harm at all in dishonesty, and they give no thought to the inherent wrongfulness of being dishonest, nor to the harm they might be doing to others. This was not the case to anything like the same extent thirty years ago." He added, "To an overwhelming extent the motto of young people to-day is, 'I see, I want, I take.' "

(*e*) The lavatory attendant in the men's cloakroom of a restaurant catering entirely for an upper middle-class and upper-class clientèle told us, "The soap, the nail brushes and the hand towels here are all mine. I have to buy them myself and I keep my eye on them. If I didn't the whole lot would go. Even then I've known customers take them when my back was turned—not often, mind you, for I don't take many risks."

(*f*) A man running a medium-sized canteen for men, most of whom are working or lower middle-class, said, "As a result of ten years' experience I conclude that the *average* customer is dishonest. For example, only a minority would ever tell you if you gave them too much change."

(*g*) A man of great experience in youth work, who had devoted some years to running residential training courses for youths who showed some natural aptitude for leadership, told us that in his experience most young people consider that pilfering and scrounging are not stealing, and are not wrong. The only thing that is wrong is to be found out. Our informant emphasized that this does not apply only to a small class of delinquents, but to the large majority of ordinary working-class lads.

(*h*) A stipendiary magistrate told us that in his court one of the most striking features is the lack of an ethical standard in contemporary life. Youths in general seem to be amoral. They say, "I wanted that, so I took it." (These words are a remarkable echo of the view expressed to us by another informant recorded in (*d*) above.)

(*i*) A senior executive officer of British Railways talked to us about losses on the railways. The facts are generally well known, and we will not repeat them here at length, recording merely that the articles stolen annually by passengers include a vast number of electric light bulbs (which are of course useless to the thieves, being the wrong voltage and being designed for a special kind of holder), thousands of mirrors, ash-trays and window-blinds (possibly used for such purposes as repairing chairs), as well as spoons, cups and almost anything that is portable. It seems to us to be a striking comment on the contemporary level of honesty that, as we were informed, British Railways cannot even contemplate putting small hand towels in the lavatories of trains because they would be quite unable to stand the rate of loss through theft.

(*j*) Having been much impressed by the way that in many towns piles of newspapers, particularly evening papers, are left unattended for customers to help themselves and leave a penny, we asked three of such vendors whether they suffered serious losses. They all gave much the same answer, which was to the effect that the papers must be left in a very public and well-lighted spot. People who might either take a paper without paying, or steal some of the accumulated pennies, are afraid of being seen. Even so, the newspaper men all stated that unless the coppers are collected when there is about a shilling's worth, the money is usually short. One newspaper man said that a favourite trick, when there is an unusually large pile of coppers, is to put down threepence and take change for sixpence.

(*k*) The managing director of a luxury hotel told us that losses from his hotel are very slight. A certain number of coat-hangers are taken and a few electric light bulbs, ash-trays, hand towels and table napkins, but not to an extent that is in any way serious.

(*l*) The warden of a provincial establishment offering advanced courses in further education told us that there is a steady, though not large, rate of loss of toilet rolls from water-closets. In this connection it is interesting that one large manufacturing firm whose products are world-famous has thought it worth while to design and market a device for holding toilet rolls, described in a pamphlet advertising it as follows:

"The holder is pilfer-proof in two senses; toilet rolls cannot be stolen from it, and its removal from the wall is a matter of the utmost difficulty. . . . Altogether the holder offers considerable saving to the buyer in eliminating waste and loss due to pilferage. It is attractive in appearance and is eminently suitable for use in factories, schools, hotels, and public lavatories generally."

Individual habits

Now we turn to consider the reverse aspect of petty pilfering of the kind we have just been discussing, with the object of showing what sort of people engage in these dishonest activities, and what they themselves think about them. Naturally, a large proportion, probably a majority, of the persons whom we approached on the subject, claim to be, and very likely are, completely honest. On the other hand a substantial number, that at least constitutes an important minority, admit freely to some form or other of minor dishonesty, of which the following are a fair sample:

(i) Two sisters, each in part-time employment, one in the forenoon and one in the afternoon, and both living at home, share one season ticket for their local bus service, handing it from one to the other at dinner time when they are both at home.

(ii) A naval officer working in a large town and living some distance away by rail said that by a judicious purchase of return tickets, third and first, he could practically always travel first-class on a third-class ticket, safe in the knowledge that if a ticket collector ever challenged him he always had a first-class ticket in reserve in his wallet. Asked to explain further, he said that on each first-class ticket that, after challenge, he had to surrender, he made about fifteen to twenty first-class journeys with a third-class ticket.

(iii) A middle-class housewife, who is normally absolutely honest, ordered her week's groceries from the local Co-operative Society branch. She said, "I'll take the biscuits, and you can send the rest." When the order arrived, it included a second supply of biscuits, which she kept because, "After all, nobody lost on it, the Co-op. belongs to us all, doesn't it?"

(iv) A waitress working in a good-class restaurant gave one of us

(G.R.L.) tea in her small and rather shabby flat. When asked if she could really spare the generous quantity of butter, sugared cakes, and so on that she offered, she said, "Blimey, you should see my kitchen. Come on, have a look." The kitchen contained butter, eggs, chicken, sugar, cheese, cakes and fruit in appreciable quantity. The waitress said, "Nobody misses it you know. It's only a bit for me and my friends. I wouldn't do it serious like, for selling or nothing of that sort."

(v) A working-class man, who was a personal friend of a builder and decorator in a small way of business, helped him when he was short of labour to decorate a house. The builder later complained that certain planks had vanished while his lorry was on its way to pick them up. The man in question helped the builder to look for them, but when all the enquiries were ended the man told one of us, "I fooled him proper. I've used the planks for my new hen-house."

(vi) When one of us was visiting a lower middle-class home in connection with our investigations, the son of the house, aged about 9, who was scribbling in a book, suddenly said, "Daddy, why do all the pencils and rubbers you bring me have 'Service Only' marked on them." The father explained that the mark was 'S.O.' (meaning Stationery Office) and that as a civil servant he was able to keep the home supplied with stationery.

(vii) One of us witnessed an altercation in a grocer's shop between a working-class woman and the shopkeeper, she maintaining that she had not had her bacon ration, he maintaining that she had. The grocer was adamant and the woman left the shop. Seen afterwards, she was quite cheerful. She said, "Oh yes. I had it last Tuesday, but it's worth trying, isn't it?"

Shoplifting

We said at the beginning of this chapter that we were not concerned here with actions recognized as criminal, but we feel obliged to make some mention of shoplifting, because we are assured that, except for a small number of professional shop-lifters, most of the persons who steal from shops are not dishonest in any other way, and indeed hardly consider shop-lifting to be theft. A London stipendiary magistrate, who was talking to us about shoplifting, said that the majority of the persons charged before him with stealing from shops were ordinary decent housewives, who had yielded to the temptation of what appeared to be an easy chance of getting something for nothing. He added that his experience, and that of his colleagues in other London courts, was that severe punishment of persons detected was the only deterrent to shoplifting.

Some idea of the magnitude of the evil is given by the fact that in one women's dress shop in the West End of London 5,000 garments are stolen every year, equivalent to 16 for every day the shop is open. In one large general store in London one of the directors informed us that they employ 12 full-time detectives without whose activities losses from shoplifting would seriously affect the successful trading of the company. His words were, "If we didn't keep the matter under strict control we should be sunk." In yet another case we were informed that a certain multiple store, with branches throughout the country, suffered losses of as much as £300,000 in a year.

A comparatively recent development in shoplifting has been its extension on a large scale to bookshops, and the same stipendiary magistrate informed us that the persons convicted by him in recent months for stealing from bookshops included a dental surgeon, a schoolmaster, a fairly senior civil servant and a minister of religion. Thefts from large bookshops have been so serious that some at least of them now employ house detectives to protect their property from ostensible customers.

What is the standard of honesty?

We are now in a position to make an estimate of what is the general standard of honesty in England to-day. Despite all the foregoing examples, most of which relate to petty thefts, there is still a great deal of reason for satisfaction. First and foremost our judicial system is second to none in the world for integrity and impartiality. Likewise the Government and the civil service are above any suspicion of corruption, and the public enquiry early in 1949, presided over by Mr. Justice Lynskey, demonstrated how the Government, Parliament and and nation are determined to tolerate no recession from the present high standard. Finally, we have had assurances from persons in different occupations, but all in a position to know the facts, that the standard of honesty in commerce and industry is high. In other words in the national and public life of Britain there is no present cause for anxiety on the score of dishonesty.

But in the private lives of the people the situation is less satisfactory for there is abundant evidence that a great many individuals, actuated by a desire to obtain goods or services without giving anything in exchange, are dishonest in many small ways. There is no means of knowing how large a proportion of the nation is dishonest in petty ways, but we have been greatly impressed by the apparently widespread nature of this dishonesty, and by the otherwise high standing of many of the individuals who yield to it. Since the theft of a book by a clergyman, or an attempt by a naval officer to defraud British Railways, has news value, it is easy to exaggerate the volume and importance of the petty dishonesty we have described. Nevertheless it is probably enough in volume to indicate some lowering of the moral tone of the nation, which bodes ill for the future. This is particularly so if we remember that young people seem to be more affected than their elders, and that their attitude has been described to us in the graphic phrase, "I see, I want, I take."

The fact that in our public life and in business the standard of honesty has not declined, although it has done so in private life, can only mean that we are living nationally on what might be called "moral capital accumulated in the past." Unless the present tendency in private life can be reversed, there seems little hope of the maintenance for many more decades of the present high standard of integrity in public life.

Why are people dishonest?

As we have already pointed out, widespread dishonesty is evidence of an unsatisfactory moral outlook. The fact that many goods are difficult to obtain, and others are much more expensive than they used to be, naturally increases the temptation to be dishonest, but we must look further for the reason why so many people are not only yielding to the temptation but also see no reason why they should not do so.

Among those whom we asked to answer this question for us was a man of 80, wise and kindly, old enough to look back over three generations, and although not highly educated, having a wide understanding of his fellow men. He said:

"I believe that unless people are restrained by some active religious belief or are disciplined by fear, they will always be dishonest. When I was a boy we were taught to be afraid of hell. When I became a man I decided that the religious teaching I had received was not true, and I became an agnostic. But even then I wished with all my heart that the religious teaching was true, because I foresaw that as more and more people ceased to believe it, every sort of crime and wickedness would grow. Looking back over eighty years I have no hesitation in saying I have watched a steady growth of dishonesty—and it is still growing. Not only has the religious belief declined, but the fear of consequences has declined, too. Prison is not so terrible a thought as it used to be. People believe that prisoners are fairly well treated and, at any rate among the class of people I know—the working-class and lower middle-class—prison is no longer thought of as something shameful. With this decline of religion and failure of discipline has come greater temptation. Not only are many things scarce, but people need more pocket money than they used to do for cinemas, cigarettes at 2d. each, beer at 1s. 2d. a pint, football pools, dog races, always travelling about by bus, and so on. All this incessant need for money puts a premium on fraud. Finally there is the effect of two wars. You can't teach people to kill, lie, cheat and steal for years on end and then expect them to be quiet, honest citizens as soon as the war is over."

We believe that our elderly friend's diagnosis is a true one and, like him, we place the principal emphasis on the decline of religious belief. Reasons for dishonesty, such as the shortage of some goods and the effect of two wars, can be cured over a period of time without undue difficulty. There is, however, no easy solution of the problem presented by the decline of religious belief, although without such a basic solution scarcely any of the major problems facing the nation can be solved. We discuss this at length in a subsequent chapter.

CHAPTER VII

THE CINEMA

THERE are about 5,000 cinemas in Great Britain[1] and they contain a total of nearly 5,000,000 seats. On the assumption, which is supported by enquiries that we have made, that each seat is occupied six times a week, the attendances in the course of a year reach the gigantic total of over 1,500,000,000.

With so huge a record of total attendances, it is perhaps surprising that 27 per cent of persons over school age never go to the cinema at all, although this is largely accounted for by the small attendance of persons over 60 years of age. This fact was among those discovered in a survey made by Kathleen Box in the spring and autumn of 1946, and published as Report NS 106 of the Social Survey. We quote from it below with the permission of the Central Office of Information, and it is the source of our figures in the next few pages, except where we indicate the contrary.

Frequency of cinema-going

The enquiry by Kathleen Box covered all parts of Great Britain, and all classes of the community. The two tables on page 229, compiled from the results of the survey, show the frequency with which persons over and under 16 years of age respectively visit a cinema.

The main bulk of those, among both adults and children, who do not go to the cinema at all are understandably found in the two extreme age groups. Thus 77 per cent of children under 4 never go to the cinema (although even at this age 4 per cent go or are taken more than twice a week). Similarly 61 per cent of adults over the age of 60 never go. If cinema-

[1] 4,692 in 1948, when many damaged during the war awaited an opportunity of rebuilding. In 1938 the number was 4,967. (*Annual Abstract of Statistics.*)

going habits are tabulated according to age group it appears that there is a steady rise in frequency from the earliest age to the 16–19 age group. Thereafter there is a steady decline, which is particularly sharp between the ages of 30 and 39, when the claims of parenthood are probably most exacting. Among persons aged 60 or over, only 11 per cent attend the cinema once a week or more often, and it is worth noting that this is a smaller percentage than in the age group 0 to 4.

PERSONS OVER 16 YEARS OF AGE

Frequency of attendance	% of sample	
	Men	Women
More than twice a week ..	3	4
Twice a week	9	10
Once a week	15	21
Once a fortnight	9	9
Once a month	9	11
Less than once a month ..	23	20
Never	32	25

PERSONS UNDER 16 YEARS OF AGE

Frequency of attendance	% of sample	
	Boys	Girls
More than twice a week ..	6	7
Twice a week	13	10
Once a week	26	26
Once a fortnight	6	7
Once a month	6	8
Less than once a month ..	9	11
Never	34	31

These figures, referring to Britain as a whole, tend to conceal the even greater importance of the cinema in the lives of urban dwellers. For example, in a special survey of the London borough of Willesden, carried out by Bertram Hutchinson for the Social Survey in the winter of 1946–7, it was found that 46 per cent of the adult population of that borough go to the cinema once a week or more often, as against 32 per cent for the country as a whole, while only 18 per cent never go, as against 27 per cent in the whole country.[1] Furthermore, in Willesden, only 39 per cent of persons aged 60 or over never go to the cinema, whereas the proportion in the whole country is 61 per cent. These differences are of some interest because they illustrate the fact that, as might have been expected, cinema-going is so frequent in an area of dense population that, in the words of the Willesden survey report, "By far the most common recreational activity was the cinema." It should not, however, be thought that because the cinema plays so important a part in the lives of those living in urban areas it is of no great significance in rural areas. Few villages are now so devoid of public transport that the cinema is inaccessible. For example, Joyce Ward, in the report *Children out of School* prepared for the Central Advisory Council for Education in the winter of 1947, pointed out that 28 per cent of children from 5 to 15 years of age living in rural areas go to the cinema once a week or more often.[2]

The cinema audience

Considering again the nation as a whole, it is possible from Kathleen Box's report already quoted to consider the composition of cinema audiences. The main fact that emerges is that having regard to educational background, occupational groups and sex, there is a remarkable parallel between the composition of cinema audiences and that of the nation as a whole. There is, however, a substantial variation in the matter of age. The proportion of young adults, particularly those between 20 and 29 years, tends to be unduly high in a cinema audience and, as already noted, older people tend to stay away. Similarly women make up 62 per cent of adult civilian cinema

[1] Social Survey Report No. NS 88, *Willesden and the New Towns*, quoted by permission of the Central Office of Information.

[2] Social Survey Report No. NS 110, *Children out of School*, quoted by permission of the Central Office of Information.

audiences, whereas they represent only 54 per cent of the population. On the whole, however, it remains true to say that to a surprising degree cinema audiences in the aggregate are composed of all sections of the community in proportions not greatly different from their relation to each other in the nation as a whole, with the exception that the proportion of young people is unduly high.

Which cinema?

Another subject about which the Box report gives information is how people decide which cinema to attend on any given occasion. The largest group of cinema-goers (48 per cent) first make up their minds that they are definitely going to a cinema, and then choose between the cinemas available to them that which is showing the film they most wish to see. The next largest group (23 per cent) go to the same cinema regularly whatever the film. Thus 71 per cent of cinema-goers are not influenced in their decision whether or not to attend a cinema by the nature of the films being shown. Of the remaining 29 per cent, the majority (19 per cent) only go to a cinema when there is a film that they particularly want to see, and they will go to the cinema in which the film is being shown provided that it is one they can reach without undue effort and of which they can afford the prices. The remaining 10 per cent always go to the same cinema but only when there is a film that they expect to enjoy.

One matter of importance concerning the choice of cinemas dealt with in the Box report should be mentioned here, namely, the extent to which parents are aware of the films which their children see. Of the mothers of children attending films, 70 per cent said, when asked, that they generally knew before letting their children go to the cinema what film they would see and 30 per cent said they did not know. As might have been expected the proportion of mothers who thus far guarded the well-being of their children was directly related to the economic class to which the mothers belonged, being nearly half as frequent again among the well-to-do as among the working-class.

Prices of seats

Naturally the price of seats varies according to the nature of the cinema. In the West End of London the charges in the principal cinemas usually vary from 4s. 6d. for the cheapest seats to 11s. 6d. for the dearest, and when there is a popular film there are long queues many times each week for all seats costing up to 9s. In suburban and provincial cinemas where the same films are shown as in the West End, but some weeks later and in rather less glamorous surroundings, prices normally range from 1s. 3d. to 3s. 6d., with intermediate prices at 1s. 10d., 2s. 4d., and 2s. 10d. In smaller cinemas, where the films are often revivals of those that were successful months or even years earlier in the larger cinemas, prices are lower, though there are now few cinemas with a minimum price of less than 1s. In the most expensive cinemas children are charged the full price of admission, but it is usual in the intermediate and cheaper cinemas for them to be admitted at a reduced price, though this privilege is sometimes restricted to children who accompany an adult. Babies in arms, who are not infrequently both seen and heard in cinemas, particularly in the afternoons, are admitted free.

In the White Paper, *National Income and Expenditure, 1946–9*, it is stated that in 1949 the public paid a total of £105 million for admission to the cinemas. This is almost exactly the same sum as was spent in that year on private motoring, and is some 45 per cent more than was spent on books and magazines of all kinds.

What do audiences see?

We now leave the statistics of cinema-going and turn to an examination of the content of films. When we started our investigations early in 1946 neither of us knew much about the cinema. We were not in any way hostile to it, but it so happened that preoccupation with other matters had prevented both of us from paying other than very infrequent visits to cinemas. We decided, however, that we must be in a position to write from first-hand knowledge, and one of us (G.R.L.) has accordingly during the course of our investigations visited

125 cinemas of all types in London (both in the West End and suburbs), High Wycombe, York, Newcastle, Carlisle, Leeds, Birmingham, Manchester, Bristol, Exeter and Exmouth. After every visit a careful analysis was made of the principal film shown, and our remarks in this section are based on those analyses. It should be added that these visits were in addition to a substantial number of visits to News Theatres, which we deal with separately on page 251.

Before discussing in some detail the nature of the films seen, we think it will be of interest to quote at length a few of the analyses themselves, so that the method adopted may be clearly understood. We have accordinaly chosen four typical ones:

(1)

1. *Name of Film* — *Passport to Pimlico.*
2. *Country of Origin* — United Kingdom.
3. *Certificate awarded by Censors*[1] — U.
4. *Length of Film* — 1½ hours.
5. *Theme* — The story of amazing happenings that follow the discovery that a street in Pimlico was granted in perpetuity to a Duke of Burgundy, as Burgundian territory. The inhabitants are in consequence still Burgundians, not subject to English law. Many amusing complications follow before the government of Burgundy negotiate with H.M.G. for the return of Burgundy to Britain.
6. *Artistic Level* — Technically excellent.
7. *Comments* — A thoroughly amusing and praiseworthy piece of nonsense. Good entertainment that is wholesome in every way.

[1] For details of censorship system and key to the letters denoting the type of certificate, see page 241.

(2)

1. *Name of Film*	*Foreign Affair.*
2. *Country of Origin*	U.S.A.
3. *Certificate awarded by Censors*	A.
4. *Length of Film*	1½ hours.
5. *Theme*	Filmed in the ruins of Berlin, this is the rather naïve story of a visiting Congressional Committee, which is charged with an enquiry into the morale and morals of the U.S. occupying troops. One member of the Committee is a woman with whom the hero—a Captain in the U.S. Army, who has a German mistress and is a regular purchaser on the black market—falls in love. When he tries to leave his mistress he is ordered back to her by his Colonel, who is using him as a decoy to draw out of hiding a leading Nazi who was a former lover of the German woman, and is jealous at being supplanted.
6. *Artistic Level*	Technically the film is raised well above average by superb acting by the female star (as the German mistress), and by the poignancy gained by exploiting the ruins as scenery. The film portrays well the deep bitterness of feeling in contemporary Berlin.
7. *Comments*	It seems curiously insensitive to put a frivolous love story against a background of such deep suffering as exists in Berlin, while the picture given of the life of the U.S. forces in the city, although presumably accurate, is unedifying. Some memory of the horror of the ruins of Berlin, and perhaps a new realization of the savagery with which the Allies fought the war, might remain with those who saw this film long after they had forgotten its plot.

(3)

1. *Name of Film*	*The Naked City.*
2. *Country of Origin*	U.S.A.
3. *Certificate awarded by Censors*	A.
4. *Length of Film*	1½ hours.
5. *Theme*	This film was made in New York and not in a studio. As a result, it is impressive in its realism. It has neither hero nor heroine and claims to be the story of one citizen of New York. In fact the citizen in question is murdered in the opening scene, and the film deals with the resolving of the murder mystery by the police. It is a factual and objective account of police work, and is not glamorized.
6. *Artistic Level*	A high level of acting and production.
7. *Comments*	An excellent example of a semi-documentary film and a significant contribution to the theme "Crime does not pay." It is also good entertainment of the "thriller" type.

(4)

1. *Name of Film*	*Copacabana.*
2. *Country of Origin*	U.S.A.
3. *Certificate awarded by Censors*	U.
4. *Length of Film*	1½ hours.
5. *Theme*	A farce with a negligible plot centering around a theatrical agent's success in passing off one singer as two separate persons—an action which leads to complications of love-making and even to the agent's arrest for the murder of one of the "two" singers, when her "disappearance" has been adopted as the only way of solving the complications.

6. *Artistic Level* — Technically the film can only be judged as a "nonsense" production of two highly specialized stars—Groucho Marx and Carmen Miranda. This film is a reasonably successful sample of their particular brand of acting.

7. *Comments* — Quite good entertainment of a kind that legitimately caters for people who don't want to be serious all the time. Nothing at all objectionable.

Our primary analysis of the 125 reports on individual films was made in two separate ways; first according to the main theme of the films, and then according to our assessment of their desirability from the national point of view.

Main theme of films seen

In analysing the main themes of the films seen, we bore in mind the classification used by H. W. Durant on page 124 of his book, *The Problem of Leisure*, where he quoted from Dr. Edgar Dale's analysis of 1,500 films produced between 1920 and 1930. We have not used quite the same system, nor indeed would our films have fitted easily into the earlier framework, but we have kept fairly near to Dale's system. The main themes of the 125 films we have considered are shown in the following table:

Theme	No.	%
Crime or mystery	36	28·8
Love story	30	24·0
Comedy	15	12·0
Adventure	19	15·2
Musical	8	6·4
Dramatized biography	7	5·6
Others	10	8·0

Under the heading "Dramatized biography" we place films that may be based on either fact or fiction, but that deal consecutively with a period of years in the life of the principal character, and not with one or two incidents only, as in the majority of films. Examples of films we have classified under this heading are *Oliver Twist*, *Fame is the Spur* (the biography of an imaginary Labour politician) and *Monsieur Vincent.*

It is always unsatisfactory in an analysis to have to include a category "Others," and it is especially unsatisfactory when it includes as high a proportion as 8 per cent of the total. We have had to do so, however, because a substantial number of the films seen could not reasonably be fitted into the chosen headings, so that the choice was between unduly multiplying the number of headings or classifying the somewhat unusual—and often praiseworthy—films under the one general heading. Examples of the films included under the heading "Others" are:

(*a*) *Servant of the People.* A documentary film, running for one hour, about the duties of a Member of Parliament.

(*b*) *It Always Rains on Sunday.* A film lasting approximately two hours. Despite a plot about the concealment and eventual recapture of an escaped convict, its chief merit in our view lies in a brilliant portrayal of life in a working-class urban home on Sundays, so that its most important function is documentary.

(*c*) *Thunder Rock.* A psychological drama dealing with and finally offering a solution to the question, "What can the ordinary man do about the apparent drift of civilization towards destruction?" The film lasts 1½ hours and is concerned entirely with the efforts of one man first to evade and then to solve this problem.

It is perhaps significant that, with only one exception, the films that could not be fitted into the conventional headings were British.

Desirability of films

So far, in this chapter, we have been dealing only with matters of fact, for even in regard to our assessments of the main themes of the films we have analysed there can be little room for difference of opinion. Now, however, we turn from matters of fact to an expression of opinion as to the value of each of the 125 films seen. We have used five classifications:

(*a*) "Broadly of cultural or educational value." Under this heading we have included not only such obviously eligible films as *Hamlet*, but any that might be expected to make a real contribution to the cultural life of an average audience, either by giving factual information on some subject of contemporary or historical importance, or by promoting thought about some such subject, or even in such ways as by the portrayal on the screen of really beautiful scenery.

(*b*) "Reasonable entertainment but nothing more." We have thus assessed films that are thoroughly wholesome and enjoyable recreation, but that make no contribution to the nation's cultural life as defined in (*a*) above.

(*c*) "Harmless but inane." These are films that contain nothing unwholesome, but in which the standard of taste and art is so low that they would be readily acceptable only to an audience whose taste and critical faculties are undeveloped, and whose cultural life is at a low level.

(*d*) "Glorifying false values." These are films in which striking emphasis is given to beliefs and attitudes of mind that reasonable and broadminded people would consider run contrary to the standards which should be maintained in civilized nations. The most obvious examples are the excessive luxury portrayed in many American films, the excessive use of night-club "shots," and the undue emphasis on drinking in some films. Although a great many films, particularly of American origin, have moments when they might be said to be glorifying false values, we have assessed them under this heading only when they persistently do so.

(*e*) "Really objectionable."

Our assessment of the 125 films under the foregoing headings is:

Assessment	No.	%
Broadly of cultural or educational value	18	14·4
Reasonable entertainment but nothing more	59	47·2
Harmless but inane	30	24·0
Glorifying false values	15	12·0
Really objectionable	3	2·4

The first fact that becomes apparent from our analysis is that 61·6 per cent of films are either of positive value in the cultural or educational sense, or at least are good entertainment such as could be enjoyed by normally cultured and intelligent people. That this should be so when the sample of films on which the analysis is based covered cinemas of virtually all categories in many different parts of the country seems to us to dispose of the view, not infrequently expressed by moralists and sociologists, that the cinema is a thoroughly undesirable influence.

It is manifestly unsatisfactory that nearly a quarter of the films seen should fall into our category, "Harmless but inane," but we feel that too much should not be made of this fact. It is true that seeing such films is waste of time, but, as we have already seen in relation to gambling, a considerable proportion of the population has never yet had the opportunity of acquiring the intellectual and cultural qualities that would enable it to differentiate between the shoddy and the worthwhile. While this is so, it is almost inevitable that a substantial proportion of "harmless but inane" films will be shown, for the most part to audiences not capable of appreciating really fine ones.

In our view, by far the worst feature of the contemporary cinema is the tendency that we have called "Glorifying false values." Not only was the tendency so strong in 12 per cent of the films seen that they were specifically assessed under that heading, but as stated above traces of it were found in many other films, especially in those made in Hollywood. We feel that the constant repetition of scenes of rather vulgar and ostentatious luxury, and the constant suggestion that "having a good time" can only mean dining and drinking champagne in expensive restaurants, dancing in night-clubs, being waited on by several servants, and living in rooms of absurdly large dimensions, must have a deleterious effect upon a nation that has, above all, to realize that its future lies in plain living, hard work and in unsophisticated pleasures.

In considering the films classified as "Really objectionable," it is at first sight satisfactory that only three films out of 125 (2·4 per cent) should be so classified. On further reflection, however, we are inclined to think that, having regard to the enormous number of people who see any given film, the situation is more serious than it seems. Lest it should be thought that we are narrow-minded and intolerant in our judgment, we think it worth quoting the analysis of the films we classify as objectionable, omitting only the title of each:

(1)

1. *Film X*	
2. *Country of Origin*	U.S.A.
3. *Certificate awarded by Censors*	A.
4. *Length of Film*	2¼ hours.
5. *Theme*	The scene is set in Texas in the nineteenth century and relates how the spoilt sons of a crippled Senator, ranching a million acres, reacted to the simultaneous arrival at the ranch of a railroad and a half-caste Indian girl. The major incidents consist of five murders, one judicial hanging, one attempted murder, one rape and two seductions. Much of the film is crudely suggestive.
6. *Artistic Level*	The technical level is moderate. The film is made in Technicolor and the colours are crude. The standard of acting is not high.
7. *Comments*	The film is coarse and unedifying in every way.

(2)

1. *Film Y*	
2. *Country of Origin*	U.S.A.
3. *Certificate awarded by Censors*	A.
4. *Length of Film*	1½ hours.
5. *Theme*	This ridiculous gangster film eventually reaches its end with the sixth violent death portrayed because there were only six principal characters to start with, and five having been murdered, and one shot by the police, the story could hardly be continued. A few large-scale thefts, and a sprinkling of "snaky" women living with "tough" men, fill in the plot.

6. *Artistic Level* — Mediocre. The "sets" are unconvincing, and smart bungalows insist on looking like wooden frames and canvas—as they very likely are.

7. *Comments* — The whole story is sordid, vulgar and silly.

(3)

1. *Film Z.*
2. *Country of Origin* — U.S.A.
3. *Certificate awarded by Censors* — A.
4. *Length of Film* — 1 hour 20 minutes.
5. *Theme* — The story of a maniac who hunts and kills humans for amusement. He indulges in his unpleasant pastime on a South Sea island, helped by a few trusted servants. He obtains his supply of "game" by wrecking ships with the aid of a false beacon. Having killed his victims, he pickles their heads. Eventually an intended-victim turns the tables, and kills the maniac.
6. *Artistic Level* — Acting and décor are good. Indeed so good that they add to the horror of the film.
7. *Comments* — The theme of this film can only be described as horrible. It is unsuitable for exhibition to anyone except adults of exceptionally strong mind and its assessment by the British Board of Film Censors as "Certificate A," meaning that children could see it if accompanied by a parent, seems inappropriate.

Censorship

In the early days of the cinema it was obvious that some form of censorship would be necessary, and in 1912 the trade itself set up for the purpose a body which, under the title of the British Board of Film Censors, is still the responsible censorship authority. Although often referred to as a trade organization, in fact persons who are, or have been, connected with the film industry are absolutely debarred from membership of the Board. Only the Chairman of the Board, who is always a person distinguished in public life, is appointed by the trade. All other appointments to the Board are made by the Chairman.

Although this is an unofficial body, the decisions of the Board about films are implemented as an indirect result of the Cinematograph Act, 1909. That Act puts upon various Local Government authorities the responsibility for licensing cinemas. As it was held in the High Court in 1921 to be *intra vires* for a licensing body to attach conditions to the licence, it is now the universal practice for local authorities to make the condition that a cinema can, in normal circumstances, only show films passed for exhibition by the British Board of Film Censors. Licensing authorities do, however, retain the power, in special cases, to permit the exhibition of films not passed by the Board, or to prohibit the exhibition of films that have been so passed. In practice little use is made of these reserved powers, though occasionally films that have aroused controversy are banned in some areas.

The Board not only examines completed films, but, if a producer so wishes, scripts on which it is intended to base films are also examined, as it is sometimes possible for the Board to ban a film before it is even made, thus saving the costly process of making a film which has no chance of being passed. Naturally even if a script is passed, the completed film still has to be presented for censorship.

The film industry pays a fee to the Board for every film examined, and these fees are the sole income of the Board which has to be self-supporting but non-profit-earning.

Films that have been examined and passed are awarded one of three certificates by the Board, either "H," "A," or "U." "H" is a rare classification and means that the film is "horrific," and children may not see such films. "U" is the classification for films that contain nothing at all that could be harmful to a child, and children may go unaccompanied to such films. "A" means that a film is what might be termed "a grown-up story," dealing perhaps with marital problems, showing crimes of violence or containing other matter to which it is not desirable to allow children uncontrolled access. Children may only be admitted to a film classified "A" if they accompany a parent or *bona fide* guardian. The widely held belief that any adult can take a child to a film classified "A" is incorrect. This classification is intended to be a warning to the parent that he or she should find out something about the film before letting a child see it.

It is perhaps relevant to mention here that the Board is not concerned with aesthetic judgment. It is no part of its work to refuse a licence to a film because it is thoroughly bad art or is utterly stupid. The Board is concerned only with preventing scenes being shown that are objectionable on broad considerations of morality (not of course only of sexual morality). The mechanism for keeping films above a minimum aesthetic level is the box office, for, at least in theory, if films are too bad the public will not pay to see them. We think that we might reasonably add that "too bad" here means very bad indeed, but at any rate there is nothing the Board of Censors can do about it.

In a normal year between 2,000 and 3,000 films are submitted to the Board for examination. In 1948, when imports of American films were restricted, 1,607 films were passed for exhibition, and they were awarded the following certificates:

"U"	..	1,230
"A"	..	372
"H"	..	5

These figures include a large number of short films, such as comic cartoons and travel films, that are almost automatically "U." Of the 1,607 films, 559 were "feature" (i.e., principal) films, and these were assessed.

"U"	..	214
"A"	..	340
"H"	..	5

In the same year, 1948, cuts ranging from single words or shots to whole sequences were imposed by the censors in 192 of the 1,607 films finally passed, while 3 completed films were rejected altogether, and 10 scripts were rejected as unsuitable as a basis for films.

Classification system in practice

After a film has been passed and classified "A," "U," or "H," the Board of Censors naturally has no responsibility for seeing that the rules concerning the admittance of children are observed. This is the duty of Local Government authorities which are legally responsible for licensing cinemas and stating the conditions on which films may be shown. In practice, however, these authorities always make the observance of the licensing rules of the Board of Censors one of the conditions of granting a licence. But even so the regulations concerning the admittance of children to the different categories of films are not always strictly enforced. In the course of his investigations G.R.L. has in several cinemas seen children being admitted, unaccompanied, to films with an "A" certificate. As a trial, he asked the women in the box offices of 18 cinemas what certificate had been granted to the particular films then being shown in those cinemas, and although 12 of them gave the right answer, 4 answered incorrectly, and 2 admitted they were not sure. One of the women who answered "U" when the correct answer was "A," added, "You see when we have both 'A' and 'U' films in one programme I always let the kids in. I don't see it does them any harm." It is quite a common practice to have both "U" and "A" films in one programme, and though few box-office attendants are likely to be as guileless as the woman just quoted, it is probable that a good many children gain admission when they should not do so.

Children's cinema clubs

We turn now to consider another side of the question of the relation of the cinema to young people. Of recent years it has become the practice throughout the kingdom for cinemas to be opened on Saturday mornings to special audiences of children admitted at low prices. At most cinemas, the children have to be members of a children's cinema club associated with the particular cinema. The two main cinema groups in the country, the Odeon and the Gaumont-British, have nearly 400 children's cinema clubs between them, and almost half a million children attend their performances each Saturday.

These figures are in addition to the number of children attending cinema clubs organized by independent exhibitors. We have no means of knowing how many children these independent exhibitors attract in the aggregate, but the number must be large.

It is quite common for cinema clubs to be criticized on grounds such as:

(*a*) The children should be in the open air playing healthy games.

(*b*) It is wrong of exhibitors to make profits out of children's pocket money.

(*c*) The gathering of large groups of children in the dark, free or largely free from adult control, and with exciting events on the screen, tends to produce hysteria.

On the whole we think there is very little in such criticisms. Of course it would be better for children to be playing games in properly equipped playing fields than for them to be sitting in a dark cinema. But the real choice is usually between the cinema and the busy streets with their Saturday morning crowds and traffic, and we believe that most people would consider the cinema preferable.

At any rate the main groups of children's cinema clubs (Odeon and Gaumont-British) are non-profit-distributing. After paying expenses, any surplus is devoted either to special club activities, of which we have something to say below, or towards the cost of making special films for children's cinema clubs. An alternative version of the criticism about making profit out of the children is to say "Ah! The cinema industry is training its future audiences to the cinema-going habit." We think that this too is difficult to sustain, for the figures of cinema attendances that we quoted at the beginning of this chapter show quite clearly that the industry has no need of devices such as cinema clubs to ensure that it has audiences.

Likewise, judging by a performance at a children's cinema club that we attended ourselves, there is not much hysteria. Children are by nature noisy creatures, and at this performance the villain of the cowboy film was booed, the hero cheered and the courting of the heroine greeted by long and derisory whistles. But we saw no evidence of hysteria; the manager of the cinema, who made various appearances on the stage to conduct community singing, and for similar purposes, seemed to us to have a remarkable degree of control over the children, of whom nearly 1,000 were present.

Although performances for children's clubs consist mainly of films, other features are introduced such as community singing. On the assumption that all the formal education that children can absorb is given from Monday to Friday in school, no directly educational matter is introduced into the cinema clubs, although not infrequently there is instruction in such subjects as road safety drill and personal hygiene.

It is recognized by the persons responsible for running the main groups of children's clubs that sufficient films entirely suitable for children do not exist. In 1944, as a practical step towards the solution of this difficulty, J. Arthur Rank, who is President both of the Odeon National Cinema Clubs for Boys and Girls, and of the corresponding Gaumont-British Junior Clubs, set up a Children's Film Department to ensure that films suitable for children were made in adequate numbers.[1] The Children's Film Department is assisted by an Advisory Council on which sit representatives of the Ministry of Education, the Home Office, the Secretary of State for Scotland, the National Union of Teachers, the National Federation of Women's Institutes, the National Associations of Boys' Clubs and of Girls' and Mixed Clubs, the National Union of Townswomen's Guilds, and others. Making films, even the unsophisticated ones suitable for children, is a long and costly process, and it will therefore necessarily be some years before an adequate supply can be available. It is encouraging, however, to note the number of these special films that have been completed, namely, 18 in 1944–5, 44 in 1946, 44 in 1947, 40 in 1948, and 28 in 1949.

To give an impression of the type of film that is being produced by the Children's Film Department, we think it worth giving some details of the 28 films made in 1949. They fall under six headings and the most striking feature is the strong

[1] We note with regret that since this chapter was written, conditions in the film industry have caused Mr. Rank to discontinue the making of children's films. We hope that it may be possible to begin again at some time in the future, in view of the high value of the work that was being done.

"travel" element that runs through them. The programme is:

(*a*) Long stories.

The Lone Climber—a ski-ing story in Austria.

The Mysterious Poacher—a country story in the Dolomites.

Trek to Mashomba—a story of early settlers in Southern Rhodesia.

The Dragon of Pendragon Castle—a fantasy-comedy.

Looking for Trouble—a school story produced in Germany.

Trapped by the Terror—a story of the French Revolution.

(*b*) A series of four travel films about Denmark.

(*c*) A coloured cartoon.

(*d*) A newsreel entitled *Remember 1948?*

(*e*) Nine editions of a magazine film,[1] and also four editions of a new magazine series dealing with matters of interest all over the world.

(*f*) Three films of general interest.

Valley of the Sun.

Beating the Weather.

Feeding on the Farm.[2]

The year's programme is of particular interest because it is based on over four years' experience of making special films for children, during which time a considerable amount of information has been amassed on the reaction of child audiences, and on such technical matters as casting, photography, length of films, and so on. These matters are beyond the scope of our present work, but anyone wishing for further information would find a good deal of interest in the annual reports of the Advisory Council on Children's Entertainment Films, and in the annual series of pamphlets entitled *Entertainment Films for Children.*

Before leaving the question of special films for children, we should point out that although the films are made by the Rank Organization for the Odeon and Gaumont-British cinema clubs, permission has been given for them to be shown in other

[1] A magazine film is one of which new editions are produced periodically and in each of which a number of unrelated subjects of interest are dealt with briefly as is done in the articles in a weekly magazine.

[2] This information has been provided by the courtesy of the Children's Film Department.

cinema clubs or in youth clubs after they have completed the Odeon and Gaumont-British circuits.

As we stated above, the activities of the cinema clubs belonging to the two main groups, and those of many clubs run by small-scale exhibitors, are not restricted to cinematograph performances. Other activities are of diverse natures, including children's orchestras, sports clubs, rambling clubs, football and cricket. Some of the football clubs are organized in leagues and compete against each other. When one remembers that a considerable proportion of the children belonging to the cinema clubs come from poor homes, it is perhaps true to say that some of the most worth-while of their activities are the simple acts of friendliness, such as sending a birthday card to each member.

To sum up our views of children's cinema clubs, we believe that they do useful work by catering for a large number of children on Saturday mornings when few other youth organizations function. We are impressed too by the special efforts to produce films suitable for children to be shown at the club performances, and we recognize that many of the subsidiary activities of the clubs are valuable.

Effect of the cinema

It is convenient at this point to discuss briefly what is the effect of the cinema on the outlook and character of regular film-goers. One well-known professional film critic with whom we discussed the matter gave it as his view that persons who see films regularly and frequently develop a sort of protective mechanism, which enables them to utilize the cinema as an escape from their daily lives, without attributing any reality to the events depicted. In his view, therefore, apart from the advantages and disadvantages of the cinema as an escapist medium, its net effect is nil.

We believe that this is true of the large majority of adults, and in our case histories no evidence was gathered from adults of staid mind that could suggest that the effect of the cinema on them is in any way deleterious.

We do not believe that the same holds good of young people, including in that term not only children but adolescents and the many young adults who for one reason or another have been slow to grow up mentally. We have no direct evidence of the cinema being responsible in any way for crime, and we doubt, for example, whether gangster films are really responsible to any significant degree for boys committing criminal actions. This is confirmed by the work done by Dr. Healy in America and quoted in Professor Cottell's book, *Your Mind and Mine*. After an elaborate investigation into the psychology of crime, Dr. Healy concluded that only 1 per cent of juvenile delinquencies are motivated directly by film suggestion.[1] But we believe the cinema has on young people effects that are much more subtle, and that infinitely the most harmful of them is the encouragement of a false scale of values to which we have already referred.

Comparatively few American films, and not as many British films as would be desirable, deal with everyday people, with humdrum problems. Wealth and luxury are constantly held out to be desirable ends in themselves, and it is extremely rare to find a film where the aims of the hero and heroine are not at least mainly materialistic. Even poverty when shown, usually as a prelude to the rise of a hero or heroine to riches, is glamorized.

In our case histories of those whom we have defined above as young people, we gathered evidence of the effect on them of films that too sharply accentuate glamour and luxury, and we quote three as examples:

(*a*) Miss A., aged about 20, a waitress: "I'm fed up. What's the good of a job like this. If a customer you know takes you out, you never go anywhere classy. Not like they do on the pictures."

(*b*) Mr. R., aged 19, in the R.A.F. : "This country's no good. It's finished. I'd like to go to America and have a car, and one of those flats you see on the flicks, with a refrigerator and a telephone, and all that. We're behind the times I tell you."

(*c*) Miss B., aged 21, a shop girl who is discontented with life and very bitter: "Marry and have kids you don't want, and live in a poky house, and not have any nice clothes? Not me! Marrying would be all right if it was the way they do it on the pictures, but real life isn't like that."

[1] *Your Mind and Mine*, published by Geo. G. Harrap & Co., Ltd.

A careful study of the effect of cinemas on their audiences was made in the immediately post-war period by J. P. Mayer, and the results of his enquiries are published in his book, *British Cinemas and their Audiences*, to which we have the permission of the publisher (Dennis Dobson Ltd., of London) to refer. J. P. Mayer's enquiries were conducted in such a way that, although they obtained highly interesting and valuable results, they were not such as could be quoted as random expressions of opinion, even in the qualitative and quite unstatistical sense that in our indirect interviews we have interpreted the word random. Nevertheless Mayer's results appear to us to be interesting because they reveal that which certain large portions of cinema audiences wish to express when they are not only off their guard, but are also eagerly responding to an invitation to talk without fear of criticism. It is difficult to quote from Mayer's book because of the range of his material. We think, however, that at least the three following quotations are of particular interest in connection with our theme:

"Miss D., aged 18, a bank clerk: 'It [the cinema] has made me despise boys of about my own age, with whom I have been out. After seeing the polished lover on the screen it is rather disillusioning to be kissed by a clumsy inexperienced boy. I have tried not to feel like that about them, but I still find I would rather go out with . . . an older man than a young boy.'

"Mr. E., aged 22, a clerk: 'My particular screen idol is Miss ——, who is adept at mannerisms and noted for her particular style of acting. I've often caught myself using her mode of speech during a conversation, using clipped phrases and highly dramatic movements. Yes, I'm sure this actress has influenced my way of thinking and doing things in everyday life.'

"Miss F., aged 20, a civil service clerk: 'I often adopt phrases used in films when joining in office chatter, in fact, it is quite the vogue to be able to quote actual speeches from films these days. . . . Sometimes by quoting such a remark I have been given praise for a quick wit and often find that conversation can be enlivened by appropriate use of such phrases. I find that by seeing so many films my vocabulary has increased and I can hold my own in conversation by sometimes unconsciously copying the attitudes and inflexion of the voice of some of the better stars, Miss —— being my first choice of a correct diction.'"

The News cinema

So much for what might reasonably be called the fictional cinema. Now we turn to another aspect of the commercial cinema, namely, the news cinema. It is not easy to arrive at a reliable estimate of the number of news cinemas operating in the United Kingdom for two reasons. First, the term "news cinema" is not a precise one, and a number of small cinemas giving continuous performances of short films might or might not be classified as news cinemas according to the definition adopted. Second, the total number of news cinemas is only a small minority of the total number of cinemas, and statistics about them are not, as far as we have been able to ascertain, published separately.

There are approximately 20 news cinemas in London, and their seating capacity varies from about 250 to 600, the usual prices of admission being 1s. and 1s. 10d. They are normally open from 11 a.m. to 11 p.m. on weekdays, and for six or seven hours on Sundays. As each performance lasts only one hour, and there is no interval between the performances, there may be as many as 78 complete performances each week.

There are very few news cinemas in the provinces, probably not more than a dozen in all. It seems as though a population of at least 300,000 is needed to sustain a news cinema, and even in some much bigger towns there is none at all.

Originally the programme of news cinemas consisted of one or more films showing current items of news, together with a brief comedy or travel film to make the total duration of the programme up to one hour. Now, however, the news films occupy only a comparatively small part of the programme, largely because public interest in news films has declined, and animated cartoons, travel films, and films on matters of general interest such as sports, fashions, and domestic economy, make up the balance.

The standard of news films is disappointing and it is not surprising that public interest in them has declined. The events to which their scenes relate are of course already known to the public through the radio and press. They are therefore not "news" and could only make a good impression either by emphasizing some new angle to the news story or by outstandingly good presentation. Too often they do neither and are content with, for example, long-range shots of wearily-smiling Royalty officiating at this or that, or with straightforward and uninteresting photographs of current events.

The standard of the other films shown in news cinemas varies greatly. Occasionally they are interesting or instructive, but the general level is mediocre. Even travel films are seldom as effective as they should be, no doubt because, not being great box-office attractions, not much money can be spent on their production.

Foreign films

There are eight cinemas in London, having altogether approximately 4,000 seats, that show films in which the speech is in languages other than English. On any given day it is usual for about five of the eight to be showing programmes composed of or including such films. French films predominate in this field, but in addition German, Italian, Czech, Danish and Russian films are occasionally shown, the last three only rarely. Since audiences only see outstanding examples of foreign films there may be a tendency to estimate them in general too highly, but it is certain that some really outstanding films have been shown in England since the end of the Second World War. The enjoyment of the films is seriously decreased by the superimposing of sub-titles in white lettering in English on the bottom of the pictures, but without this device they would naturally be unintelligible to the majority of the persons in the audiences.

Foreign films make little appeal in the provinces, although the best known of them are occasionally shown in a few of the larger cities.

Religious films

There is only one further type of film with which we wish to deal, namely, religious films. It appears to us, *a priori*, that these could be of two kinds, namely, those designed to give specific teaching in religious dogma or in Bible study, and those designed to teach an ethical doctrine without direct reference to religion. Either of these kinds of films could theoretically be exhibited either in places of worship as part of a service, or in such places as church halls, or even in commercial cinemas.

We have discussed this question with various bishops and with persons high in authority in the Free Churches, as well as with a small number of enthusiastic ministers of religion who have actually experimented with films for religious teaching. We have been in touch with the officers of organizations interested in religious films, and we have seen some religious films specially made by a non-profit-distributing organization. Although a few ministers of religion have apparently made successful use of films, the consensus of opinion was against them. In any case the religious films we were shown were so imperfect, artistically and technically, that they could not conceivably have impressed favourably a generation that has become used to a high technical level in the cinema.

Film societies

There are rather more than 200 film societies in Britain,of which the members are persons interested in the cinema as an art, rather than as a mere means of entertainment. In most of these societies a proportion of members own their own cinematograph cameras and societies usually own their own projectors. They are thus able to make and show their own films. In addition, film societies frequently hire commercial cinemas on Sundays and show there to their members commercially produced films of high quality that have not proved to be a box-office success. Foreign films, in particular, are often shown on such occasions. Film societies also organize lectures and discussions on matters of interest connected with the cinema.

Cultural organizations

The immense importance of the cinema as a means of providing information and helping to form public opinion has led responsibly-minded persons inside and outside the industry to form various bodies, the joint and several aims of which amount to assisting the development of the cinema as an art, whilst ensuring that such development is not along lines that are contrary to the public interest. Two of these bodies of which we particularly wish to make a brief mention are the British Film Institute and the British Film Academy.

The British Film Institute receives a large proportion of its income from public funds but it is free from any direct official control. Its principal aims may be summarized as being:

(*a*) To encourage the development of the art of the film, to promote its use as a record of contemporary life and manners and to foster public appreciation and study of it from these points of view.

(*b*) To advise educational institutions and other organizations and persons as to sources and conditions of supply, types of films and apparatus, and the conditions of production, distribution and exhibition.

(*c*) To act as a means of liaison between the trade (producers, distributors and exhibitors) and cultural and educational interests.

(*d*) To develop the National Film Library in order to form a comprehensive collection of significant films; to arrange for the loan and exhibition of films from such library, and generally to evolve facilities for individual and group study of films and the showing of special programmes.

(*e*) To act as a clearing house for information on all matters affecting the production, exhibition and distribution of films at home and abroad.

Within its special field we are confident that the British Film Institute is doing valuable work, although much of it is necessarily of an unsensational nature that will not attract public attention. For example, the work of the film library, where a collection is being made of the scripts of important films and "still" photographs of special significance, as well as complete copies of films, is of considerable value in the artistic development of the industry and will be of still greater value as the collections become more complete.

As far as the relations of the British Film Institute with the man in the street are concerned, it is only necessary to quote two examples, first the work of the Institute with film societies and second that of the information section of the Institute.

It is probably not too much to say that the 200 or so film societies in Britain could hardly exist without the help of the British Film Institute, which acts as their central booking agency for the hire of films. Not only does the Institute obtain films from commercial renters for the film societies, and sometimes lend films out of the loan section of its own national film library, but it is also constantly seeking, through its special agents at foreign film festivals in Europe, to obtain information about films which it can obtain abroad especially for the use of film societies.

The information section of the Institute deals in the course of a year with many thousands of enquiries, which have in common only the fact that they relate to the cinema. Many of them are trivial questions from members of the public about their favourite "stars" or films, but many others are about matters of substantial importance from such organizations as Governmental agencies, libraries, the British Council, the B.B.C., theatrical agents and various sections of the film industry.

The British Film Academy is an organization set up by film-makers in the United Kingdom, and is financed by them. Its objects are:

(*a*) To further the advancement of the art and technique of the film.

(*b*) To stimulate exceptional creative work and to encourage experiment and research in all branches of the industry.

(*c*) To co-operate with organizations in this country and abroad which advocate similar ideals.

The Academy works in close contact with the British Film Institute as well as with other bodies connected with the film industry, but it differs from them all in that it is primarily concerned only with the British film industry, and it has a membership exclusively of persons professionally engaged on the production side of the industry. The Academy has its own library of film scripts, books dealing with the cinema, and "still" photographs, and it deals with a substantial number of enquiries on technical matters and on specialized subjects. It encourages the publication of books, and facilitates research into technical subjects connected with the cinema.

The best-known of the Academy's activities is the granting of annual awards for certain categories of specially meritorious film work. These awards have the particular value that they are the judgment of film technicians on films, but although the awards are much publicized they are not the major part of the Academy's work.

SUMMARY

The most impressive fact about the cinema is its immense power for good or evil that results from its staggering popularity. We believe that the cinema industry in Britain is in the hands of persons alive to their responsibilities, and that such subsidiary organizations as the British Film Institute and British Film Academy are helping in a total effort to improve the cultural, technical and educational value of the cinema without detracting from its entertainment value.

We are less happy about American films, and wish to repeat and emphasize what we have said earlier, that the worst feature of the cinema is the glorification in many films of false values, and that this evil occurs far more frequently in American than in British films. We believe it would be for the public good if this evil quality were considered by the Board of Censors to be sufficient justification, in extreme cases, for withholding a licence altogether, and in less extreme cases for the granting of a licence only after cuts to the film.

We are impressed with the work of the Children's Film Department.

On the whole and considering that the popularity of the cinema is such that hundreds of millions of visits would be paid annually whatever the nature of the films shown, we believe that the country has reason to be pleased at the standard generally maintained, particularly by British films. Although a good deal of progress has been made in recent years, there is naturally still plenty of room for improvement and, despite the financial difficulties of the industry, we are confident that, in Britain at any rate, a good deal of further progress in both the artistic and technical sides of the cinema will be made in the next ten or fifteen years.

CHAPTER VIII

THE STAGE

In England and Wales theatrical productions, using the term in a broad sense, are of four different types, namely (*a*) the legitimate theatre, i.e., drama, comedy, and musical plays, (*b*) opera and ballet, (*c*) music halls, (*d*) special entertainments such as ice shows given on the stage of buildings licensed as theatres. In addition to these there are the concert parties that are popular at holiday resorts in the summer.

To obtain information about the number of theatres presenting entertainments of the four types mentioned above, we consulted a man who is engaged in organizational work in the theatrical world, and who is fully conversant with all the intricacies of what is to us largely *terra incognita*. He informed us that without a detailed survey covering the whole country, it would be impossible to say how many theatres there are, how many musical halls, and so on. He stated that the main difficulties in providing accurate figures are, first, the number of theatrical companies operating in buildings not classified in the directories as theatres; second, the number of "mixed policy" houses where straight plays, variety and, less frequently, repertory are all presented at one time or another; third, the number of seasonal theatres.

To obtain a rough indication, however, of the total number of places where there are professional theatrical productions of one kind or another, we have examined *The Stage Year Book, 1949*, from which it appears that there are rather less than 400 theatres and music halls in England and Wales, of which 89 are in London. In addition there are a substantial number of places, such as the pavilions of piers at seaside resorts where in summer, and sometimes in winter also, there are stage performances by concert parties of which we give a brief description later in this chapter. There are almost certainly not less than 100 places, other than theatres and music halls, where performances are given by these concert parties. Finally there are a very small number of places, such as two open-air theatres in London parks, and the theatres at Glyndebourne and Aldeburgh, where highly specialized performances, Shakespeare's plays in the first two mentioned and opera in the second two, are given for brief seasons each year.

To show how the productions in the principal theatres and music halls of London are divided between the various forms of theatrical entertainment, we chose two weeks at random, one in the summer and one in the winter, and recorded the type of entertainment at each of the 42 main theatres and music halls in Central London and the West End. The results are shown in the following table:

	Number of places of entertainment presenting	
	Summer	Winter
Opera	Nil	1
Ballet	2	2
Musical plays	10	10
Drama	11	16
Thrillers	2	1
Farce or straight comedy	11	7
Ice revues	2	1
Variety	2	3
Non-stop revue	1	1

In addition, during the summer week, Shakespeare's plays were being produced in two open-air theatres.

Opera

Since the end of the Second World War, several new English operas have been presented in London, and in some cases subsequently in the provinces, and on the whole they have enjoyed a not insignificant degree of artistic success.

Presentations of Italian, and to a lesser extent German, opera, sometimes sung in the original language and sometimes in English translations, have of recent years become a normal part of London's theatre programmes, although frequently they have to be subsidized by the Arts Council. With the exception of one or two cities, there appears to be insufficient support in the provinces to make the presentation of opera a feasible proposition even when it is subsidized. A recent attempt to present opera in one of London's large suburban theatres was also a failure, and the production was withdrawn after a few days, despite the inclusion in the cast of singers of international reputation. It seems, therefore, that although opera has made sufficient progress in popularity in England to justify its production in the theatres in the West End of London that draw their audiences from all over the country, it does not make sufficient appeal to the public taste to draw purely local audiences, even in areas of dense population. Since opera, with its combination of vocal and instrumental music and décor, is an important form of musical and theatrical art, its comparative neglect over large portions of Britain is a reflection on our national level of culture and is a sad contrast to, say, Germany and Italy, where opera flourishes and is eagerly appreciated in even quite small towns.

Under the term "opera" we have not included the comic operas of Gilbert and Sullivan, which continue to be so much to the public taste that they are certain of playing to full houses in almost any city in the kingdom.

Variety

The theatrical productions most widely supported in England and Wales are what are broadly called "Variety," and this is particularly true of the provinces, where many large towns, some with populations of a quarter of a million, cannot support a theatre devoting itself all the year round to the presentation of plays, but can readily support one or more places of entertainment devoted to variety.

Variety takes various forms. It is often of the music-hall type, in which the programme consists of a number of individual "turns" with no more connection between them than a belief that they make up a balanced whole. Another favourite type is the revue, where there is a thread of story, often hardly discernible, to hold the contributions of individual actors together.

The popularity at the present time of variety of the music-hall type is astonishing and some American "stars" who have visited England for seasons in London and tours of the principal cities have had remarkable successes. For example, in one large provincial city some people actually queued continuously for more than twenty-four hours to obtain seats to see one American star.

In order to be able to speak about variety from first-hand knowledge, one of us (G.R.L.) has attended a number of variety performances in different parts of the United Kingdom. His total of fifteen attendances included two in the West End of London, three in the suburbs of London, and the remainder in provincial towns including Reading, Portsmouth, Bristol, Plymouth, Birmingham, Manchester and Newcastle. Outside the West End of London, performances tend to follow a standardized pattern. The basis of a variety show is usually the dancing team of highly trained and attractive girls. The highlight of the programme is provided by one star of considerable eminence, who might be a raconteur, a singer, a dancer, or something of all three, or perhaps by two or even three stars of somewhat lesser brilliance. There must of course be at least one comedian in every show, and usually one or more turns devoted to "specialities," such as xylophone playing, acrobatics or trick cycling.

It is no more possible to dogmatize about the variety theatre than it is about any other form of legitimate entertainment. At its best, it provides wholesome, amusing and sometimes interesting entertainment that never even pretends to be of any "highbrow" value in the educational or cultural fields. At its worst, it is dull and stupid and sometimes vulgar, without, as far as we know, ever being so bad as to be positively vicious. The vast majority of programmes lie between the two extremes.

Concert parties

Concert parties constitute a special branch of the variety stage. They consist of small groups of people who give straightforward performances, in which songs and various types of humour predominate, relieved, perhaps, by an occasional simple sketch. Although not entirely restricted to holiday resorts, concert parties are mainly concentrated at such resorts during the summer season.

We know of 121 concert parties, and we have reason to believe that our list includes the great majority of those that exist. The parties vary in size from six or seven artists to as many as sixteen. Some parties remain the whole summer season at one resort, others change at weekly or fortnightly intervals.

Concert parties have to perform with a minimum of scenery and properties, and often on inconvenient or improvised stages. The audiences to whom they play are certainly neither critical nor sophisticated, but, after making full allowance for this, the fact remains that the artists have to display considerable personality and technical skill to overcome the shortcomings of their "pitches."

It is not possible to do much more than guess at the number of persons who attend concert party performances in the course of the summer season, but on the basis of 120 companies, each giving twelve performances a week in a four-month season, the total number of attendances can hardly be less than two million, and may be more. Children form an important proportion of concert party audiences, and the programmes must be judged accordingly.

Neither of us has been able to attend enough performances to give a final opinion, but so far as our experience goes we believe that whereas, naturally enough, none of the concert parties makes any significant contribution to the nation's cultural life, few of them include turns that are objectionable. If, as we believe, their main function is to provide harmless relaxation at holiday time for people, mostly of the working- and lower middle-classes, who have worked hard all the rest of the year, they can reasonably be said to achieve this quite useful end.

Repertory

The essence of the repertory theatre is that there is a resident company which presents a series of plays of different types, a change of play normally being made each week. There are approximately 200 repertory theatres in the United Kingdom, including those in the non-profit-distributing repertory theatre movement to which we refer below. A substantial proportion of the 200 theatres are small, some having only two or three hundred seats.

The frequency with which the plays are changed imposes a great strain on the actors, who are not infrequently learning the lines of one play, rehearsing a second, and playing in a third, all in one week. To overcome the difficulty a few repertory theatres have exchange arrangements with a company in a neighbouring town so that each play is presented for a week in each town in turn. In this way double the time is available for rehearsals and the strain on the actors is halved, but the system is costly because of the high charges for the transport of the sets and properties, as well as the fares of the actors.

Non-profit-distributing repertory theatres

For the most part the repertory theatre, like any other theatre, is run for the purpose of making a profit. But such theatres cannot always be successfully run, particularly in towns of small or medium size, where they are in competition with cinemas and possibly also a music hall. Up to a fairly recent date the alternative to making a profit as a theatre was to shut down, or to become a music hall or cinema. Yet any one of these alternatives, involving the loss of regular presentations of drama, amounts to a definite decline in the cultural life of the locality.

It was to solve the problem of how to present worth-while drama when a profit could not necessarily be anticipated that the non-profit-distributing repertory theatre came into existence. Its basic principle is simple, namely, that a small number of local inhabitants, some at least of them with business experience, should form themselves into a non-profit-distributing limited liability company, of which they are the directors, for the purpose of running a repertory theatre. Experience has shown that such undertakings can provide first-class theatrical productions and be financially sound in every way, charging the same prices of admission as the local cinemas. The directors, who receive no fees, employ professional advisers to guide them on all technical matters relating to the theatre and they concern themselves entirely with the business side of affairs and with keeping general control to ensure that adequate artistic and cultural standards are maintained.

Non-profit-distributing repertory theatres, provided their articles of association are drawn up so as to cover certain matters, can obtain exemption from the payment of entertainment tax. But even without such benefit repertory theatres of this type have operated without loss in some towns.

The size of town which can support a non-profit-distributing theatre depends on the size and rent of the theatre. We know of one town with a population of only about 6,000 where such a repertory company, playing in a theatre seating only 230 people, has beenconducted without loss for the last twelve years, presenting plays of such a quality that the editor of *Picture Post* thought it worth while to give a full and well-illustrated account of it in his paper. There is a cinema in the town but no music hall.

We know of another town with a population of about 40,000, where a non-profit-distributing theatre has been carried on without loss for five years, although it has to face the competition of four cinemas.

In both these towns the charge for seats is higher than in the cinemas.

Our personal knowledge points to the fact that in large towns, say towns with a population of 80,000 or 100,000, it is possible to run successfully a non-profit-distributing repertory theatre in competition with several cinemas and a music hall and charging prices no higher than those of the cinemas, if its plays are well presented and if its articles of association are such as to enable it to obtain exemption from the payment of entertainment tax.

In general we cannot but think that here is a field in which public-spirited citizens in scores of towns could, with no vast effort or financial risk, enrich the cultural life of their neighbourhoods. It is to be hoped also that many local authorities will take advantage of the power given to them by recent legislation to open civic theatres and to levy a rate of up to sixpence in the pound to finance them. Well-run theatres putting on good plays could open new worlds of pleasure and understanding to the millions of people in Britain who have never been to a theatre.

Since the aim of the non-profit-distributing repertory theatres is frankly cultural we have had to use that word several times in the preceding paragraphs. We wish, however, to say in explanation that we do so in no "highbrow" spirit. Theatres devoted only to works by, say, Shakespeare, Ibsen, Strindberg and Chekhov would not only be non-profit-distributing; they would also be non-profit-earning, non-wage-paying and would soon be non-existent. Naturally the directors of theatres of the type of which we write wish to put on as high a proportion as practicable of plays by the great dramatists and not infrequently they will put on such works knowing that the costs of production or the limited appeal are likely to result in a net loss. But over a period not only must current costs be covered, but there must be a sufficient balance to pay for maintenance work, and for capital expenditure generally. Nor are the directors likely to forget that a primary function of a theatre is to entertain. Therefore, thrillers, comedies, satires and dramas of every kind all have their place in the repertoire of non-profit-distributing repertory theatre companies. The actors speak good, unaffected English, against a background of scenes designed with careful but unostentatious taste. We believe that that alone, even if the play is light in content, is a cultural mission, and one all the more important in a generation devoting so much of its leisure to watching, and listening to, American films.

We know of 45 non-profit-distributing repertory theatres in the United Kingdom and as their clearing house for information, and as an instrument of mutual help they have an association, the Council of Repertory Theatres, of which more than one-half of them are members.

An unsatisfied demand

Although a non-profit-distributing theatre can prosper even in very small towns, and in competition with cinemas, if they can secure a suitable building on reasonable terms, there are of course a great number of small towns and large villages with no theatre. In one district with which we are familiar these are catered for by occasional visits by a mobile non-profit-distributing theatre company, which travels round, carrying with them the sets, costumes and other requisites, and playing in village halls, and in schoolrooms.

The amateur stage

Although when speaking of the theatre, one first thinks automatically of the professional stage, we must not forget how many plays are put on by amateurs. There are a large number of amateur dramatic societies, which put on two or three plays a year, and there are also many amateur operatic societies which perform one or more operas a year. But these societies account only for a small part of the total of amateur theatrical productions. To a steadily increasing extent over the last 20 or 30 years, groups of people who come together primarily for other purposes have formed the habit of regularly putting on plays of various kinds. Thus community centres, youth clubs, women's institutes, social and sporting clubs, and many other diverse groups have made amateur theatricals a regular part of their activities. Even some public libraries have sponsored drama groups as part of their general cultural work and, as we state in Chapter XI, some large and efficient public libraries maintain special drama libraries from which groups of persons intending to put on a play can borrow sufficient copies of the text for the actors and producer. Workers in factories, too, not infrequently organize theatrical productions, and so do many of the small societies that exist within the membership of most churches.

There is no possible means of ascertaining quantitatively what this widespread and diverse amateur theatrical effort amounts to in the nation as a whole, but it is safe to say that it constitutes an important cultural achievement, and this is all the more true when it is remembered that frequently amateur dramatic groups, especially the smaller ones, make their own own sets and costumes.

Effect of the theatre

It is not easy to estimate the effect of the theatre on contemporary British life. We cannot even estimate with any certainty the total number of attendances each year, beyond saying that without doubt it is numbered in tens of millions.

The proportion of theatrical productions that are directly cultural is not large, but it is on the other hand by no means negligible. For example, out of 41 now being given daily in the West End of London, we would say that five have some direct cultural value, using the word in a broad sense. On the other hand many plays have indirect cultural value, and we mentioned an example of this above when writing of the non-profit-distributing repertory theatres. Variety performances of various kinds cannot be called cultural, but on the other hand they give a good deal of pleasure and it is seldom that they are seriously objectionable.

CHAPTER IX

BROADCASTING

THE number of wireless licences issued—11,931,000 in 1949, as against 8,908,000 in 1938[1]—indicates that there is a receiving-set in more than 90 per cent of all the dwellings in Britain. Not only does this provide an unrivalled means of disseminating factual information by means of news bulletins and talks, but it also means that those who control the broadcasting system have at their disposal a more powerful and effective means of influencing national culture, for better or for worse, than has ever previously existed. It is our aim in this chapter to try to estimate the effect of broadcasting on our national life, and to discuss some of the benefits, and some of the disadvantages, that accrue from it. We are not concerned with the organization of the broadcasting system as a monopoly under the control of a public Corporation, which is free, within the terms of its charter, to shape its policy and provide its service without interference from any Minister or Department of State. We believe that the present system, although possibly it may not theoretically be the most satisfactory one that could be devised, has much to recommend it, and in particular is preferable to any system of privately sponsored broadcasts containing advertising matter.

The effect of broadcasting upon listeners in general, which, as indicated above, is the principal theme of this chapter, is an extremely difficult matter to discuss briefly because, with listeners numbered in tens of millions, the effects produced must be so varied as to render any generalization meaningless.

For our source of information we have relied mainly upon our case histories, and in particular upon that substantial number of cases where G.R.L. in the course of compiling the

[1] *Monthly Digest of Statistics*, September 1950.

case histories was invited into the homes of the persons he was interviewing. In this way we have had an opportunity of observing at first hand the effect of broadcasting in the homes of persons belonging to widely different classes of the community. We have supplemented our knowledge by direct enquiries from various groups of youths and girls. Finally, we have discussed the whole question with two professional radio critics. We are thus able to give a good qualitative picture of the situation, meaning by the word "qualitative" that we are convinced that our description is fairly accurate, but that we are unable to make any statistical assessment of the various opinions and trends we describe.

What is listening?

The first question to which we turn our attention is, "What is listening?" Quite clearly if a man, after consulting the *Radio Times*, closes his book, switches on the radio and concentrates his attention on a programme of his choice, he is "listening." Clearly, too, if he switches on the radio at random and then goes into another room, he is not "listening," although he may be conscious of hearing "noises off" which may give him satisfaction. Between the two extremes there are many variations, of which the following are a few examples:

(*a*) Mr. C., aged 70, a retired postman, switches on the radio each evening about 7 p.m., settles himself in an armchair beside it, and goes to sleep. He likes a certain type of variety programme and if items of the kind he likes are broadcast, he wakes up automatically.

(*b*) Mrs. D. is a working-class housewife, aged about 40. She has the radio on for the major part of the day because it is company for her when she is alone. She switches from the Home to the Light Programme, or vice versa, several times a day so as to receive as much music and as little speech as possible. Is seldom in the same room as the radio set during the day.

(*c*) Mr. E. is a doctor whose hobby is writing one-act plays. He cannot concentrate on writing unless he has the radio switched on, playing music softly. The type of music is not important.

(*d*) Mr. F. is a labourer who supplements his income by cobbling for friends. When mending boots he sits in the kitchen with the radio playing very loudly in the next room, so that he can hear it. He appears, however, to be concentrating his attention on the cobbling.

(*e*) Miss G., a shop assistant, says her main hobby is reading books which she borrows from the public library. She says "of course" she always has the radio on. She is aged 21, and cannot remember a time when there was no radio. She says, "When it's switched off the house is so quiet it makes me feel funny, it's so queer."

Another class of persons about whom it is difficult to judge at what point their "listening," as opposed to "hearing," begins and ends, are those who listen regularly to one particular programme that they enjoy but either leave the radio switched on when the programme of their choice has ended, or perhaps switch on a considerable time in advance of what they want to hear. Specific examples are:

(*f*) Mr. and Mrs. H., a middle-class couple, aged about 50, always listen to a certain variety series on the Light Programme. It is followed each week by a broadcast of good music to which the H.'s would not ordinarily listen. Mr. H. says, "We leave it on because it's not worth getting up specially from my chair to switch it off. Besides, that music sometimes has some nice tunes in it."

(*g*) Miss J. is a typist, living in a bed-sitting room in London. She always listens to the weather forecast broadcast in the Home Service at 7.55 a.m. To be sure of not missing it, she always switches on well in advance and so hears some or all of the short religious broadcast that precedes the weather forecast. She says she pays no attention to it as she is always washing up her breakfast dishes or making her bed. Nevertheless enquiry on three separate occasions showed that on each occasion she remembered the theme of the morning's broadcast and some at least of the ideas put forward by the speaker.

Yet another group of persons about whom it is difficult to say whether or not they "listen" are those unfortunate persons, very numerous in the aggregate, who have to hear radio programmes chosen by somebody else in the household and which they themselves would not have chosen. Thus:

(*h*) Miss K. is a university graduate, with cultured interests. She is employed in a bank and lodges with a lower middle-class couple. In winter the communal living-room is the only warm room in the house and Miss K. shares it with her hosts. They have the Light Programme on every evening. Miss K. says, "I try not to listen, but it's not easy."

(*i*) Mr. L. has a strong dislike of variety programmes but his wife likes them. On two or three evenings each week Mrs. L. insists on listening to her favourite programmes. On these evenings Mr. L. sometimes goes out to the public house (which he does on no other occasion) but usually he tries to read a book and not to pay any attention to the radio. He says that he finds it very difficult to disregard the radio.

The examples that we have given, although by no means exhaustive of the possible variations of habit and taste, illustrate the extreme difficulty of answering the question, "What is listening?" and therefore of the further question, "How many people listen?"

How many listeners?

Various organizations, with the Listener Research Department of the B.B.C. pre-eminent among them, seek from time to time to answer statistically the question "How many people listen?" but we feel doubtful, because of the difficulty of knowing what constitutes "listening," whether the results they obtain are much more than good general indications of the listening habits of the public. We believe that the matter is too vast, and subject to too many personal variations, to be capable of a reliable answer without much detailed investigation and research on a large scale.

No doubt some general deductions can safely be made, and it is easy to pick out programmes that will attract a vast number of listeners and those that will attract but few. This does not, however, throw any light on the highly important question of how far broadcasting is influencing substantial numbers of persons by causing them to listen to programmes either above or below their intellectual and cultural level. To that question we are inclined to think that probably no reliable statistical answer is possible.

What is the general level of programmes?

There is ample evidence from the public statements of its senior officials that the British Broadcasting Corporation is fully alive both to the potentialities of broadcasting as a factor in raising the nation's cultural level, and of the Corporation's particular responsibility for ensuring that that opportunity is taken. On the other hand it would be unrealistic to suppose that at any given moment the level of the programmes could be much in advance of public taste. The only practicable means of stimulating the critical faculties of listeners and developing their taste is to provide alternative programmes for persons of different tastes, and at different levels of cultural development, and to seek to improve the taste of the least critical groups of listeners by the introduction into the broadcasts to which they listen of a certain amount of material of a better quality than they would normally choose. In such an endeavour two factors must be taken into account. First, that such a task can never be finished, because, in any foreseeable future, there will always be new listeners, some of them young people, others persons who previously "just hadn't bothered to listen," to take the places as listeners to the simplest programme of those who have graduated to something better. Second, that as broadcasting is so powerful an instrument for influencing opinion, absolute intellectual integrity and impartiality are essential in those responsible for it; in other words it must not become an instrument of propaganda, nor in matters of controversy must any one view be presented without equal opportunity being given to those who hold opposite views to express them.

To all of which should perhaps be added the fact, which will be uppermost in the minds of a large section of the public, that the main purpose of broadcasting is to provide entertainment which the hearers regard as being worth the price of the set and the annual cost of the licence.

In our endeavour to assess how far the wireless programmes broadcast in Britain conform to the standards we have outlined above we have made a threefold approach. First, listening ourselves to programmes broadcast over a period of some months; second, a study of the *Radio Times* and of *The Listener* over a period of several weeks; third, discussion of the problem with two professional radio critics.

Broadly our impression is that the B.B.C. performs its task remarkably well. We offer below a few criticisms as well as mentioning a few items in the B.B.C. programmes that seem particularly praiseworthy. In general, however, we believe that broadcasting in Britain is making a significant contribution to the raising of the cultural and intellectual levels of the nation, and that virtually nothing is broadcast that could be considered seriously objectionable.

We have been particularly impressed by:

(*a*) The annual series of Reith Lectures, particularly those broadcast by Bertrand Russell in 1949. These lectures provide an opportunity once a year for an eminent person to enrich the lives and thoughts of, presumably, millions of people by discussing at length some fundamental problem of living.

(*b*) The Children's Hour broadcasts, which show great skill in blending education in a broad sense with entertainment, and introducing a high moral tone without "preaching."

(*c*) The manner in which good music has been introduced by the radio into millions of homes, so that even where the names of Haydn, Mozart, and many others, are still not much regarded, their music exercises a cultural influence.

(*d*) The skilful blending of the Light Programme to include cultural items, such as excerpts from operas, and brief concerts of classical music.

(*e*) The contribution made by series of talks such as Fred Hoyle's "Nature of the Universe," of which it is probably not too much to say that they provide many hundreds of thousands of people with a new basis for the thoughts and ideas by which they regulate their lives.

(*f*) The high level of dramatic broadcasts and the great interest that these arouse. Through broadcasting, the works of some of the world's greatest dramatists, past and present, are presented each year to very large numbers of persons who would otherwise be ignorant of them.

(*g*) The broadcasting of the unrehearsed and uncensored discussions of groups of informed persons exchanging views on topics of current political, economic or social interest. Such discussions must have a powerful effect in helping listeners in general to form balanced judgments on contemporary problems.

On the other hand, the B.B.C., like every other human organization, is open to criticism in some respects. Particularly in our view for:

(*a*) Too many recorded repetitions of broadcasts which are

not of the highest quality. This applies particularly to routine repetitions of variety broadcasts of various kinds.

(*b*) Although, on the whole, scripts are kept "clean," there are a good many cases of *double entente* and of slightly vulgar jokes that are not worthy of the B.B.C.

(*c*) Fairly numerous joking references to alcoholic drink and in particular to drinking too much. These references are usually certain of a cheap laugh from the audience, and they help to dull the minds of listeners to the seriousness of the drink problem.

(*d*) Too great an intellectual gap between most of the programmes in the Home Service, and most of those in the Third Programme. Entirely praiseworthy as the concept of a Third Programme is, it seems to us often to go so far in its aim of appealing to intellectuals that it becomes obscure to the substantial body of persons who find that they want something more satisfying culturally and intellectually than the Home Service but for whom the Third Programme is simply incomprehensible. Whilst we believe that it would be a great improvement if the Third Programme catered a little more for normally intelligent people, and a little less for the highly intellectual, an alternative might be to reduce the gap by a substantial improvement in the intellectual level of some Home Service programmes.

Machinery for criticism

As we stated above, we believe that the B.B.C., on the whole, is doing a difficult job remarkably well. But, as a monopoly, should a set of officials rise to power in the Corporation less conscientious than those who now hold office, there is a danger that they might become neglectful of the views and interests of listeners, seeking only some purpose of their own.

At present ordinary listeners have extremely little chance of putting forward their views effectively, or of influencing the policy of the B.B.C. Because the Corporation is wisely governed and efficiently run, that is not of any great immediate consequence, but it might conceivably become so in the future.

If a citizen's legitimate interests are disregarded by the officials of a Government department, a letter from his Member of Parliament to the responsible Minister quickly ensures that the private citizen's views are taken properly into account. Because the B.B.C. has rightly been divorced from ministerial control, this safeguard does not exist.

We believe that some special machinery should be devised to safeguard the interests of listeners should they ever conflict with those of the officials of the Corporation. It would not be easy to devise, although the very fact that there are at present no outstanding major problems would make its establishment less difficult than it would be if a conflict of interests actually existed. The form we have in mind is that of a Council on which the B.B.C. and listeners would be represented and of which there would be an independent chairman appointed by, say, the Lord Chancellor. Since it would be extremely difficult to choose individuals to act as listeners' representatives on such a Council, the best plan would probably be to invite such bodies as the National Federation of Women's Institutes, the British Council of the Churches, the T.U.C., the British Legion, and many others, to nominate representatives. Once established, the function of the Council would be, in short, to ensure that broadcasting remains, as it is now, the faithful and efficient servant of the community, and to provide against the contingency, however remote it now seems, that broadcasting controlled by undesirable persons might become an instrument for the overthrow of democracy.

In making this proposal we have not overlooked the existence of the General Advisory Council of the B.B.C., which advises on general programme policy. It is not, however, a body that could readily fulfil the function we have in mind, for its members are appointed by the B.B.C., and so would not in any future clash of interests necessarily represent those of listeners; it has no executive powers and meets only three times a year. The establishment of a Council that reflected the views and wishes of listeners, and provided a democratic safeguard, but which did not interfere unreasonably with the normal work of the B.B.C., would undoubtedly be a difficult task. But the alternative of accepting permanently a broadcasting system organized as a monopoly, free from effective Parliamentary control, involves so grave a risk that in our view the difficulty of establishing a Council, and giving it effective powers, should be faced. We repeat, however, that in putting forward this suggestion we are concerned only with what *could* happen. We offer no criticism at all of the persons at present in positions of responsibility in the B.B.C., for whose work, on the contrary, we have the deepest respect.

Broadcasting and the home

Except for a small minority of persons with radio sets in their motor cars, or owning portable sets for use in the open air, broadcasting is a form of entertainment that is enjoyed exclusively in the home. Unlike most other forms of entertainment, it is capable of being enjoyed whilst the listener is occupied also on some other pursuit. We have already given some examples of this when examining the question of what constitutes listening. Other examples are:

(*a*) Miss S., aged 18, a member of a working-class family, likes to have the radio on while reading.

(*b*) It is so well known as to need no proof (although we have obtained confirmation by a substantial number of enquiries) that a considerable proportion of children have the radio on while they are doing their homework.

(*c*) It is a normal arrangement in a great many homes to have the radio on during meal times. Naturally this habit becomes less frequent the higher one ascends the social scale.

(*d*) Mr. and Mrs. T., a working-class couple, both aged about 50, play cribbage together every evening. They always have the radio on while they are playing.

(*e*) Mr. V., a clerk, aged 35–40, is visited every Saturday evening by a neighbour and they play chess together for two or three hours from about 8 p.m. They always have the radio on, even if the two of them are alone in the room.

During our enquiries we rarely met persons of lower middle- or working-classes who recognized that a radio set is a device for listening to selected programmes. It appears to be the attitude of most persons in these classes, and of many who are better educated, that the function of radio is to provide an almost constant stream of programmes, which can, at the individual will, be treated as "noises off," or as an object for serious listening. Although this tendency is apparent in both town and country, it is noticeably less frequent in the country, where appreciation of the value of quiet has not yet been so completely lost as in most urban areas.

Although this indiscriminate "listening" is no doubt to be deplored, it must not be overlooked that within the general pattern of "continuous radio" there is a great deal of genuine listening, and many broadcasts of cultural value may be heard through the prevalence of "continuous radio" that would be heard by much smaller audiences if everyone selected only that which appealed to him. Indeed, if listeners were punctilious in switching off their sets as soon as a programme was not to their present taste, the B.B.C. would find its task of raising the level of taste even harder than it is, for the listeners to their "uplift" programmes would be drastically reduced.

Nevertheless, "continuous radio" imposes real hardship in not a few cases where one or more members of the family are more sensitive, or more refined, than the others. Over a long period this involuntary listening can have serious effects; indeed, we came across one household where, solely because of the prolonged and loud playing of the radio by her husband, a woman had had a nervous breakdown, so that, on the doctor's instructions, the radio set had been sold. This is, of course, an extreme and very rare case, but a degree of mental strain is not infrequent.

It occurs in many houses where, although the radio is not in use continually, it is used regularly, and the programmes are usually chosen by one person without consulting the rest of the family. In a large majority of houses there is in effect only one living-room,[1] and a member of the family who dislikes the particular programme chosen, or who would prefer not to have the radio on at all, has no means of escape. Examples which we have come across include:

(*a*) Miss A. is a highly intelligent woman of 30. She comes from a lower middle-class family and is employed as a shorthand-typist in a Government office. She is keenly interested in politics and in drama.

[1] Probably some 75 per cent of working-class and about 50 per cent of middle-class houses built in England and Wales since 1919 have only one living-room, and even where there are two or even three living-rooms the cost of heating them normally prevents the use of more than one of them for seven or eight months in the year.

At home the radio programmes are chosen by her father. They consist exclusively of variety, brass-band music and such occasional items as commentaries on boxing matches. Not only is Miss A. prevented from hearing the programmes—talks, plays and music—which she would like to hear, but the programmes of her father's choice prevent her from reading or studying, which she desires to do. The only alternative room where she could sit is her bedroom, which is unheated, and in any case from her bedroom she can hear the radio sufficiently for it to be a distraction.

(*b*) Mr. M. is 25, the son of a bank clerk. He is unmarried and lives with his parents. Has been studying economics for some years in his spare time in the hope of getting an external degree of London University. His parents and sister have the radio on every evening from 6 p.m. to 11 p.m. Formerly he went to the house of a friend each evening to study in quiet, but the friend has left the district. As the radio prevents Mr. M. from studying at home he has now abandoned his efforts to obtain a degree.

(*c*) Mrs. C., aged about 25–30, is a rather simple, kindly person, and a great chatterbox. She says, "Tom [her husband] is so inconsiderate. I am alone here all day and when he comes home I want to talk and have a little fun. But he sits by that blessed radio and listens to ever such dull programmes—symphony concerts and the Third Programme, and never a bit of variety to liven us up. And if I say anything he says, 'Hush'."

It is perhaps relevant to add here that, although we have not dealt in this chapter with television, because it is not yet sufficiently developed to be an important factor in the spending of leisure, its future development is likely to increase the discomfort caused by selfish listeners of the kind to whom we have been referring. For, when their homes are equipped with television sets, they will no doubt insist on the light in the room being dimmed for their better enjoyment of the picture. Thus, not only intellectual pursuits such as reading, but also manual ones such as knitting and darning will become impossible.

Without underestimating the enormous benefits conferred on the community by broadcasting, it remains true that in a great many homes lack of consideration for others offsets the benefits. Indeed, the full beneficial effects of broadcasting will not be enjoyed until in every home three rules are observed which are now, in our experience, very widely disregarded.

First, never to use the radio as an instrument for making "noises off." Second, never to have the volume of sound greater than is necessary for the programme chosen to be heard in the room where the set is located. Third, never to use the radio as an instrument of domestic tyranny, by means of which one member of a household makes it impossible for others to enjoy their own particular leisure-time pursuits.

CHAPTER X

DANCING

THERE are 450 halls in the United Kingdom used exclusively for ballroom dancing, which takes place in them on each weekday, and sometimes on Sundays also. Admission to these halls on weekdays is open to anyone on payment of a small fee, usually between 1s. 6d. and 2s. 6d. On Sundays admission is restricted to persons who, by virtue of the payment of a small annual subscription, have formed themselves into a Club for the purpose, since the admission on Sundays of the public as opposed to club members would infringe the law. In an article entitled "Britain Off Duty,"[1] Mark Abrams estimates that some 3,000,000 persons are admitted each week to the 450 halls. Naturally there is no means of knowing how many separate individuals make up the total of admissions, nor indeed does Mark Abrams claim that the total of 3,000,000 is an even approximately exact figure. It does, however, indicate the importance of dancing as a means of spending leisure.

This becomes even more apparent when it is added that the halls used exclusively for dancing, although the most important places where dances regularly take place, are supplemented by a very much larger number of places used for the purpose only occasionally. These include the ballrooms of hotels and restaurants, assembly halls of the kind that exist in most towns and that can be hired for an evening, and publicly owned buildings such as town halls and village halls, as well as in the recreation rooms of many factories.

All these halls, whether used regularly or occasionally for dancing, have to be licensed for the purpose by the local authorities if the general public are admitted.

[1] Published in *The World Off Duty*, an anthology compiled by Contact Publications Ltd.

The dancers

Our information about the whole subject of dancing has been obtained partly by personal observations, for in the course of our investigations one of us (G.R.L.) has been to a number of dance halls of different kinds both in and out of London, and partly in the course of conversations with persons concerned in a variety of ways with the organization of dancing as part of the amusement industry, as well as with individual dancers.

A large majority of dancers are young people, mostly between the ages of 16 and 24. Although many people in the well-to-do sections of the community dance in the more exclusive restaurants and hotels, and at private parties, for the most part dancers are drawn from the working- and lower middle-classes, to an extent greater than the numerical preponderance of those classes in the nation as a whole.

Of recent years, however, on account of a revival of styles of dancing that were fashionable before the First World War, after which they were superseded by various forms of "jazz," older people have again been taking an interest in dancing. It is now a frequent practice in the principal dance halls for one night a week to be set aside for what is called Old Time Dances. On these evenings many of the persons present are over 50 years of age and dancers of over 60 are by no means rare.

Places where people dance

We do not think it worth giving extensive descriptions of the different kinds of places where people dance from time to time but not regularly. On the other hand, because there are often mistaken notions about them, we think it worth referring briefly to the places that are used regularly and exclusively for dances. Often, although by no means always, these halls are known as "palais-de-danse," or simply as "palais."

In a typical palais-de-danse there are two sessions of dancing each day, the first from 3 p.m. to 5.45 p.m., and the second from 7.30 p.m. to 11 p.m. The price of admission is 1s. 6d. from Monday to Friday, and 2s. on Saturday. On Sundays there is a dance organized by a club consisting of regular weekday patrons; only club members may attend and the price of admission is 2s.

The palais-de-danse has no licence to serve intoxicating liquors, but it has a restaurant where good meals are served at quite reasonable prices, as well as snacks. Soft drinks are also on sale.

Strict supervision is exercised in the entrance hall to ensure that no undesirable persons are admitted. For example, neither an intoxicated person nor a known prostitute would be allowed in. Supervision inside is also strict, and any unruly behaviour would result in the persons concerned being asked to leave. As the manager of one palais expressed it, "I can't afford to take chances. If I allowed drunkenness or any other form of rowdiness here, I should lose the licence. This place is a business premises. We supply clean entertainment to people who want it. To get a bad name would ruin us."

Many customers of the palais arrive in pairs, male and female, or in parties balanced numerically between the sexes, and they dance together the whole afternoon or evening. Many others of both sexes arrive singly, and it is the recognized practice that girls or women without a male escort may be asked to dance, without a formal introduction, by a man who has no partner. A majority of such casual meetings go no further than a few dances; some lead to enduring friendships and even to marriage; a few no doubt lead to sexual promiscuity.

Formerly, at the large palais-de-danse, professional dancing partners of both sexes were provided, who could be hired for a small fee for a dance. Although this practice, in the vast majority of cases, was quite harmless, it has, on the whole, proved repugnant to those who frequent palais-de-danse, and partners are now seldom provided for hire.

Local Government authorities have power to provide dance halls, and organize dancing, and a few of them have instituted what amount to municipal palais-de-danse.

Liquor licences at dances

From the foregoing it will be recognized that palais-de-danse are, in ordinary circumstances, well conducted and orderly places. Making every allowance for the high standard of management, we believe that the principal reason why they are well conducted and orderly is that they have no licence to sell intoxicating liquor. Conversely, we believe (both from what we have been told and from our own observation) that public dances, particularly those catering for the less educated sections of the community, tend to become rowdy and objectionable when they are licensed for the sale of liquor.

Modern ballroom dancing may easily degenerate into a sensuous form of entertainment, and if self-control is weakened with alcohol it is more than likely that it will do so, which might easily lead at least to unruly behaviour and not infrequently to sexual immorality.

We stress this point because licensing magistrates often grant liquor licences to halls in connection with particular dances and, not infrequently, such licences permit the sale of liquor for two, or even three, hours after the closing time of other licensed premises. As a result, not only can the dancers obtain alcohol in almost any quantity that they wish, but there is also a tendency for men and women who have been drinking in public houses to go to such a dance when the public houses close, so as to continue drinking. We are convinced that many licensing magistrates are not nearly alive enough to the dangers inherent in enabling dancers to obtain alcohol.

Individual opinions about dancing

In order to illustrate the views that persons of different ages and backgrounds have about dancing, we now give a few individual opinions, most of which we gathered in compiling our case histories, but a few of which were obtained by special enquiry:

(*a*) Mrs. C. is a working-class housewife of about 60. She says, "These young people nowadays are always out for pleasure. When I was young I stayed home and looked after my children. Take B (Mrs. C.'s daughter-in-law). She's off dancing four or five nights a week. Just puts the baby to bed and off she goes."

(*b*) Mr. D., a post office clerk, aged about 35. "Oh yes, I'm very keen on dancing. It's good exercise and I meet some nice young women. I go to the palais two or three times a week, and sometimes also to the special late dance they have there, that starts at midnight on Fridays and ends at 5 a.m. on Saturdays."

(*c*) Miss E., aged 16, a clerk. "I love dancing. I'd go every night if I could, but daddy only lets me go twice a week."

(*d*) Miss F., aged 17, a shop girl. "I think dancing is the best form of pleasure there is. I like dancing with other girls just as well as with boys."

(*e*) Mrs. G., aged about 26, a miner's wife on holiday. "I met my husband at a palais. I shouldn't like to be married to a man who wasn't a good dancer. We can't go often now because of leaving the kids, but my mother comes in about once a week to look after them, and then we go to the palais."

(*f*) Mr. H., aged about 25, an undergraduate. "I can't really say I care for dancing. It's just a thing one has to do if one is going to have any social life at all."

(*g*) Mr. J., aged 19, a lorry driver's mate. "I'm jolly glad I learnt to dance. It's good sport. I go to the palais every Saturday."

(*h*) Miss K., aged 22, a nurse, living in a small town. "This is a dead-and-alive place to be in. There's a dance only once a week. I like a bit of life. I'd go dancing every night if I could."

(*i*) Mrs. L., aged about 35. "When I was younger I used to dance a lot, but I can't get my old man to go much now. I still like it, when I get a chance."

(*j*) Mr. M., a railway porter, aged about 25. "I don't care for the palais. I like a dance with a bar. I'm not all that keen on dancing really, but if there's plenty of beer it's all right. It's a good place for picking up a girl."

(*k*) Mrs. N., a working-class housewife, aged 50, or perhaps more. "When the children were small, I never had a chance to go out much. Now I go to a dance every week with my eldest son. It's the only pleasure I ever get, and I love it. He's very good to me; you don't often see sons nowadays looking after their mothers like he does."

Dancing as a business

Although the teaching of dancing, and the provision of facilities for people to dance, do not constitute a major part of the nation's amusement industry when measured by the turnover or by the number of persons employed, yet in the aggregate they probably amount to more than is ordinarily supposed. On the basis mentioned earlier in this chapter of the 3,000,000 attendances each week at palais-de-danse, the total charges for admission over a year would amount to about £15 million. To this must be added the gross takings at dances in the much larger number of halls which are not devoted exclusively to dancing. A national authority on the organization of ballroom dancing whom we consulted estimated that there were at least 2,000 halls in England and Wales, in addition to the palais-de-danse, where dancing takes place regularly. They vary from expensive restaurants, which are licensed for dancing on six days a week, to village halls, where on the average there may only be one dance a fortnight. It is impossible even to guess at the takings in these places, but they must amount to millions of pounds a year.

Similarly professional teachers of dancing are more numerous, and their professional qualifications more difficult to obtain, than is ordinarily supposed. Teachers of dancing are organized into professional associations, of which the most important has over 8,000 members. It needs three years' study and practice of ballroom dancing in its various forms to become an associate of one of the teachers' societies, another three years to become a full member, and another three years to obtain a fellowship. These qualifications, associate, member and fellow, are much sought after, since they are recognized by such bodies as the Central Council of Physical Recreation and most Local Government authorities, as the professional qualifications without which persons are not competent to act as teachers of ballroom dancing.

Besides the qualifications mentioned above, the associations of teachers of dancing hold regular examinations throughout the country to test the skill of amateur dancers, that is to say, of those who merely dance for recreation but are keen enough to wish to measure their skill against some standard test. One association alone examines between 18,000 and 20,000 persons each year in this way. Naturally the dancing schools, staffed by professional teachers, and giving instruction to persons who either wish to learn to dance, or to improve whatever skill in dancing they already possess, encourage their pupils to enter for the examinations held by the professional associations.

Another aspect of dancing as an industry is provided by the large dancing competitions that are organized, both in London and the provinces, throughout the year. In these competitions there are separate classes for professional dancers (i.e., teachers) and amateurs. The winners of the main competitions are recognized as the champions of their various districts and classes, and in connection with some competitions there are valuable prizes, amounting sometimes to as much as £500. The most important championship dances are watched by large crowds of spectators, not infrequently numbering some thousands of persons.

Folk dancing

No account of dancing would be complete without some mention of folk dancing. The principal organization of folk dancers in Britain is the English Folk Dance and Song Society, but the total number of folk dancers does not exceed 100,000.

The greatest concentration of folk dancers is in London, but there is considerable interest in parts of the North Country. Women folk dancers outnumber men by nearly two to one, and most folk dancers of both sexes are between 25 and 35 years of age.

There is no English national costume for folk dances, but there are certain conventional articles of dress, such as the bells worn by male Morris dancers.

CHAPTER XI

READING HABITS

THE reading habits of a nation have a double significance, for what a man reads not only reveals his present intellectual and cultural standards, but also helps to determine what they will be in the future.

Reading matter falls broadly into two categories, first newspapers and magazines, and second books, and it is under those headings, subdivided as necessary, that we deal with the subject in the following pages. Books, newspapers and magazines have two main functions, to give wholesome recreation and to instruct. Each function is legitimate, and indeed, the functions overlap, for good fiction is not infrequently instructive, nor need technical works be dull. It is important to bear in mind when reading the factual descriptions that follow, that printed works have this double chance of justifying themselves.

Illiteracy

Before proceeding to our detailed description of reading habits, we must however point out that the widely held belief that every adult in England can read, unless he is mentally defective, is a fallacy. There is still a substantial measure of illiteracy, the extent of which we estimate below. For persons in this unfortunate state, books, magazines and newspapers are incomprehensible, and as we pointed out in the chapter on gambling, such persons tend to turn to more simple and often less desirable activities.

As our definition of illiteracy we take that given by Sir Cyril Burt in his article, "The Education of Illiterate Adults," in *The British Journal of Educational Psychology* for February 1945. There he writes:

"Broadly I would suggest that (i) an *illiterate* may be defined as meaning one who in everyday life is able to make no practical use whatever of reading or writing, and (ii) a *semi-illiterate* as one who is able to make no *effective* use of these activities, that is, one who is debarred by his disability from using the ordinary literary machinery of a civilized country (e.g., he will not be able to read with any understanding a short paragraph in a newspaper, or to write an intelligible letter home, or to comprehend simple printed instructions)."

On the basis of his definitions Burt concludes from experimental work that in Britain 1½ per cent to 2 per cent of persons aged about 21 are illiterate and a much larger group, probably 15 per cent to 20 per cent, are semi-illiterate.[1]

A senior officer of the Army Directorate of Education with whom we discussed the question told us that in his experience many illiterates get around perfectly well in their daily life. For example, a man going to work by a bus running on a certain route knows as a picture in his mind what the letters composing the name of his destination look like on a bus indicator. The officer also quoted a master-barber who had six assistants in his shop, and being completely illiterate, employed a girl at £6 10s. per week to keep his accounts and write his letters. Similarly one of us once knew intimately a ship's steward who was absolutely illiterate, but who carried out scores of buying and selling transactions each week, amounting to many hundreds of pounds' worth a month, all without any written record except for a few crude pictures that he drew in a notebook.

Rather surprisingly, the percentages of the different categories of illiterates are not different for the National Service men now being called up from what they were for the volunteers of whom the Army was composed before the war. Thus

[1] In 1947 the Minister of Education set up a Committee to investigate illiteracy among young people. The Committee has not reported as we write (June 1950), but we are informed that their estimate of illiterates is much the same as Burt's, but that their estimate of the proportion of semi-illiterates is much lower than Burt's, namely 4·3 per cent as against 15 per cent to 20 per cent. As semi-illiteracy is an imprecise term, part of the difference is possibly due to a different standard of definition. Enquiries we have made from persons of experience make us believe that, using Burt's definition quoted above, the proportion of semi-illiteracy is probably very much as he estimates. Even if, however, the much more favourable estimate of the Committee proved to be correct it would still mean that more than 2,000,000 persons in Britain over the age of 16 are either illiterate or semi-illiterate.

the interruption of schooling to which the present generation of young adults was subjected by evacuation and other disturbances of war has not led to the large increase in illiteracy which might have been expected. This is no doubt because the number of children whose education was handicapped by the war is counterbalanced by the number who were evacuated to homes where their hosts were of a higher cultural and intellectual level than their own parents, with a consequent gain to the children.

The introduction of women into the Army (in the Auxiliary Territorial Service, now renamed the Women's Royal Army Corps) enabled the Directorate of Education to make a comparison between the standards of literacy of the two sexes. Their tests established that illiteracy of either the complete or the partial types is less frequent among women. This is probably due to the greater interest women have in printed matter in their daily lives, for example in recipes, ration books, instructions on tins and on beauty preparations, as well as their acute interest in the doings of other people, particularly in female "royalty" and male film stars, as reported in the popular press and pictorial magazines.

Considerable experience in the methods of teaching adult illiterates of both types has been gained by the military authorities, who have established special training centres for the purpose. Provided that the individuals concerned want to learn, and are reasonably industrious and persevering, most illiterates can be taught to read and write. The problem is therefore capable of solution and the County Colleges authorized by the Education Act of 1944 will, when circumstances permit of them being set up, provide an opportunity for teaching those who are almost illiterate. The Colleges will also help to prevent the growth of illiteracy through the loss of skills acquired at school but not consolidated. That it will be necessary to undertake such elementary teaching for an important proportion of the students at County Colleges may, when the time comes, prove a shock to those responsible for working out in detail the curriculum and methods of teaching at County Colleges.

Having thus briefly outlined the subject of illiteracy, we are now free to deal with the reading habits of the much larger number of persons who are fully literate.

Newspapers and periodicals

There are approximately 150 daily, evening and Sunday newspapers in the United Kingdom, but only a small proportion of them have circulations large enough to give them any great significance. These are the national dailies, the London evening papers, the principal Sunday papers and a few of the main provincial papers such as *The Manchester Guardian.* The nature of the contents of the important papers is too well known to need any lengthy description, but some reference is necessary to those that are most widely read.

From the Hulton Readership Survey, made by Research Services Ltd., for the Hulton Press, which we quote by permission, we are able to give not only the circulations of certain papers but, what is far more important, a scientifically determined assessment of the number of persons who actually read them.

Sunday newspapers

The *News of the World*, which was established in 1843 and is published on Sundays, is read by more people than any other paper in Britain. During the period covered by the Hulton Readership Survey in 1949 it was seen each week by 17,770,000 persons over the age of 16, approximately one in every two of the population over that age. It had a slight absolute preponderance of women readers, but not to an extent proportionate to the excess of women over men in the adult population. A typical number of the *News of the World* is before us as we write. It consists of ten pages containing a total of 80 columns. These are allocated approximately as shown on p. 290.

The emphasis is heavily on sensational news stories, and the enormous sales of the paper are proof that they are what the public want on Sundays. We have no definite information about the division of the readers of the *News of the World* into social class and income groups, but such facts as we have suggest that whereas there is a substantial proportion of

NEWS OF THE WORLD COLUMN ALLOCATION

	Columns
Sensational news stories	25·5
Advertisements	21·75
Sports (cricket, football, boxing, athletics, etc.)	8·75
Two serious articles by prominent persons	3·0
Horse-racing	2·25
Greyhound-racing	1·5
A report on a floral exhibition	2·0
Competitions (£1,500 prizes)	2·5
Gossip column (mainly political and social)	1·0
Parliamentary news	0·5
Correspondence	0·5
Leaders	0·5
Miscellaneous	10·25
	80·00

readers in all classes and groups, they are relatively less frequent among the best-educated and the well-to-do generally.

On the credit side there is the fact that each week the *News of the World* devotes three, or sometimes more, of its columns on the centre page to instructive and important articles by well-known and often eminent persons. This offsets to some extent whatever is unworthy in other parts of the journal.

We have dealt with the *News of the World* at length because of its enormous circulation. But although pre-eminent it is not the only Sunday newspaper that reaches vast numbers of persons. In 1949 *The People* was read weekly by 12,060,000 persons and *The Sunday Pictorial* by 11,430,000. We have not the space to describe these and other important Sunday papers at length, but some further mention must be made of these two.

The People first appeared in 1881. It is a smaller paper than the *News of the World.* It devotes about the same proportion of its space to advertisements, substantially more to sport, does not normally have articles by persons of importance equal to those who write for the *News of the World*, but its news stories are less sensational. Many parents who might doubt whether the *News of the World* was entirely suitable reading matter for their adolescent children, however much it was to their own taste, would not mind their children reading *The People*.

The Sunday Pictorial, as its name implies, is devoted mainly to pictures, but each week it prints an article, one column in length, by one of the most prominent "intellectuals" of the Labour Party. *The Pictorial* relies for its attraction mainly on "human interest" pictures and news items. It can hardly be a serious factor in forming public opinion but, although not reflecting a high cultural standard, it is not in any way objectionable.

If the *News of the World*, *The People* and *The Sunday Pictorial* represent the popular Sunday press, the principal organs of the "serious" press on that day are *The Observer* and *The Sunday Times*, which at the time of the Hulton Readership Survey in 1949 were read respectively by 1,290,000 and 1,680,000 people each week.

The Observer is a paper of which any nation might well be proud. It is a non-profit-distributing enterprise, organized as a Trust, of which the Trustees are men of high purpose, devoted to the public interest, and all of them experienced and distinguished in one or other sphere of public life. The paper is objective in its presentation of news, whilst in the expression of opinions it is non-political, dignified in tone, and it marshals its facts with scientific accuracy and detachment. It devotes an important part of its total space to criticisms and reviews of books, to art, music, radio, plays and television, and makes a real contribution to the cultural life of its readers.

The Sunday Times is a frankly right-wing political paper, but it too includes articles of merit, whilst its purely cultural features—book and radio reviews and so on—are equal in importance to those of *The Observer*.

Statistics show that, as might be expected, the "popular" papers find their greatest concentration of readers among the working-class, and the "serious" among the well-to-do and the more highly educated classes. In the Hulton Readership Survey the population was divided for statistical purposes according to income and occupation into three classes, AB (well-to-do and middle), C (lower middle) and DE (working and poor). The following table shows a comparison between the proportion of each class in the population, and how the total readers of each of the five Sunday papers mentioned above are divided between the classes:

Class	AB	C	DE
Proportion of the population	15%	20%	65%
How total readers of these papers are divided	%	%	%
News of the World ..	6·4	16·3	77·3
People	7·7	18·2	74·1
Sunday Pictorial	9·0	19·4	71·6
Observer	48·2	28·3	23·5
Sunday Times	55·0	27·5	17·5

Daily newspapers

Among the daily newspapers two have completely outstripped their rivals in the number of their readers. According to the Hulton Survey the number of readers each day of the principal daily papers during the period covered by the Survey in 1949 were:

	Readers
Daily Express	9,830,000
Daily Mirror	9,320,000
Daily Mail	5,380,000
Daily Herald	4,060,000
News Chronicle	3,420,000
Daily Telegraph	2,670,000
The Times	699,000

The two papers claiming the greatest numbers of readers achieve their results by widely different methods. The *Express* relies on bold headlines and highly efficient journalism of a kind easily read, and perhaps equally easily forgotten, by a generation brought up on film captions and advertising slogans. The *Mirror* on the other hand relies on "human interest" stories, and plenty of pictures. The *Express* is a right-wing paper, following a political line that often varies considerably from the official policy of the Conservative Party. The *Mirror* is, if anything, left-wing in sympathy. But, whatever the owners of the two papers might wish, it seems that many, and very likely most, of their readers buy them for reasons quite unconnected with their politics. The following examples demonstrate this:

Mr. X. is a London taxi-driver. He and his wife are keen Labour Party supporters. Mr. X. reads the *Daily Express* because, he says, "It's a live paper with plenty of go about it."

Mr. Y. is a retired civil servant. Once a Liberal, he is now a staunch Tory. He always reads the *Daily Mirror* because, he says, "It's the best pennyworth I know. There's something interesting every day."

Miss Z. is a schoolmistress. A member of a local Fabian Society and a reader of the *New Statesman*. Her daily paper is the *Expresss* because, she says, she wants a paper that will interest her, with news stories well written in a modern way. She has made up her mind about her politics, and no paper will change them. Facts she gets from the B.B.C. It is interest she wants from a newspaper.

The foregoing illustrates an important general principle that newspapers do not form the political views of their readers and probably do not influence them as much as is popularly supposed. Although persons holding strong political views no doubt choose the paper that corresponds with their opinions (Communists for example usually read *The Daily Worker*), many and perhaps most readers choose a paper because they are attracted by something other than its politics. "Slick" journalism, a successful racing tipster, a popular cartoon strip,[1] or a "sob-stuff" series of articles dealing with the family problems of individual readers, are all examples of what really decides the average person to buy this or that paper. Further examples of this tendency are:

Mr. A. is the hall porter in an hotel catering for well-to-do people. He is a Tory, but buys the *Daily Herald* because he follows the "tips" of "Templegate," the *Herald's* racing correspondent.

Mr. B. is a Liberal by inclination, but votes Labour. He buys the *Daily Mail* (a right-wing paper) because his son, aged 7, follows the adventures of a certain "Teddy Tail," an animal in a child's cartoon.

[1] We discuss these cartoon-strips below.

Mr. C., a dental surgeon, has no politics and never votes. He buys the *Daily Mail* because he follows the adventures of Rip Kirby, a detective in a strip cartoon serial.

Mr. D., a Trade Union official and active member of the Labour Party, buys the *Evening Standard*, a right-wing paper, because he is reading a serial play, *A Streetcar named Desire*, which the *Standard* is publishing.

Mr. E. is a shipwright in a Royal Dockyard. He is a Communist sympathizer, although not a member of the Party. He reads *The Daily Worker*, but in addition buys the *News Chronicle* once a week in the winter because he believes they give the most helpful football forecasts which he uses when filling in his pool coupon.

Newspaper reading habits

We have so far discussed the question of newspapers as though people made a simple choice between one paper or another. This is an over-simplification. As will be seen from the table (page 295), based on the Hulton Survey, some people read no daily paper at all and others more than one.

Strip cartoons

Before leaving the subject of newspapers mention must be made of two further matters. First, the growth in popularity of the strip cartoons, to which we have already referred, and second, the importance of articles on sporting events, including forecasts of results and reports on games and races.

The strip cartoon is a comparatively new feature in British newspapers. It has little in common with the long-established and still popular cartoons that are pictorial comments on real persons or events of public interest. The strip cartoons have more in common with children's "comics" that tell simple stories in a series of pictures, but whereas the children's "comics" deal with admittedly fabulous creatures—talking animals, giants, fairies and such-like—the strip cartoons are meant to be taken seriously. They tell humorous stories and stories of adventure and love-making, often in serial form so that a whole story needs many issues of the paper to complete. They are, for the most part, naïve both in conception and execution. Had they not achieved such popularity that virtually all the newspapers with huge circulations regard them as an essential feature, one would have thought that they would have appealed only to the least educated sections of the community. It is certain that their growth and popularity constitute a reflection on the nation's cultural level.

NEWSPAPER READING HABITS OF ADULTS[1]

	Men and Women together	Men only	Women only
Morning papers	%	%	%
Reading no national daily	21·7	18·6	24·7
No national nor semi-national daily ..	19·2	16·0	22·0
No morning paper at all	13·1	10·0	15·7
Reading one only ..	63·6	63·6	63·6
two ..	18·8	20·7	17·2
three or more ..	4·5	5·7	3·5
Reading one or more national dailies ..	78·3	81·4	75·3
Sunday papers			
Reading no national Sunday paper ..	10·1	7·5	12·
Reading no Sunday paper at all ..	7·5	5·2	9·4
Reading one only ..	32·5	31·7	33·3
two ..	36·5	37·2	35·8
three or more ..	23·5	25·9	21·5
Reading one or more national Sunday papers	89·9	92·5	87·6

[1] This table is compiled from the Hulton Readership Survey, 1947. The term "semi-national paper" refers to papers, such as *The Manchester Guardian*, which are widely read but not so widely as the national dailies. The line "No morning paper" includes purely local dailies.

Sports news

It is hard to assess the real importance of the sporting news in newspapers. Those national penny daily papers that consist of six pages usually devote rather less than one of the pages to sport, including under that heading all tips about and information relating to horse and dog races. From the analysis of a copy of the *News of the World* given above (page 290), it will be seen that rather less than one-sixth was devoted to sport. Even the more expensive daily and Sunday newspapers devote an important part of their space to sport—*The Observer*, for example, varies from one-sixth to one-eighth—although most of them, wisely we think, do not include greyhound racing under the heading of sport, nor do they publish programmes of greyhound racing meetings, or the results of greyhound races.

We saw above (page 293) that a racing correspondent whose forecasts are believed to be reliable can increase the circulation of a paper. So, however, can sporting writers, even when no gambling is involved, as the following shows:

> Mr. X. is an artisan, aged 35. Not much interested in politics, but a staunch Trade Unionist, and always votes Labour. His hobby is cricket, both playing and watching. Every summer he gives up the *Daily Herald* and instead buys the *Daily Telegraph* because he likes E. W. Swanton's articles on cricket.
>
> Mr. Y. is an estate agent's clerk, aged about 30. Very keen on all games. Used to be a regular reader of the *Evening Standard*, but gave it up in the summer of 1949 in favour of the *Star* because of articles on cricket by W. R. Hammond.

Periodicals for adults

The term "periodicals" covers a large range of publications, including such widely different ones as *The Argosy*, a monthly publication specializing in short stories written with a high degree of literary skill, *The Tatler*, published weekly and reporting the activities of people in Society, *The Red Star*, a cheap weekly paper for women, *The Amateur Gardener*, of which the scope is obvious, and *Beano*, a "comic" for children and youths. Together the periodicals make up a vast body of reading matter, some of which is excellent, a good deal harmless if sometimes foolish, and very little in any way vicious. We have examined 217 periodicals, of which 77 are intended primarily for children or adolescents.

Naturally the periodicals attracting the greatest number of readers are those devoted to matters of general interest, such as *Picture Post* with its 9,560,000 readers a week, *Illustrated* with 6,390,000, and *John Bull* with 4,500,000. Of the monthly publications in this category, *Lilliput* is the most widely read with 4,360,000 readers. *The Listener*, published weekly, which we have included in this group, has 950,000 readers. It reproduces the best talks broadcast by the B.B.C. in the preceding week and costing only threepence seems to us to be the best value for money of all the periodicals. Indeed, some of the most valuable broadcast talks, such as Bertrand Russell's series of Reith Lectures in 1948, and Fred Hoyle's series on "The Nature of the Universe" in 1950, can hardly be appreciated fully at one hearing and *The Listener* enhances greatly the value of such broadcasts.

Periodicals specially written for women are another important type. Quite apart from the ultra-romantic weeklies that are intended primarily for adolescent girls, there are a substantial number of weekly and monthly women's journals of good quality. Although no single one of them has a really large circulation, their aggregate circulation is such that one or other of them is to be found in most middle and working-class homes. Furthermore, it is a usual practice for women to exchange their periodicals among a circle of friends or neighbours, so that, each buying one, they are enabled to read several. In this way the influence of these periodicals is considerable. They are wholesome, if rather naïve, productions, usually containing two or three romantic short stories, and articles on clothes, dressmaking, cooking, and other matters of interest to women.

The largest group of periodicals, although their circulations are more restricted, are those devoted to hobbies, such as *The Amateur Photographer* and *The Motor Cycle*. Another important group, such as *Practical Engineering*, is devoted to technical subjects and is intended primarily for technicians.

Apart from the religious papers, which need no description, the foregoing comprise the large majority of periodicals meant primarily for adults, and though occasionally one or other might lapse from what most people would consider to be in good taste, in general they contain nothing objectionable. Nor, except again in a few cases, do they contain undesirable advertisements—an important matter in itself. On the other hand the positive contributions made by these periodicals to the nation's cultural life is considerable. Not only is this true of such obvious examples as *The Listener* or *The Argosy* (for its literary quality), but the encouragement of hobbies (for instance stamp collecting, poultry keeping and the building of model aeroplanes) is an important factor in developing worth-while ways of spending leisure time.

Periodicals for young people

Periodicals published especially for children and young people follow much the same general pattern as is described above for those intended for adults. A few, such as the *Children's Newspaper*, are excellent. The large majority are harmless but not very elevating, and a few are positively shoddy but not vicious. No doubt children from 10 or 11 years of age upwards also begin to share the interest of their elders in some of the magazines devoted to hobbies.

As might be expected, the predominant theme in periodicals for boys is adventure, and in those for girls is romance. Both sexes are eager readers of school stories. They do not like these stories to be about children of their own type, in schools such as they themselves attend, but prefer that the whole subject should be glamorized, so that the scene of the school stories is invariably set in expensive boarding schools, which innocent piece of snobbery adds to the enjoyment of the readers and does nobody any harm.

Magazines devoted entirely or mainly to cartoons, often described as "comics," are popular with both youths and girls. These magazines are cleverly designed, and the stories told in the pictures are by no means devoid of humour nor lacking in an understanding of human nature. The pictures themselves, however, are for the most part not well drawn and are often crudely coloured.

Some of the magazines for young people are widely read. As the Hulton Readership Survey was concerned only with persons over the age of 16, we are unable to give comprehensive figures, but in 1948 three of the romantic weeklies intended mainly, but not exclusively, for adolescent girls had circulations of 487,052, 451,057 and 320,000 respectively. At the same time one of the leading adventure magazines for boys had a weekly circulation of 302,903. A rough indication of the number of actual readers can be obtained by multiplying the circulation by 2·5.

Erotic magazines

In view of the sensational covers and titles of some magazines and paper-backed "novelettes" displayed for sale in certain shops, and occasionally offered by itinerant vendors or displayed at railway-station bookstalls, we thought it necessary to ascertain whether their contents were objectionable. In fact there seems to be so little really objectionable literature on sale that, with the exception mentioned in the next paragraph, its volume can fairly be described as negligible. Quite harmless, simple and unsophisticated stories are contained within nearly all the lurid covers which are presumably designed as "catchpenny" devices.

Objectionable magazines

There is nevertheless one class of magazines on sale which seem to us to be thoroughly objectionable. They are of transatlantic origin, most of them coming from the United States, but some from Canada. They contain highly sensational stories of crime, which purport to be true. These publications are deplorable from every moral and aesthetic point of view, for their literary style is as crude as their subject matter, and the advertisements they contain are hardly less objectionable than the stories.

We have no means whatever of knowing how many of these magazines are sold in England, but the total number must be considerable because they are sold throughout the country by one of the multiple stores, and they are often obtainable on bookstalls, and in street markets, and in a number of the smaller and low-grade bookshops. Whatever the number, however, we believe that the importation and sale of these maga[illegible]s most undesirable. Their influence can be nothing but evi[illegible]

Books

Some 15,000 books are published every year and though comparatively few of them have large sales the total number of books bought each year is measured in millions. Even so, the purchases represent only a small fraction of the books actually read because the large majority of them are obtained from libraries and not by purchase. For example, one publisher informed us that approximately 80 per cent of the copies of the average new novel are sold to libraries, and not to individual purchasers. With the exception therefore of certain special classes of books, which we discuss both because of their intrinsic interest and because they do not conform to the general rule of being normally obtained through libraries, it is to libraries of various kinds that we devote this section.

Public libraries

Incomparably the most important library system in Britain is that maintained by Local Government authorities and paid for out of the rates. We think it safe to claim that the British public libraries are the best in the world. In the whole of Great Britain and Northern Ireland only 62,000 persons, approximately one-eighth of 1 per cent of the population, live in areas where no free public library is available to them.

Although the free public libraries service in Great Britain started as early as 1850, its period of greatest development has been since 1919, in which year a statutory restriction of the library rate to one penny in the pound was removed. Some of the libraries have a really large number of books; for example, in Cardiff, with a population of 240,000, the lending library contains 534,000 books, with another 262,000 in the reference library. On the other hand, in another town of 62,000 inhabitants, the public library contains only 67,000 books. The exact number of books in any given library is, however, not of great significance because the National Central Library established under Royal Charter in 1931 not only itself maintains an extensive library from which other libraries can borrow books required by their readers, but also acts as a clearing house through which libraries borrow fre[illegible] om one another. Thus, Mrs. X., living in an isolated town or village in the Highlands of Scotland, or Mr. Y., living in a remote fishing village of Cornwall, have at their disposal every library book in the United Kingdom. We have ourselves experienced the benefits of this service during our work in preparing this book for, through our local public library in High Wycombe (although neither of us is a ratepayer in that borough), we have been able to consult books from many different parts of Britain, some of them books for which there can be so little demand that only a library service organized on a comprehensive national scale could possibly include them in its collection.

In 1949 the total number of books borrowed from public libraries in Britain was 289,726,183. A further large number of books were consulted in the reference libraries attached to the lending departments, but it is impossible to say exactly how many because not all libraries are able to keep records of the books consulted in the reference libraries, as wherever practicable free access is given to the shelves, readers taking down the books they want and putting them back when finished with.

To obtain sufficient facts to bring our information about public libraries into perspective, we obtained detailed information from the librarians of a number of towns in different parts of the country and from several metropolitan boroughs. One of the most striking facts that emerged is the consistently large increase in the numbers of books issued in comparison with the numbers issued a quarter of a century ago, and this remains true even when allowance is made for the increased population. For example, in Plymouth, where owing to the destruction of a vast number of houses during the war the population in 1948 was less than it was in 1924, the number of books issued by the library had, nevertheless, increased from 364,215 to 1,111,113.

Although no statistics are available, there is no doubt that a considerable proportion of works of fiction issued are not of first-rate quality. The most popular "non-fiction" books are those classified as "History, Travel and Biography," and this is true for every library for which we have figures. The two next most popular categories are "Fine Arts" and "Useful Arts," the preference between them varying from place to place.

Although no comprehensive figures are available to support the contentions, two interesting trends have been mentioned to us by several of the librarians with whom we have been in touch. The first is that not only is the total volume of reading increasing steadily and fairly rapidly, but also a larger and increasing proportion of people are reading serious books—the best fiction and works of cultural interest. The second trend is that public libraries are being used now by persons belonging to classes, such as the professional class, who would seldom or never have used them a quarter of a century ago, with the result that the users are becoming a cross-section of the community. Both these facts are no doubt partly due to the improved standards of the libraries, and particularly of the librarians' staffs. Although the practice varies from place to place, it is now generally regarded as part of the librarian's duty to ensure that one of his staff is available to give advice and guidance to those who seek it about books to read.

Reference libraries—answers to questions

As stated above, reference library statistics are incomplete because so many books are available to the public without restraint or record. But mention must be made of one function fulfilled by the staffs of most reference libraries, namely, to answer questions on general subjects, or to indicate where the answers can be found, or to seek the answers. That this is a formidable task is shown by the experience of the staff of the reference library at Plymouth, who in 1948 answered 65,000 personal enquiries. No question went unanswered, and they included:

"What is the weight of 18-gauge sheet aluminium per square foot?"

"Can I have a list of the white fish-cake manufacturers in the Liverpool area?"

"What is the average relative humidity of Plymouth over twenty years?"

"What is the formula for diabetic marmalade?"

Lest it should be thought that persons in the West Country

housed in a special room, fitted with a stage and dressing rooms and seats for 150 persons to enable the plays to be rehearsed there.

(*d*) In Plymouth a system of children's libraries has been instituted. These are used exclusively by children and are staffed by children under the guidance of a qualified librarian. At present (May 1950) two children's libraries are open, two more are planned for 1951 and a fifth for 1952. They contain study rooms where special lectures are given and educational film strips are shown, and where exhibitions of the children's own paintings and handicrafts have been arranged from time to time. One of the children's libraries is being specially designed with facilities for children's concerts and drama.

How much do public libraries cost?

As we have been extolling the public libraries, it is as well to come down to earth and examine the cost of the excellent and varied facilities that they offer. It is not heavy. Generally speaking, about nine-tenths of it is borne by the ratepayers. Though there are naturally considerable local variations, in the majority of areas the library rate is not less than 3d. nor more than 5d. For many of the best libraries the rate is about the latter figure, although Bristol, with an exceptionally good library, manages on 3·81d. Perhaps a better idea of the cost of the library is given by saying that the cost per annum for each inhabitant of the area served is: Bristol 2s. 3·3d., Birmingham 2s. 10·57d., Liverpool 3s. 1·2d., and York 3s. 5d.

Public libraries in rural areas

On page 300 we stated that only a small fraction of 1 per cent of the population of the United Kingdom was not provided with a public library service. So far, however, our descriptions have all been drawn from urban areas. We turn now to consider briefly the provision made and projected in one large rural area, selecting for the purpose the West Riding of Yorkshire. The population of the area administered by the County Council of the West Riding is 828,500 and the administrative centre is Wakefield. In 1948–9, the latest year for which we have information, 255,762 separate individuals borrowed a total of 5,295,251 books from the public County Library. Of these books, 16·5 per cent were non-fiction.

The aim of the Council is to establish a branch library in every area where there is a community of 1,000 persons or more. On this scale, 135 branch libraries will eventually be needed, of which 85 had been provided up to March 1949.

In areas with a population of less than 1,000, a library service is provided through 441 library centres. These consist of collections of books, changed at intervals by the County Library, and housed in public buildings, such as village halls, schools and Miners' Welfare Institutes. The library centres, which are open for a few hours each week, are under the control of local librarians, who are usually voluntary workers. In 1948–9 the library centres in the West Riding issued 1,201,378 books.

In common with other authorities that are concerned with upplying library books in rural areas, the West Riding County Council is building up a system of mobile libraries that will eventually replace the library centres, although it will be a number of years before they do so. The projected fleet of specially designed motor-vans carrying the mobile libraries will consist of nine large enough to serve the needs of villages with a population up to 500, and twelve to serve isolated dwellings and small hamlets. The villages will be visited once a week, and the hamlets and isolated dwellings once a fortnight. A start was made with this scheme three years ago, and it is said to be very successful. It offers readers in rural areas not only a far greater choice of books than can be maintained in a library centre, but also the help of the trained librarian, who travels in the van, in making a selection from the books carried.

In a rural area it is not possible to provide many of the cultural activities organized by the libraries in large towns, nor, indeed, where men and women can draw on the traditional and long inherited culture of a countryside, are the external activities so necessary. But even so a good deal of useful work can be done. For example, the County Library in the West Riding has a collection of sets of plays for loan to amateur dramatic societies, and it also has a music library with 112,869 scores, which has been built up largely in response to specific requirements of societies and interested persons. There is also an organization for sending books by post to students and others who need specific works for serious courses of reading. 37,917 books were lent in this way in 1948–9.

Libraries run for profit or privately maintained

In addition to the books borrowed from free public libraries, a large number of books are also borrowed from libraries run for profit, and from those that are privately maintained by organizations of many different kinds for the benefit of their members.

For the reasons given below, it is impossible to make any estimate of the total number of books borrowed from subscription libraries, but the two largest concerns between them lend approximately 100,000,000 books a year. It seems a reasonable guess (though we offer it only as such) that all the other libraries together are unlikely to lend less than another 50,000,000 books, and equally unlikely to lend more than another 100,000,000. Some of the most important libraries and types of libraries are:

(*a*) Nearly 1,000 branches maintained (in friendly rivalry with one another) by two well-known firms. They both offer alternative kinds of subscriptions, namely, a preferential rate of 25s. od. per annum, for which subscribers can borrow up-to-date books and may send in lists of books they wish to read, and an alternative of 12s. 6d. per annum, for which subscribers must take their chance of what they find on the shelves. One of the two offers the third and more expensive alternative of a guaranteed service of new books. Each of the two firms issues approximately 50,000,000 volumes a year, non-fiction accounting for somewhat less than 10 per cent in one case and rather more than 10 per cent in the other. Between them, the customers of the two firms represent almost all classes of the community, although one of the two caters mainly for the middle classes. Women account in each case for some 70 per cent of customers, but a proportion of them are almost certainly borrowing books for their husbands or male relatives to read. Both firms report large increases in the number of books borrowed in 1949 as compared with 1939, and still larger increases as compared with 1929. In this their experience is parallel to that of the public libraries. The Head Librarian of one of the firms told us that he noticed no great change in the taste of their readers except that "people are more broad-minded than they used to be." The Head Librarian of the other firm was inclined to think that there had been a very definite improvement in taste. He said that one of their most successful recent books had been the biography of Cosmo Gordon Lang, the former Archbishop of Canterbury. He added that his firm could no longer, as used to be the case, stock their libraries in the big industrial areas with cheap fiction and stories of the Wild West. In his experience working-class men to-day want good solid fiction that is of some educational value, for example, a well-written historical novel. Women are still great readers of romantic fiction, but they too seem, in his view, to want a better standard of writing than previously.

The librarians in the libraries maintained by both these firms are available to give advice about books if asked, but their task is not considered to be in any way cultural, nor is their duty to improve taste. They are simply there to give the customers the kinds of books they want.

(*b*) Chain libraries, also known as 2d. libraries. The essential feature of these libraries is that there is no method of "joining" them or becoming a subscriber. A person requiring a book simply walks in, pays a small hiring fee, and walks out with the book of his choice. It is impossible to say how many 2d. libraries exist because many of them are individual ventures. Others are owned by companies formed for the purpose, the largest of which has 120 branches. It is certainly safe to say that in the aggregate there are many hundreds of these libraries. Although the term 2d. libraries is a convenient one, it is not altogether accurate, as in fact the fees vary from 6d. per book for three days to 2d. a week. Fines in respect of books retained too long are usually levied at the same rates.

At least two-thirds of the customers are women. The vast majority of the books borrowed are fiction, and indeed comparatively few of the libraries keep any other kind of books.

Most of the customers are working-class or lower middle-class, and we learnt from one company, operating on a large scale, that a branch could be made to pay provided it had a population of not less than 15,000 on which to draw. To some extent the trade is seasonal, being appreciably heavier in January and February than in other months, and slackest in June and July.

There is a pronounced element of competition between the 2d. libraries, and they are understandably reticent about the number of books they issue.

(*c*) Corporate libraries. Bodies of persons who band themselves together for a special purpose, whether formally incorporated or not, not infrequently establish libraries, and some of these are on a considerable scale. As an example, we were given some facts about the library of the Polytechnic in London. It contains 28,000 volumes in the lending library and nearly 4,000 more in the reference library. In the year 1948–9, 4,704 separate individuals borrowed 66,373 books from the lending library, fiction accounting for approximately 44 per cent of them. The next most popular categories were fine arts (12 per cent), literature (9 per cent) and useful arts (7 per cent). In addition to the lending and general reference sections, there are also special libraries for the Polytechnic's School of Architecture, Survey and Building, for the School of Commerce, and others. Polytechnic lending library is directly linked with the National Central Library (see page 300), so that its members are able to borrow books from any public library in Britain, and likewise people anywhere in the United Kingdom can obtain books from the Polytechnic Library if they are not available elsewhere. Few, however, of the "corporate" libraries are linked to the National Central Library in this way.

It is impossible even to guess how many of these "corporate" libraries exist, but the number must be very great, although many of them are restricted to technical works on one main subject and on subjects subsidiary to it.

(*d*) British Museum. In dealing with the question of libraries, we have not included the library of the British Museum because it is not intended for the free and normal access of casual or curious readers. It is intended for the serious work of students of specific subjects who cannot obtain elsewhere the information which they seek. It is an excellent "last resort" for the student and the learned, but any detailed consideration of it would be out of place in this book.

Purchases of books

For reasons that we have stated at the beginning of this chapter, we do not deal with books sold to the public, except for three special categories about which there are features that should be mentioned. These categories are:

(*a*) Penguin books. The object of publishing these was to provide books that were cheap in price but not in content, and through them to enrich the cultural and intellectual lives of large numbers of people who cannot afford to buy expensive books.

Penguins started in July 1935 with ten books. The intention of the publisher was that they should exercise a definite cultural influence, but should not be so highbrow as to alienate the general reader. The authors of the first ten books included André Maurois, Eric Linklater, Dorothy Sayers, Beverley Nichols and Compton Mackenzie.

Penguin books were at once a success, and nearly 800 had been published by December 1949. At first the major emphasis was on reprints, but now it is on new books, specially written or specially edited.

In May 1937 Pelican books were introduced by the same publishers. Whereas the original Penguins might be described as impinging on culture, the aim of the Pelicans was definitely cultural. Again, Pelicans started with reprints, but a large majority of them are now specially written. Up to date some 220 volumes have been issued in this series. There are also other series, such as Penguin Specials, which deal with current affairs, mainly but not exclusively in politics (157 volumes up to date) and editions devoted to Shakespeare, translations from the classics, English poets, modern painters, and so on.

One of the features that specially distinguish the series of books described above is the careful planning of the works in advance. If it is intended to deal with some specific subject, a person eminent in that subject is approached and asked to act as adviser and editor, and an informal team of experts is gathered round him, so that the books written and published dealing with the subject conform to a coherent and predetermined plan.

During the years that Penguins have been in existence, not only has the total demand for books increased, but there has apparently been some change in public taste. Nowadays a much larger proportion of the public than ever before are well informed about events and are interested in cultural books. Among the best-selling titles in the Penguin and Pelican series at the present moment are *The Symphony*, *The Meaning of Art* and the *Iliad*. The books on ballet and opera are constantly being reprinted. This concentration of interest on purely cultural books does not mean that there is a falling-off in the sales of fiction. For example, in August 1948 ten novels by Agatha Christie were published in the Penguin series and in a year each of them sold 100,000 copies.

Penguin and Pelican books are sold at 1s. 6d. a copy, and we were informed by Allen Lane, whose original idea they were, and who founded the company responsible for their production and is still its managing director, that "over 10,000,000, but less than 20,000,000 copies" are sold each year.

Great importance is attached to making Penguin books attractive to the eye, and their typographical and general presentation receive as much care as is devoted to the production of expensive books.

(*b*) Mail order books. These are books sent by post, direct from the publisher to the customer. They are not obtainable in bookshops, nor through normal wholesalers or retailers. It is an important but comparatively unknown part of the book trade. We have discussed the matter with the senior executive official of a firm which deals largely in this trade, and we give below a resumé of the information he gave us. He prefers that his firm should remain anonymous and we therefore refer to it as "Messrs. X."

The mail order business deals almost entirely in practical works (i.e., non-fictional works that may be either academic or technical, but which are intended for the use of laymen), reference books and children's books. Within these limitations they cover almost every conceivable subject. They are specially written and are designed to be read by the "masses." These books do not cater for technicians, nor for highly educated people.

Messrs. X. get into touch with present and potential customers by advertisements and by circularising. Once a person writes to them about a book he or she is circularised about every subsequent book that is likely to be of interest.

Before the war the firm used to sell a very large edition of a book in a short time. A few popular books would sell 100,000 copies in six months. Under existing conditions an equally large edition could only be sold over a much longer period of time.

On an average, about 25 new books are produced each year. Messrs. X. are not prepared to say how many they sell a year, but said it was "many hundreds of thousands." They lay stress on the fact that a very high proportion of these books are bought by people who do not normally visit bookshops.

Messrs. X. are concerned mainly with meeting an existing demand for books. They do not consider their task is to create a demand for any particular kind of book. They have a staff whose job it is to carry out research work to ascertain what kinds of books the public want, and also approximately how many books dealing with the different subjects can be sold.

The readers of their books are approximately 60 per cent men, and the large majority of the readers, both male and female, are between 21 and 35 years of age. For the most part they are working-class people earning about £6 or £7 a week.

Messrs. X. seek the views of their customers, not only on the contents of the books, but also on such matters as whether the type in which they are set is clear and on the layout generally.

It is difficult to estimate how much the demand for books through the mail order service has grown, but Messrs. X. state that they are constantly trying to reach what they call a "fringe market," meaning those people who seldom or never buy or read books, but who could make use of practical books if they could once be persuaded to acquire the habit.

As far as the nature of books in demand is concerned, there has been a definite change since before the war. People are no longer so keen to obtain general knowledge for its own sake. The trend is sharply in favour of books that will tell people how to do something that they want to do.

Messrs. X. advertise that any customer not satisfied with a book after receiving it can obtain a refund of the total cost. In practice the money is refunded without question as even though a customer may make an unreasonable claim it would not pay the firm to argue about it. In fact, considerably less than 1 per cent of persons to whom books are sent subsequently avail themselves of Messrs. X's. guarantee to refund their money.

(*c*) "Books as tools." The phrase "books as tools" was first used during the war years to indicate the place that technical works whether advanced or elementary could have in the practical day-to-day life of the people. They are important for our purpose of portraying the pattern of the nation's cultural life for two reasons. First their sale has increased enormously since pre-war days. Second, they often reach people who read no other type of book.

Sales of these books do not reach vast proportions, but they represent in the aggregate many hundreds of thousands of volumes a year, all helping people who would otherwise remain devoid of technical knowledge to master the practical affairs of their lives, and so encouraging them to spend their leisure in useful and active ways.

Reference books of this type are widely sold to persons who would never think of going into a bookseller's shop. The practice has therefore grown up of selling them in shops selling equipment for various kinds of hobbies. Thus books on motor cycles are sold through motor cycle shops, those on photography and gardening through shops selling respectively photographic materials and garden requisites. This tendency, which is naturally disliked by the retail book trade, emphasises the conception of "books as tools," and helps to make people think of them as essential pieces of equipment.

SUMMARY

There is still a large class of adults in Britain, possibly as many as 20% of the whole, who are unable to make any effective use of reading matter of any kind. The bulk of these are men. They are not in any way mentally defective although a good many of them are dull, and experience in the Army has shown that most of them can be taught to read if they are prepared to make a determined effort. Their illiteracy is both a reproach and a challenge to educationists.

For the normal 80% of the adult population, reading of all kinds plays a large and increasing part in their lives. A few newspapers and some periodicals, particularly those devoted to hobbies of various kinds, make an important and entirely beneficial contribution to national culture. Many papers and periodicals are foolish but harmless, but the sensational news stories of some newspapers make them undesirable. Though they probably reflect the standard of public taste, they certainly do nothing to raise it. A certain type of magazine usually imported from North America, and dealing with sex and with crime stories in a grossly sensational way, is thoroughly undesirable. The illustrations in these magazines are in bad taste, the literary style is bad, and the advertisements are sensual, suggestive, and unpleasant. We would like to see their import prohibited.

The reading of books has increased to a great extent over the last thirty years. It is impossible to say how many books are read during a year because it is impossible to cover some important sources of supply, e.g., borrowing from friends. It is safe to say, however, that it is not less than 12 or 13 per head of the literate population, and it may be substantially greater.

There are two sources of supply of books in Britain of which we feel proud, certain that they have no equal anywhere in the world. They are the Penguin venture, with Allen Lane's motto of "Cheap in price but not in content," and the public libraries. The value of the work done by these, each in its own field, in enriching the cultural and spiritual life of the nation cannot easily be exaggerated.

CHAPTER XII

ADULT EDUCATION

SINCE this book is concerned primarily with leisure time activities, and their effect upon character, we do not deal with the education of children during the years that schooling is compulsory, nor with adolescents and young adults in secondary schools and universities, since for them the educational process cannot reasonably be said to constitute a leisure time activity. Our attention in this chapter is directed to the men and women, millions in the aggregate, who, often at a sacrifice of money as well as time, devote a portion of their leisure to improving their understanding, or to acquiring useful skills, through one or other of the many varied forms of adult education. We use the term adult education to include all broadly educational activities from the age when compulsory schooling ends onwards, excepting only secondary schools and universities. In our definition, therefore, adult education includes the term further education, which is sometimes used by writers as being synonymous with adult education, and at other times is used to describe educational activities, such as day continuation schools, that fill in the three or four years after the end of compulsory schooling.

Of the high importance of adult education there can be no doubt, and there is a strong element of truth in Sir Richard Livingstone's forceful statement, "To cease to be educated at 14 is to die at 14."

Our investigations into the subject of adult education have been conducted by the threefold method of discussion with a substantial number of well-informed persons, many of them men and women of national reputation in this particular field, by visits to representative centres of adult education, and by extensive reading. In this chapter we shall seek, first to establish the true aim of adult education, seco current practice, and third, to assess the exten practice is likely to achieve the desired end.

The aim of adult education

One man whose advice we sought, and who occupies an important organisational post in the field of adult education, described its aim as being "to produce a knowledgeable citizen, who has an understanding first of the framework of life (i.e., broadly speaking, of politics), second of the means of life (i.e., economics), and third of the nature of life (i.e., ethics)."

Another man with considerable experience of adult educational work has written, "In this interim period when the churches, once the source of a working philosophy covering all fields, have lost much of their grip, it is the duty and opportunity of adult education to set about the gradual establishment and strengthening of civilizing influences throughout national life." He has also written, "The task of adult education is not to teach but to evoke and set upon a civilizing mission the latent energies and aspirations of men."[1]

Yet a third expert has written, "Most social problems are at bottom problems of human relationships. . . . Adult education is a group activity. The success of an adult class depends largely on good relationships between its members, and between the class and the tutor." And later in the same article, "Democracy is unworkable unless there is widely spread throughout the community a respect for truth, a capacity to think outside one's own interests, a willingness to learn from experience, and to adjust one's attitude accordingly, and (perhaps the most difficult of all) the ability to combine conviction with tolerance. All this demands high qualities of head and heart alike, for social judgment involves feeling as well as thinking. In a word, what we need most in our citizens is maturity. A knowledge of the facts is important but is not enough. We have to adjust ourselves to knowledge and to each other. It is in this power to achieve adjustments that adult

[1] Guy Hunter, warden of Urchfont Manor, in an article, "1950—A New Dedication," in *Adult Education* for March 1950, the quarterly review issued by the National Institute of Adult Education in London'

education at its best makes a major contribution to the problems of personal relationship."[1]

From the three foregoing opinions, the true scope of adult education can be deduced. It is a communal enterprise, deriving an essential part of its strength from that fact, and concerning itself with the development of culture and wisdom, rather than with the imparting of factual knowledge. Indeed, since it is often said with a good deal of reason that many of the world's difficulties to-day arise from the fact that technological development has outstripped the development of the social and moral senses which are necessary to ensure that technology is harnessed for good and not for evil, it follows that adult education, as outlined in the passages we have quoted, is, in so far as it remains true to its ideals, a force for good of which the potentialities can hardly be exaggerated.

Few men and women attending classes at an Evening Institute or joining a drama group in an Educational Settlement, or attending meetings of a Women's Institute, or joining a discussion group in a Community Centre, will think of themselves as engaged on what Guy Hunter calls "a civilizing mission." Yet, allowing for variations in quality, adult educational activities in general aim at nothing less, and it is with this in mind that the value of the work described in the following pages must be assessed.

Adult education in practice[2]

Although later in this chapter we shall have cause to remark on ventures, such as Community Associations, where persons, without the help of any exterior organizing body, come together for purposes that involve adult education, it is nevertheless true that most of the adult educational facilities in England and Wales are provided, usually in anticipation of demand which they help to stimulate, by organizations that exist wholly or in part for that purpose. These organizations can be divided into four categories:

[1] John H. Nicholson, Principal of University College, Hull, writing on "Adult Education and Personal Relationships," in the Winter 1949 edition of *Common Room.*

[2] In this and succeeding paragraphs we have taken many facts and figures from a handbook, *Adult Education in the United Kingdom,* a document prepared by the National Co-operating Body for Education at the request of Unesco, for inclusion in an eventual international handbook on the subject.

(1) The Ministry of Education. The function of the Ministry in regard to adult education is restricted to advising Local Education authorities, and to providing money to assist suitable schemes of adult education, whether such schemes are instituted by Local Education authorities or by voluntary bodies.

(2) Local Education authorities. Under Section 41 of the 1944 Education Act, Local Education authorities are required "to secure the provision of facilities for the leisure-time occupation, in such organised cultural training and recreative activities as are suited to their requirements, for any persons over compulsory school age who are able and willing to profit by the facilities provided for this purpose." The phrase in the Act, "to secure the provision of facilities," means that each Local Education authority can choose between providing facilities itself, and helping voluntary organizations to provide facilities. In practice Local Education authorities usually do both, reserving certain fields to themselves and encouraging voluntary organizations in others.

(3) Extra-mural departments of universities. Seventeen universities, or university colleges, in England, and four in Wales, engage in extra-mural work. This takes many forms, but the basic principle of each is that lecturers of university standard should be made available to guide the studies of persons to whom university standards of culture and understanding would not otherwise be available.

(4) Voluntary organizations. These are extremely numerous and are of three types, namely (i) those, such as the Workers' Educational Association, that are recognized by the Ministry of Education, or by Local Education authorities, and are supported by them, (ii) those, such as certain educational settlements, of which the aims are definitely educational in an academic as well as a cultural sense, but which receive no official support, (iii) those, such as the Women's Institutes, of which the aims are educational in a broad sense but which ordinarily provide no academic teaching.

Such is the diversity of the adult educational work carried out under the aegis of the four types of organizing bodies referred to above that no estimate, or even useful guess, can be

men's. Although naturally the educational activities centre more around such activities as home nursing and infant care, there are courses on current affairs, and on foreign languages, and discussion groups are popular.

Both these groups of institutes suffer from having normally to use in the evenings buildings that are used during the day as schools. This causes a great deal of inconvenience and discomfort, as neither the buildings themselves, nor the furniture, are suitable for the purposes of adult education.

Although some 250 of London's 3,000 youth clubs receive financial help from the London County Council, the direct work of the Council for youth is concentrated principally in its 21 recreational institutes which have 30,000 members of both sexes up to the age of 20. The amenities that they offer are social and recreational but a condition of membership is that every member must take part in at least one educational activity. The institutes are open every evening for approximately nine months of the year. Membership costs 1s. 6d. or 3s. 0d. a year, depending on whether the member is under or over 18 years of age. The activities at a typical recreational institute include woodwork, cookery, drama, fencing, ballroom dancing, boot repairing, photography, boxing and musical appreciation.

In the course of our investigations we have ourselves visited examples of each of the different kinds of institutes described above and we can testify to the excellent work they are doing. Those attending them were obviously being influenced for good, not only by the intellectual development resulting from their studies, but also by the gain to their characters resulting from the communal activity of pursuing a course of study as one of a group under the direction of inspiring teachers.

A particular word of praise is also due to those in charge of the recreational institutes, most of which are established in areas that might fairly be called urban deserts, for nothing flourishes but seemingly endless rows of mean streets, cheap cinemas, public houses and poor shops. Our enquiries have convinced us that the recreational institutes are true oases in these deserts and are carrying out a truly civilizing task.

It must not be thought that the description we have given is in any way a full summary of all that is being done in the field of adult education by the London County Council. We have merely sketched the outline of the work that the Council is doing in the direct promotion of non-vocational adult education. We have no space to deal with the other parts of its work, including the vocational training of both sexes undertaken by the technical colleges, and the vast amount of work done by voluntary organizations receiving aid from the Council. To obtain an indication of the magnitude of this work it is only necessary to remember that the Polytechnic alone has some 21,000 students and that the London County Council pays £200,000 a year towards the cost of their instruction, equivalent to two-thirds of the total.

Before leaving the subject of the London County Council, brief mention must be made of its work in relation to Community Centres and Associations, the whole subject of which we discuss at greater length later in this chapter. Before the recent war the Council had planned an extensive programme of Community Centres, but owing to conditions arising out of the war the programme has been abandoned. At present the Council maintains one Community Centre and gives financial assistance to eight others. In addition it has let it be known that it will provide instructors whenever Community Centres or Associations in London wish to form educational classes and in such cases the Council will also meet the maintenance costs of the accommodation used by the classes. In a few cases advantage has already been taken of this offer.

Provision by the Local Education authority in Plymouth

In a few other of the greatest cities in England, both because of the financial strength of the local authority, and because a great concentration of population enables each of a great many diverse demands for courses to become significant, provision for adult education can be, and sometimes is, on a scale comparable to that in London. There are, however, a still larger number of cities of considerable, but not great, size where local authorities are doing excellent work within the limitations that size and finance impose upon them. As an example of these we take Plymouth.

In that city in the autumn term, 1949, 8,497 persons were taking part in adult educational activities organized by the local education authority. Of this number 374 were still at school and in their case the activities consisted of evening classes in folk dancing, ballet and ballroom dancing, and in gymnasium clubs. The remaining 8,123 persons represented well over 5 per cent of all those in the city above school-leaving age. The main media of adult education were the classes at the Plymouth and Devonport Technical College, where, at the time of our enquiry, there were 2,915 students following over 50 separate courses of which the large majority were vocational. 1,344 persons, of whom 789 were women, were undergoing courses at evening institutes, where the courses of instruction were not greatly different from those at the London institutes. Almost 1,000 persons were receiving adult education in a rather more academic form in classes organized by voluntary bodies, and for which lecturers were provided either by the local educational authority, or by the University College of the South-West, or through the Workers' Educational Association. Other large classes for adults were organized under or through the local education authority by the School of Art, the Technical School of Housecraft, the youth organizations and the community centres movement.

Overall it seems to us that the adult educational movement in Plymouth is virile and alive to its opportunities, and this is particularly so if, in addition to the official arrangements which we have outlined, account is taken of the voluntary organizations, such as the Educational Settlement at Swarthmore Hall, with its 400 members, which work independently of the local education authority but in close touch and harmony with it.

Adult education in rural areas

Although the provision of modern bus services means that most persons in rural areas could, if they were so disposed, take part in the adult educational activities in nearby towns, in fact few actually do so, and those few are mostly young.

people concerned primarily with the vocational aspect of adult education. In many parts of rural England, village halls and women's institutes are live centres of cultural and social life, and provide a good deal of indirect education. But in most areas direct adult education in anything even remotely resembling the form it takes in even quite small towns is entirely lacking.

It is true that the countryside has its native culture, and that its inhabitants, though sometimes untutored, have a wisdom that their sharper urban cousins often lack. But it is equally true that, generally speaking, countrymen are deprived of many, indeed of most, of the educational advantages that adult townsmen enjoy, and which could enrich their lives and restore a dynamic culture to the countryside, where the dangers of stagnation and sterility become steadily greater as the most active young people leave the country to seek their fortune in the towns.

County Councils, in their capacity as Education Authorities, have, for more than a quarter of a century, had all the legal powers that they need to make adult education in rural areas an effective reality. In some few areas there has been real achievement; in many little has been attempted. This is doubtless because the numbers who would take advantage of educational facilities in a village or small rural area would not be large enough to justify, or indeed to render possible, the setting up of an organization to meet their requirements. This difficulty has been successfully overcome in Cambridgeshire where the completion of a comprehensive and imaginative scheme has demonstrated the potentialities of a new system of village colleges.

The scheme had its origin in a memorandum presented to the Education Committee of the Cambridgeshire County Council in February 1925, by Henry Morris, the Council's Secretary for Education. The subject of his memorandum was "The provision of educational and social facilities for the countryside." Morris perceived that the facilities that were needed could not be based economically on a single village as a unit, but that what was required was, in his words, "the adoption of the rural region as a cultural and social unit."

In practice this meant the choice of large villages in which could be built centres, to be known as village colleges, which would be the cultural, educational and social headquarters not only for the village itself but for eight or nine smaller villages around.

Four of these village colleges were completed before the declaration of war in 1939. It had been intended that 11 should be built.

Following a discussion of the whole project with Henry Morris, we were taken by him round the Village College at Impington, the latest of them to be completed.

Impington Village College is, in the words of the brochure describing it, "A Community Centre housing a Secondary Modern School." The building is plain and even severe, but it has a beauty of its own, for it is finely proportioned and in good taste. It is true that a modern school and community centre are under one roof, but there is a wing kept chiefly for adult use, consisting of a common room, lecture room, library, committee room and games rooms, while the school rooms and their equipment are designed for use by adults as well as children. The hall of the college, which seats 320 persons, has a cinema projection room and a properly equipped stage; by day it serves as an assembly hall and gymnasium for the school.

The area, of which the Impington Village College is the centre, consists of 10 villages, having a total population of 10,000. In winter the Warden estimates that over 1,000 persons a week (i.e., equivalent to 10% of the population of the villages) use the facilities provided in the evening.

The College is democratically run by an elected council. In addition to providing a local headquarters for voluntary bodies of various kinds such as the Young Farmers' Club, the Workers' Educational Association, and the United Nations Association, courses are arranged for members in a large variety of subjects. The programme for the winter session, 1949–50, provides courses on 38 different subjects, the wide diversity of which can be gathered from the fact that they include courses on "Leading Ideas of the New Testament," "Local Government and Public Services," "Engineering Metalwork," "Cookery," "Needlework," and "Beekeeping." There are also music and drama groups and so many other activities that the fortunate local inhabitants have a positive *embarras de richesse.*

The cost to those who take part in the College's educational work is trivial, the maximum being 12s. od. for a session of nearly five months. Special buses are run to and from the outlying villages three times a week; some four-fifths of the cost of this transport is borne by the Education Authority.

We understand that the idea of village colleges on the Cambridgeshire pattern is now being taken up in Somerset, and in a slightly modified form in Peterborough.

Centres for adult education

Quite apart from the direct provision made by local education authorities, there are throughout England and Wales a not inconsiderable number of centres of which the main, and often the whole, purpose is to provide adult education on a broad basis. A large proportion of the centres are linked together in the Educational Centres Association and we cannot better develop the statement of the aim that we have just given than to quote briefly from a pamphlet of the Educational Centres Association, headed "Education for the New Community."

"Few of us have had time or opportunity to win from the world's storehouse even a fraction of the accumulated knowledge and experience that lies ready to help us, or to work out with others how it can be used, or to enjoy our heritage of beauty and learning.

"Education can help us to use our time and gifts to more advantage both at work and leisure, to be more effective in the community as citizens and it may be to influence the course of national and international events.

"The Educational Centre movement for over 30 years has sought to provide a special kind of education appropriate to the needs of grown men and women. In an atmosphere of democracy and friendship you can join with groups of like-minded people who are engaged with experienced tutors in finding out what they want to know about the world in which they live, in studying languages and other subjects which interest them, in gaining new understanding and pleasure from music, drama and the arts, or who are together enjoying recreational activities.

"Educational Centres are self-governing communities of adults engaged in education in its broadest sense and enjoying the companionship and stimulus of people of all ages and differing opinions drawn from all walks of life."

Educational centres are of three kinds—long term residential, short term residential, and non-residential, and we must consider each in turn.

Long -term residential centres. There are eight of these in England and Wales. The numbers of persons attending them at any one time is necessarily small, for example Ruskin College has never at any one time had more than 90 or so students, but the courses in all cases last one year or more, and though the annual output of students from all these colleges may be a mere trickle if compared with the vast numbers that are denied the experience of such a period of study, it is nevertheless a trickle that enriches the whole.

The Secretary of the Educational Centres Association, with whom we discussed the matter, strongly emphasized the value of the long term residential colleges, and he added that for manual workers in particular three terms are necessary for any really effective educational work, as so much of the first two terms is inevitably occupied in the workers adjusting themselves to new habits, for example to regular and serious reading and to expressing their thoughts in writing.

One of the difficulties encountered by long term residential centres, and to a lesser extent by short term establishments, is the difficulty of getting men released by their employers to take the courses.

Short term residential centres. We know of 18 of these in England and Wales. They are a comparatively new medium for adult education, and the length of courses normally varies from two or three days to two weeks. We have no reliable means of assessing the value of the work done in these establishments, but they are highly thought of by many of those whose lives are devoted to the cause of adult education. Several of these colleges are connected with the extra-mural departments of universities, and there is a great diversity in the subjects studied. The programme of one is before us as we write; its courses vary from six to twelve days, and the subjects include "The Reading and Writing of English," "The Rights of Man," "Introduction to Psychology," "The English Educational System," and a course in the French language, to be conducted entirely in French!

Since the short term residential centres are of such recent introduction, it is too early yet to say whether they will become a permanent part of the nation's system of adult education. One might reasonably suppose that the amount of factual knowledge gathered in an intensive six or twelve days, and subsequently retained and applied, would not be significant. On the other hand the very experience of communal living and communal study might have beneficial effects which we are in no position to measure.

Non-residential centres. Excluding the literary institutes in London and the village colleges of Cambridgeshire, both of which are sometimes considered as non-residential educational centres, we know of 31 such centres in England and Wales. Naturally the arrangements in them vary from place to place but as representative of a good centre we describe below the Swarthmore Educational Settlement in Plymouth.

This Settlement originated as an old type Adult School but it started its present broader type of work in 1921. Its curriculum varies little from session to session, and indeed it has a remarkably wide sweep from puppetry to philosophy and embracing such courses of study as "Social and Economic Problems," modern languages, "Film Appreciation," "Marriage and the Family," "Trustworthiness of Sources for the Life of Jesus," and marine biology.

No handicraft work of any kind is carried on at the Settlement, because ample local provision for it is made elsewhere in Plymouth by the local education authority.

In addition to the formal courses at the Settlement there are also informal discussion groups, play reading groups, a badminton club, and a drama group which presents three full length plays every year.

Various bodies, not directly connected with the Settlement, use its buildings and by their presence contribute to the communal, as opposed to the academic, life of the Settlement.

The Settlement has approximately 400 members, but nearly twice that number use the buildings regularly because of the visiting organizations mentioned above. The tutors, of whom there are normally 17 or 18, are either lecturers from the University College of the South-West at Exeter, or local schoolmasters, or local inhabitants with special qualifications.

The 400 enrolled members of the Settlement represent both sexes and all classes of the community, but the majority are middle-class and there is a substantial preponderance of women. A majority of them are in the 30–40 age group.

There is a resident Warden, whose influence is a decisive factor in the work and life of the Settlement, but who exercises his office by example, tact and persuasion, and not by an assumption of "headship," which would be resented and would damage the feeling of being engaged in a communal enterprise, upon which the success of the Settlement depends to a considerable degree. This communal spirit is greatly strengthened by the exchanges of views, and the sharing of experiences, that take place in the common room. Indeed, it is hardly too much to say that a common room is a vital feature of any such place and one that transforms it from a lecture room block into a Settlement.

Fees at the Settlement are small, a typical charge being 10s. 0d. for a session of 20 weekly lectures. The local education authority makes an annual grant which was £200 in the year ending 31st July 1949, when total expenditure at the Settlement was £1,817.

There is no doubt that the Settlement meets an important need in the life of the people of Plymouth, for it provides for the intellectual and social needs of persons living over a wide area. It is by no means uncommon for members to travel five or six miles each way for a lecture.

Other organizations concerned with formal education

Besides the centres of Adult Education which we have described, there are also a number of organizations of national importance which, though normally possessing no premises of their own where classes can meet, nevertheless play an important part in promoting courses of study.

The most important of these organizations is the Workers' Educational Association. It has well over 100,000 students organized in over 6,000 classes, and the general aim of the Association has been described as "Teaching people how to think, not what to think." It works in close co-operation with the universities and nearly one-third of its courses are provided in conjunction with the universities. Although a majority of the courses are, in content and duration, very similar to those given in a non-residential educational centre such as we have described, on the other hand an important minority of them (14% in 1948–9) are three-year courses which require considerable self-discipline as well as intellectual effort from the students. In addition to its other work the Workers' Educational Association organizes single lectures, study circles, discussion groups, conferences and week-end and one-day schools on a considerable scale. Despite its name, the Workers' Educational Association, which from its foundation in 1903 did, for a considerable number of years, cater mainly for manual workers, has of recent years attracted non-manual workers in increasing numbers. Even so, manual workers still constitute approximately 20% of all the students.

The National Adult School Union is an old-established organization that has somewhat diminished in importance as the system of public education organized by local education authorities has developed. Nevertheless the Union still has some 13,000 members organized in 700 groups. The Union has a strong religious background to its class-work.

The Co-operative Movement maintains its own Educational Association, through which help and advice in educational matters is given to 450 Co-operative Societies. The Co-operative College which it maintains is one of the long term residential centres mentioned above. The Association's main interest is in social studies, particularly with reference to the Co-operative Movement, and in studies of managerial and secretarial work.

Community centres and associations

We turn now to those organizations of which the contribution to adult education is indirect although often important. Probably the most important of these are the community centres and associations. Their contribution cannot be measured and recorded in terms of "so many students in so many classes," for at their best they are making an immensely useful but intangible contribution to what might be described as "education for living," at their worst they are mere places of amusement of no educational significance. The fact that community centres have an educational function has received statutory recognition in two Acts, namely, the Physical Training and Recreation Act, 1937, which authorizes the Ministry of Education to make a contribution towards capital costs, and the Education Act, 1944, under which local education authorities can make a grant for running expenses. Many community centres organize classes of instruction, the instructors or lecturers frequently being provided by the local education authority. Other centres house branches of the Workers' Educational Association, or organize lectures and discussion groups from among their own members.

It is impossible to say how many community centres there are in England and Wales, since the term is an imprecise one and many independent establishments, some of long standing, described by their members as "clubs" or "institutes" are similar in function to community centres.

The National Council of Social Service, which has done a great deal to stimulate the community centre movement, know of the existence of 1,110 community associations, of which 437 own their own buildings (community centres). The Council wisely recognize that community centres cannot successfully be established by simply placing a building, however well designed and furnished, where some local authority or well-meaning individual thinks there ought to be a centre. The only practicable method is to allow the need for a centre to grow by first establishing a community association, that is an association of people living in one neighbourhood who are anxious to share their interests, experience and leisure with a view to the mutual enrichment of all their lives.

courses of lectures and demonstrations in subjects such as handicrafts, cookery, or household tasks.

In some institutes the members have developed a remarkable interest in educational activities, for example, in one village, where most of the members were the middle-aged wives of agricultural labourers, they selected medieval history as the subject for a course of six lectures.

Townswomen's Guilds

Townswomen's Guilds, which, as their name implies, exist only in urban areas (defined for the purpose as places with a population greater than 4,000) are somewhat analogous to Women's Institutes. Their aim is, "To encourage the education of women and to enable them as citizens to make their best contribution to the common good." There are 115,000 members in England and Wales, organized in a National Union. Each Guild holds a monthly meeting, which is divided between business, educational and social activities. Drama, music and handicrafts play an important part in the Guilds and sometimes groups of members are organized to study social conditions generally.

As an illustration of the activities of Guilds we describe below those of three Guilds during a recent month in a large provincial city:

Guild 1.—The social studies section organized a "mock council" meeting to demonstrate the working of the local government authority.

Members went on an outing by coach to Bournemouth (an annual event).

The drama group presented three-one-act plays.

The choir entertained some of the aged people of the city.

The handicraft group carried on candlewick and embroidery.

Guild 2.—Several members gave brief lectures at the monthly meeting. The subjects included "The glory of being a housewife," "Childhood Days in Belgium," and "Equal Pay for Equal Work."

Guild 3.—Drama, handicraft and social groups met during the month, and one group studying civic organization visited the telephone exchange and the office of the local newspaper.

Since the Guilds attract women of widely differing backgrounds, it will be seen that they are doing valuable educational work.

Youth Hostels Association

The aim of this organization is "To help all, but especially young people, to a greater knowledge, care and love of the countryside, particularly by providing hostels or other simple accommodation for them in their travels." The Association has some 300 hostels in England and Wales and a membership of 225,000 young people, who, travelling on bicycle or on foot, enlarge their knowledge of the countryside and thus raise their cultural standard.

The Arts Council

The Council was incorporated under Royal Charter in 1946 for the purpose of developing the appreciation of fine arts by the public throughout Britain. It gives financial help to existing orchestras, theatrical companies, opera companies, art societies and kindred bodies, and frequently succeeds in organizing or supporting successful concerts and exhibitions in areas where such events have previously been virtually unknown.

Outward Bound

Important pioneering work in the field of adult education is being done by the Outward Bound Trust, which exists to provide short term character building courses for youths between the ages of 15½ and 19. The name "Outward Bound" is symbolic and, having particular regard to the fact that the Trust's first school was by the sea on which a good deal of the training was given, is a reminder that the youths at the schools are outward bound on the voyage of life. The first Outward Bound School, the Sea School at Aberdovey, was founded in 1941. A second school, a Mountain School, was opened at Eskdale in the Lake District in 1950.

Youths from all classes of the community attend the schools for 26 days, and the concentrated and exacting training that they receive is designed to develop their bodies and to strengthen such qualities as self-reliance, endurance and courage. More important still, however, is the fact that the training and the experience of communal living and effort that are an essential part of the course, evoke a spiritual response in a large majority of the youths who attend an Outward Bound school, so that in the duration of a course they grow in spiritual stature, and return to their factory, school or home, finer persons and more useful citizens than they were a month earlier.

In the nine years since the first beginnings of the work, the Outward Bound Trust has not yet solved all its problems. It has demonstrated that the training produces an enduring strengthening of character but it has not found a way to reap the whole harvest by a careful follow-up of each youth so that he can be strengthened and encouraged to keep and spread his ideals in his normal, often far from idealistic, environment. Yet we know that the Trust recognizes the need for some form of follow-up and we are confident that in due course it will be achieved. In the meantime the two Outward Bound schools, which can cater for 2,000 youths each year, are an important demonstration of what can be done in the field of character training, and it is to be hoped that the Trust will expand its activities, and that other organizations will think their work worth copying.

We are informed that at present over 150 industrial concerns, including many of the largest in the country, and over 60 local education authorities, are supporting the Outward Bound Trust by sending youths to the schools. In the House of Commons on the 17th July 1950, the Minister of Education described the Trust as "A voluntary body which is doing a great work."

Broadcasting

It is difficult to assess the place of the B.B.C. in the field of adult education. Its influence is informal rather than academic. One professional radio critic, with whom we discussed the matter, expressed the view that broadcasting is the most important single cultural force in adult education and he pointed out that good music, drama, serious talks, and the unbiased presentation of world events in news bulletins, had entered millions of homes for the first time. On the other hand a great deal of broadcast material would not raise anybody's cultural level, although perfectly legitimate and reasonable entertainment, and many people listen to nothing but these "popular" programmes.

Broadcasting has undoubtedly done much to relieve the monotony of life for housewives in small houses, who are often alone for most of the day, and who have little change from routine duties. Some of the programmes specially broadcast for them contain what might reasonably be called educational matter. but it seems, at best, doubtful whether much is achieved in this way.

In our view there are two serious objections to the acceptance of the British Broadcasting Corporation as a decisive influence in adult education. First, listening makes very little demand on a listener. It is easy to switch on a radio set, and hearing the resultant sounds (as opposed to listening attentively) needs no concentration; nor can the speaker be questioned or challenged. The second objection is that listening is an individual and not a communal enterprise and we saw earlier in this chapter that educationists usually maintain that an important part of the value of adult education is derived from the fact that it is a communal enterprise.

SUMMARY

We do not claim that the outline we have given of the nature of adult educational work in England and Wales is comprehensive. Indeed it could not be so within any reasonable limits of space, but to have expanded the chapter further would have made it out of proportion with the rest of our work. Within the limits we have allowed ourselves, we have concentrated largely upon pioneering projects and may therefore seem to have done less than justice to such long-established and large scale activities as the Workers' Educational Association. Nevertheless, on the whole we believe that we have said enough to give a fair picture of the volume of adult educational work. Although we have not been able to make any direct appraisal of its quality, we have been informed by those who, without being directly concerned with the day-to-day work of adult education, are nevertheless in close touch with it and are therefore in a position to know, that the general standard is high, particularly in urban areas. This has been borne out, as far as our own observation goes, by what we have seen in the substantial number of adult education establishments of different kinds that have been visited by one or other, or both, of us in counties as far apart as Yorkshire, Hertfordshire, Gloucestershire and Devonshire, and in London.

The weakness of adult education work in England has apparently been hitherto in the rural areas. It seems reasonable to believe that the village college system will provide the solution to the problem, although at the most optimistic estimate, decades will elapse before the colleges become normal features of the English countryside.

CHAPTER XIII

RELIGION

In the preceding chapters dealing with ways in which people spend their leisure, we have been building up a picture from which it is possible to deduce with some accuracy what is the philosophy of life of people in Britain[1] to-day. Now we deal with the extent to which religion is a dynamic factor in determining their thinking and behaviour.

What is our problem?

By religion in this chapter we mean Christianity, since Western civilization has been built mainly upon it, and since it has provided both the ideals at which men and nations have aimed, and the spiritual power which has impelled them to seek their attainment.

The problem which we seek to elucidate is, therefore, what influence does Christianity exert on the lives of British people to-day and what are the prospects for the future. To resolve this problem it seems to us that we need to answer three questions:

(*a*) How far do people in Britain believe that Christianity is relevant to life in a scientific age?

(*b*) Since, in the late Sir George Newman's words, "The value of any religion depends upon the ethical dividend that it pays," what is happening to the character of the people of Britain to-day? Is it improving or deteriorating?

(*c*) If our factual investigations support the general belief that there is a decline in the observance of the formalities of religion, such as church-going, how far does this decline

[1] As stated at the beginning of this book, our studies have been restricted to England and Wales. To avoid wearisome repetition of the words "England and Wales," or the corresponding adjectives, we have used the words "Britain" and "British" with some freedom. As Scotland may differ markedly from England and Wales in the matter of religion, we wish to reiterate that whatever we write here does not refer to Scotland.

represent a real deterioration of the nation's religious life? If it is a sign of real deterioration, how can it be reconciled with the growth of humanitarianism, including the vastly increased care now given to even the least vocal sections of the under-privileged, such as the aged?

If we can make a fair show of answering these three questions, we believe that we shall provide a basis for an assessment of the true level of religion in Britain to-day.

Our method of examining the problem

In an attempt to measure, even approximately, the religious life of a nation, it is necessary to know both the extent of the formal observance of religion and the effect of such observance on people's lives. We determined therefore upon a threefold approach:

(*a*) Carefully organized church censuses in two towns, with the aim of relating the number of attendances by adults at places of worship on a normal Sunday to the total adult populations of the particular towns. As one of us (B.S.R.) had already carried out similar censuses in 1901 and 1935 in one of the towns (York) selected for our census, we were further able to examine differences of church-going habits in that city over the course of half a century.

(*b*) Examination of our 975 case histories (of which 220 typical ones are printed on pages 1–121) to ascertain both what the individuals concerned said about their religious views, and the apparent relation of these to the general quality of their lives.

(*c*) Discussions with 125 men and women especially qualified to advise us on various aspects of our problem. These 125 persons have included members of the Cabinet, Bishops, persons in authority in the Free Churches, senior police officers, professional psychologists, workers in many branches of social service, magistrates, parish priests and ministers of religion of various denominations, at least two convinced atheists, agnostics, university professors, directors of education, persons active in adult education, schoolmasters from schools of different kinds, journalists, and men whose interests are industrial or commercial. With their help we have managed to get our problem into perspective by seeing it in turn from many different angles.

As a matter of convenience we proceed below to discuss under six headings the information we have gathered, but this division is an arbitrary one which we adopt only to help in clarifying an extremely complicated picture. Later in the chapter, when we attempt to answer the three questions we posed on page 339, we shall have to look at the evidence as a whole. Our six arbitrary divisions are:

(1) Matters relating to church attendance.

(2) How non-church-goers regard the clergy and their congregations.

(3) Attitude to the Church of both church-goers and non-church-goers.

(4) Matters relating to the state of belief in the Christian doctrine.

(5) Social and political measures reflecting the Christian ethic.

(6) Religious activities other than church services.

(1) *Matters relatin to church attendance*

Church censuses.—Church censuses were held in York on two consecutive Sundays at the end of October 1948, and in High Wycombe on two consecutive Sundays in November 1947. Our aims were to ascertain how many attendances were made by adults at places of worship, and to classify those attending according to sex, and approximately according to age. In most places of worship where the clergy were willing to give their assistance, the enumerators selected were active church members and were well acquainted with the members of the congregation. They were furnished with specially-prepared cards, and were stationed at the doors inside the churches. In a few cases where the clergy did not wish this method to be adopted, other arrangements were made. Since, as stated above, we are able to compare the York census with others made by B. S. Rowntree in 1901 and 1935, using an identical procedure, we deal separately with York and High Wycombe, for we have no earlier records with which to compare those obtained in 1947 in the latter town. In each case the results of the census refer to total attendances by "adults" (i.e., persons of 17 years of age or over). Since we have no means of knowing how many persons went to church more than once on a given Sunday, we cannot say how many individuals make up the total attendances.

York.—The number of places of worship of the different denominations in York in 1948 was:

Anglican		29
Nonconformist:		
Methodist	18	
Congregationalist	2	
Other sects	11	
	—	31
Roman Catholic		5
Salvation Army		2
Missions		2

This total of 69 places of worship is equivalent to one for every 1,137 adults. In 1935 there was one for every 1,032 adults and in 1901 one for every 941.

The three censuses of church attendance in York were made in October, March and November respectively. From the point of view of the weather, there was nothing to render a comparison of the results of the censuses unreliable. All figures are the averages of censuses taken on two Sundays, and in each case the term "adults" has been taken to mean 17 years of age or over.

NUMBER OF ATTENDANCES AT PLACES OF WORSHIP IN YORK BY ADULTS IN 1901, 1935 AND 1948

	1901	1935	1948
Anglican	7,453	5,395	3,384
Nonconformist	6,447	3,883	3,514
Roman Catholic	2,360	2,989	3,073
Salvation Army (indoor services)	800	503	249
Totals	17,060	12,770	10,220

The first striking fact disclosed by his table is the steady decline in church attendances, notwithstanding the fact that the adult population of York increased from 48,000 in 1901, to 72,248 in 1935 and to 78,500 in 1948. In other words the attendances which represented 35·5 per cent of the adult population in 1901, fell to 17·7 per cent in 1935 and to 13·0 per cent in 1948. This means that the proportion of attendances at church by adults in 1948 was only a little over one-third of the proportion of attendances in 1901.

The total attendances were divided between the various denominations in the following proportions:

	1901 %	1935 %	1948 %
Anglican	43·7	42·2	33·1
Nonconformist ..	37·8	30·4	34·4
Roman Catholic ..	13·8	23·4	30·1
Salvation Army (indoor services)	4·7	4·0	2·4

To be fully significant this table should be read in conjunction with the previous one, which shows the total numbers of attendances. If this is done, it will be seen that in the thirteen years from 1935 to 1948 the Roman Catholic Church improved its position substantially relative to the other churches, but the attendances in 1948 represented a somewhat smaller proportion of the adult population of the city in 1948 than in 1935, and thus its real position is slightly less favourable than in 1935. The Anglican Church has lost ground sadly in the same years, both relatively and absolutely. It is indeed startling that in an archiepiscopal city the total attendances at Anglican Churches is less than that at the Free Churches, and only 10% more than the attendances at the Roman Catholic Churches. Nor can the relatively improved position of the Free Churches since 1935 be a great source of consolation to their members, for they too have lost ground in terms of total attendances.

Further interesting facts emerge from an examination, first of the proportion of males in the respective attendances, and second of the approximate distribution of the attendances into age groups.

The proportion of males of 17 or over in the population of England and Wales as a whole is approximately 47·6%. The proportions in the total attendances in the various denominations during the York census were:

	%
Anglican	40·3
Nonconformist	39·0
Roman Catholic	44·3
Salvation Army	32·1

There was thus an undue preponderance of women in all cases, although the Roman Catholics came near to properly balanced congregations.

Since, as far as age is concerned, the most important question is how far the churches, severally, are attracting an adequate number of the younger age groups, it is sufficient for our purpose to divide the attendances into "Under 50" and "50 or over." In England and Wales as a whole approximately 64·6 per cent of the adults are under 50, and 35·4 per cent are 50 or over. The percentages in the York census were:

	Under 50 %	50 or over %
Anglican	63·8	36·2
Nonconformist	54·9	45·1
Roman Catholic ..	77·4	22·6
Salvation Army ..	67·0	33·0

This is, of course, only a rough classification, but it is based on more than pure guesswork, for, as already stated, nearly all the investigators were themselves members of the churches concerned, and knew most of the attenders. It follows from these figures that the Roman Catholics have an excellent chance of maintaining a vigorous and expanding congregation for some decades, because the proportion of younger adults attending their churches is substantially higher than the proportion in the nation as a whole. No particular change in attendances is to be expected in the Anglican Church and Salvation Army arising solely from the distribution in age groups of their attendances, but the long term prospect for the

Nonconformists in York appears to be distinctly bleak, for these figures indicate that they are not attracting sufficient of the younger age groups.

High Wycombe.—As stated on page 403, there are 35 churches in High Wycombe, which is the equivalent of one for every 834 persons of 17 years of age or over.

Detailed figures of attendances on the Sundays of the census are given on page 404. The total of 3,427 attendances, equivalent to approximately 10·5 per cent of the adult population, were divided between the denominations in the following proportions:

	%
Anglican	20·7
Nonconformist	54·4
Roman Catholic	19·5
Salvation Army (indoor services)	5·4

Sub-divisions of the attendances according to age groups is given on page 413. In all the congregations there was an undue proportion of women but in no case was their preponderance really striking.

(2) *How non-church-goers regard the clergy and their congregations*

In the preceding section we have given evidence about church-going habits in York and High Wycombe and there is no reason to suppose that if censuses were made in other towns the results would be very different. In this section we are concerned principally with the persons who do not go to church, in order to ascertain their views on the clergy and on the lay members of congregations. We have discussed this question with informed individuals among both laymen and clergy but the main source of our information is our case histories. We think we should make clear at this point that we are recording the views expressed to us. We do not thereby imply that the criticisms made are necessarily justified. It is important, however, that whether people are right or wrong, their views should be known.

Quite apart from any question of belief or disbelief of the Christian religion, which is a separate matter which we discuss later, we have found so widespread a dislike of the ministers of religion of the Anglican and Free Churches that it can only be described as anti-clericalism.

How great a handicap the mere fact of being a clergyman can sometimes be is illustrated by a story told us by a Methodist parson of unconventional ways, who is doing work of the highest value in running a club for young people in the East End of London. He is careful never to wear clerical dress in the club, not even at the Sunday evening services, but returning from a funeral one day he was seen in a "dog-collar" by a group of lads in the club. They looked horrified, and one exclaimed, "Boys, we've been had. He's a bloody parson." The lads left the club never to return, deprived by their anti-clericalism of all the benefits of which they were in need.

One of the strongest criticisms of the clergy is that they are parsons "just for a job," as another man might be a bank manager. In a remote village with which one of us is acquainted, a new vicar stopped a man in the village street with a friendly greeting and said brightly, "I'm the new vicar." He received the reply, "Ah, tha' has a right good job. Stick to 'un, lad."

We have come across many other examples of this distrust of the motives of the clergy of which we quote three as typical:

(*a*) A working-class man in early middle age. "Nobody believes all the nonsense they read out in church. The parsons just do it to earn their living."

(*b*) A middle-class man in middle age describes the attitude of both church-goers and clergy as a "mixture of superstition, sentimentality, hypocrisy and—in the case of the parsons—pure chicanery."

(*c*) A working-class widow in late middle age. "Don't talk to me about parsons! They've got a pretty soft job, if you ask me. Telling decent working folk how to behave! What do they know about it? Never done an honest day's work in their life, most of them."

Besides their anti-clericalism, non-church-goers not infrequently express a dislike for people in general who do go to church. Often this goes no further than some such sneer as, "Fat lot of good it'll do them," but in a good many cases charges are made by the non-church-goers that churchmen do not live up to their principles. For example:

(*a*) A bus conductress said that when she brings people home from church on Sunday they don't look any different to her from what they did when she took them there, and she hears them gossiping about one another just as spitefully as usual.

(*b*) A working-class housewife said, "If parsons and church people practised what they preach there would be no need for political reforms."

(*c*) A working-class woman, "We're not church-going class. Anyway I'm too busy, and from what I see of people who do go it makes no difference to them."

(*d*) A working-class housewife, "What good does this chapel-going do? My old man never goes, but he doesn't do the dirty tricks some of these chapel people are up to six days of the week."

(*e*) A professional man, a bachelor, in middle age. "Thank God people *are* hypocrites. Life would be intolerably uncomfortable if people started practising their religion."

(*f*) A working-class man. "When I had T.B., mate, and was off work for fourteen months I can tell you who looked after me and the missus. It wasn't all those —— people from the chapel. It was my mates from the boiler shop. They'd sooner go to a pub than a church, and so would I."

(*g*) Male shop assistant, in early middle age. "My boss is a great man for the chapel but he'll give short weight if he can, and he makes plenty of mistakes adding the bills—all on his own side. Does a little in the black market line, too—nothing serious, but enough to give him a tidy bit of pocket money."

(*h*) Middle-class housewife, speaking about her landlord: "It doesn't encourage you much to go to church, does it, when you see an old skinflint like him? He'd squeeze the last penny out of anybody, and then up he gets on Sundays bold as brass and reads the lessons. I think they're all the same."

In this connection we think it relevant to quote the views expressed to us by two of the distinguished men whom we have consulted—one a minister of religion occupying a high administrative post in one of the Free Churches, the other a layman, whose life is devoted to social service.

The minister said, "The judgment of the community on Christianity will be more the judgment on the lives of people who call themselves Christians than on what is said from the pulpits. The layman should certainly get his inspiration in church, but he has a duty to spread Christianity by his daily behaviour."

The layman said, "The basic disease in the moral and Christian witness of the day is the lack of real integrity. People do not realize that the philosophic concept of integration demands that those people who bear a Christian witness should make that witness supreme in every activity of their life, at all times of the day."

From our enquiries we believe that a large majority of those who do not go to church judge churchmen by the standards of the two distinguished men whom we have just quoted, and find them wanting—"They do not practise what they preach."

Quite apart, however, from any question of sincerity of purpose, another factor which has tended to lower the esteem in which Protestant, and particularly Anglican, clergy are held, is the reduction in the difference between their degree of learning and social position and those of the average member of their congregations. This has come about in two ways. First, the general standard of education in the country has risen to a marked extent over the last half-century, and the economic position of wage earners has improved even more strikingly. Second, because of the difficulty of getting enough men of university education and high culture, a great many individuals have been accepted for ordination whose educational standard (apart from a period of intense but specialized study at a theological college) is not above secondary school standard, while the economic position of the clergy—not generally too favourable at the beginning of the century—has become desperate through sharply rising costs, and stipends that have either remained stationary or at best have increased proportionately less than the cost of living, that so a curate is often paid scarcely more than an errand boy, and a vicar less than an artisan. One Anglican bishop with whom we discussed this, pointed out that one of the evil effects in the decline of the status of the clergy was a corresponding decline in the quality of men offering themselves for ordination, so that the situation would be likely to deteriorate further. Indeed he went so far as to say that, with individual exceptions, young men from the universities were not in general turning to the Church as a career unless they had a poor opinion of their chance of making a way for themselves in any other sphere of activity.

We have no doubt, as a result of our enquiries, that, as we have recorded above, there has been a real decline in the esteem in which Protestant ministers of religion are held. It would not, however, be right to leave the subject without pointing out how readily the public responds to a man of more than ordinary spiritual power and ability. The picture is not all black. Men such as the late Archbishop Temple and Dick Sheppard exercised a great influence, and so too do a great many individual ministers whose names are never "headline news" but who are loved and respected in their particular areas. This we know to be true of both Anglicans and Nonconformists, many of whom are doing fine work, particularly in poor parishes. It is unfortunately true of the clergy, as of so many other categories of people, that one individual who fails to reach an expected standard is remembered and quoted, to the detriment of many who are all that could be desired but who in consequence receive less than justice.

What about the Roman Catholics?

Remembering that our church census of York showed that the Roman Catholic Church even if it were not quite maintaining its position was very nearly doing so, we think it worth digressing briefly at this point to see what is the position of the priests in the Roman Church, what are their duties, and how they maintain their hold upon, and the respect of, their congregations—tasks in which so many of the Protestant clergy are manifestly failing. As an example of how the Roman Catholic priests work we give below a description of Father X and his duties in a large and poor urban parish. We have made enquiries in Roman Catholic circles about how far this account can be considered typical, and although Father X is recognized as a man of high ability, we are told that our account does not go appreciably beyond what might be expected from an efficient parish priest in a parish similar to his. We doubt, however, whether many parishes are as well served by the priest as this one is.

The first striking fact about Father X is the strictness of the training he had to undergo before he could become a parish priest. He started with one year as a novice in the Order to which he belongs, and the training during this year was so strict, and the discipline so stern, that only five out of eleven novices who started with him completed the novitiate. Then followed three years' study of philosophy, and the other four novices dropped out leaving only Father X. Then followed a further four years' study in a theological college in Rome. He was then ordained, but was not considered ready for parish work, being sent for three years to teach philosophy in a seminary. This was followed by three years as an assistant priest in an urban parish, and then a further spell teaching canon law in another seminary. It was only then—sixteen years after starting his novitiate—that he was considered sufficiently experienced and wise to be entrusted with the charge of a parish. Of those sixteen years he was under training for eight years before being ordained.

His parish contains 1,200 Roman Catholics, of whom between 700 and 800 attend church on a normal Sunday. Father X devotes four nights a week to taking groups of parishioners for religious instruction, about 70 or 80 persons attending each night. He runs two youth clubs, and every Sunday evening, to keep the young people off the streets and out of the public houses, he has a dance in the hall under the church, attended by about 120 to 150 young people.

Father X is concerned in the administration of a large Roman Catholic school in the parish, in which he says openly that secular teaching is subordinate to the teaching of the Roman Catholic doctrine.

Great importance is attached to the visiting of parishioners. Every Sunday from noon to 4 p.m. Father X and his two assistant priests make house-to-house visitations. The parish is divided into four parts, and one part is dealt with each Sunday, so that every parishioner is visited in his home once every four weeks. Each priest visits approximately 30 houses every Sunday. He does not interrupt whatever is going on in the house—except in so far as father may have to wake up from his after-dinner nap—and Father X states that the families welcome these visits, even when they are backsliders from church attendance. In many houses the priest only stays a minute or two. In houses where there are troubles of any kind, or where the family are backsliders, the priest stays longer.

Father X considers that no priest can even begin to do his job until he knows personally every Roman Catholic family in his parish in their own homes, so that he can understand their difficulties, help in their troubles, guide them, and make them realize that the Church cares for them. There can be no doubt about the success of his methods, nor does there seem to be in them anything that a Protestant clergyman of adequate learning and experience, and comparable energy, could not copy. It is, however, relevant to add that Father X himself said that he could not carry out his heavy programme (including much private study and prayer) unless he had given himself completely to the Church. In his view, apart from any doctrinal consideration, celibacy is a practical necessity for the priesthood, so that the priest is free from the distractions, worries and divided loyalties inherent in domesticity.

One question which Father X could not help us to answer, for he could not be unbiased, is "What in terms of behaviour is really the effect of his successful ministrations? Are his Roman Catholic parishioners better citizens than their nominally Anglican, and often actually pagan, neighbours?" Father X claims that they are. The opinions of persons qualified to judge (magistrates and social workers) whom we have consulted are divided. It seems reasonable, however, to suppose that there should be some "ethical dividend" from so much effort.

(3) *What do people think about the Church?*

We have already in this chapter discussed the views which many people hold about the clergy, and about church-goers in general. We come now to a related theme. What do people think about the Church as an institution?

Perhaps the first interesting fact in this connection is the large number of persons in positions of great responsibility, persons with much learning, wisdom, and experience of the world, who are devoted and active members of one or other of the churches. Nor do an undue proportion of these men come from the privileged classes, which might have a special interest in preserving so important an institution as the Church. On the contrary many have reached their positions of authority from humble beginings.

At a time when so many people are perhaps a little premature in their eagerness to "write off" the churches, it is salutary to remember, for example, that the Minister of Education is a lay preacher, that the Chancellor of the Exchequer sometimes finds time to preach church sermons, that the Prime Minister gave his support publicly to the launching of the Christian Action Movement, and that two of our great war-time ambassadors to the United States—Lord Lothian and Lord Halifax—were deeply religious men, and active members of their respective churches. These examples could be multiplied many times as a reminder that many of the great men of the day still find the Church relevant in their lives.

Yet despite the encouragement and example of men such as those just named, and despite the devoted adherence to the churches of millions of ordinary men and women who make up church membership, it remains true that in the lives of a large majority of people of all classes of the community the Church is no longer relevant. As one distinguished Free Church leader said to us, "There is no doubt that the speaking, publications, and even way of thinking of the Church are simply not in harmony with the way of life of the people." To a great extent this is for the reason given by H. G. Wood in his contribution to the book *Has the Church Failed?* where, on page 153, he writes, "In spite of the contribution of many profound, honest and courageous Christian thinkers and teachers during the last hundred years, in general the Christian mind has not yet adequately come to terms with the scientific temper and with modern knowledge."

The Church is generally regarded with tolerance and indifference, and with little or none of the hostility which, as we saw above, the clergy so often evoke. Yet perhaps, in the long run, this indifference is more difficult to overcome than active enmity.

But even among people who are indifferent to the Church, and find that it has no answers to their problems, there is not infrequently a spiritual hunger, a wish that there was something in which to believe. It was put well in one of our case histories by an elderly man of the lower middle-class who said, "Is there nothing for me to believe? It's no good going to church where people read out prayers they don't really believe themselves. But there must be something. There is so much love and unselfishness in the world among all the evil things. And just look at those (pointing to a row of sweet peas in full bloom). You can't tell me that's all just accident. After all, people know the difference between right and wrong; and what's beautiful and what's ugly. I'm old now, and I'm not afraid to die, but I wish I could understand more clearly what this 'good' is that we can feel and see. It would be a help to people to get it organized a bit. But the churches will never do it. They're too much out of touch."

(4) *Matters relating to the state of belief.*

In his contribution to *Has the Church Failed?* J. Middleton Murry, writing of the spiritual beliefs on which the authority of the Church was founded, says, "The fundamental belief without which the rest could not have existed was the firm belief in a life after death. The belief in 'the resurrection of the body' was, from the sociological point of view the *unum necessarium.*" Yet it is precisely this fundamental belief which is partly or wholly rejected by a large proportion of people to-day. In order to throw some light on this matter we addressed a question to about 150 persons of both sexes, between the ages of 18 and 30, all of them interested in problems of community living and social questions. They all answered the question and only 49% of them said that they believed in any form of life after death, and a half of these so modified their answers as to make it clear that they had in mind various forms of survival that did not necessarily amount to a continued personal existence. In other words only one-quarter of the whole subscribed to what J. Middleton Murry has called the *unum necessarium.*

To some extent it is surprising that so large a proportion as a quarter were willing to commit themselves without qualification to this belief, for our case histories would certainly suggest that the proportion of persons holding a positive view is undoubtedly less. Much the most frequent type of answer was that given by a middle-aged male teacher in a secondary school who said, "I don't know, and I don't see how anybody can know. If there is a future life it is only reasonable to suppose that in some way it would be a continuation of this one, or influenced in some way by this one. I don't worry about it. I do my best here and now, and I'm not afraid of death. It seems impossible sometimes to imagine another life, but it's impossible, too, to imagine just going out like a candle and leaving nothing. My son (aged 14) was asking me the other day what I thought about it, and I could only tell him the same as I'm telling you. I know one thing, there aren't many people about who behave as though they really believed in heaven or hell!"

Besides his own typical attitude of "I don't know," the schoolmaster touched on two other important matters in his reply—first, his inability to imagine the complete extinction of his being and second, the lack of belief in hell. In our case histories we have found repeatedly that people of all classes and degrees of education, unless they have embraced atheistic creeds with the corresponding dogmas, find it virtually impossible to grasp the idea of their own complete extinction. Likewise, too, only a merest handful of people believe in hell, whether with or without everlasting flames. This latter state of disbelief is of the greatest practical importance, for it means that people can no longer be frightened into conversion. As a consequence, the task of large-scale evangelism has become immeasurably more difficult.

The question of a religious revival in England is often debated as though it were synonymous with a restoration of the power of the Churches, that is to say, as though large masses of Christians had strayed absent-mindedly from the fold, but still retained their general belief in the Christian doctrine as expounded by the Churches. If this were so, it would be comparatively easy either to win them back to the Churches or, alternatively, to form new religious groups within which they could practise their Christian rites. The reality is far different. Large numbers of people, certainly the majority of those outside the Churches, and very likely a majority of the whole population, have either explicitly, after careful thought, or instinctively, after little or no thought, rejected so much of the Christian story as related in the New Testament that no Church could recognize them as Christians at all.

By way of illustration of this, we give some further extracts from our case histories to show the state of belief of large sections of the population:

(*a*) A working-class housewife. "A working-class family that is religious is working against its own interest. Everyone knows religion isn't true, but the nobs try to make working folk believe it is, so that they won't kick up a fuss."

(*b*) A middle-class woman, who has obviously thought seriously, and calls herself an agnostic. "Religion is nonsense. The Church is run by the feeble in body for the benefit of old women and men who won't face facts."

(*c*) An upper middle-class man, who declares he is indifferent to religion. "I have travelled too much and seen too many different religions to believe that there is such a thing as a true religion."

(*d*) A serious-minded man of the professional class. "I believe Christianity cannot be sustained as a theological system, and doubt whether its ethics, and therefore the civilization built on Christianity, can survive the decay of belief in their supernatural sanction."

(*e*) A working-class man (seriously minded and spending much of his leisure time in doing voluntary social and political work). "It stands to reason, doesn't it, that the Christian doctrine isn't true? The basic idea's a fine thing, but it needs bringing up to date."

(*f*) A lower middle-class man. "I don't know what I believe, but I don't believe all this 'God is Love' stuff. When I was a kid I had a text in my bedroom, 'God is Love.' Since then I've been in two wars, been unemployed eighteen months on end, seen the missus die of cancer, and now I'm waiting for the atom bombs to fall. All that stuff about Jesus is no help."

(*g*) The headmistress of a girls' secondary school. "When you have simple people—children or nearly illiterate grown-ups—you have to teach them in simple terms, by stories and so on. It seems to me that the New Testament does just that. It was, as it were, a text book for a very elementary stage of human understanding. I don't believe now it is true, in the sense that I believe the theorem of Pythagoras to be true, any more than I believe nursery rhymes to be true. What is needed now is what I would call an advanced text book, a sort of Newer Testament, fit for the twentieth-century level of thought."

(5) *Social measures with a spiritual basis*

So far in this chapter, despite recording the existence of a spiritual hunger which we believe to be widespread, we have been dealing mainly with religion in a negative way—showing how small is the proportion of people who go to church, remarking on the hostility to ministers of religion, dealing with disbelief, and so on. This by itself gives a quite distorted picture of the situation, for the proper understanding of which it is necessary to recall the vast amount of positive work that is going on, of which the driving force is some form or other of religious belief. In this and the next section therefore, we intend to deal with this aspect of the question.

In Britain to-day so much effort is expended in caring for and helping people in every kind of need that it would be a major task to give an adequate impression of what is being done by a great number of agencies varying from individuals to Departments of State, and including a host of societies of different kinds. All these individuals, departments and societies are actuated by one common purpose, to minister to human need. They recognize an obligation to their fellow men and seek to fulfil it. They do not ask whether the recipients of their help are Christian or non-Christian, nor about their politics, nor about their views on any of the other numerous questions that often divide men into separate camps. Their aim is simply to give help where it is needed. This seems to us to be evidence that even if church congregations are small, there is a substantial measure of practical Christianity in the way men deal with men.

As we said above, it would be quite beyond our scope to give any sort of comprehensive list of the activities we have in mind, but they include such as the Discharged Prisoners' Aid Society, the St. John Ambulance Brigade, Dr. Barnardo's Homes, the National Assistance Board, and perhaps we should add the tens of thousands of anonymous men and women who contribute their blood to the Blood Transfusion Services.

It seems to us to be largely pointless to discuss the question of whether the agencies we have mentioned, and the large number of others that are actuated by a similar spirit, are providing an example of practical Christianity, or whether they are the expression of something called "humanism." The difference seems to us to be only one of nomenclature, for the humanism that acts in the way we have indicated, even if it calls itself "scientific," is expressing what is recognized as the best and highest of man's behaviour to man, and in our Western civilization that has its roots in the teaching of Jesus.

(6) *Religious activities other than church services*

We consider next some activities, other than church services, of which the aim is to impart religious instruction:

(*a*) *Parental teaching.* It is usual nowadays to decry the home as a place where no religious influence is exercised and to draw a picture of "the good old days" when in every home the family and servants are assumed to have gathered together daily for family prayers. In fact, the proportion of homes where that was the case was never more than a small minority of the whole. Even where family prayers were the custom, it seems legitimate to doubt whether, in many cases, they were of much real value. Certainly they did not stop most of the families concerned from grossly exploiting the maids who prayed with them, but whose lives otherwise alternated between basement and attic. To-day there are certainly bad homes in all classes of the community, and in many homes the discipline, which certainly used to be too strict, is now not strict enough. But on the credit side there are plenty of good homes, where the parents' influence is entirely wholesome, and where the children learn to live good and useful lives through love and example rather than through fear, as used too often to be the case. Specific religious instruction is certainly rare in the home to-day, often for the reason given by several parents among those whose stories are related in our case histories, namely, "It isn't fair to teach as a fact something I am far from sure about, and children's minds are simply not developed enough to take in the doubts and reservations that I make in my own mind." On the other hand it may well be that the practice, as opposed to the profession, of Christianity is now quite as highly developed in home life as ever before. It takes such forms as tolerance, unselfishness and mutual respect between parents and children and a recognition of the value of personality, even of the personality of the very young, in the place of the despotism, often far from benevolent, of earlier generations.

(*b*) *The school.* Under the Education Act, 1944, religious instruction is now compulsory in schools, but this is in itself no more than making into a statutory requirement what was previously a general practice. The two main changes caused by the Act are, first, that each local education authority is made responsible for the drawing up of an agreed syllabus of religious instruction, and, second, that to obtain an adequate supply of men and women qualified to give instruction it has been made possible for teachers to specialize in religious instruction as a main subject at their training colleges.

We have seen specimen agreed syllabi and three—those of the London County Council, the City of Plymouth and the Cambridgeshire County Council—are before us as we write. They are impressive documents, drawn up by representatives of the Anglican and other Protestant Churches, of the various teachers' associations, and of the local education authority itself. They indicate the outlines of a comprehensive course of biblical and religious study, and show praiseworthy courage and integrity in facing the difficult questions which they obviously anticipate that the teaching will provoke.

We have discussed the matter with the Minister of Education, the Permanent Under-Secretary of the Education Department, the General Secretary of the National Union of Teachers, various Directors of Education, and a number of headmasters and masters from schools of different grades. It is probably not unfair to say that we found optimism as to the result of the scheme to vary directly with the importance of the office held by the person discussing it. At a high level we have found confidence and optimism, although naturally there is a recognition that any beneficial effects cannot possibly be seen in the adult population for at least ten years. Among the rank and file we have found doubts whether the new arrangements will really lead to any great change. A master or mistress of first-class personal qualities, high ideals and having a desire to pass on his convictions, already achieves much. It is not easy, in the absence of proof, to believe that a new syllabus, plus some extra training in religious instruction as "a subject," will turn the average run of teachers into evangelists.

In some respects teachers stand to their pupils *in loco parentis*, and their difficulty in giving religious instruction is the same as that encountered by parents, to which we referred when dealing with religion in the home. They cannot give what they haven't got. The new arrangements seem to us to suppose, to some extent, that effective religious instruction can take the form of purely intellectual teaching, without coming from the heart. We were greatly impressed by the wise and cautious statement of one Director of Education, who said to us: "A great many teachers are in a state of religious bewilderment. They know they want something, they do not know quite what it is, and they cannot find it in the Church. Like many persons outside the teaching profession, they find it impossible to accept the Creed as it stands, and they do not like making subtle mental reservations when they say it. A great many modern churchmen are groping their way to understanding through a re-reading of the Testaments, but religious thought is in a highly fluid state and it is impossible to be sure that any professional conclusions that are arrived at are valid. For this reason it is extremely difficult to teach religion in schools, because people who are not certain that their ideas are valid dare not teach them to the young."

We would ourselves make one further criticism of religious instruction in schools as organized under the Education Act, 1944. It is that necessarily the agreed syllabi—excellent and courageous documents as we have already testified that they are—are based on precisely that doctrine which, as the empty churches testify, people are not prepared to accept. We see no reason to suppose that a new syllabus is likely to make the doctrine acceptable to a new generation.

(*c*) *Sunday schools.* General views about Sunday schools are of two kinds. Some persons—wisely we believe—consider them to be potentially a powerful source of good. Others regard them as outmoded institutions, from which no good is-to be expected except for their traditional function of keeping the children quiet on Sunday afternoons while working-class fathers sleep.

The approach of the Church of England and the Free Churches to Sunday schools is somewhat different, and we intend therefore to treat them separately. We give a separate account, too, of the Roman Catholic practice, in which Sunday schools, in the Protestant sense, play little part.

There are no statistics to show how many children belong to Anglican Sunday schools, nor by how many teachers they are taught. We were told by an informant closely in touch with Anglican Sunday schools that the number of children is much lower than in 1939, but that some recovery has been made from the low level of the war years.

Most of the children in Anglican Sunday schools come from the lower middle-class. Parents of a higher class do not often send their children, nor do those of the working-class, unless almost the whole of a parish belongs to that class. We were informed that the reason was that the working-class parents do not wish their children to stand comparison with the somewhat better dressed children of the lower middle-class.

In Anglican Sunday schools teachers are difficult to obtain and are recruited mainly from the same class as the children, often beginning to teach as early as 14 years of age. Despite an inter-diocesan training scheme, supplemented by regional training classes for Sunday school teachers, correspondence courses and summer schools, the large majority of Anglican Sunday school teachers still have quite inadequate training, and so can hardly hope to be effective. Another weakness in the relation between Anglican Sunday school teachers and their pupils is that the former are seldom sufficiently in touch with the children during the week. Ideally they should, through informal visits, know the children in their homes, and should also organize weekday activities for them.

Perhaps rather oddly, it is assumed in Church of England Sunday schools that children obtain elsewhere, mainly in their day schools, all the basic religious knowledge they require, and all they need to know of the Bible. Anglican Sunday schools therefore concentrate on instruction about Church practice, and worship in the Anglican Church.

We were informed that very few children continue in Church membership after they reach an age when they are able to break away from the Sunday school. The official reason given is family influence, but we cannot avoid the belief that the Sunday schools themselves are, at any rate in part, responsible for this.

Unlike the Anglicans, the Free Churches have comprehensive statistics of Sunday scholars and teachers. In round figures there were in 1949 about 1,500,000 children and 160,000 teachers in the Sunday schools of the principal Nonconformist Churches of England and Wales. These numbers were much lower than in 1939, but higher than the low level reached in the war years. The children come mostly from the working- and lower middle-classes. Teachers are difficult to obtain, and the same question of adequate training arises as in the Anglican Church. Our impression, however, after discussion with persons having authority in the Nonconformist Churches in matters relating to Sunday schools, is that, on the whole, they fare better in this matter than the Anglican Churches. We were informed that one reason for this is that they are fortunate in being able to attract a significant leaven of men and women whose weekday occupation is that of school teacher.

Nonconformist Churches have undoubtedly made great efforts to bring their Sunday school teaching up to date by use of the methods employed in modern day schools. They have also, despite denominational differences, achieved a substantial measure of agreement among themselves about the content of Sunday school teaching. The training is concentrated largely on the Scriptures, and seems to follow very much the same lines as the agreed syllabi for the day schools, which we criticized on page 359 on the ground that they were seeking to instil into children precisely the doctrine which experience has shown to be unacceptable to adults.

There is therefore little cause for surprise that the Nonconformist Churches, like the Church of England, find that only a small minority of the Sunday scholars (the estimates of the different churches varied from 10 per cent to 20 per cent) enter into Church membership.

In the Roman Catholic Church the prevailing atmosphere is one of spiritual totalitarianism, by which we mean that doctrine and the method of inculcating it are decided by a centralized authority, whose decisions are enforced by a rigorous discipline imposed at the local level by the parish priest who, with his assistant priests, concerns himself directly with the spiritual life of all his parishioners, whatever their age. As the influence of the parish priest is exerted in the home, in the Catholic day schools, and through weekday and Sunday services in the Church, as well as through such additional media as clubs and social gatherings, it is not surprising that the conception of Sunday school (the very name of which suggests that religion is something apart from weekday life) plays a less significant part in the organization of the Roman Church than in that of the Protestant Churches. Children of the Roman Church are admitted to their first communion while mere infants, eight being a common age, and thereafter they play a more complete part as Church members than Protestant children of similar ages.

The organization for dealing with young people differs in the Roman Church from parish to parish, In the parish of Father X, which we described on page 349, there was no specific Sunday school, the instruction considered desirable being given through the day school, the evening study groups, the Sunday Masses, the home visitations, and through the social activities. In another parish which is known to us there is a special children's service in the church each Tuesday evening, which all Roman Catholic children are expected to attend, and which is less a meeting for worship than a period of instruction. In general it may be said that Roman Catholics, through their organization and discipline, contrive to keep religion, or at any rate the forms of religion, constantly in the minds of their young people, so there is little need for special instruction on Sundays.

(*d*) *Religious broadcasting.*[1] In Britain religious broadcasting

[1] We desire to acknowledge the factual help given to us by the Rev. Francis House, Head of Religious Broadcasting of the B.B.C. Mr. House is in no way responsible for any opinions we express.

is highly developed, and there are religious broadcasts every day, including services, talks and discussions, as well as occasional musical programmes and presentations of drama. In the average week the total duration of religious broadcasts is approximately eight hours, this total being made up by nearly thirty separate broadcasts. The Listener Research Organization of the British Broadcasting Corporation has estimated that as many as 6,000,000 persons listen to the most popular religious programmes on Sundays. It has also revealed the fact that the majority of listeners belong to the working-class, and are non-church-goers. Radio therefore often represents their only contact with organized religion.

The religious broadcasts of the B.B.C. represent an important effort at evangelism, which is all the more commendable and effective because it is the result of joint planning by the Anglican, Free and Roman Churches. Few of the broadcasts are straightforward reproductions of the normal services held in churches. The majority of the programmes are broadcast from the studios of the B.B.C., and can therefore be made more effective by the use of the most up-to-date technique of radio presentation.

In planning religious broadcasts, the B.B.C. consider three separate categories of listeners, namely, convinced and practising Christians who are confined to their homes by sickness or infirmity, normal church-goers who may through the radio supplement the teaching they obtain in Church, and non-church-goers. Separate programmes are provided to meet the needs of each of these three categories of listener.

Like all other departments of broadcasting, the quality of the religious programmes varies a good deal and indeed opinions about individual programmes are often matters of purely personal judgment. Three facts are however certain. First the Religious Affairs Department of the B.B.C. shows real initiative and courage in its constant readiness to try out new methods of making its contribution to the nation's religious life more effective. Second it succeeds, not infrequently, in bringing to the microphone preachers of the highest quality, some of them laymen. Third, it succeeds in turning to religion the minds of millions of non-church-goers who would otherwise be untouched by any corporate religious influence.

It would be a stupendous task of social research to ascertain with accuracy what is the real effect of religious broadcasting, and indeed so powerful an instrument is the radio that many persons may be influenced by what they have heard without themselves realizing the fact. There is, however, not the slightest doubt that the influence of religious broadcasting is thoroughly wholesome. Our only criticisms are that the broadcasts might be even more effective if a greater percentage of the time available for religious broadcasting were allocated to laymen and laywomen and if rather less time were devoted to liturgical broadcasts. We do not, however, pretend that these criticisms are based on any certain knowledge of the situation. They are rather deductions from the general knowledge about the national outlook that we have gathered in the course of our work.

(*e*) *Recent attempts at evangelism.* We do not concern ourselves here with the work of the Churches and organizations (such as the Salvation Army and the Church Army) for whom evangelism is a part of their normal work—a part indeed which is often carried out with great devotion and energy and which undoubtedly leads to a steady, if not dramatic, flow of converts. Our purpose is rather, at the moment, to endeavour to estimate the prospects of success of large-scale evangelism by *ad hoc* bodies, of which there have in recent years been several examples. Probably the most important of these, because of the scale of the effort, the length of preparation, and the importance of the "target," was the Christian Commando Campaign carried out in London between the 14th and 23rd April 1947. This campaign was the culmination of four years of planning and preparation, and of experience of similar but smaller campaigns in the provinces. In the London campaign 3,000 clergy and laymen took part. They came from all over the country, and included representatives of nearly all the Protestant Churches. The laymen included professional men, students, journalists, politicians, men engaged professionally in sport, manual workers, and men from the managerial side of industry. The Commandos were organized into 34 teams, which in turn split into smaller groups. Besides holding over 12,000 meetings in the ten days of the campaign, the Commandos went into shops, factories, cinemas, markets, dance halls, public houses, clubs, private dwellings, and indeed into any place where people were likely to be congregated.

The Commandos were received politely, with many questions, with occasional hostility, but with little realization of the urgent and vital nature of the message that they were trying to convey.

One or other of us spoke during or after the campaign to six of the Anglican clergy who had taken part, and each of them stated, without any pressure, that they considered that they had achieved very little. Nevertheless, there is always the hope that words uttered during such a campaign will start trains of thought in the minds of the hearers, leading to beneficial results that remain unknown to the original speaker. But it can hardly be denied that the direct results of the campaign appear to have been distinctly meagre, despite the very thorough and efficient preparation. There are probably two reasons for this. First listeners were repelled by an unacceptable doctrinal approach, for example, the not infrequent use by Free Church ministers of the phraseology of nineteenth-century evangelism. Second—and perhaps more important—so great an effort should not have been allowed to exhaust itself in one wave; it needed months, or perhaps even years, of patient follow-up, even if the need for this "advance in depth" necessitated the adoption of a narrower front than the whole of London for the first assault.

We have no information about the cost of the Christian Commando Campaign in London, but the scale of preparation was such that it must have been extremely high. Neither this particular campaign, nor the other evangelistic efforts that have been made in recent years, should be judged as failures, nor indeed should they be judged at all, at this stage, merely by the standard of how many persons were persuaded to accept the Christian faith.

For a long time the man-in-the-street has been saying that the Churches, entrenched behind their own traditions, have not been entering in any significant or relevant way into his daily life. We believe that these evangelistic efforts are a most hopeful sign that, possibly, the Churches may stir themselves to accept the challenge. New techniques, new phraseology, and new thoughts about the doctrine to be presented, would be needed to make twentieth-century evangelism an effective reality. But it would be foolish to under-estimate the possibilities. Every such evangelistic experiment deserves sympathy and support.

(*f*) *Societies and organizations with a specifically religious purpose.* We do not propose to describe the work which each of them is doing. There are a great many of them, and the sum total of their efforts is a highly important part of the nation's religious life. They include such diverse organizations as the Society for Promoting Christian Knowledge, the Council of Christians and Jews, the Student Christian Movement, and a considerable number of Church Societies, formed for the purpose of fighting specific social evils, for example, the Churches' Committee on Gambling.

Can we now answer our earlier questions?

At the beginning of this chapter we asked three questions which we should now be in a position to answer in such a way as to enable us to form an opinion about the present position and future prospects of Christianity in Britain. Our original questions were:

(*a*) To what extent do people in Britain believe that Christianity is relevant to life in a scientific age?

(*b*) Is the character of the British people becoming stronger or weaker?

(*c*) How can we reconcile an apparent decline in the nation's religious life with an apparent growth in the practice of the Christian ethic, for example, in the care of the under-privileged?

Our answers are:

(*a*) Most people in Britain do not believe that the *Churches* are relevant to life in a scientific age because they observe that the Churches are in a double strait-jacket of clerical domination and rigid dogma. Since a considerable proportion of the clergy are respected neither for their learning nor for their personal qualities, and since much of the dogmatic belief is considered to be simply untrue, and since persons outside the Church consider that, in general, laymen within the Church do not live up to the ideals that they profess, there is a deep and widespread conviction that the Churches are of little practical account in modern life notwithstanding the fact that most children are baptized, many people are married in Church, and in most cases clergy conduct funeral services. At the same time there are three favourable factors. First, spiritual hunger. Many men and women feel the need of a supernatural religion that will reconcile the contradictions inherent in a purely secular and material conception of life. Second, vestigial Christianity. The time when open renunciation of the Church was so shocking as to be almost unthinkable is still sufficiently recent for the idea to linger at the back of people's minds that, whatever the state of the Churches, and however much the dogma may be disbelieved, there is still "something in Christianity." Third, the fact that people have a vivid sense of right and wrong, a deep sense of decency, ideals about what the pattern of family life should be, and how their country and the world should be organized. Speaking generally, the standards are Christian.

Since, therefore, many people have a real, although seldom expressed, hunger for a supernatural religion, which is related to the general inability to conceive of utter extinction at death, and as so many people still accept the ministrations of the Church in the baptism of their children, in marriage, and in funerals, and as Christianity, in the sense of behaviour rather than belief, still provides the standards of right and wrong, we conclude that people to-day still believe that Christianity is a relevant and vital force, although they no longer accept the idea that the Church is the "chosen instrument" for the expression of that force. The situation, in our view, is therefore somewhat brighter than is popularly believed, and brighter indeed than we believed when we began our studies. But there is still a grave danger. It is, in our view, certain that people will never again seek from the Churches *in their present form* the inspiration that they should obtain from them. It is, perhaps, not much less certain that the general level of spiritual life is not yet high enough to dispense with some central institution, even though it may not need a large professional priestly class.

(*b*) Our second question was whether the character of the British people is getting stronger or weaker.

It is almost impossible to give a clear-cut answer to this question. The first difficulty is that the past is wrapped in a nostalgic mist, which often conceals an extremely brutal reality.

If we remember that as late as the latter part of the eighteenth century there were 165 crimes punishable by hanging, and a number of them also by the unspeakably horrible process of quartering, and that these executions were public spectacles much enjoyed by crowds of both sexes, we must feel that to-day we are living in another world. During the same period infant mortality of children cared for in public institutions in London was between 80 per cent and 90 per cent (or 99 per cent of children admitted to the institutions under the age of 1 year), and gin shops amounted to 1 in 8 of all houses in Westminster, and 1 in 5 of all houses in Holborn. The influence of these gin shops can be judged by a contemporary advertisement for one of them that stated, "Drunk for 1d., Dead drunk for 2d., Clean straw free." This could surely only have been tolerated by a nation in whom the finer traits of Christian character were not developed.

In the nineteenth century, too, there was a long story of brutality—in schools, prisons, lunatic asylums, workhouses, factories and private dwellings. Brutality that gives way steadily through the century as Christian character develops. It was a century of exploitation of women. Even as late as 1870 married women could still own no property, all of which passed automatically to their husbands. It was mainly a century of illiteracy, with the real assault on that evil not beginning until 1870. It was a century of poverty. Even at the end of the century 15·46 per cent of the wage-earning classes of York, equivalent to 9·91 per cent of the whole population of the city were, through no error or omission of their own, living in poverty.[1]

[1] The level below which a family was considered to be in poverty was described by B. S. Rowntree, in *Poverty: A Study of Town Life*, in the following terms:

"A family living upon the scale allowed for in this estimate must never spend a penny on

It was a century, too, of destitution. In 1876, in a paper read before the Social Science Congress in Liverpool, Dr. Barnardo estimated that in London alone there were 30,000 completely destitute children, either orphans or, more often, children thrust out and abandoned by their parents, having no shelter but the streets, no food but what scraps they could scrounge, and no clothes but rags. Despite the glories of the Victorians, it was probably a thoroughly disagreeable century for all except the eminent, learned and well-to-do. With such remarkable exceptions as Dr. Barnardo, the Earl of Shaftesbury and Elizabeth Fry, the privileged classes did not care overmuch about the large and unhappy minority who were often too debased to care about themselves. In the matter of neighbourly love and unselfishness, and in the practice, as contrasted with the profession, of Christianity, it was decidedly inferior to our own time.

But what about the twentieth century, now half-way through? It is difficult to find a means of measuring our character to-day against that at the beginning of the century. It is always hard to be objective about the time in which one lives, and although we have sought the advice of many wise and informed persons of both sexes in our endeavours to solve this problem, their opinions have been by no means unanimous.

It is impossible in our view not to take most seriously into account the great resurgence of brutality which was not only tolerated, but encouraged, praised, and rewarded, during the two world wars, but to a very much greater extent in the second than in the first. We believe that the systematic

---

railway fare or omnibus. They must never go into the country unless they walk. They must never purchase a halfpenny newspaper or spend a penny to buy a ticket for a popular concert. They must write no letters to absent children, for they cannot afford to pay the postage. They must never contribute anything to their church or chapel, or give any help to a neighbour which costs them money. They cannot save, nor can they join sick club or trade union, because they cannot pay the necessary subscriptions. The children must have no pocket money for dolls, marbles, or sweets. The father must smoke no tobacco, and must drink no beer. The mother must never buy any pretty clothes for herself or for her children, the character of the family wardrobe, as for the family diet, being governed by the regulation, 'Nothing must be bought but that which is absolutely necessary for the maintenance of physical health, and what is bought must be of the plainest and most economical description.' Should a child fall ill, it must be attended by the parish doctor; if it die, it must be buried by the parish. Finally, the wage-earner must never be absent from his work for a single day.

"If any of these conditions are broken, the extra expenditure involved is met, *and can only be met*, by limiting the diet; or, in other words, by sacrificing physical efficiency."

destruction by bombing of the German cities was a series of acts of savagery that not only marked a sharp regression in the national character, but has also had a brutalizing effect that it may take years to expunge. Men and women cannot be taught for six years to admire the bestial standards of total war, and then turn in a few months into highly civilized persons of fine character.

Besides its brutalizing effect, the war was a demoralizing force in other ways, for with money plentiful, goods short, and death round the corner, it encouraged a tendency to live selfish and superficial lives. As we have shown earlier in this book, there has undoubtedly been a deterioration, too, in honesty, and perhaps in truthfulness also.

Furthermore, there has been a great increase in gambling and an increase in the use of alcohol and tobacco.

Perhaps we still do not fully realize the importance of housing in matters of morals and character, for even now there are horrible slums, in which hope ebbs away from human lives in an environment of leaking roofs, broken windows, rats, bugs, and the remains of the day-before-yesterday's meal. Yet those places are much less numerous than they were and but for the catastrophe of the two wars they would virtually have been abolished to-day. The nation is awakening to the evil consequences of bad housing, and men and women of all classes of the community have been devoting themselves throughout the century not only to fighting it, but by the exercise of intelligence and goodwill, to the prevention of a comparable evil growing up in the future.

This has been, too, a century of enlightenment, not only through progressive extension of public education of the young, but also through the adult education movement expressed in Educational Settlements, Adult Schools, University Settlements, movements such as the Workers' Educational Association, and more recently through the Arts Council. Britain has become increasingly conscious of books, of music, and of the natural beauty of the countryside. These yearnings for good literature, good music and beautiful scenery, are stirrings of intangible qualities; they constitute a search for beauty, which is closely related to a yearning for God. They could not in our view appear in a decadent or thoroughly materialistic generation.

Furthermore, this century has brought a great upsurge of care for the weak and needy in Britain; for old people, children deprived for one reason or another of their parents' support, mental defectives, indeed for all the casualties of civilization. Poor Smike of *Nicholas Nickleby* would to-day be classed as "educationally sub-normal"; he would be cared for in a school adapted to his needs, and would be turned into as efficient a person as his capabilities allowed.

These instances of an improvement in the national character during this century could be multiplied, but enough has been said to illustrate the twofold dilemma. First, it is almost impossible to judge the present accurately in comparison with the past. Second, as far as we can judge, the picture is one of deterioration in such virtues as truthfulness, honesty and so on, and improvement in those other virtues to which we have referred. Without attempting to strike a balance, which would be a meaningless subjective judgment, we record our opinion that the situation has real perils on account of a decline in certain essential virtues, but that there are also important signs of a deepening of other virtues, and a strengthening of the national character. Certainly all is not well, but equally certainly, all is not ill, and we believe the balance may be on the side of "well" rather than on that of "ill."

(*c*) Our third question was how to reconcile the contemporary decline in formal religious observance and the rejection of much of the dogma of the Church as being untrue, with the considerable increase in the Christian practice of care for those in need, even when they are in no position to press their claim for it.

The contradiction is in some ways more apparent than real and—as is clear from the form in which we have put the question above—it arises from the fact that people no longer regard the Church as being the repository of all that represents religion or the good life. The Christian ethic on the other hand, and this is indeed to some extent a measure of the past success of the Churches, is so deeply impressed upon people's minds that, even for those who would not call themselves Christians, it is in fact the Christian solution to any practical problem that more often than not they instinctively recognize as the right one. The situation was put clearly to us by one of the wise men whom we consulted, a man who has devoted a lifetime to helping and guiding the least privileged classes, among whom he has chosen to make his home for the last thirty years. He said, "As far as my experience goes, I believe young people to-day have a deep desire, that I can only call a craving, for religion and for faith, but they are bored by the institutional religion offered by the Churches. Young people are just as potentially spiritual as they ever were, but religious leaders are failing utterly to capture their imagination and to satisfy the yearning."

It would, however, be highly imprudent to believe that all is well because there is in many quarters a greater readiness than ever before to consider and resolve problems in terms of the Christian ethic. As we stated previously, the situation is indeed one of real, although not immediate peril. The Christian ethic is instinctively regarded to-day as the standard of values over wide spheres of public and private life, because for long periods in the past those values were accepted as having the supernatural sanction of Christianity as a revealed religion. We are in fact living on the spiritual capital of the past.

If our view of the situation outlined above is correct, there can be no certainty that the community will continue over a long period to be guided by the Christian ethic. If the spiritual vacuum is filled in the future by an atheistic and totalitarian belief, the standard of public behaviour will be according to the ethic of that belief.

What action is possible and desirable?

In writing this chapter, the fact has been constantly in our minds that we are not qualified to go beyond an examination of the state of things as they are. We believe however that the central problem is clear. It is:

How can the great spiritual truths of Christianity be presented in a form which will win response from the mass of people who, although they accept the Christian ethic and are for the most part in a receptive state for spiritual teaching, nevertheless reject much of the dogma of the Christian Church, and in many cases are hostile to ministers of religion?

From the enquiries that we have made, we believe that the need of the present time is not a new religion, but a new presentation of the true values of Christianity, shorn of the embellishments and dogmatic assertions it has picked up from the time of its first revelation onwards.

For men with finite minds (especially when those minds are filled with vague echoes of an immense conglomeration of scientific facts which are often imperfectly understood) it is difficult to have a conception of God so clear and vital as to be a dynamic force in their lives. But when men cannot make their conception of God a reality, they can still draw inspiration and strength from their understanding of Jesus and from their perception that He drew His power from a deeper and more intimate understanding of the eternal mysteries than normal men can attain. Nor do the inspiration and strength that men can draw from Jesus need to be formalized by any dogma or interpreted by a priest.

Though the Protestant Churches, with the prestige that attaches to much of their ritual because it maintains traditional practices that in some cases go back to the Early Church, will no doubt continue to exist as a symbol of the enduring nature of the Christian religion, it is inconceivable to us that they will ever again be a dominant force in the religious life of the nation, although the corporate worship that they make possible will remain a source of strength and inspiration for a great many individuals.

In so far as the Roman Catholic Church is concerned, we have given earlier in this chapter the reasons for believing that it will remain vigorous. In all probability it will continue to attract a steadily increasing proportion of the nation's total diminishing Church membership. But the reason for the success of Rome is, we believe, also the reason for what we consider to be its inevitable ultimate decline, namely, the spiritual totalitarianism to which we referred earlier in this chapter. Its success to-day is gained by removing from individual minds all sense of fear, doubt and uncertainty, and by giving instead a feeling of security. Like totalitarian organizations in other fields of human activity, spiritual totalitarianism can produce satisfactory results over a considerable period of time. It might indeed provide a permanent solution, if the minds of those whom it sways were closed to all other influences. But in fact men's minds and spirits, however imperfect they may be, cannot for ever be forced or persuaded to eschew the critical functioning of intelligence which asks of dogma, "It is true?" and of priests, "Are they necessary?"

Individual men, as we have pointed out, can regulate their lives, if they so wish, according to the precepts of Jesus, and many persons of all classes of the community do in fact habitually seek to do so. Such persons, by the high standards apparent in their lives, will always influence others for good, and therefore spread their beliefs. It has several times been suggested to us during our work that the influence of such individuals would be enhanced, and they themselves would be reinforced in their beliefs, if they found it practicable, without any formal organization, to form themselves into small groups, similar to Communist cells. In such groups common problems of the relevance of Christian belief to daily life might be worked out by a co-operative effort that would both enrich and strengthen the religious lives of the individuals, and we believe that the idea has much to commend it. It has incidentally much in common with the organization adopted in the Early Church when that Church faced the twin problems of maintaining itself and converting a pagan world.

Such an idea may seem a slight one on which to base a hope of a re-conversion of England, but its rests on a powerful basis, namely, on the faith of individual Christians in whom a belief in the teaching of Jesus is the dominant force of their lives. As Dean Inge writes in *Mysticism in Religion*, "A rebirth of spiritual religion . . . as in former revivals . . . will be very independent of the Churches and not too kindly regarded by ecclesiastics. . . . Christianity began as a lay prophetic religion. There was not a single priest among the Apostles . . . It is on the laity that the future of Christianity depends though we must have organization to prevent the fruits of the Spirit from being lost."

CHAPTER XIV

LEISURE TIME ACTIVITIES IN HIGH WYCOMBE

In the previous chapters of this book we have dealt functionally with various ways in which people spend their leisure time devoting a chapter to each of them. We thought that it would help readers to obtain a clearer view of the picture we are attempting to draw if we selected a typical town and gave a full description of *all* the facilities provided in it for spending leisure, and the extent to which people took advantage of them.

We have selected High Wycombe for this purpose, primarily because we both live there, but also because it is particularly well suited to our purpose.

Before describing the facilities available, a few words must be said about the general characteristics of the town. It grew up in the narrow east-west valley between two steeply rising ridges which in several places form almost isolated spurs of land. As a small country town there was no difficulty in finding sufficient sites on level ground for commercial or residential building, but the great growth in population has pushed the residential areas on to the slopes of the valley, and the spur-like nature of the hills has in many cases resulted in comparatively isolated residential units of population. This has produced a slightly unusual social pattern, resulting in these outlying areas in many cases retaining a village spirit. It should also be noted that east-west the town boundaries are five miles apart, whereas north-south they are, at some points, only two miles apart. High Wycombe is about 30 miles from London and 28 from Oxford. In 1948 it was officially estimated that the population was 40,580. At the time of the last official census in 1931 it was 27,988. This abnormal growth in population has had repercussions on many aspects of the

..e and is one of the chief factors to be taken into ..unt when considering a survey of its leisure time facilities.

High Wycombe is an industrial town. By far the most important industries are furniture and chair-making. Other industries include: light engineering and scientific instrument making, in which some thousands of workers are engaged, printing, including the printing of stamps for countries all over the world, the manufacture of cigarettes, cosmetics, handbags, biscuits, pipes, clothing, etc.

Although there are more than 200 factories in High Wycombe, very few of them are large enough to organize recreational facilities for their employees. The number doing so is about 24, and between them they employ about 5,000 men and 1,100 women. About half-a-dozen of them either have sports grounds of their own, or rent land for the use of their employees. Some of the sports grounds which belong to factories are the best all-round sports grounds in the county. They have well-kept cricket pitches, football and netball fields, either grass or hard tennis courts, and bowling greens. All the cricket teams play weekly on Saturdays and some on Sundays, and the football teams weekly in winter.

Some of the factories have angling clubs; they fish in the Thames and hire private waters.

The indoor recreational facilities provided by the factories vary, of course, from one factory to another. They include dramatic performances given in factories where there is a room with a stage, table tennis, billiards and bar billiards, concerts, facilities for handicrafts and hobbies, dances and physical culture. In some factories there are rooms where people play chess, dominoes, darts and card games. Two or three of the factories have full licences to sell alcoholic drinks, either in the canteen or the sports pavilion.

It will thus be seen that, taken as a whole, the factories make a considerable contribution to the recreational facilities available in the town.

Coming now to the other facilities available for recreational activities, we will deal first with those that take place indoors. Our enquiry showed that a good many of these are seriously hampered by lack of suitable and adequate accommodation.

There are 10 halls which can be hired, in addition to a few church halls which are not large and where the type of activity allowed is restricted. The largest of the halls is the Town Hall, which seats 958. It is not very suitable for plays, and is used chiefly for dancing and occasionally for meetings. Five schools let their assembly halls (all of which have stages) for dramatic performances, concerts and dancing. Four other halls, seating from 150 to 200 people, are let, principally for dancing, but also for meetings. They have no stages. The charges for these halls vary from £16 for the Town Hall to under £1 per evening; the Repertory Theatre, seating about 309, can be hired for concerts on Sundays only.

Social clubs

High Wycombe British Legion and Ex-Servicemen's Club.—This is by far the largest club in High Wycombe. It owns fine premises in a central part of the town. There is a billiards room with four tables, a dance hall with maple floor, with accommodation for 100 couples, a large ladies' room where refreshments are served and where ladies can play darts and cards, a room for men where cards, darts, dominoes, etc., can be played. There are bathrooms, steward's quarters, and a room for meetings. This is sometimes lent, without charge, to outside bodies such as the Blind Institute and the Old Men's Club.

There are about 1,000 male and 200 female members. The women members organize various activities such as whist drives, dances and concerts, to raise money for charitable purposes connected with the Legion. The average daily attendance of members at the club is about 300. The club is open every day of the week. It is licensed to sell beer and tobacco. It does not serve meals but sells sandwiches, cakes and other light refreshments.

The weekly programme of club activities is as follows: Mondays and Saturdays, whist drives (50–55 tables); Tuesdays, Ladies' Day, socials, concerts, Old Time dances (open to the public); Wednesdays, modern dances (open to the public); Thursdays, table tennis; Fridays, modern dances (open to the public).

The club organizes cricket matches, billiards and snooker

competitions, darts teams and fishing competitions. Many cups and prizes are played for by club members.

There is no doubt that this club fulfils a useful purpose in providing its members with facilities for spending their leisure time in wholesome ways.

Club of the Wycombe Marsh Branch of the British Legion.—This club meets in a large army hut of the 1914–18 war. It is owned by the branch and consists of a room with two billiards tables and a bar billiards table. There is a bar and eight small tables, and dart boards. There is also a hall with a stage. The hall has seating accommodation for 200 people.

The club is open every weekday from 6 p.m., and on Sundays from 7 p.m. In winter there is a whist drive every Wednesday, attended by about 35 people. On Thursdays the women run Old Time dances fortnightly, the attendance being about 30. Every month there is a social, and the club plays matches with other clubs in indoor games. Coach trips are arranged to big football matches, to the seaside and to theatres.

The club has a beer and spirit and a catering licence.

Club of the Terriers and Totteridge Branch of the British Legion.—This branch was formed in 1946 and soon afterwards a women's section of the branch was instituted. The membership is about 100 men and 85 women. The purpose of the branch is to watch the interests of ex-service personnel resident within its boundaries.

In addition to money-raising efforts for carrying on the work of the branch by way of whist drives, dances, fêtes, etc., meetings of the branch are held quarterly, and of the women's section monthly, when at times, if business permits, addresses are given on varying topics of general interest, followed by discussion.

A drama class and also a choir were formed in 1947, and have successfully produced plays and concerts.

A service committee deals with pension queries and benevolence, and all sick members are visited.

Gifts are sent at Christmas to all widows of ex-servicemen, and at Easter every mother in the district who lost a son in the wars is presented with a bunch of violets for remembrance. New babies to members of the women's section are each presented with a gift of savings stamps.

Social evenings are arranged and are well attended, and coach trips to theatres and national events are organized.

The branch is handicapped by not having headquarters, and often committee meetings are held in members' homes.

Liberal Association Club and Lincolnshire Memorial Hall.—This club has about 320 members, of whom 40 are women. The club owns the building, which comprises a games room with four billiards tables, a reading room, also used for cards and darts, seating about 30, a tea room, steward's quarters, and a hall seating about 300. This is the only room let to outside bodies. It is let three times a week for dances, and is let for Liberal meetings without charge. About 70 members use the club daily, and 100 or more on Saturdays.

The club is not licensed to sell intoxicating liquors nor has it a full catering licence, but sandwiches, cake, tea, coffee and mineral waters are sold.

The club is well conducted and is much appreciated by the members.

Trades and Labour Club and Institute, Ltd.—This club, which is a member of the Club and Institute Union, has about 260 members including about 60 women, who pay the same subscription as the men (5s. a year) and have exactly the same rights except that they cannot go to the convalescent homes run by the Club and Institute Union. Although not a political club, most of the members belong to the Labour Party.

The premises are rented at an annual cost of £166 for rent and rates. They consist of a social hall, which has a stage, and seats about 250 people, a games room nearly as large as the social hall in which there is a billiards table, a bar, four meeting rooms and living accommodation for the steward and his wife. The meeting rooms and hall are let whenever possible to outside bodies; several Trade Unions meet there, and also the Communist Party and two branches of the High Wycombe Labour Party. The charge for small meetings is 2s. 0d. per hour, and for meetings in the hall, 5s.

The meeting rooms and hall are so largely used by Trade Unions that the club is not a club in as full a sense as the Liberal, British Legion and ex-Servicemen's clubs. No doubt many members go there to attend Trade Union and other meetings, and take advantage of the recreational and refreshment facilities by the way. About 40 members use the club daily, except at week-ends when the number rises to 100–150.

As far as the club is concerned, its activities are entirely social. Concerts are given nearly every Saturday and Sunday night, and members play billiards, darts, cribbage, chess, dominoes, etc. Coach trips are arranged for members and their friends. The club is open daily from 10 to 2 and 6 to 11. It is licensed to sell beer, wine, spirits, and tobacco. No meals are served except teas on special occasions. Sandwiches and cakes are served nightly.

The Totteridge and District Social Centre.—This Social Centre caters for people of all ages over 17. It is situated in a thickly-populated district 1½ miles from the centre of High Wycombe, and is run by a most enthusiastic and enterprising committee.

At the present time its activities are carried on in premises which are not satisfactory, and so the committee has bought about two acres of land and is erecting a building which will be really adequate. The whole of the money for the land and building has been raised by members. The building will have a large hall with a stage, and dressing rooms which will also be used as committee rooms.

On the ground there will be football and hockey fields, tennis courts, and a bowling green.

At the present time the activities of the club include a weekly whist drive, with an average attendance of about 50 people, and a drama section which meets weekly with an average attendance of about 45. The members make all the costumes, build all the scenery and do all the work connected with stage lighting. Once a week there is a ladies' night, when about 50 women members meet for a chat and light refreshments.

Every month there is a social evening, to which members bring their friends. About 150 attend. The centre circulates a monthly bulletin.

The great event of the year is a fête held on the sports ground of a local factory. It is attended by some thousands of people, and sporting events of different kinds are arranged in which any person or club within a radius of 30 miles may compete. There are about 20 side-shows. Many of the prizes are given by members of the social centre and the whole of the catering is done by them. Much of the food is given, the non-perishable articles having been saved in small quantities over a long time. The centre makes a profit of about £450 on the fête.

Descol Social Club.—This club started in a "getting together" of the residents of DESborough Avenue and COLville Street, hence the name of "Descol." Its main aim is to foster neighbourliness and to make newcomers to the district feel at home. The club helps anyone in the district who is in need. There are about 170 members, rather more than half of whom are women. The club meets every Saturday night for a whist drive, the average attendance being about 25. For the time being they meet in a room of the High Wycombe Girls' Club, but they are raising funds to erect a building of their own.

They organize trips to the seaside and to London theatres, and social evenings for the children.

This is an interesting case of an attempt made by ordinary people to provide their own means of spending their leisure time happily and wisely.

High Wycombe Boys' Club.—This club has 90 members—54 aged 14–20 and 36 aged 11–14. The premises are very poor. They stand on a small patch of very untidy land, too small for games, but the boys practise high and long distance jumping. It belongs to the County Council, and no rent is charged for it. The club building was built by voluntary effort with some financial help from the County Council. It is a poor building, with thin concrete walls, and consisting of one fairly large room with a concrete floor and two small rooms—an office for the whole-time leader (whose salary is paid by the County Council), and a room used by boys who want to talk or read or play quiet games. In the hall there is one quarter-size and one miniature billiards table, a bar billiards table, and two table tennis tables.

Occasionally there is a concert. A discussion group meets once a week. On Sunday evenings there are brains trusts, quizzes, "Twenty Questions," and always a short talk by the leader. The programme for the juniors consists mostly of games. In winter the average attendance is about 25 seniors and 34 juniors. It is much less in summer.

The building is likely to come down shortly as it stands on land on which it is proposed to build a new Technical Institute.

High Wycombe Girls' Club.—This club meets in premises belonging to the County Education Committee. They were previously used as a school and are lent to the club rent free. The accommodation consists of a main hall, kitchen, lounge, games room, committee room, and a dark room for photography. There are 55 members, aged 15–21. The club leader is paid by the County Council.

The club is open six nights a week, from 7 p.m. The activities include table tennis, keep-fit classes, tap dancing, dressmaking, ballroom dancing and dramatics. On Sundays there are talks, debates and lectures. The average attendance is about 25, except for the night when there is ballroom dancing and boys are invited, and the night when there are keep-fit classes and tap dancing. On these nights the attendance rises considerably. In summer the leader organizes cycle rides, sometimes going to a Youth Hostel where the girls sleep.

In addition to the above activities, the club is open for girls aged 10–15, two days a week, from 5.30 to 7.30. There are about 55 members in this section. The average attendance is about 40. Their activities include cooking classes, folk dancing, handicrafts, games, both indoors and on a public recreation ground.

About 15 girls who are too old to remain in the club meet twice a week in one of the club rooms in the afternoons to play table tennis.

Totteridge Youth Club.—This meets twice a week in three classrooms of a school. The rooms are not available on other nights. Members may also use the school gymnasium on one day a week and (for special occasions) the concert hall. A nominal charge is made for the classrooms, but £3 is charged for the hall for a concert or dance if a charge is made for admittance.

There are about 65 members, aged 14–18, of whom 10 are girls. The average attendance is between 30 and 40. The subscription is 3d. a week. The club activities include table tennis and other indoor games, drama (attended by 11 members) and a keep-fit class (attended by about 30).

There are two football teams, one for boys under, and one for boys over 16. They play on the public recreation grounds.

There is a paid club leader. The club is not open during school holidays.

Boy Scouts.—There are approximately 400 members of the Scout Movement, including those mentioned later in this chapter in the section on Religious Activities. They are organized in 16 groups, and include Rovers, Scouts and Cubs.

Girl Guides.—350 girls in the Guide Movement are divided into 16 Companies, and they comprise Rangers, Guides and Brownies. The total of 350 includes those mentioned later in the section on Religious Activities.

Sea Cadet Corps.—There is a Company of the Sea Cadet Corps consisting of some 44 youths.

Army Cadet Corps.—High Wycombe provides one Company, consisting of 35 youths, in the Second Buckinghamshire Cadet Battalion of the Army Cadet Corps.

Cinemas.—There are four cinemas in High Wycombe, with a seating capacity of 4,300. We are informed that their weekly attendances amount to about 24,000. The price of seats varies from 1s. 3d. to 3s. 6d.

A branch of the Odeon Cinema Club for children has about 1,250 members, aged between 7 and 15. About 800 attend the Odeon Cinema regularly on Saturday mornings. The charge is 6d., but on their birthdays children are admitted free and may bring a friend. The programme varies from week to week, but it includes community singing, the words of the songs being flashed on the screen. Several of the songs, which are all set to well-known and particularly "catchy" tunes, are about the need for care in crossing the roads. After the community singing the children sing the National Anthem and repeat the Club Promise, which is:

> "I Promise to tell the truth, to help others, and to obey my parents.
> "I Promise to be thoughtful of old folks, to be kind to animals, and always to play the game.
> "I Promise to try to make this Great Country of ours a better place to live in."

The films shown fall into two categories. One consists of films specially produced for children, under the direct control of an advisory council which includes representatives of the Home Office, the Ministry of Education and the National Union of Teachers. The other consists of a commercial film which must have a "U" certificate. This is only given to films which children under 16 may go to see unattended by an adult.

A football team for the older children has been organized, and it plays against teams organized in connection with other children's theatres in adjacent towns.

Every year a choir of 30 boys and girls is entered in the National Carol Competition, which, during the last three years, has been organized by the Odeon Cinemas throughout the country in conjunction with the *Star* newspaper. The choir has been in the finals each year, and has won the trophy twice.

There can, we think, be no doubt that the children's cinema makes a really worth-while contribution to the recreational facilities in the town.

Educational Activities.—Under this heading only educational facilities provided for people in their leisure hours will be described.

Excellent work is being done by the Technical Institute, which provides evening educational facilities for young people and adults. It provides both intra- and extra-mural courses in a wide variety of subjects. The former courses are provided for those who join them as individuals. The extra-mural courses are run by the Institute at the request of various organizations such as youth clubs and the Townswomen's Guild.

In the 1949–50 session intra-mural courses were provided in commercial subjects, art, modern languages, chair-making, cabinet-making, engineering, carpentry and joinery, plumbing, radio, boiler-house practice, industrial management, dress-making, bread-making and flour confectionery, as well as courses to prepare students for the matriculation and intermediate examinations in Science and Economics for the London University degrees. Extra-mural courses were provided in drama, ballroom dancing, keep-fit, madrigals, cookery, crafts, choral singing, folk-dancing and photography. If a group wishes the Institute to provide a particular course, application is made to the Principal of the Institute, who then investigates the need for such a course, and if he is satisfied that a need exists, arranges staff and accommodation.

The total number of students availing themselves of the facilities offered by the Institute (both extra- and intra-mural) in the session 1949–50 was 1,600, analysed as follows: technical courses 425, commercial 375, arts and crafts 400, miscellaneous 400.

Both the number of students and the variety of courses are seriously limited by lack of accommodation. Nearly every night of the week the building is full to capacity, especially at the beginning of the session. Nevertheless, no reasonable demand for a course is refused by the Principal, provided that a minimum of ten will enrol for ordinary classes, and seven for advanced classes. With the sanction of the Chief Education Officer, the Principal will recommend the provision of classes where enrolments may be even fewer.

The standard of work is high, in spite of the handicap of poor accommodation and the fatigue of students and teachers, consequent upon having done a full day's work before evening classes begin.

Fees for the courses, often dealing with different subjects, and involving three or four lectures or lessons per week. range from 2s. 6d. to 30s. 0d., according to the age of the student and the nature of the course. Only for the University courses is the charge 30s. 0d. per session. Youth club classes cost 1s. 0d. per member for the course.

Classes are not normally held in the summer months, but

generally speaking, art classes, advanced classes and youth club classes do continue during the summer. There is no hard and fast rule.

Plans exist and will be implemented as soon as possible for the building of a new College of Further Education, whose functions would be similar to those of the Impington Village College, only much wider in scope. The need for this is very great, not only in order to provide accommodation for students but also to provide accommodation for many local voluntary organizations to hold some of their meetings as is, for instance, done in Chelmsford by the Technical Institute there.

The Workers' Educational Association.—The local branch of this Association has a membership of 65, half of whom are men. Members pay 5s. 0d. annually, and are then entitled to attend the lecture courses arranged during the winter months. W.E.A. members can attend summer schools organized in Britain and abroad. The local branch does not appear to attract many factory workers, the majority of its members being clerical workers or teachers. Occasional rambles and socials are arranged, and a large dance is run from time to time as a source of income.

The Association is constantly faced with the problem of finding suitable lecture accommodation at a rent which it can afford.

The National Council of Labour Colleges.—There is a branch of this national body in High Wycombe Classes are held fortnightly, dealing with such subjects as economics, the Co-operative Movement, Trade Unionism, problems facing Labour in Britain, etc. The average attendance is about 25.

The Young Farmers' Club.—This has 60 male and 30 female members. Half of them live in the borough, and the others in the immediate vicinity. It is an active body doing good educational work. In summer the members meet fortnightly, either at farms or in schoolrooms, or the games room of a public house. The programme for meetings includes lectures, demonstrations, judging members' stock, and occasional social gatherings. In winter, meetings are held weekly in a school hall in High Wycombe.

National Book League.—The object of this league is to encourage the reading of good literature. The High Wycombe branch of the league has 60 members. They meet monthly, the average attendance being about 40. Lectures are given by authors and poets, and discussions are held on all matters connected with books.

Library Facilities.

The reading public can borrow books from the public library, from two subscription libraries, and from the chain or "2d." libraries. The public library is housed in an excellent modern building in the centre of the town. In 1949 it had about 49,000 books, including 8,600 children's books and 450 books in the reference library. In 1948–9, 441,100 books were issued, including 64,100 issued to children. Of the books issued, about 362,500 were fiction, including about 58,000 issued to children. Of the non-fiction books, 36,000 were books on history, biography and travel, 8,800 on literature, 12,050 on fine arts, and 13,400 on useful arts.

The cost of the library in 1949 was £8,535, of which £1,840 was made up by income from a large bequest and from fines on overdue books, and £6,695 paid from the rates. The library rate in 1949 was 5½d.

Although no accurate figure is available, our investigator, after discussing the matter with the librarians of the different libraries, came to the conclusion that probably about 16,500 persons in the town borrow books with varying degrees of regularity, and that about 80% of the books are fiction.

Rotary Club.—This meets weekly. There are 55 members and 25 members of the "Inner Wheel" which consists of the wives of Rotarians. It also meets weekly. In addition to these there is an organization called the "Round Table," which is in effect a junior Rotary Club. There are 50 members, aged from 25 to 40 years. They meet in the evenings, and after supper speakers address them on matters of social and public interest. The addresses are followed by discussion. They meet fortnightly in winter and monthly in summer.

Royal Air Force Association.—The object of this association, which has about 330 members of whom 30 are women, is to foster comradeship begun during the war. Meetings are held monthly, the average attendance being about 40. The club has no permanent headquarters, and this seriously handicaps its activities, which are now confined largely to welfare work on behalf of club members.

Royal Naval Old Comrades Association.—This association has 100 members of whom 40 are women. About 70 members live in the borough, the rest in the immediate vicinity. Its object is similar to that of the one named above. It meets monthly in a room in a public house, which affords very inadequate accommodation. The average number attending is about 20, including 5 women. Social activities are the chief feature of its meetings.

Old Contemptibles Association.—Membership is limited to soldiers who served in the 1914–18 war. It has about 35 members and meets fortnightly in licensed premises. Its object is similar to that of the two associations named above.

Water Rats.—This is the National Fire Service counterpart of the Service associations. It has about 60 members, of whom 40 live in High Wycombe. Meetings are held four times a year.

Old People's Welfare Clubs.—There are five clubs for old people in High Wycombe. One of these is run by the United Council of Social Service of High Wycombe and four by a sub-committee of the Central Aid Society, which is a local society formed in 1906 to undertake social work in the borough.

Three of the clubs run directly by the Central Aid Society are for women. They meet weekly and have a total membership of about 180. One is a club for men. It has 60 members and meets fortnightly. The Central Aid Society pays the rent of the rooms in which the clubs meet; apart from this the clubs finance themselves, either by a subscription of a few pence a week or by money-raising efforts of one kind or another.

Most of the clubs have a sick visitor from among their members. A card is sent to members on their birthdays. There are two day-outings in summer. The Secretary of the Central

Aid Society visits the clubs from time to time in order to find out whether any of the members are in need of help.

In addition to the clubs named above there is a men's club with 140 members, run by the United Council of Social Service of High Wycombe. It has a club room of its own, with a billiards table and other games equipment, piano, bathroom and kitchen, and is open daily. Every fortnight there is a social entertainment and tea.

Each of the clubs has a group of members who not only give entertainments—songs, recitations, etc.—in their own clubs, but visit the other clubs in the town.

The following is a description of a visit paid by our investigator to one of the women's clubs, which is typical of the other two:

"The programme consisted of the singing of 'Jerusalem,' the repetition of the club motto, and then an hour or two of entertainment, usually provided by the members themselves in the form of songs, recitations and community singing. This club has a choir of 14, all over 70, the oldest being 83. Before I visited these clubs I was sceptical of the ability of the members to entertain themselves. However, I was wrong. On the occasion of my visit they sang songs and recited their own and other people's poetry, all remarkably well. The personal note thus introduced was very much appreciated by the members, who made remarks such as the following to me: 'You'd never believe she'd remember like that, miss, she's four years older than me.'

"When asked, some of the members admitted that they had not wanted to come at first, but now they never miss except in very bad weather. 'When you come together, miss, it makes you realize there are lots worse off than you are. Now that poor soul there lives all by herself, whereas I've got my old man.' This particular old lady is unable to walk any distance and is regularly fetched to the club in a car."

Arrangements for transport are made whenever possible for the crippled, by the kindness of interested friends.

We have been much impressed by the fine spirit shown by the leaders of these clubs and by the amount of hard work done by them and their helpers. There is no doubt that their efforts are very much appreciated by the old people. In a letter received from one of the leaders she says, "We have just had two new members who told me they had been looking forward to being old enough to join."

The Townswomen's Guild.—This is a local branch of the National Union of Townswomen's Guilds. The object of the Guilds is "to encourage the education of women to enable them as citizens to make their best contribution towards the common good." The Guilds are non-party and non-sectarian.

The local Guild has 125 members. Meetings are held monthly, the average attendance being 70 to 80. They usually begin with a lecture, and this is followed by "a social half-hour." Then follows tea, and various kinds of entertainment.

The Guilds have other activities besides the monthly meetings, such as sewing parties held weekly at members' homes to make garments for children, a choir which gives concerts for charitable purposes, dramatic performances, and handicraft classes. Outings are also arranged for Guild members.

Wycombe Women's Co-operative Guild.—This is a branch of a national organization, which has 1,700 branches and 60,000 members. In an official publication it is stated that "The Guild is a movement which exists to serve the interests of the working housewife and, while its educational facilities should help women to give better service in both the co-operative and the civic field, these facilities should not be considered solely from this angle. Its primary work is to fit the ordinary housewife to take her full place in the Co-operative Movement and in the State, and to enable her to understand the problems of everyday life and to exercise judgment in regard to them. Democracy can only function satisfactorily if individual democrats are competent to play their part, and the purpose of the Guild is to make the ordinary housewife a democratic co-operator and an informed citizen."

The local branch has 73 members. They meet weekly, the average attendance at the meetings being about 50. In the High Wycombe branch addresses are given on topics of general interest, such as Local Government, Nursery Schools, Food Rationing, Germany, Austria, etc.

Every year the High Wycombe and three other Guilds attend a district school. The lectures at a recent school were on the Human Rights Charter, Our National Heritage, How the Law affects Women, and Co-operation in other Lands. Cookery demonstrations were also given.

The local Guild assists with flag days for charitable objects, organizes collections for the blind, and has collected a large number of old garments for displaced persons in Europe.

Although the aims of the national Guild are primarily educational, in the message sent to members by the Central Committee in January 1950, it is stated that "the effort of every Guild branch must be concentrated behind Co-operative and Labour candidates."

Women's Institutes.—There are four Institutes in High Wycombe, with a membership of 355. It is anomalous for these to exist in a town, for they were formed to meet the needs of village life. The anomaly is accounted for by the fact stated on page 375, that the borough includes some country districts.

Meetings are held monthly, the average attendance being about 250. Lectures are given on many subjects of general interest, and in addition to these, demonstrations are given to show the best ways of preserving fruit and other foodstuffs. After the lectures and demonstrations, members have a cup of tea and games and music.

Drama groups have been formed which have been particularly successful at Drama Festivals.

The members are also encouraged to engage in handicrafts of different kinds, and efforts are made to revive old crafts, such as lace making and traditional quilting.

St. John Ambulance Brigade.—The High Wycombe and District Corps is a very active body. It has an adult membership of 109, 40 of whom are nursing personnel, and a "cadet" membership of 95, of whom 50 are nursing cadets. In addition to a membership fee of 4s. 0d. a year, further funds are raised by social activities organized by the members of the brigade, and by donations from other organizations for services rendered. It has a lecture room and an office. The garage for six ambulances is provided rent free by the local authority. Training classes are held weekly, and the efficiency of the members is maintained by an annual examination in First Aid and Home Nursing.

Night duty staff are housed in adjacent premises. The first aid post is manned night and day. During 1949 the ambulances travelled 81,770 miles and transported 6,647 sick and injured persons to and from hospitals and nursing homes. All the work is done gratuitously.

Young People's Political Associations.—The Conservatives have a very active association, with nearly 300 members, of both sexes in about equal numbers, mostly between 15 and 30 years of age. They meet weekly for general meetings, and have one or two sub-committees a week and social meetings fortnightly. Their object is to encourage young people to join the Conservative Party and to educate them in Conservative principles. In addition to meetings they have socials, brains trusts, quizzes, film shows and musical evenings, dances, supper parties, and in summer tennis parties and river trips.

The Young Liberals have a League, but it is not well organized and has only a few members.

The Labour Party League of Youth (Young Socialists) has between 60 and 70 members, aged 16–25, of both sexes. They meet weekly in the hall belonging to the Co-operative Society, the average attendance being about 30. Except about once in six weeks, when a social evening is held, the purpose of the meetings is purely to train the young people in Socialist principles. Talks are given by different people.

Model Engineering Society.—This society has 64 members, of whom 15 are under 16 years of age. Most of the other members are under 40.

The members make models of all kinds of mechanical contrivances—locomotives, aeroplanes, boats, motor cars, radio-controlled boats and aeroplanes, motor bicycles, and many other things. All are made to scale, and actually work.

They meet fortnightly in the hall of the Trades and Labour Club, the average attendance being 35. The models are made at home, and tested in the club room.

Music and Drama

For the size of the town there is an unusually large number of musical activities of a fairly high standard.

The Oratorio Choir, with a membership of 60, of whom about 20 are men, meets in a church hall weekly during nine months of the year. They study choral works and rehearse for public concerts, of which a number are given annually. About 40 of the members live in the town and the others in surrounding villages.

There is a Symphony Orchestra with about 40 members, of whom 30 live in the town and 10 just outside it. Run in conjunction with it there is a junior orchestra with about 25 members, training to join the adult body. The orchestra usually gives two concerts a year in the Town Hall, and it also accompanies the Oratorio Choir. It meets weekly for rehearsals.

Many of the symphony orchestral concerts are sponsored by the Musical Entertainments Society, which has a membership of about 45. This Society produces annually a comic opera which gives four performances. Since it was started in 1941 it has given over £500 to charities.

There is also an Operatic and Dramatic Society. It was formed nearly 50 years ago and has 127 members, of whom 86 are women. They are primarily interested in drama. They read plays, have lectures, and produce a few plays each winter in the Town Hall and elsewhere. They also organize coach trips to London theatres, usually filling a 30-seater coach.

Masque Players

This is a small Dramatic Society with a membership of from 15 to 20. Its object is to encourage members to take an interest in stage management, design and lighting, and to present to the public plays of an educational nature which are not often to be seen in a commercial theatre. Although the members have no accommodation except a derelict loft reached by a ladder, they build their own sets and make their own costumes. They meet weekly throughout the year. The plays are performed in church and other halls and in surrounding villages. Any, Ta[illegible] are given to charities.

Dancing

There are three halls in High Wycombe which can be hired for dances.

The Town Hall provides comfortable accommodation for 250 couples, but 300 couples often dance there on Saturday nights. Dances are held practically every Saturday and often on Fridays also. The rent of the hall is £16. The dances are sponsored by different organizations and the cost of the tickets varies from 3s. od. to 4s. od. There is no bar, but those who organize the dances sometimes arrange with a caterer to provide alcoholic drinks. Permission for this must be obtained from the licensing magistrates.

The Liberal Club Hall provides accommodation for 60 couples. Dances are held three times a week. The dances are organized by a professional dance band. Tickets cost 2s. od. for mid-week dances and 2s. 6d. on Saturdays. Light refreshments are provided but no alcoholic drinks.

The British Legion Hall provides comfortable accommodation for 100 couples. Dances are held twice a week, and in addition an Old Time dance is held fortnightly. Tickets cost 1s. 6d. for British Legion members and 2s. od. for non-members. Refreshments are provided for all, but only members of the British Legion may use the bar.

Probably the number of people going to dances is in the neighbourhood of 1,000 a week pretty well all the year round. The great majority of them are young—from 16 to the early 20's. The numbers attending dances at the Red Lion Hotel are not included in this estimate—they are about 400 a week from October to March inclusive. Scarcely any people dance there in the summer.

Chess Club

This has 31 members, all of whom are men. Meetings are held weekly in a room in the Town Hall. Matches are played with other clubs. Subscription, £1 1s. od.

Camera Club

This has 56 members, of whom three-quarters the

town. They hold fortnightly meetings, when there are lectures and demonstrations.

Radio

The number of holders of wireless and television licences in High Wycombe at the end of 1949 was 7,875 and 1,310 respectively.

Repertory Theatre

This is a non-profit-distributing theatre and the directors are not paid. It seats 300 persons, and the prices of seats vary from 2s. 6d. to 4s. 6d. The plays are well presented and the acting is good. The theatre undoubtedly makes a significant contribution to the cultural life of the town.

Squash

A Squash Club was formed in 1947 and has 50 playing members who pay a subscription of £3 3s. 0d. The Club facilities include the court, changing rooms fitted with showers and constant hot water, a club room, and a bar which is only open on special occasions. The Club is open every day of the week.

Billiards

There are two large billiards clubs in the town, one with 10 tables and about 800 members and another with 8 tables and about 500 members. The tables are not much used in the day-time except on Saturdays and Sundays. Various social clubs in the town have between them 16 tables, only three of which may be used on Sundays.

Badminton

There is no Badminton Club in the town except the one run by the Congregational Church, but 16 High Wycombe people play at one five miles away. The club meets once a week.

Table Ter

This is ery popular game in High Wycombe. There are two Tal ennis Leagues—a Senior League, affiliated to the

English T.T. Association, and a Youth League. Together they comprise at least 500 playing members. The clubs comprising the League are drawn from all sections of the community—social centres, British Legion clubs, church and chapel organizations, boys' and girls' clubs, service teams, municipal clubs, working men's clubs, and so on. On an average, each of these clubs plays twice a week, one League match and one practice night. The number of players would be much greater than it is if there were more accommodation. There is no central table tennis club where all the players can get together.

Public Houses

There are 77 licensed premises in the town. The ratio of public houses to population is 1 to 527 as compared with 1 to 592 for the country generally. The public houses are well conducted. Most of them are inspected by the Police every week. In 1949 only seven persons were arrested for drunkenness in High Wycombe. Of these, four were Poles, one a visitor and only two were local residents.

An immense number of men and women play darts in public houses. There are 64 men's darts clubs with rather more than 2,000 registered members, and 22 women's clubs, with about 330 members.

These clubs meet once a week and sometimes oftener, and matches are played alternately at home and away, "away" meaning in another public house. Occasionally coaches are hired and matches are played with clubs outside the borough. Some of the clubs raise money, by raffles and subscriptions, for an annual outing to the seaside or a pantomime.

Betting and gambling

Within 30 miles of High Wycombe there are three greyhound racing tracks and three race courses. One of the greyhound racing tracks, not affiliated with the National Greyhound Association, is quite near to the town. Races are held there every Saturday and are attended [illegible] about 100 people. Only very occasionally is a coach book[illegible]or a greyhound racing track. There is no means of [illegible]ssing the number who go regularly by private car, but i[illegible]robably very small. On the other hand, the police estimate that 25 per cent of the street betting is on greyhound races.

There is no basis for estimating the amount of money spent on gambling. There are five bookmakers in the town, each with about a dozen runners, and there is a great deal of illegal betting done with the runners and others, often newspaper vendors. The difficulty of preventing street betting is widely known. A police officer said that to deal with it at all effectively it would be necessary for about half the police force to do nothing else, and even then a great deal of it would go unchecked.

The newest form of widespread gambling—football pools—is the easiest about which to obtain information. During the football season 1948–9, the average number of postal orders sold weekly in High Wycombe was 6,196. During the months of 1949 when there was no football, the average number of postal orders sold weekly was 2,611, so it may safely be assumed that the average number of persons doing football pools during the football season 1948–9 was certainly not less than 3,585. Allowing for the fact that in many cases coupons, and therefore postal orders, are shared by two or more persons, the figure will be considerably larger than this, but how much more we cannot say.

Outdoor recreation

High Wycombe is well provided with open spaces and publ recreation grounds. The four recreation grounds cover acres, and two woods and the land adjoining, exte to 37 acres, are open to the public, as well spaces.

One of the recreation grounds, the centre of the town. It has ground with a whole-time the children to ride on pool and wel track with

Anothe ren's pla

Alto

pitches, 8 cricket squares, 3 hockey pitches and 3 tennis courts.

Games are played on Sundays as well as weekdays.

Football

With the exception of one senior rugby club, with 70 or 80 playing members, which runs four fifteens throughout the season, all the football teams in High Wycombe play association football.

There is one senior amateur association football club, and in the town and its immediate vicinity there are about 40 junior and minor clubs, with nearly a thousand playing members. Throughout the season a score or more games are played in the borough every Saturday.

About half the town's football clubs have grounds of their own. Others play on the public recreation grounds, where they have to pay 12s. 6d. a game if they are over 16 years of age, and half-price if they are under 16. The charge includes preparation of the pitch, erection and hire of goalposts and use of dressing accommodation.

About a dozen football clubs play on sports grounds belonging to factories in the town. They are among the best appointed grounds in the county, many of them with facilities for a wide range of sporting activities apart from football.

The one senior club (Wycombe Wanderers) attracts most of
spectators in High Wycombe on Saturday afternoons.
average attendance is between 4,000 and 5,000 with
of as many as 16,000 for important cup-ties.
t some of the leading junior games in the town
res of close supporters of the team to
for local cup-ties between old

he's population of about
and 7,000 watching
on.

winter.
club,

league, "friendly" or "scratch" games of one sort or another. They play on private grounds, on factory sports grounds, on public recreation grounds or sometimes in the open fields. On the public recreation grounds clubs have to pay 6s. od. for the use of a cricket pitch, including the preparation of the "square."

The principal senior club in the town is the High Wycombe C.C. It is more than 100 years old, and runs four teams on Saturdays and one on Wednesdays, with occasional Sunday matches, on its own ground.

A dozen Wycombe clubs play in the High Wycombe and District Cricket League, which has about 1,000 members. Apart from the High Wycombe League, many "friendly" matches are played in High Wycombe each Saturday and Sunday.

A dozen or more of the furniture factories in High Wycombe have, since the end of the war, organized a Factories' Cricket League, with evening matches on local recreation or factory grounds.

Cricket attracts substantially fewer spectators than does football. High Wycombe's main club attracts several hundred on a fine sunny Saturday to their ground. A county match may attract a crowd of possibly up to 1,000. Some local matches in the Wycombe League may attract attendances of 300 or 400.

Netball

The High Wycombe and District Netball Association has about 180 members. During the winter they play on Saturday afternoons and in summer on Tuesday and Thursday evenings. A team consists of seven members. Most of the teams play once a week, but some only once a fortnight.

In 1949 the High Wycombe team won two games out of three in an All-England rally.

Hockey

There are three women's hockey clubs with a total of about 50 members. Matches are played weekly during the season. The subscriptions vary from 7s. 6d. to 12s. 6d. a year. One of the clubs, which consists of "Old Girls," uses a school playing field. The others use the public pitches, at a cost of 10s. od. a match.

The men's club also has about 50 members, and three teams play every Saturday during the season. The first and second teams play on the High Wycombe Cricket Ground, and the third team on a public recreation ground. The subscription is 25s. od. a year for adults and 15s. od. for youths under 21. All three teams use the cricket pavilion for changing.

Tennis

There are two tennis clubs. One, with 66 members, has two hard courts, and a somewhat inadequate pavilion. The subscription is 30s. od. a year. The other club has 150 playing members, about half of whom are women. It has seven hard courts and a pavilion. The subscription is £3 3s. od. a year.

Tennis is also played on three public grass courts, the charge being 3s. od. an hour on weekdays and 4s. od. on Sundays. Three factories have excellent sports grounds, including grass and hard courts, and a few of the churches have tennis courts for the use of their members.

Bowls

Of the four bowling greens in the borough, three are on factory sports grounds; the fourth is an open club with a membership of 70 playing members, all men. Weekly matches are played from May to September. The green is surrounded by a garden and there is a large pavilion. In 1949 a Social Club was formed in connection with the bowling club. It is open every day of the year except on Christmas and Boxing Days. Two whist drives are run each week, and once a month there is a special concert and social evening.

Harriers

The Harriers' Club has an active membership of 60 and a total membership of 85. Senior members pay 5s. od. a year, and juniors 3s. od. The members are active throughout the year. They engage in cross-country and road races, and training on a running track on one of the public recreation grounds on two days a week. During the summer they hold four athletic meetings for members, and promote races for novices and children.

Golf

Two hundred High Wycombe residents belong to a club which has an excellent 18-hole course and is only 3½ miles away. About 75 High Wycombe residents belong to two other clubs, one 9 holes and another 18 holes. Both are about 9 miles away.

Cyclists' Touring Club

This Club has only 10 members living in the borough.

Motor Cycle Club

This Club has about 100 members, most of whom are riding members. Most week-ends the Club either organizes an event itself or else supports another club's event. Occasionally in the summer members go camping at week-ends. Every summer the Club organizes grass track races which attract about 5,000 spectators. Members compete in races in different parts of the country. They have a club room, where films of motor cycling events are shown.

Sailing

About 50 residents in the borough own yachts and belong to the Upper Thames Sailing Club. The reach of the Thames on which they sail is about 5 miles away.

Swimming

An old and rather out-of-date open-air swimming bath has recently been closed. The Corporation has plans for a new one but cannot build it until the present building restrictions are withdrawn. Residents in High Wycombe can swim in the Thames, but this is about 5 miles away.

Angling

Notwithstanding the fact that there is no fishing except in the Thames, which at the nearest point is about 5 miles away, angling is a popular sport in High Wycombe, several hundred people indulging in it. There are several angling clubs, some of which rent the fishing rights on stretches of the Thames, paying rentals as high as £50 a year. Some of these preserved waters are 10 or 15 miles from High Wycombe.

Beagling

Thirteen people living in the borough belong to the local Beagling Club. The subscription is £4 4s. 0d. for men and £3 3s. 0d. for women. Meets take place twice weekly.

Naturalists' Society

This Society, which has 40 members, is a branch of the British Empire Naturalists' Association, whose object is "to bring naturalists and nature lovers into helpful communication, to secure the protection of wild life, and objects o interest to the nature student, and to promote the preservation of the natural beauties of the countryside." It arranges field meetings, rambles, talks and exhibitions. Members have the use of a church hall for indoor meetings.

Allotment gardens

The Town Council has devoted 68 acres to allotments, but 24 acres are allotted only temporarily. Of the 917 allotments, 89% are let. There are two societies interested in gardening and horticulture. The more active of these has a membership of 853. Members pay 1s. 0d. a year and are then entitled to facilities which include the loan of spraying machinery, the purchase of seeds and fertilizers on wholesale terms, help in obtaining security of tenure and the prevention of trespassing and pilfering. In particular Old Age Pensioners are helped. The Town Council loans an old malt house to the Association for use as a store.

Coach trips

There are nine coach operators in the town. In summer, each Saturday and Sunday, between 40 and 50 coach loads go into the country, almost all of them to coast resorts between Clacton and Bournemouth.

In spring, autumn and winter, a great many coaches take

people to the theatres, pantomimes and other attractions in London, Oxford and Reading.

One of the largest companies sends on the average 20 coaches a week to London from October to the end of April. In 8 weeks they sent 100 coaches to London filled with people going to see "Skating Varieties." They took 32 coach-loads of people to see a fight for the heavy-weight world championship.

The coach companies buy tickets for popular attractions, and make a composite charge for these and for the coach fare. In five weeks one company bought between 1,500 and 2,000 tickets for the Bertram Mills circus, taking the people there in coaches.

During June 1949, one of the largest companies sent 367 coach-loads of people to the coast and to attractions in various towns. In May they sent about half this number.

Most of the coaches hold 32 people, but a few are rather smaller.

Religious activities

There are 35 churches in High Wycombe. In November 1947, on two Sundays when the weather was fine, we took a census of the number of attendances by adults, i.e., persons of 17 years of age and over. The average for the two Sundays was as shown in the table on the following page.

The average number of church attendances by persons of 17 years of age and over is equal to about 10·5% of the adult population. This does not mean that the average number of persons attending church on the two census Sundays represented 10·5% of the adult population, because we do not know how many persons attended more than once on a Sunday.

In the case of the Anglican churches the figures refer to the attendances at Matins and Evensong. They do not include attendances at Holy Communion services. The average total number attending these services was 16 men and 34 women. In the case of the Roman Catholic church they refer to the five Masses held at 7.30, 8.30, 9.30, 10.15 and 11.0 in the morning and Benediction at 6.30 in the evening. A church census we took in York in 1948 showed that attendances by persons of 17 years of age and over equalled 13% of the adult population.

	Men	Women	Total
11 Methodist ..	294	433	727
2 Free Methodist ..	68	83	151
10 Anglican	324	386	710
1 Roman Catholic ..	266	404	670
3 Baptist	210	244	454
1 Strict Baptist ..	21	51	72
1 Congregational ..	100	204	304
1 Salvation Army ..	90	96	186
1 Christian Scientist	17	46	63
1 Christadelphian ..	17	14	31
1 Quaker	14	15	29
1 Spiritualist ..	4	12	16
1 Plymouth Brethren	7	7	14
Totals ..	1,432	1,995	3,427

The churches make so valuable a contribution to the cultural and spiritual life of the community through the activities they sponsor other than the formal church services that we have thought it important to give a brief description of those provided by the different denominations.

Methodists

There are 11 Methodist churches in the town. Our census of attendances taken on two Sundays in November 1947 showed an average attendance of 727 persons aged 17 or over.

The large number of churches is due to the fact that previously there were many Free Methodist sects which are now united. Most of the services are conducted by laymen, for there are only 4 ministers to serve the 11 churches in the town and 15 outside it. Between them, the 4 ministers supervise the religious and social activities of all the churches. These activities are so many and so varied that we cannot do more than give a few brief facts about some of them.

The detailed description of them, furnished by our investigator, fully justified the remark with which she closed her report. "It can thus be seen that the Methodist churches are literally bristling with activities for all ages, and the ministers are all eager and full of devotion to their churches."

There can be little doubt that the Methodist churches are very much alive, and this raises the question of whether they do not benefit from the fact that so much of the responsibility of conducting church activities of all kinds rests on the shoulders of laymen, supervised, and doubtless inspired, by ordained ministers.

Among the churches' many activities, apart from the church services, probably the most important centre around the Sunday schools. These are much more than places where children meet on Sundays. Altogether about 1,100 people of ages varying from the very young to young adults attend these schools. In nearly all the schools the children are prepared for scripture examinations, and they are encouraged to take part in many of the churches' activities. They take part in musical festivals, in dramatic performances, and school anniversaries where children from several churches meet together and individual children read verses from the Bible or recite verses of hymns. The school children are active in raising funds for foreign missions and they collect about £1,500 to £1,600 a year. They do this not merely by asking people to subscribe, but by bazaars, concerts, plays and socials.

All Methodist churches have afternoon meetings for women. Almost all of them are held weekly throughout the year, and have an average total attendance of over 400. The meetings begin with a prayer and the singing of a hymn. Talks are given, sometimes on matters connected with the home and sometimes on religious matters. Members are visited when they are ill. There is no doubt that these meetings lead to a real sense of fellowship.

Six of the churches have choirs, in which about 200 people of all ages from about 15 upwards take part. Practices are held weekly. In one church, after the evening service, there is community singing led by the choir.

Six churches have organized mixed youth clubs which are attended by young people from other churches.

In addition to the above there are many and varied activities

—religious, educational and recreational. It would occupy too much space to describe these, but some idea of what is being done can be gained from the list of activities other than the Sunday services of one church with about 100 members. It is as follows:

Activity	*Frequency*	*Regular attenders*
Women's Meeting ..	Weekly	40
Men's Institute (Social)	Each weekday	25
Youth Club ..	Twice weekly	20
Young People's Fellowship ..	Weekly	20
Cricket Club	2 weekly practices and matches on Saturday	16
Sick and Poor Fund ..	Occasional	—
Christian Endeavour ..	Weekly	16
Choir	Practice weekly	40
Junior Missionary Association ..	Occasional	—
Sunday School ..	Weekly	130

This same church organizes a thrift club, into which participants pay a weekly sum, drawing out benefits at Christmas and being eligible also for payments at set rates during the first 12 weeks of sickness or on the death of a spouse. In certain cases of need loans are also made from the funds and interest is charged on them. This club started more than 50 years ago among members of a young men's Bible class, but it has been so successful that its membership has extended far beyond that of the church and now numbers 5,500 persons from High Wycombe and the surrounding villages.

Free Methodists

There are two Free Methodist churches in High Wycombe. Only one has an ordained minister, services in the other being conducted by laymen. The sect is very fundamentalist in its doctrine and did not join in the union of Methodist churches.

The average attendance on the two Sundays of our census was 151. The two Sunday schools have an average attendance of about 165.

Although the churches are small there are a number of weekday activities. There are choirs in both churches, with a total membership of about 24. They compete annually in the Free Church Union Choir Festival held in the Albert Hall, where they have won diplomas and awards. One of the choirs frequently gives concerts in High Wycombe.

There are branches of the Girls' Life Brigades in both churches. About 50 girls meet weekly, the programme of the meetings including handicrafts, mothercraft, first aid, and physical training. There is also a short religious service. The girls go camping, celebrate their anniversary, and organize rummage sales in aid of church funds.

Weekly women's meetings are held, with a total average attendance of about 50. They are mostly devotional in character. At one church, women's and men's Bible classes are held every Sunday, with an average attendance of about 24 men and 10 women. This church also has a mixed adult Bible class held weekly, with an attendance of about 12.

Three times a week about a dozen young men meet to play billiards and table tennis.

In summer a cricket team plays in a local league.

A Junior Christian Endeavour holds weekly meetings attended by about a dozen young people, and a Young People's Fellowship meets weekly.

Anglican Churches

There are 10 Anglican churches in the town. Our census of attendances taken on two Sundays in November 1947 showed an average attendance of 710 persons aged 17 and over.

All the churches have Sunday schools. The total number of children attending them is about 600, a figure which is in somewhat startling contrast to the 1,100 attending the Sunday schools in the 11 Methodist churches.

About 150 people belong to church choirs, and practices are held twice and in some cases three times a week.

Six of the churches run a Mothers' Union, which is the Anglican women's weekly meeting, having the particular aims of upholding the sanctity of marriage and the Christian upbringing of children. About 200 women regularly attend the meetings, where talks are given and bazaars, jumble sales and other means of raising money for church funds are organized. As not many younger women came to these meetings, each of the six churches has organized a Young Wives' Group for mothers with young children. Each group meets weekly, and talks are given on subjects connected with children. The members are encouraged to bring their children, and a nursery is run in connection with every meeting, which is followed by tea. Over 200 women belong to these groups.

Altogether about 155 boys belong to Church Lads' Brigades, Boys' Brigades and Scouts and Cubs, and 126 girls are in Guides and Brownies. These meet weekly, and besides the usual activities undertaken by these uniformed groups, concerts are organized with sketches, songs and dances, and one Guide Company has an orchestra.

Three churches have mixed Fellowship Groups, in which about 60 people between the ages of 16 and 50 meet weekly. Talks are given, socials arranged, and at one of them there are occasional dances. In all the groups members undertake to do some church work, such, for instance, as dusting the church and arranging flowers for the altar.

One church has an active girls' club which meets weekly with an attendance of about 25 girls between the ages of 10 and 14. The same church has a dramatic group with about 20 regular attenders aged from about 18 upwards who meet weekly. Both groups do a great deal to raise money for church funds.

Two churches have boys' clubs, meeting weekly, attended by about 44 boys aged between 13 and 16. In one of these churches there is a club for boys between 15 and 20. This has suffered through the call-up to the Forces, but about 16 meet weekly.

In eight of the churches there are a number of very small groups of people meeting for different recreational activities. The total number meeting weekly is about 120.

One church has a weekly women's fellowship meeting, attended by about 30 people. This meeting is definitely devotional.

Much interest is taken by the different churches in foreign

missions. One church in a small parish contributes about £100 a year. About 100 women spend a good deal of time in organizing bazaars and sales of work.

Roman Catholics

The one Roman Catholic church draws its congregation from neighbourhoods extending some miles outside of High Wycombe, a fact which must be borne in mind when comparing the numbers attending the Roman Catholic and the Protestant churches. The average attendances by adults on the two Sundays on which we took a census was 670, of whom probably from two-thirds to three-quarters were residents of High Wycombe.

There are no church halls, and this virtually renders the organization of weekday activities impossible. Occasionally, however, a room at the Catholic School is made available, and about 40 women belong to a sewing guild which makes articles for bazaars.

The church choir, with a membership of 24 boys, has attained so high a standard that it has broadcast.

Baptists

There are three Baptist churches in the town and one branch church in a temporary building in charge of a layman. Our census of attendances taken on two Sundays in November 1947 showed an average attendance of 454 persons of 17 years of age and over.

Two of the churches have particularly good accommodation, and the church halls are well occupied nearly every night of the week.

About 650 children attend the Sunday schools. The children are encouraged to take part in various activities besides attending the school on Sundays. For instance, in 1949 one school collected £230 for a missionary society. The schools also take part in musical festivals, and occasionally organize concerts for the benefit of church objects.

Two churches have a Young People's Fellowship, holding weekly meetings throughout the year, and one holding them weekly in the winter. They have all sorts of activities—socials, rambles, talks, Bible quizzes, discussions, devotional meetings. One has a good choir and took complete charge of the services in the church on one Sunday. The average attendance of the fellowship meetings is 55, when all three meet, and 45 in summer when only two meet.

All three churches hold fortnightly meetings during the winter, when talks are given by highly qualified people on a variety of subjects—religious, political and social. These are followed by questions and discussion. The total average attendance is a little over 100.

All the churches have mixed choirs, which altogether number about 80 people. There is a choir practice every week.

A good many recreational activities take place in the church halls of all three churches on week nights. In no cases are they very largely attended, but in the aggregate the attendance is not inconsiderable.

Two churches have afternoon women's meetings weekly, with an average attendance of 100. In one of these, talks are given and discussions held and there is a good choir which practises once a week. Every month there is a sewing meeting to make articles for the foreign and home missions. The other meeting is almost purely devotional.

In connection with one church a Young Wives' Fellowship meeting is held weekly in the afternoon. Sometimes it is devotional, at other times a nurse, or welfare officer or psychologist will speak. The average attendance at these gatherings is about 40. Wives may bring their babies or young children, who are looked after by volunteers.

About 250 young people are in companies of Scouts, Guides, Brownies and Cubs associated with the churches.

Altogether the Baptist churches give evidence of real life—not only in their definitely religious work, but in the great variety of their weekday activities.

Strict Baptists

This sect is extremely fundamentalist in its outlook. They have only one church in High Wycombe and our census showed that the average number of attendances on the two Sundays of our census was 72.

Although the membership of this sect of Baptists is not large, there is a mixed youth club run by the church which meets weekly and has an average attendance of 25. Billiards, table tennis and the usual indoor games are played. For the last 15 minutes there is always a religious address.

A mid-week devotional afternoon service is attended by 30 women, and a mixed fellowship meeting is also held weekly, attended by about 25 people aged from 15 upwards. The meetings are sometimes devotional, at other times there are talks, socials and discussions. Bible classes are attended on Sunday evenings by about 12 men and 20 women, and a preaching service on a week-night is addressed by the minister and attended by about 50 people.

Sunday schools are held in the morning and afternoon, attended by about 60 people of all ages.

Congregational Church

There is only one Congregational church in the town. It seats 600 people and has two church halls capable of seating 500 and 60 people respectively. Our census of attendances taken on two Sundays in November 1947 showed an average attendance of 304 persons aged 17 and over.

The average attendance at the Sunday school is about 145. There are 19 teachers and the school is exceptionally well managed. Nativity plays are performed and scripture stories are frequently dramatized in order to bring home their significance. The children have won honours in musical festivals and are active in raising funds for foreign missions. In 1950 they won the Sunday School Union shield awarded for the best school performance at scripture examinations.

A women's meeting held weekly has an average attendance of 35. It opens with a prayer and a hymn, and addresses are given on child welfare, cookery and other subjects. The meeting has a good choir which gives many concerts in the town and outlying districts. It has its own provident club.

A working party of about 20 meets weekly to make articles for sales of work and bazaars in aid of church objects. The working parties sometimes meet in members' homes, and are regarded as pleasant social occasions.

The church has a mixed choir of about 20 members, which practises every week. It organizes occasional musical events with augmented numbers. In addition to the choir, a music group of about 25 adults meets weekly in winter; gramophone records are played, and occasionally someone will play or sing.

One of the halls has been fitted up as a gymnasium and many people use it. There is a qualified but unpaid instructor, and senior and junior classes are held weekly, with an average attendance of about 60. A gymnastic display was given recently in the Town Hall, and competent judges said that the standard of work was very high.

A dramatic group with about 24 members frequently produces plays to raise money for some church object.

There are senior and junior mixed youth clubs. The senior club meets twice and the junior once a week, the average attendances being 45 and 30 respectively. Apart from the club meetings, a variety of activities are fostered, such as cricket, football, netball, tennis, swimming, table tennis, debates, lectures, concerts, and folk dancing. In the winter an adult badminton club meets weekly with an average attendance of about 12.

The church has companies of Scouts, Rovers, Cubs, Guides and Brownies, with 93 members in all.

There is no doubt that this church is very much alive. Apart from the Sunday services, there is a wide range of week-day activities, in the running of which the young people take their full share.

The Salvation Army

There are about 200 members of the Salvation Army in High Wycombe. They have a meeting hall in the centre of the town. The average number attending the two indoor services on the two Sundays when we took our census was 186. An open-air service is usually held preceding the evening service.

About 70 women regularly attend the weekly women's meeting. Apart from this, the week-night activities of the Salvation Army reflect its musical interests. There are almost nightly practices for the adult and junior bands and choirs, each of which has about 30 members. On Saturday evenings the band and choirs give a concert attended by about 100 people.

Christian Scientists

This body has an excellent modern building with a hall and reading room. There are two meetings on Sundays. On the two Sundays of our church census, the average attendances by adults were 17 men and 46 women.

There is a Sunday School and a mid-week testimony meeting.

Other sects

The Quakers, Christadelphians, Spiritualists and Plymouth Brethren are not large enough bodies to organize week-day activities but many of them take an active part in various kinds of social work in the town.

General remarks

It should be pointed out that the bare statistical summary of the activities of the various churches only tells half the story of the leisure time activities of church members, both young and old. In church and chapel work there are always bazaars, pageants, preparation for scripture examinations, musical festivals, concerts and so on, which are often not sponsored by the groups described, but by the Church as a whole. There is no doubt whatever that the week-day activities of the churches play a very important part in enabling and encouraging people to spend their leisure happily and wisely.

Age of persons under church influence

When taking the census of attendances by adults (i.e., persons of 17 years of age and over), our investigators made an estimate of the proportion of the church attenders who were over 50 years of age. This was, of course, only a rough classification, but it was based on more than pure guesswork, because nearly all the investigators were themselves members of the churches concerned and knew most of the attenders. They estimated that the proportion of attenders over 50 was 35·6 per cent in the Anglican churches, 44·8 per cent in the

Nonconformist churches, and 20·9 per cent in the Roman Catholic church. Of the population of England and Wales as a whole, 35·4 per cent are over 50.

These figures suggest that the proportion of the rising generation who are coming under religious influence is smaller in the Nonconformist than in the other churches.

The description given of the activities of the Nonconformist churches appears, however, to point to the fact that although the proportion of young people attending church services may be small, a much larger proportion come under religious influence through the week-day church activities in which they take part. Church attendance is not an acid test of spiritual life.

CHAPTER XV

LEISURE TIME PURSUITS IN THE SCANDINAVIAN COUNTRIES

DENMARK, Norway, Sweden and Finland have done so much to encourage and enable people, and especially young people, to spend their leisure rationally, that we thought it worth while to investigate the matter on the spot. Accordingly in 1947 B.S.R. visited them. He was accompanied by Christian Gierloff of Norway, the distinguished economist and sociologist, who knew all the countries intimately, and who had made arrangements in advance for him to meet groups of people who had intimate knowledge of the different matters on which we sought information. Although the main purpose of his visit was to gather information about the positive steps taken to encourage people to spend their leisure wisely, he also enquired into other matters which have a bearing on the character of the people as a whole. Thus he sought information about the direct influence of the churches and of religious belief, and the extent of gambling, drinking and sexual promiscuity. He also made enquiries about Communism because this is more likely to spread in countries where the people feel frustrated, rather than in those in which they are pretty well satisfied with their living conditions.

His report, which follows, shows that we have much to learn from all the countries visited about steps which might be taken in England to encourage people to make good use of their leisure.

DENMARK

In 1948 the population of Denmark was 4,190,000, of whom about two-thirds live under urban conditions—nearly 1,000,000 of them in Copenhagen. In 1947 Aarhus had a population of 107,393, and Odense 92,436. Except for Aalborg (population 60,880) and Esbjerg (population 43,241), none of the other towns had a population of more than 36,500. Just over one-fourth of the population live exclusively by agriculture and about one-half by manufactures and trade. Denmark is a country with a high *per capita* income, and her wealth is more evenly distributed than in many other countries. In the words of Grundtvig, "Few have too much and fewer too little." About half the workers employed in industry are professionally trained. Their standard of craftsmanship is high and the output per worker is higher than in many neighbouring countries.

(Prices are quoted in Kroner. In 1947 the rate of exchange was about 20 Kr. to the £. 1 Kr. = 100 øre.)

Education

So far back as 1814 an act was passed that made in compulsory to provide elementary schools in all towns and rural districts. It laid down the aims of the schools, describing them as Christian and Civic Schools, in which the children were to be "brought up to be good and honest in conformity with the Evangelical Christian doctrine, and where such knowledge and proficiencies were imparted to them as to make them useful citizens." The National Education Act of 1937 definitely puts the development of character before the dissemination of knowledge. Under that act, children must attend school from 7 to 14. Games and gymnastics were made compulsory in all schools, and were to be placed on the same level as the principal subjects. Every school with pupils of 12 years old and upwards must have a gymnasium with changing room and baths. The teaching of carpentry to boys, and sewing and housework to girls, is also compulsory.

The teaching of religion was also made, and still is, compulsory, except in the case of children whose parents object to this. The general opinion of those knowledgeable people whom I consulted was that this formal teaching is not of great value.

Although parents may send their children to private schools, or educate them at home, 90% of the children go to the State elementary schools. They come from all social classes. University training is free. Anyone may attend lectures, but only those who have matriculated may sit for an examination.

So great is the importance attached to education that school teachers are often regarded as the leading personalities in the social and political life of the neighbourhoods in which they live.

Folk High Schools

The emphasis placed in the elementary schools on the formation of character has an important effect on the pupils, but this applies with even greater force to the Folk High Schools. These are residential schools for young people, usually between 18 and 25. The first of these was founded in 1844—now there are 58 of them, with a 5-months' course for young men in winter, and a 3-months' course for young women in summer. Between 8,000 and 9,000 pupils attend the schools each year, including about 2,500 in the 24 agricultural high schools, which are run on very similar lines, but in which a large part of the syllabus is devoted to agricultural subjects. The Folk High Schools "are founded on Grundtvig's ideas of free popular education, aiming more at developing personality and moulding character than at imparting knowledge. 'To awaken, cherish and enlighten that human life which should and must be expected of the young of Denmark' was his intention for the people's high schools, whose aim in more modern times, but in accord with that first principle, has been expressed thus: 'Not to impart real knowledge first and foremost, but to educate the human being, give him a proper attitude towards life, not in the form of a cut-and-dried philosophy, but by helping the pupils to think for themselves and to distinguish between real and false values.' Instruction at the people's high school consists of the preaching of an idea, and its purpose is *inspiration towards an outlook on life*."[1]

Almost all of the schools are quite definitely Christian in character, although no religious instruction is given. They have prospered chiefly in rural areas. During the last 30 years over one-third of Denmark's agricultural youth attended Folk High Schools or Agricultural Schools, and many have attended both. In the autumn old students and people influenced by the Folk High Schools gather in different localities for meetings, some only attend for a day, others for two or three. The total number attending in a year may be as many as 25,000 or 30,000.

The women's course in the Folk High Schools includes

[1] *Social Denmark*, p. 361.

instruction in domestic science. In addition, there are 30 domestic science colleges, modelled on the Folk High Schools and attended by young women of about the same age. They are residential colleges and the courses last from three to five months. A certain amount of general education is included in the syllabus.

The cost of building the Folk High Schools has been met by private subscriptions, but the State makes grants for their upkeep and also gives bursaries to pupils who cannot afford to pay the whole of the school fees.

Until quite recently the Folk High Schools were confined to rural districts, but there are now two residential high schools in towns, started by the Workers' Educational movement. This movement was established in 1924, and has widespread activities. It provides a large number of lectures, organizes study circles, evening schools, schools for shop stewards and for unemployed workers. It organizes the distribution of a large amount of wholesome and useful literature, arranges for visits to art galleries and industrial plants, and in many other ways seeks to carry out its objects of spreading enlightenment among the working population of Denmark.

"Students and participators in the many branches of this work run into thousands every year, members of study circles for example number about 10,000, evening schools 16,000–18,000, summer courses about 2,500, attending lectures in the country 35,000–40,000, in the towns 75,000–100,000, and so on. All the same, the Union strongly emphasizes the importance of self-study, and encourages book reading and discussions in small groups, for which reason the study circle is considered to be the best working method within the workers' educational movement.

"It is beyond question that the educational movement has its great share in the high standard reached by the Danish labour movement. By its means all problems arising have been discussed without bias, whereby a large number of leaders and representatives have acquired knowledge and schooling of great help to them in the exercising of their functions.

"For the upkeep of the Educational Union, and for the advancement of its work, the trade unions and the Labour

Party pay an annual contribution of a few coppers per member (in 1945 15 øre), and special grants are made by the Workers' National Co-operative Union and the Social Democratic Youth Association. In addition, the Educational Union receives an annual grant from the State."[1]

There are 3,200 evening schools in Denmark, run either by the local authorities or by private associations. Although attendances are voluntary, 160,491 pupils attended the local authorities' schools in 1946–7. In Copenhagen the pupils receive facilities for attending museums under competent guidance, attend concerts and get cheap tickets for the Royal Theatre.

In addition to the schools referred to above, there are agricultural classes attended by 13,000 pupils.

Religion

There were two great religious revivals in the second half of the nineteenth century, but none since. The situation to-day with regard to religious beliefs is very similar to that in Great Britain. The Churches no longer play the important part in developing the social and religious life of the people that they used to do. Church attendance is very much smaller than it was in the latter half of the nineteenth century. As stated above, religious instruction is given in the day schools by the ordinary class teachers, but I gathered that most of it is very formal and amounts to little. Many of those who give the teaching do not themselves believe in the Christian doctrine. On the other hand, thoughtful and knowledgeable people told me that people are not more materialistic than they used to be, and although few parents give religious instruction to their children, they are more interested than they were in their all-round development.

As in Britain and Norway, Sweden and Finland, sexual promiscuity is much more common than when the influence of the Churches was stronger than it is to-day, and much more common than in Norway, Sweden and Finland.

Sport

In 1948 the membership of different sporting organizations

[1] *Social Denmark*, pp. 370–1.

amounted to 564,000, but the number of active athletes and sportsmen is less than this, for some of them belong to more than one organization. There is, however, no doubt that the number of active sportsmen is very large. This is due, in part, to the importance attached to gymnastics in the schools, and partly to the facilities for engaging in different kinds of sport and in gymnastics which are provided, often with financial aid from the State.

In addition to the State elementary schools, in all of which (as stated above) if there are pupils of 12 years or over, there must be a gymnasium with changing room and bath, there were 1,500 public gymnasia in 1943, and about the same number of football fields, so distributed that there is a football field and gymnasium in every rural area.

Both the State and the local authorities contribute to the cost of laying out sports fields, tennis courts, swimming pools, and the building of boat houses and halls for indoor games.

There are four gymnastic colleges where, every year, about a thousand men and women attend courses in gymnastics, lasting from three to five months. Some are trained to become gymnastic instructors and others take the classes just for their own physical well being.

Waste material playground in Copenhagen

On a piece of waste land near a number of working-class houses, there is a children's playground which was opened in 1943. It represents an attempt to solve one of the problems of children's playgrounds. It covers an area of 6,000 square metres (7,130 square yards), and is surrounded by an earthen embankment 2 metres high, which is planted with shrubs. The interesting thing about this playground is that there is no equipment, such as swings, see-saws, etc. The only thing with which children can amuse themselves are waste materials—old bricks, old cases, poles, old boards, old straw matting, pieces of canvas, clay, etc.

There is one man as supervisor, a trained educationist. He may suggest to children what they might make, but more often they decide this for themselves. When I visited the playground, some children had built little houses of bricks, with or without clay, some had built houses of straw mats raised on poles. Some had dug caves, and some had made a clay model of a man on horseback, more than half life-size. Some had made a series of dolls' heads, many with different coloured hair, which were to be used for a kind of Punch and Judy show, the building for which was being made by two boys, aged about 10, and consisting of posts driven in the ground with pieces of dark green cloth, rather old and shabby, nailed to them.

The ages of those using the playground varies from 5 or 6 to 20 or 21. The old ones naturally go in for ambitious projects, for instance, they had made a concrete surround for a sand pit for the youngsters.

Unlike the usual mechanized playground, a waste material playground affords the children every opportunity for developing their talent for self-education. The one I saw was opened by the Workers' Co-operative Housing Association in 1943, as part of their large housing developments in the neighbourhood, where there are about 1,500 children up to 15 years of age. The cost of maintaining the playground (that is, pay for the supervisor, and the amortization of the cost of the land) is distributed as follows: 40 per cent from the State, 30 per cent from the municipality, and 30 per cent from the tenants in the neighbouring houses, whether they are parents or not.

Open-air entertainments

In summer, bands play in the parks in Copenhagen and Aarhus, and in Copenhagen dramatic performances are given. This is rendered possible by a mobile unit with stage and dressing rooms.

In "Tivoli," Copenhagen has what is probably the finest amusement centre in the world, though "Liseberg," in Gothenberg, is almost, if indeed not quite, as fine. Certainly there is nothing like it in England.

It was originally designed in 1843 by a young architect and has been open ever since. In 1948 it was visited by 3,117,000 people, not counting nearly 12,000 season-ticket holders. It is owned and financed by a private company, but the charges for admission are only sufficient to cover costs. They are 30 øre (3½d.) for adults before and 60 øre after 2 p.m. Children half price. On Saturdays the admission charges are doubled. It is open from May to September. The grounds, extending to very many acres, are beautifully laid out, and entertainments are provided suitable to all tastes.

Writing about it in the *News Chronicle* of July 1st, 1949, Mr. J. B. Priestley said:

"Old folks go there in the morning to saunter among the trees and flower beds. Children rush to the playground or the lake or to see the clown and the harlequin at the Pantomime Theatre.

"In the evening, highbrows go for Beethoven and Brahms, and lowbrows go to jitterbug. You can stare at coloured fountains while the promenade orchestra plays Strauss waltzes, or can scream your head off on the Balloon Wheel or the switch-back or among the scooter cars or in the Crazy House.

"You can entertain your friends to a cheap snack or sandwiches and beer or give them the most elaborate and expensive dinner in the city. At one place they are wolfing sausages and at another they are nibbling caviare.

"This, I trust, suggests not only a wide variety of attractions but also a genuinely democratic institution. And this is what Tivoli is, a place for everybody, not only all ages, but also all classes."

Holidays

Since 1938 employers are compelled by law to give their employees 12 days' holiday annually with pay.

An association called the Dansk Folke-Ferie was set up by the trade unions in 1938 with the object of promoting the healthful enjoyment of holidays by the general population. This association has acquired or built a number of hotels and camps. I visited a typical camp at Gilleleje. It is on the sea-shore, and its area is about 20 acres. There is a building with a restaurant, a shop, and a large room used for social purposes. Social gatherings are held there twice a week. There are 60 bungalows, each capable of housing four people, the rents of which are 50 Kr. a week.

Trade unions gave 500,000 Kr. towards the cost of establishing this holiday centre. The rest of the money has been borrowed. Nearly 3,000 people come to the camp yearly.

Altogether the Folke-Ferie has 10 holiday centres—six hotels and four camps with bungalows and a central hall, as at Gilleleje. There are 2,000 beds in the holiday centres, and they can give one week's holiday to about 33,000 people during the summer.

In addition to establishing camps and hotels, the association canvasses farmers and other country dwellers to ask if they will let rooms to town dwellers. It then acts as an agent bringing farmers and town dwellers together.

The erection of holiday resorts is subsidized by the Ministry of Social Affairs, municipalities, private firms and other organizations.

The normal length of the working week is 48 hours, but in agriculture the hours are longer, particularly in summer, when they are often from 54 to 60 hours.

Cinemas

A pointer to the ways in which people spend their leisure is provided by the number of people who visit cinemas. The following table gives the facts with regard to this for persons over 10 years of age, for 1945:

	Number of Inhabitants over 10 years old (thousands)	Attendances at Cinemas (millions)	Attendances per Inhabitant over 10 years old
Copenhagen ..	870	19·0	24
Country towns	955	19·5	23
Rural parishes	1700	8·5	5

It will be seen that the total number of attendances for the country as a whole was 47,000,000. A somewhat rough calculation shows that in Great Britain the number of attendances by persons over 10 years old in 1946 was about 1,270,000,000, and as the population of Great Britain is about 12 times that of Denmark, it would seem that the proportion of people attending cinemas is about twice as high in Great Britain as in Denmark.

Reading habits

In 1946–7 there were 1,276 public libraries, owning about 4,300,000 books, and 226 children's libraries, owning rather over 770,000 books. The number of persons borrowing books was about 622,400 and 104,000 respectively, and the number of books borrowed was about 14,000,000 and 2,000,000 respectively. This is equivalent to just under 4 books borrowed per head of the population, as compared with 5 for Great Britain and Northern Ireland. In addition to the public libraries, there were 57 hospital libraries owning about 587,000 books, as well as school libraries in 2,216 schools. It is estimated that about one-third of those borrowing books are working-class people.

In the second half of 1946 the circulation of weekly illustrated papers was about 2,000,000. This gives an average of nearly two illustrated papers a week per household.

Broadcasting

There are a few facts about the Danish Broadcasting Corporation which are worth mentioning.

There is youths' brains trust once a week, and a broadcast for young people when they "try to smuggle some education among the entertainment."

The Corporation has organized a large number of listener groups. It prepares text books for the groups and sells them cheaply. Recently a series of talks was given on "What is Christianity?" A text book was written about these talks and 25,000 copies were sold. About 30,000 young people, members of 3,000 listener groups, hear the talks and discuss them. The listener groups are encouraged to ask questions of the Broadcasting Association. More questions are asked about religious subjects than about any others.

The number of licences in 1948 was 1,163,272, equal to 280

per thousand of the population, as compared with 236 in Great Britain.

Housing

As stated previously, a quarter of the population of the country live in Copenhagen.

Out of 327,500 houses and flats in that city 8 per cent have 1 room, 43 per cent have 2 rooms, 24 per cent have 3 rooms, and 25 per cent have 4 rooms or more.

The number of houses and flats in provincial towns is about 313,500. Of these 6 per cent have 1 room, 37 per cent have 2 rooms, 32 per cent have 3 rooms, and 25 per cent have 4 rooms or more.[1] Kitchens are not included in the number of rooms. They are too small to use for sleeping purposes.

It will thus be seen that the proportion of houses and flats with only one or two rooms is much greater than in England, but it is much lower than in Norway, Sweden and Finland.

In Copenhagen and the larger provincial towns the modern practice tends to be to build large blocks of flats, four or five storeys high.

Allotment gardens

The principal organization concerned with allotment gardens is "The Association of Colony (i.e., allotment) Gardens in Denmark," which has 60,000 members. Other Associations have 40,000. The average size of an allotment is about 600 square yards. During the summer months 24 advisers are at the disposal of allotment holders. The State pays a head adviser to aid local allotment organizations. The land for allotments is rented by the local Associations or the central Association on leases of 25 years, but recently the central Association has begun buying land.

On many of the allotments the tenants have erected small wooden bungalows in which they often spend week-ends during the summer, or even stay in them for longer periods.

The State gives to the two Associations an annual grant of 1 Kr. per member, and local authorities let land in their possession at one-fourth or even less of the rent which they

[1] *Social Denmark*, p. 417. The figures refer to the year 1940.

charge to other tenants. The Associations buy tools and seeds on wholesale terms for allotment holders, and make loans to them for the erection of their bungalows.

Drinking

The control of the drink traffic is based on the Licensing Act of 1939. Under that Act licences to sell alcoholic liquors are granted by a special licensing board in the towns, and by county and parish authorities in the country. A licence is granted for a period of from five to eight years. If it is refused, the question may not be reconsidered until after a lapse of five years. In country districts, if so desired by 35% of the electors or 33% of the parish council, a plebiscite may be held to decide whether a given licence shall be granted, but more than half the licences are granted without a plebiscite.

As in Norway, Sweden and Finland, there are no public houses or bars in Denmark—alcoholic drinks are taken in restaurants, which may be open from 5 a.m. until midnight, or bought for home consumption from grocers or wine merchants.

The taxes on alcoholic drinks are very high. There is a tax of 34 Kr. per litre of pure alcohol levied on the producers, a tax of 22½ per cent on the wholesale price of sales to restaurants and retail dealers, and a tax of 33⅓ per cent on restaurant sales of alcoholic drinks. All alcoholic drinks are taxed, no matter how small is the amount of alcohol.

The consumption per head of alcoholic liquors in Denmark and in England and Wales in 1947 was as follows:

	Denmark	*England & Wales*
	Litres	Litres
Spirits ..	1·9 ..	0·9
Wines ..	3·1 ..	9·0
Beer ..	68·3 ..	60·5

Expressed in terms of absolute alcohol, the annual consumption per head of the alcoholic liquors shown in the foregoing table is equivalent to 3·3 litres in Denmark, and 3·9 litres in England and Wales.

No comparison can be made between the amount of drunkenness in Denmark and England and Wales, because the official statistics for Denmark only publish the arrests for drunkenness, and those for England and Wales only the number of persons prosecuted.

Gambling

Gambling is not a serious evil in Denmark. The total amount of authorized gambling in 1946–7 was 46,000,000 Kr. Of this 29,000,000 Kr. was gambling on trotting races, 7,000,000 Kr. on horse racing, 5,000,000 on bicycle racing, and 5,000,000 on pigeon flying.

A State Lottery was established in 1753. The total sum invested in 1948 was 25·7 million Kr. Of this 20·5 million Kr. was paid to those who drew lucky numbers, administrative costs were about 2·2 million Kr., and about 3 million Kr. went to the National Exchequer.

Football pools were introduced in 1949. They are strictly controlled by the State. No one is allowed to spend more than 12 Kr. a week on them, and winners are taxed 15 per cent on all winnings over 200 Kr. The gross income in 1949 was 25·7 million Kr. Of this the State took 15 per cent, 42½ per cent was paid to the winners, and after meeting the costs of administration and the fixed interest on the capital, most of which was provided by athletic associations, the remainder was kept in reserve. When an adequate reserve has been built up, any surplus income remaining after meeting administrative costs will be given to athletic associations and other social organizations.

Communism

There are not many Communists in Denmark. In the General Election of 1945 they got 255,256 votes and won 18 seats. In the 1947 election, out of a total of 2,064,141 votes only 141,094 were cast for Communists, and of the 148 seats in the Lower House they only secured 9.

Norway

Population in 1948, 3,198,000, of whom about 28 per cent live in towns and 72 per cent in rural districts. Oslo (after extension in 1948), population 428,000, Bergen 109,320, Trondhjem 57,128, Stavanger 50,320, and 15 other towns with populations between 10,000 and 27,000. Only about 3 per cent of the country is cultivated; forests cover nearly one-fourth, and the rest consists of highland pastures or uninhabitable mountains. 30 per cent of the population are engaged in agriculture and forestry.

(Prices are stated in Kroner. The rate of exchange in 1947 was 20 Kr. to the £. 1 Kr.=100 øre.)

No one investigating social conditions in Norway can fail to be impressed by the great amount of care and thought that is given to the provision of means which will enable and encourage people, especially young people, to make good use of their leisure time.

Education

Education is compulsory for children from 7 to 14 years. In elementary schools it is free. Naturally the quality of the school varies, but on the whole it is not dissimilar from that of the schools of Britain. Children of all classes, including members of the Royal Family, go to the State elementary schools. In 1945–6 there were 230,027 children in the rural and 57,363 in the urban schools.

In some of the schools in Oslo a man and a woman teacher have been appointed to give children who are leaving information as to the openings before them in industry and the professions, the qualifications called for in each of them, and the cost of education. The school doctors also advise the children about the kinds of employment suited to their physical fitness.

The Oslo municipality in 1946–7 granted 100,000 Kr. to provide bursaries to talented pupils, to enable those who could not otherwise have done so to qualify for skilled trades and professions.

As an illustration of the kind of things being done in the more go-ahead schools, I may describe what I learnt on a visit to Bjölsen school, on the outskirts of Oslo. This is an old school, with 900 children, both boys and girls. From mid-September to mid-April there are evening classes, attendance at which is entirely voluntary. The subjects taught include eurhythmics, ballet dancing, folk dancing and folk songs, singing and painting. For older children the programme also includes handiwork, sewing, knitting, embroidery and carpentry. On the average children attend two or three times a week. The demand to join the classes greatly exceeds the numbers for which teachers and accommodation can be found. In the year prior to my visit, not a single child who had joined the evening classes had stopped coming.

All children from 7 upwards have to do homework. They demand to do it for they say they do not feel they are real school children without it!

All the children are given a meal before they start classes, and most children bring food with them to eat at midday.

The size of classes varies from 22 in the lowest class to 24 in the highest.

Folk High Schools

There are 83 Folk High Schools in Norway, very similar to those in Denmark, both in their methods and their aims (see page 417). In 1948–9, 1,742 young men and 2,892 young women, mostly between 18 and 25 years old, attended these schools, almost all of them coming from rural areas. The winter session lasts for five months and the summer sessions for varying periods.

Anyone may open a Folk High School. Fifty-four of them were started by private enterprise, but 29 were started by local authorities. As in Denmark, the cost of building schools started by private enterprise has been met by public subscriptions, but when the number of pupils reaches a certain figure, the school automatically qualifies for a State subsidy. In 1948–9 these subsidies amounted to 3,500,000 Kr., and municipal authorities paid 700,000 Kr.

Fees are charged for attendance at the schools, but for about 60% of the pupils these are met by bursaries. In 1948–9 the State granted 450,000 Kr. towards the cost of these.

The schools fulfil a very useful function in qualifying the young people for leadership in youth associations and other activities.

Some Folk High Schools are run by religious sects and the Co-operative Movement, and some by the trade unions. The trade union schools study the history of the Labour Movement and the problems it has to face. The educational work done by the Party has a strong ethical tendency; the students are urged to work hard, to help in the reconstruction of the country, and to lead good lives.

There are no statistics of the number of Study Circles in Norway. Particulars were given me about Circles with a total membership of 28,500 but the number of members in Norway is much greater than this. In addition to these non-political Circles, the Labour Party in 1948 had 1,073 Study Circles with 13,220 members.

Independently of the Study Circles, a large number of lectures on cultural subjects are given, both in towns and rural districts. These are organized by the Ministry of Education and the work is done by 250 People's Academies. The State pays 25 per cent of the lecturers' fees and 40 per cent of their travelling expenses.

Religion

Except for a very small minority, the Norwegians belong to the Lutheran Church. As in Sweden, Denmark and Finland, church attendance is very low. On the other hand, there were in January 1949, 3,825 Sunday schools, with 219,464 children on their registers.

As having a bearing on the moral state of the country, reference may here be made to the growth of sexual promiscuity which has occurred in recent years.

Care of Youth

There are 250 committees of the urban and rural councils in Norway which are responsible for dealing with matters concerned with the care of youth.

The activities of the Committee of the Oslo Council will give a picture of the kind of work these Councils are doing, although naturally that Council can do much more than the smaller ones.

The Committee has published a book (illustrated, 176 pages)

which is given to every young person on leaving school, and to every youth coming to live in Oslo. It gives a history of the town, tells how it is administered, a survey of all the opportunities for youth to get the right kind of work, and the facilities available for the wise use of leisure—sports, libraries, lectures, athletics, and so forth. It is written in a colloquial style, with the obvious goal of making the readers more conscious of, and more interested in, not only their *rights*, but also their *duties* as citizens. It gives information about all kinds of youth clubs (except sports clubs), and also about the entertainments in the parks. It tells them of the newly-founded City Orchestra, where they will hear good music, and about the theatre.

The Council helps to arrange cultural evenings in the city's parks—there are concerts of good music, short lectures and drama. For the dramatic performances, there is a mobile unit with a small stage and dressing rooms. The attendances at the cultural evenings amount to about 900,000 during the summer.

The Council devotes about 2,000,000 Kr. a year to parks, bathing places and open-air sports activities. It is planning to build a central institute for all activities concerned with the care of youth. There is to be a club room, gymnasia and rooms for youth societies and study circles to meet in. There will be a branch of the municipal library, especially aiming at providing books for study circles, and the librarian will advise on books to read.

The Union of the National Youth Associations (Noregs Ungdomslag) is a body which has far-reaching influence throughout Norway. It was founded in 1896, and in 1949 consisted of about 2,000 local associations, with a total membership of about 60,000, of both sexes in about equal proportions, and mostly between 15 and 20 years of age.

Originally the movement was confined to the rural districts; as the number of members who went to work in the towns increased, they formed urban branches, so that now the movement is spread throughout the country. The subscriptions vary. In rural districts they are usually 1 or 2 Kr. a year, and in Oslo, where there are 5,000 members, the subscription is 4 Kr. The great majority of the members are active and, once formed, associations seldom die out. As a rule meetings are held every Sunday afternoon from mid-September to mid-May. During the summer, meetings are only held occasionally. Some meetings are for members only, others are open to the public. The programmes of activities at the meetings vary greatly. They include lectures, reading of prose and poetry, music—including community and solo singing—dramatic entertainments, folk dancing—which is a great feature—and ordinary dancing. In 1949 about 3,500 lectures were given and about 1,200 dramatic performances.

In most local associations a newspaper is written, and read at the meetings. There are two editors to prepare these papers and other members contribute some of the articles. The central association publishes a weekly newspaper which is sent to the chairmen of all the local associations.

A great feature of the movement is to revive and maintain old national customs, such as the song-dance, and the wearing on Sundays and festive occasions of the old national costumes. The Oslo association has a workshop where these are made.

Nearly 700 of the local associations have a youth house of their own, and a still larger number have built houses in collaboration with other organizations in their districts. The members not only collected the money for these houses, but also helped to build them. The urban associations have acquired about 20 hotels and about 50 popular restaurants, which are open not only to the members of the local associations but to the public generally. They serve as meeting places for members visiting the towns, and the profit derived from them makes a significant contribution to the funds of the associations.

A large proportion of the local associations have libraries and, in addition to the weekly meetings open to all members, there are groups studying political and social questions, singing clubs, and clubs for different kinds of sports, and for other forms of activity. The central association has, for long, agitated for the development of the country's forests and every spring many rural associations arrange a planting day.

Recently a Folk High School has been established to train leaders for the local associations.

The importance of combating the growth of materialism is strongly felt by those responsible for the movement. Indeed, I was informed that it has probably done as much as the churches to deepen the spiritual life of the nation. "Christianity and Patriotism" is a motto used in the movement.

In addition to the youth associations here described, there is a youth federation in the Labour Party, with about 700 local associations and about 45,000 members. The Oslo section has about 2,000 members. Amongst other things, outdoor activities are encouraged. Children join the movement at 8 years of age. Until they are 14 no politics enter into the movement, but after that there is Labour Party propaganda, along with social activities, both in the city and in the country. It is largely a training ground for people who will take an active part in the Labour Movement.

Sports

The cultivation of outside sports is strongly encouraged in Norway. All educational and social organizations emphasize the importance of outdoor recreation. Norwegians say "We are a nation of sportsmen." People are urged to indulge in sporting activities themselves, rather than to watch others doing so. There is no professional football. In 1948 the membership of sporting associations amounted to about 300,000 persons, of whom 90,000 were under 17 years of age.

A State Sports Office was set up in 1946. It is responsible for all the work which had previously been done by different ministries to encourage sports and other open-air activities, and it gives financial aid for fields, pavilions and so forth.

There is a National Sporting Association, which is a union of all local sporting associations. It employs people to organize local associations, and among other things to encourage them to build sports stadia. Every town of any size has a stadium. In Oslo there are five municipal ones and one private one. Privately owned stadia are financed by contributions from the local associations and by State subsidies, which are now drawn from the profit on the State-controlled football pools.

As there are only two towns in Norway with a population of over 100,000, it is much easier for young people to go hiking or camping in the country than it is for the dwellers in England. where two-thirds of the population dwell in conurbations of not less than a million. Even from Oslo, electric trains take one into lovely country in about a quarter of an hour. Moreover the winter climate in Norway is such that people can ski and skate for months on end. From early childhood people learn to ski and it is almost as rare to find an adult who cannot ski as to find one who cannot walk. 75% of the population live within 15 or 20 miles of the sea, so sailing is a very popular pastime, and a good many working people have their own boats.

Gymnasia

There are gymnasia in practically every town in Norway. In small towns the school gymnasia are open to all associations which include gymnastics in their programmes. For three generations no schools in Norwegian towns have been built without a gymnasium, and in every school from 2 to 4 hours of gymnastics per week is compulsory.

In almost all towns there is a local association for gymnastics financed by a small membership subscription, the sums subscribed being spent on equipment for the public gymnasia and for administrative expenses. The national union of the local associations receives a subsidy of about 1,000,000 Kr. from the State which is partly devoted to the training of gymnastic instructors, and partly to grants to individual gymnasia. Members of the local associations belong to all classes. They are of both sexes and of all ages, from 10 to 90. I visited a gymnasium in Oslo and was introduced to a man of 80. He was stripped to the waist and perspiring freely. He did a hand-spring for me! There were several old men there—one with a long grey beard was circling on a horizontal bar!

Holidays

Employers are compelled by law to give their employees three weeks' holiday with pay. In addition there are 12 public holidays for which wages are usually paid, either by agreement between trade unions and employers or by legal enactment.

There is a holiday association (Norsk Folkeferie) much like that in Denmark. It is financed by the trade unions and Co-operative Societies and has a State guarantee. It has two hotels, each with 45 beds, and is building one with 175 beds.

Cinemas

Of the 280 cinemas in Norway 114 are run by municipal authorities. The attendances in 1947 amounted to 25,393,840 adults and 3,152,678 children. The attendances at cinemas in England probably amount to about 1,270,000,000 per annum, and as the population of Great Britain is roughly 16 times that of Norway, the number of attendances at cinemas per 1,000 of the population in Norway is about one-third as high as it is in Great Britain. The number of attendances per capita per annum in Norway was 25·4 in towns and 2·9 in rural districts.

The profits of the municipally-owned cinemas are used for cultural purposes and amenities of one kind or another; in Oslo they are used for concerts, lectures and dramatic performances in the parks, and a large sum is given annually to a luxurious home for old people.

Theatres

In addition to the State Theatre in Oslo, three towns in Norway have permanent theatres. About 30 towns have assembly halls used for different purposes and suitable for theatrical performances. Amateur companies give plays in them occasionally, and during July and August, when the theatres in the large towns are closed, the professional companies give performances in the small towns, playing in the assembly halls.

In 1947–8 the State and local authorities' subsidies to all theatres, great and small, amounted to 775,000 Kr., and 873,000 Kr., respectively.

Public libraries

In 1946–7 the number of books issued by the public libraries and by libraries which provide books for the pupils in the State schools, was 4,740,369—equivalent to about 1·3 per head of the population. This compares with just over 5·0 per head in Great Britain and Northern Ireland in 1948, but the Norwegians are great readers of newspapers, and one sees more books in working-class houses than one does in England. Moreover, the fact that so many more people than in England indulge in out-of-door activities both in summer and winter will naturally reduce the time spent in reading.

In 1948–9 the Government grant for public and school libraries was 918,500 Kr. The local authorities' grant was 1,658,047 Kr.

There are 18 "central" libraries which circulate books in rural districts throughout the country. They send out boxes of books, which are changed from time to time. Anyone can order a book from the central library in the district in which he lives, and it is mailed to him free of charge. Boxes of books are also sent to fishing vessels.

A law which came into operation in July 1949 makes it incumbent on the 700 local authorities to establish a public library, but many of these will only have a comparatively small number of books, and there will still be need for books from the central libraries.

Domestic arts and crafts

The domestic arts and crafts of Norway reached a high degree of excellence in olden days, but the number of people engaging in them fell off when industrialism became predominant in the nineteenth century. This was regrettable, for not only did the money received for the articles sold make a useful addition to income, but their manufacture provided a highly desirable way of using leisure time.

In 1891 an association was formed with a three-fold purpose—to stimulate interest in domestic industries, to give help to those engaging in them to produce articles which were both artistic and well made, and to provide a market for their products. This association, whose patroness is the Crown Princess of Norway, has met with striking success. It has 17 shops and 3 wholesale stores. In 1946 the sales amounted to about £175,000, and it is believed that goods to about the same value are sold every year through other channels, and that the value of goods made by people for their own use may amount to two or three million pounds per annum.

The goods made include metal work, textiles, tapestry, rugs, carpets, embroidery, furniture, carving, dolls, knitted sports wear, national costumes, etc., etc. Most of the goods are made in the workers' leisure time, and by farm workers in winter, when they have little farm work to do.

Broadcasting

The number of wireless licences in Norway is rather more than 600,000, equal to about 189 per 1,000 of the population as compared with 236 in Great Britain.

Housing

In 1938 23 per cent of the houses had only one room and a small kitchen, 27 per cent had 2 rooms and a kitchen, and 50 per cent had 3 rooms or more. It is probable that these figures are approximately true to-day, but no official statistics are available. During the war the number of houses built was insignificant. Although the number of houses with only one or two rooms is much higher than in England, it is much lower than in Finland and Sweden, but not so low as in Denmark. As in Denmark, Sweden and Finland, the modern tendency is to build large blocks of flats rather than cottage houses.

In considering the housing conditions, it should be borne in mind that about three-quarters of the population live in country districts. Cramped living accommodation is less serious in the country than in the towns.

Gardens and allotments

There are very few allotments in Norway—probably not more than about 3,000. This does not mean that few people are interested in gardening, it is due to the fact that the great majority of the population live in rural districts or in quite small towns, and have gardens attached to their houses. A number of schools have acquired land and divided it up into small plots, in which the children grow flowers and vegetables, thus implanting an interest in gardening in their minds.

Drinking

The consumption per head of alcoholic drinks in Norway and England and Wales in 1947 was as follows:

	Norway Litres	*England & Wales* Litres
Spirits ..	3·27 ..	0·9
Wine ..	0·83 ..	9·0
Beer ..	17·2 ..	60·5

Expressed in terms of absolute alcohol, the annual consumption per head of the alcoholic liquors shown in the foregoing table is equivalent to 2·37 litres in Norway and 3·9 litres in England and Wales.

No comparison of the amount of drunkenness in the two countries can be made, for the Norwegian statistics only give the number of arrests for drunkenness, not the number of persons proceeded against. But in Norway many people drink spirits with the definite object of getting drunk, and drunkenness has become a somewhat serious evil. This is remarkable because the licensing laws in Norway are very strict. Production, import and wholesale trade in spirits and wines of all kinds are vested in the "wine monopoly." Licences to retail wine and spirits, or to serve them in restaurants, are granted by the local authorities. In the case of spirits, the retailers must charge the customers the price they pay for them, and the monopoly makes a fixed allowance for the trouble taken in retailing it. Thus the retailer has no inducement to push the sale. This regulation does not apply to wine.

Most of the rural municipalities are prohibitionist, but the residents can buy liquor for home consumption from a neighbouring town. In 1948 there were 12 "dry" towns and 533 "dry" rural districts.

Throughout the country, no spirits may be served in restaurants before 3 p.m. Wine can be bought between 11 a.m. and 5 p.m., and on Bank Holidays and Saturdays between 9.30 a.m. and 1 p.m. There are no restrictions on the sale of beer, but a licence to sell must be obtained from the local authority.

Gambling

This plays a much smaller part in the life of the people than it does in Britain. It is not regarded as a major evil. Football pools are State controlled. In 1948 the income of the pools was about 18,200,000 Kr. Half of this was paid to the winners, 3,000,000 Kr. were given to sporting organizations, and 2,000,000 Kr. to cultural objects. The rest was spent on meeting the costs of administration.

There is a State Lottery. In 1948 the total gross income was 40,050,000 Kr. Of this 25,632,000 Kr. were distributed to the winners and the rest went into the National Exchequer.

Communism

Communism is not very influential in Norway. In the 1945 General Election the Communists got 176,500 votes and won 11 seats in the Storting. In the 1949 election they got about 100,000 votes and lost all their seats in the Storting. Strikes and lock-outs are almost negligible. The number of working days lost is less than before the last war. I mention these facts because they go to show that there is little feeling of frustration among the Norwegian people. They are, on the whole, pretty well satisfied with the conditions under which they are living.

Sweden

In 1949 the population of Sweden was 6,924,888. The three largest towns, with their suburbs, are Stockholm (725,714), Gothenburg (343,983), and Malmö (185,947). 25 other towns had populations of more than 20,000. Altogether 60 per cent of the population live in towns of 20,000 or over. 28 per cent of the population are engaged in agriculture and forestry, about 300,000 being owners, and 60,000 tenants of the land they cultivate. More than half of the country is covered by forests.

(Prices are stated in Kroner. In 1947 the rate of exchange was about 14·5 Kr. to the £. 1 Kr. = 100 øre.)

Education

As in Norway, Denmark and Finland, practically all the schools are State schools, and are attended by rich and poor alike. "Elementary education became compulsory in 1842, but it was long before the ideal of a school for each community was actually realized. For many years the period of compulsory school attendance remained fixed at 6 years, plus 2 years continuation school, and in the course of time this evolved into 7 full school years, plus 1 year continuation school, providing 180 hours of instruction. In some areas (representing one-fifth of the population) a compulsory period of 8 years was introduced as from the school year 1947, and in some towns elementary schooling covers a period of 9 years. Children usually start at the age of 7, and therefore, unless they go on to a secondary school they leave school at 15 or 16. The eighth and ninth school years are chiefly devoted to vocational training."[1]

Gymnastics are obligatory in every school.

In Stockholm school children of 13–15 are given a four-page pamphlet about different ways in which they could spend their leisure, and on leaving school children are given a pamphlet about the opportunities open to them in different industries.

Adult education

There are about 70 Folk High Schools in Sweden, the first of which was founded in 1868. They are very similar to those in Denmark, but whereas the Danish Folk High Schools were the outcome of a religious national movement and are quite definitely Christian in character, the Swedish Folk Schools place their emphasis on civics and general culture. Some 30 years ago their objective was stated by Torsten Fogelqvist as being "to develop a historical mindedness among the pupils, a sense of relativity, respect for facts, self-criticism, a widened outlook on life and a formal training," and this, I am assured, accurately describes the objective of the High Schools to-day.

Another way in which the schools differ from those in Denmark is that whereas the overwhelming majority of the pupils in the Danish schools are engaged in agriculture, that is not so in Sweden, where a considerable proportion of the pupils are engaged in industry.

The schools are residential. The winter course lasts for 21 to 24 weeks—the summer course for 13 to 16 weeks, and is for

[1] *Education in Sweden*, published by The Swedish Institute, 1949.

young women only. Most of those attending these schools are 18 to 20 years of age or over. The fee for the winter course is about 825 Kr. The State gives bursaries to all pupils who cannot afford to pay this, varying according to their needs. In addition trade unions and other bodies grant bursaries to their members. About 6,000 students attend the schools each year, rather more than half of them being women. In 1947, 2,500 young persons who wished to attend the schools were turned down, owing to lack of accommodation.

In order to obtain a Government grant, the schools must include in their curricula Swedish language and literature, Swedish history and sociology, mathematics, geography, singing and gymnastics. Other subjects are chosen by the school itself. In July 1947 Government subsidies for adult education covered half the administrative costs. There is abundant evidence that the schools play an important part in the development of the cultural life of the nation.

Important though the Folk High Schools are, they are only one of many organizations which are concerned with adult education. Most of these devote their energies principally to forming study circles, providing libraries and giving lectures. Altogether 263,217 individuals were enrolled in 22,915 study circles in 1946–7. Another 45,342 students were enrolled in 3,325 discussion groups. In addition to the study circles and discussion groups, about 300,000 students register for correspondence school courses each year, and (in 1945) about 823,000 persons attended lectures.

It is not possible to compare accurately the proportion of the population engaging in adult education in Sweden and England for available statistics are drawn up on very different lines, but from such information as I have been able to obtain, with the kind help of the National Institute of Adult Education in England, I think there is little doubt that adult education plays a more (possibly a much more) important part in Sweden than it does in England. In making this statement I do not take account of the relative quality of the teaching given in the two countries. Even if in Sweden this is not so high as in England (and I have no definite evidence that this is so) it is nevertheless true that people attending study circles and classes are spending their leisure time wisely, and the provision made for doing this, and the extent to which it is done, were the objects of my investigations in Scandinavia.

A large number of young people belong to political organizations, 40 per cent of the members of which are under 20 years of age. They usually meet every two, three or four weeks, political discussions being interspersed with social activities such as singing and dancing.

There are not many social clubs for boys and girls which are open every day. They seldom have their own accommodation and none have canteens.

Religion

My opinion regarding the situation, based on discussions with a number of people, is that the present attitude to religion in Sweden is much the same as it is in England. Church attendances have declined markedly during the last 50 years, and the same is true of the proportion of the population who accept the Christian doctrine. Over 95 per cent of the population of the population belong to the Lutheran Church.

Dr. Alberg, who has been the director of the Brunnsvik Folk High School for over 20 years, during which time many thousands of young people have passed through his hands, said to me that very few of his students accept the Christian doctrine. "Most would say that Jesus was a model man, and that they would like to live like him, but belief goes no further." "The Church," he said, "has lost out more in Sweden than in England, but," he said, "the pupils discuss religious questions among themselves; indeed they take more interest in such questions than in any others. The longing for religion is growing among labour youth. Socialism was largely a religion at first. The position to-day is serious, people seeking and not finding. If a great economic crisis occurred, the situation might be the same as it was in Germany in 1933. The people there were longing and were seeking, *and they found Hitler*!" Dr. Alberg was, however, hopeful that people would come to realize that the evils from which the world is suffering to-day can only be overcome by spiritual means.

Everyone with whom I discussed the matter said that the

religious instruction in schools has little, if any, effect, and very few children get any religious teaching from their parents. On the other hand, I was told that the Protestant Sunday schools of the different denominations are now co-operating instead of competing with each other, and that there are about 400,000 Sunday school scholars.

An indication of the weakening of religious influence is the growth in recent years of sexual promiscuity. I was told that this has become so common that prostitution has almost died out.

Outdoor recreation

In the Stockholm area (population about 726,000) there are nearly 5,000 acres of parks, and there are 42 playgrounds, in each of which there are one or two people who look after the children and try to encourage their initiative and comradeship.

Concerts, dramatic entertainments and song recitals are given in the parks and in 19 of them games are organized in the evenings for school children. There are 21 open-air nurseries where mothers can leave their children while they do their shopping.

In Gothenberg there is an amusement centre, "Liseberg." This is a park of some 250 acres, much of it laid out in quite extraordinarily beautiful gardens. I need not describe it in detail for it is very similar to "Tivoli" in Copenhagen, Mr. Priestley's description of which is given on page 422. It is owned by the municipal authority and managed by a board of directors. It is open from the 1st May to mid-September, and is visited by about 2,000,000 people annually. The cost of admission is 50 øre for adults and 25 øre for children. It is run at a profit, which, after setting aside a reserve for improvements, goes to the local authority. If a town with a population of 344,000 can support so fine an amusement centre, it should certainly be possible to have many such centres in Britain.

In almost every small town the trade unions and the Social Democrats have an assembly hall and usually a library. Originally these were used only for trade union and political meetings, but more and more they are coming to be community centres. The trade unions also, in many towns, bought small plots of land on the outskirts of the town, which are used for dancing and theatrical and other performances. Touring companies, subsidized by the State, give plays. These pleasure grounds are fenced in, and a small charge is made for admission, e.g., 2 Kr. for the best seats for a theatrical performance.

Sports and Athletics

Under the authority of the City Council of Stockholm, there is a board responsible for promoting athletic and open-air life. It gives financial help to the athletic associations, and provides them with trained leaders. It manages 14 sports grounds, about 40 places for ball and other games, 3 gymnasia and 19 tennis courts. Some of the sports grounds have Finnish steam baths for the use of the players, but they are also open to the public generally. No charge is made for the use of the playing fields.

Under the Board's management there are 14 open-air swimming baths, in which swimming instruction and sports are arranged. At one of them special arrangements are made for children aged 4 to 14 to assemble at fixed meeting places in the city once a week, from which they are taken to the bath in buses. They have swimming lessons and each child is given a glass of milk and some bread. In 1946 41,900 children took advantage of these facilities. The Board also stimulates interest in gymnastics and athletics among women. On one day each week three of the athletic grounds are reserved for their use and women instructors are provided.

For winter sports the Board has provided about 80 skating places as well as a large number of ski-ing slopes, toboggan runs, and about 140 miles of permanent ski tracks.

In order to encourage young people who have not joined an athletic club to indulge in outdoor sports, the Board gets well-known athletes to come and address them. It also organizes competitions in the different athletic associations, and it has training courses for youth leaders and other instructors in the different sports. It arranges for excursions in the country and for summer camps. Stockholm is fortunate in that there is much lovely country in the vicinity of the city. "Not half-an-hour's journey from the city by bus, tram or train there are far-stretching forests where the moss spreads a soft carpet and where one can come upon both shy forest birds and elk if he has luck and makes as little noise as possible. Several such areas have been acquired by the city of Stockholm. Others belonging to the State have been declared nature reservations. All are intended to be preserved in their wild and unspoilt condition."[1]

Of course, not every town in Sweden provides such lavish facilities for athletics and outdoor activities as does Stockholm, but there are in the country no less than 10,000 athletic and gymnastic clubs.

Many associations collaborate with schools to organize athletic activities, and there is a central organization to encourage employers to develop sporting organizations in their factories. The membership of these organizations amounts to 400,000 male and female, young and old. The central organization has a depot for sporting equipment which is sold at wholesale prices, or if necessary, it is given.

Holidays

In 1938 the granting of 12 days' holiday with pay was made compulsory, and fortunately a very active organization called "Reso" had been founded in the previous year, with the object of providing facilities to enable people, especially those of slender means, to make the best use of their holidays.

The capital required was loaned by a number of organizations, such as the Trade Union Federation, the Co-operative Union, and the Workers' Educational Association. In addition to making arrangements for those wishing to travel in Sweden, and organizing conducted tours and study trips abroad, it has acquired hotels, which in the aggregate have 1,200 beds. The cost of board and room varies, but it averages about 70 Kr. a week.

In addition to these, Reso has (in four holiday resorts) erected a main building, with a restaurant, lounges and kitchen and instead of building bungalows has rented rooms in neighbouring cottages for the guests. Beds for 1,800 people are

[1] *Stockholm of To-day*, p. 110.

provided for in this way. Altogether Reso can provide a week's accommodation for 25,000 people during the summer.

The rents payable in the cottages include board as well as lodging. The directors of Reso think this plan is preferable to that adopted in Denmark, where those living in bungalows in the camps have to cook their own food, as they consider it essential that the women should have a holiday free from all household cares.

Reso has ambitious plans for extending its activities, and intends to have kindergartens in its new tourist centres, where mothers can leave their children and so be able to take part in the excursions and other activities organized for the benefit of the guests.

Children of families with incomes not exceeding 2,500 Kr. a year and taxable property not exceeding 20,000 Kr., can travel freely when going on holiday, and their mothers can also do so if accompanied by two children or more.

Since 1946 the obligatory vacation period with pay has been extended to three weeks for workers under 18 and those engaged in certain kinds of trying work. The working week is 44 hours and the average amount of overtime weekly is 2·7 hours.

Cinemas

On January 1st 1949 there were 2,500 cinemas in Sweden, of which 567 are open on every week-day. The others are only open on two or three days a week. The number of people going to cinemas is about 50,000,000 per annum.

Theatres

There are seven permanent theatres in Sweden—two each in Stockholm and Gothenburg, and one each in three smaller towns. They receive a State subsidy of 4,285,000 Kr. The State also contributes 500,000 Kr., to touring companies which put on plays in small towns and in rural districts, and 87,000 Kr. to two organizations which put on plays in small theatres.

Libraries

In 1949 there were 1,524 municipal libraries and about

10,500,000 books were borrowed. The State contributed nearly 1,500,000 Kr. toward their upkeep. Various educational associations own and operate public libraries. In 1945 there were very nearly 5,000 of them, and about 2,600,000 books were borrowed. The number of books borrowed per head of the population per annum is therefore about 1⅜, as compared with just over 5 in Great Britain, including Northern Ireland, where 280,000,000 books were borrowed by 50,000,000 people in 1948.

Housing

A factor which cannot fail to have an influence on the social life in Swedish towns is the large proportion of the people who live in flats, many of them in blocks of flats with five storeys. In Stockholm 90 per cent do so, and over 50 per cent of the population have not more than one room and a kitchen or two rooms with no kitchen.

In 1935–6 39 per cent of the population of Sweden as a whole lived in houses having only one room and a kitchen, and 28 per cent in houses with two rooms and a kitchen.[1] In that year an official enquiry revealed the fact that 500,000 urban and 1,000,000 rural dwellers, equal to a quarter of the population of the country, were living in sub-standard houses. Energetic steps have been taken since then to raise the standard of housing, but progress has been rendered difficult, first owing to the war, and subsequently by the shortage of building materials and labour. At the end of 1945 an investigation showed that about a quarter of the population were still living in overcrowded conditions, (i.e., more than two people per room).[2]

Although the number of rooms per house is small, many of them are kept very clean, and are artistically furnished, not a little of the furniture being made by the tenants.

There are arts clubs in many factories in Sweden. The members subscribe a small sum weekly and good pictures are bought, and when there is enough in hand to buy one, mem-

[1] *BO Bättre* ("Better Housing"), a handbook of the Better Homes Exhibition in Gothenburg.

[2] *Social Welfare in Sweden*, published by the Swedish Institute.

bers draw lots for it. Thus really valuable pictures may occasionally be seen in working-class homes.

Drinking

Sales of hard liquors and wines are controlled in Sweden by a Government monopoly. In order to buy them, individuals must have personal permits or ration books, in which all purchases are recorded. No one under 25 years old can get one. Quantities are rationed according to sex, age, income and social obligations. Heads of middle-class families, for instance, can get as much as four quarts of hard liquor a month, a single man one quart a month, and a single woman one quart every four months. Habitual drunkenness, failure to pay taxes, bootlegging and various forms of criminality, including driving while under the influence of drink, usually lead to revocation of the right to buy. Wines are sold to permit-holders without quantity limits, except in cases of obvious over-indulgence. Beer is served without restrictions, except in communities with local option. There are no public houses or bars in Sweden. In restaurants and hotels spirits and wines are sold only with meals and in restricted amounts. Men can get 15 centilitres (about one-tenth of a gill) of spirits, and women 10. All profits from spirits, beyond a certain fixed and modest maximum, go to the State, and so there is no financial motive to make extra sales. Usually the national liquor consumption varies in accordance with the country's economic condition, but on the average both sales and prosecutions for drunkenness have declined considerably since the new system went into effect at the beginning of the First World War. Prohibition has never been tried, except temporarily, as for instance during the general labour strike of 1909. In 1922 it was rejected by a small margin in a public referendum.

The consumption of alcoholic liquors per head of the population was equivalent to an intake of 5·4 litres of absolute alcohol in 1901–10 and of 3·8 litres in 1947. The arrests for drunkenness were 9·29 per 1,000 in 1913–15, and 4·43 in 1947. In England the persons prosecuted for drunkenness in 1947 were 0·56 per 1,000, and in 1948 0·73. This does not, however, necessarily mean that drunkenness is more prevalent in Sweden than in England, for the circumstances leading to arrest are entirely different in the two countries. In Sweden a man who has the smallest accident when driving a car, such as scraping his mudguard, or that of another car, although he is perfectly sober, is liable to be taken to the nearest police station for a blood test, and if more than a very small amount of alcohol is found in his blood he is fined, and counts among the "arrests for drunkenness."

Gambling

This is not regarded as a serious social evil. Football pools were started in 1934. They are all run by one company, which is strictly controlled by the State. The interest on capital is limited to 5 per cent. The profit earned in excess of this goes to the State. In 1945 the turnover was 45,600,000 Kr. The State took 16,000,000 Kr., plus 4,000,000 Kr. tax on all winnings over 25 Kr. Out of the money gained from football pools, the State makes grants for swimming baths, sports grounds and running tracks. Even the smallest towns have running tracks, where men practise speed and long-distance running. The track must have a certain consistency and be well kept.

There is a State Lottery which has monthly draws with prizes up to 100,000 Kr., and which brings in about 120,000,000 Kr. a year. Of this the State takes 40 per cent, plus 11 per cent tax on winnings. The rest is given to cultural objects such as philharmonic societies, the Royal Opera House, art galleries, and so forth.

In addition to the State Lottery there are Government Prize Bonds Loans. Money has been raised by the State in this way for a great number of years. The loans are made for a period of 10 years. No annual interest is paid on them, but at the end of the period they are repaid with a half per cent added for each year. A draw takes place every six months and a great many prizes varying from quite small amounts up to 250,000 Kr. are won by bondholders drawing lucky numbers.

Communism

This has never been a powerful force in Sweden. In the

1944 General Election Communists received 318,000 votes out of a total of 3,086,000 and obtained 15 seats out of 230 in the Second Chamber of the Riksdag. In 1948 they received 245,000 votes out of 3,879,000 and obtained 8 seats.

Finland

In 1949 the population of Finland was 4,175,000. In 1948 Helsinki had a population of 394,000, and two other towns just over 100,000. All the others were appreciably smaller. About one-third of the people live under urban conditions. At the end of 1940, 51·5 per cent of the population derived their living from agriculture, only 21 per cent from industry, 10 per cent from commerce and transport, and 17·5 per cent from other occupations and public services.

(All figures about finance are given in pounds sterling, calculated at the rate of exchange at the date this enquiry was made, viz., 547 Marks to the £.)

Education

Education is compulsory for children aged 7–15. Rich and poor go to the same schools. Education is free in the primary schools and inexpensive in the secondary ones; poor children can attend them without payment. Free meals are provided in the primary and in some secondary schools. Except for a few schools in the north where the population is very scattered, few children go to boarding schools.

Headmasters and mistresses of primary and secondary schools are elected by the teachers, a system which often results in the appointment of second-rate persons.

In 1945 there were 71 People's Colleges in Finland, with 4,299 students. They are similar to the Folk High Schools in Norway, Sweden and Denmark. Although no exact figures are available it is probable that the total number of students in the 60 workers' evening schools is about 40,000. The one in Helsinki has over 5,000 students aged from 16 years upwards. Two-thirds of them are women, most of whom are employed in industry, but there are also shop assistants and domestic workers. The headmaster assured me that the students come because they believe that knowledge is power, but he said that, as many of them have no other means of cultural or spiritual development, membership of the school is their main source of inspiration. The school is a municipal one and gets a large State grant. The teachers are not whole-time; they are professors and other qualified people. The building is used as a primary school during the daytime. The school is almost free—25 F. Mks., equal to about 11d. a year!

There is in Helsinki a "University of Social Sciences," attended by 600 or 700 students of both sexes. In addition to activities which are very similar to those of the School of Economics in London, there is a section of the University devoted to the training of group leaders, such as scout masters and club leaders.

Religious teaching is given in all primary and secondary schools, and school usually opens with prayers. The class teachers give this teaching in the primary schools; in grammar schools it is often given by the clergy. I was told that much, if indeed not most, of the teaching is formal and ineffective.

Teaching of domestic science

Very thorough arrangements have been made by the State to increase the knowledge of domestic science. There are 68 rural domestic science schools, and 580 instructors, under the direction of 99 experts who travel about the country, going into the houses to advise housewives, arranging model cottages, and so on.

343,000 women belong to local associations created to spread the knowledge of domestic science. This is equal to over 15 per cent of Finland's female population.

In 1948 the State granted a subsidy of about £131,000 towards the cost of this work, and the members of the local associations pay fees amounting to about £15,600.

Social settlements

There are 17 social settlements in Finland, run very much on the same lines as the Kalliola Settlement in Helsinki, which inspired them. The activities of that settlement are two-fold—a social club and an evening school. The only difference between this school and the workers' evening school is that the settlement, including the school, is conducted on definitely Christian lines. There are about 1,000 pupils in the school, mostly belonging to the working class, and aged 16 and upwards.

In addition to the school there are, in the building, boys' and girls' clubs, with a membership of about 1,000. They engage in all kinds of activities—music, discussions, games, handicraft classes, choral singing, readings about national heroes, and so on. The evenings end with a short religious address or prayer.

The club is divided into 80 groups, each under a leader. They meet once a week. Members may join more than one group. The leaders of the different groups are university students, aged about 20, of both sexes. Twelve of them live in the settlement and take part in the teaching. The settlement gets State and municipal grants for classes and for temperance work.

Religion

Almost all Finns are Lutherans, but although they are baptized and married in church, and will be buried by the church, they very seldom attend church.

A recent census of church attendance showed that only 4 per cent of the people in Helsinki went to church. I was told by a man who had been at a holiday resort that only 20 out of a population of 2,500 attended on the Sunday when he was there. However, when pastors go to the houses of their parishioners they get a good hearing and they get good attendances at open-air meetings.

Four Sundays in the year are nominated by the Government as "prayer days," and cinemas close at six o'clock on the preceding Saturdays. In Helsinki youths have, for sometime past, held religious meetings in some of the cinemas on the Saturday evenings, conducting them themselves, and youths from Helsinki have organized similar meetings in country districts.

Formerly the Labour Party was opposed to religion, but their attitude is now changing. Indeed, there is a Christian Association in the Social Democratic Party.

Sexual promiscuity, the extent of which is an indication of the moral state of a country, is about as common as it is in England.

Finnish Youth Association

This movement was started in 1881 and its aim is to encourage young people of 16 years and over to make good use of their leisure time. A Central Committee in Helsinki supervises 22 regional committees throughout the country, each of which has a full-time organizer.

There are 1,500 local societies with 103,000 members, and 896 study circles. If a village wants a local society, one of the whole-time organizers will help it to start one. Sometimes, too, the regional committees take the initiative. The activities of the local societies vary; a society may have a library, folk dancing and choral singing, a drama group (interest in drama has always been a main form of activity), an athletic association for those indulging in wrestling, cross-country running, ski-ing and long-distance running. The widespread interest in sport in Finland is demonstrated by the fact, stated in the Finnish Year Book, that in an international walking match held against Sweden in 1941, no fewer than 1,507,111 Finnish entrants completed the march; the oldest one was 94!

The youth movement has a marked influence on rural culture. It seeks to encourage people to live good lives, but there is no definite Christian teaching. The Church used to criticize the movement because of this, but now it takes a broader view. The movement is non-political. The Workers' Educational Association comprises societies with aims very similar to those of the national movement. These are chiefly in industrial districts, and have altogether 17,387 members and 1,073 study circles. In the study circles the workers' point of view on political matters naturally influences the character of the discussions.

There are other youth movements in addition to those described above, but the National and Workers' movements are the principal ones engaged in cultural and educational work.

In 1946 the "Finnish Council of Voluntary Youth Associations" was formed. It embraced practically all voluntary youth associations in Finland, religious, athletic, political, recreational, cultural, educational, in all 49, with a total membership of about 1,000,000[1] aged between 7 and 30, of both sexes.

The main objects of the Council are to keep in touch with the work being done by all the youth organizations, and to place at their disposal information gathered, both in Finland and abroad, which will enable them to function more effectively, and also to give them financial aid where necessary. The governing body of the Council is a central committee of 16 members, elected by a general assembly of the Council, a body to which each affiliated organization sends representatives.

In 1947 it organized a Youth Cultural Week in Helsinki, when there were cinema performances of films showing the activities of youth organizations, competitions between different youth organizations in prose, drama, orchestras, choirs, folk dancing, duplicated and hand-written journals. There were also competitions between individuals in poetry writing, musical competitions, violin and piano playing, singing, drawing, painting, sculpture, photography and public speaking, and an exhibition of work done by the different organizations. The Council is seeking to get the Broadcasting Corporation to include in its programme more items appealing especially to youth, and it has begun to make a detailed investigation into the social and economic conditions of youth, the educational facilities offered to youth, the need for further education, and the character and extent of the leisure-time recreations and amusements at present available to young people.

The finance required to run the various activities of the Finnish Council of Voluntary Youth Associations comes from various sources. The Athletic Associations draw their main income from the profits of the football pools, which are controlled by the State. Some of the organizations get grants from the State and from local authorities, but the greater part of the money needed to run the different organizations has to be raised by the members.

[1] The number of individuals is less than this, for a person may belong to two or more organizations, each of which includes him in its membership. The Finnish Youth Association and the Workers' Educational Association just described are now included in the Finnish Council of Voluntary Youth Associations.

Finnish Culture Foundation

The Finnish Culture Foundation was founded in 1937, when, as the result of a very vigorous effort in all parts of the country, contributions were received from about 200,000 people, representing all classes of society. The sum thus collected has since been added to by donations, so that the funds now amount to about £365,000. The Foundation supports the arts, and helps research workers by granting yearly scholarships from the interest on its funds, and from yearly donations made by various firms. In 1947 scholarships were given to the value of about £22,000.

Since university students and young people studying at other institutions had lost their ideals during the war, the Foundation started a series of weekly meetings, with talks by well-known persons representing various aspects of cultural life. One result of these meetings is demonstrated by the steadily-growing interest in the yearly art competitions among students. The Foundation also sends well-known representatives of Finnish cultural life to speak at meetings in rural districts. With a view to meeting the growing demand for instructional books, the Foundation is publishing a series of books under the general title of "The Culture of our Day." The intention is to publish between 150 and 200 books of about 150 pages. These will be popular accounts of the latest achievements of modern research. In addition to the above activities, the Foundation arranges for persons engaged in research and in various fields of cultural life, to contribute short articles to newspapers in all parts of the country. They appear to be widely read, and make a useful contribution to popular education.

Sport

There are two large voluntary associations for encouraging sporting activities—the Workers' Athletic Association, with about 150,000 members, and the Finland Athletic and Gymnastic Association, with about 300,000 members. The latter is a bourgeois association. Both associations have separate branches for school children (7–15) and for young people of both sexes. They both have full-time paid organizers and both get large grants from the State. The two associations have different branches for different sports. Every parish in Finland has a number of athletic societies, but it must be remembered that parishes are large, some extending to 40 Km. from the centre. Both the associations publish weekly newspapers and some newspapers run for profit devote all their space to sport. The news given is about sport, not about betting.

If anyone wants to gain an impression of the importance which the Finns attach to sports, he should visit the training centre at Vierumaki. It is an immense building with sleeping accommodation for 142 pupils, of both sexes, and adjacent houses for the teachers. It has two lecture rooms, a library and reading rooms, a gymnasium, and rooms for different kinds of athletic activities. There are shower baths, a swimming bath and, of course, a number of Finnish steam baths. It was built in 1929, and stands on a beautiful estate of about 220 acres presented by the State, which also contributed to the cost of building the institute, by allowing this to be done by prisoners. There are playing fields on the estate, and a lake to swim in. It is owned by a trust, the capital having been found by various sports associations and private individuals interested in the promotion of sport.

Its main object is to train teachers of athletics and gymnastics. There are two courses yearly; the one for men lasts for 5½ months and that for women 4 months. In addition to the training courses for teachers there are brief courses, lasting for a week or so, for young men and women athletes. In 1946 there were 3,766 pupils. Half the cost of running the institute is borne by the State.

There are a number of centres for athletic and gymnastic training in different parts of Finland, but that at Vierumaki is far and away the most important.

The welfare work undertaken in Finnish factories

The social work of Finnish industry during 1946 was examined by the Economic Research Institute. The enquiry covered 526 firms which together employ more than half of the 220,000 workers in all the Finnish industries. It showed that a great deal of work has been done in connection with the housing of the workers. 22 per cent of the workers and 42 per cent of the officials and other executives in the 526 factories live in houses or flats owned by the firms. In addition to this, the firms make loans on generous terms to workers wishing to build their own houses, and in rural districts they sell land at a nominal figure.

I went into some of the workers' houses at the United Paper Mills, Myllykoski. The rooms were much larger than in the usual workers' houses in England. Every house has a good garden, and in every house there was a library of books. The houses were clean and tidy, and furnished with taste.

Half of the 526 factories referred to above have Finnish steam baths for their employees, and a great number have wash houses and bakeries for the free use of the workers. More than half of them have given up land for allotments, which are let to more than 20 per cent of the employees.

Some of the industries in the country have farms of their own, the products of which are sold exclusively to their employees. The welfare conditions in the Myllykoski factory were extraordinarily good. The dining-room had a polished wooden floor, tables for four with white tablecloths made of paper, which looked like linen, and a vase of flowers on every table. Every worker had a steel lock-up for his clothes, and shower baths were provided in a room fitted up in a way that one might expect to find in a first-rate hotel.

Ample provision is made by many factories for encouraging sports and gymnastics, and a number of firms have paid instructors.

Forty-six firms provide large houses where workers can go for the holidays. No charge is made for the accommodation. Workers can provide their own food if they wish, or they can buy it at a canteen.

Twenty per cent of the factories have between them 300 social clubs of one kind or another. Factories also have libraries and 50 of them have factory magazines. Fifteen firms provide technical schools.

Altogether these 526 factories spent in 1946, voluntarily, over £3,000,000 on welfare work. This represents about 7 per cent of the wages paid in the industry, about 1½ per cent of the total sales made by the industry, and about 3½ per cent of its total capital. The amount is a little more than half the total profits of the industry.

Before calculating profits, a sum roughly equivalent to the amount spent voluntarily, had already been spent on social services required by law.

To a certain extent the high expenditure on welfare work is due to the fact that a number of factories are concerned with industries in which wood is the raw material. Consequently they are in remote forest regions, and have to provide not only houses, but hospitals and other amenities for their workers.

Holidays

The following annual holidays with pay are compulsory for all workers:

3 weeks after 5 years' service,
2 weeks after 1 year's service,
1 week after 6 months' service.

There is also a compulsory holiday (paid for) on Independence Day (December 6th), and ten public holidays not paid for.

The usual length of the working week is 47 hours.

There is an association ("Holiday Union") to facilitate and encourage the wise use of holidays. Its activities are very similar to those of associations with similar objects in Norway, Sweden and Denmark. The finances have been provided by trade unions, the Employers' Federation, Co-operative Societies, and State grants. It has nine holiday centres; some are hotels, where workers and their families can live very cheaply, and others are holiday camps similar to the one at Gilleleje in Denmark, described on page 422. In 1948 these provided accommodation for 28,000 persons—less than half the number who applied to go to them.

"Housewives need holidays, too," is a point of view to which the Union attaches great importance. Steps have been taken to persuade housewives to take a holiday, and deputies are provided to look after their homes and children while they are away. The Union has made it possible for a number of housewives with large families to spend holidays in their holiday centres free of charge; 2,700 did so in 1948. Some holiday camps cater especially for women.

In the holiday centres, in addition to entertainments of various kinds, there are lectures, community singing, discussions on housekeeping and the education of children, religious services, etc. Attendance at these functions is of course entirely optional; usually some form of light entertainment is provided simultaneously with the lectures and religious services.

The association also organizes tours for groups of working people, not only in Finland, but in foreign countries.

In addition to the above activities, quite a number of firms (20 of them in Helsinki) provide simple homes or hotels to which their workers and their families may go, free of charge but paying for their own food. Provision is made for young people in tents. In addition many business firms have homes in the country near their factories, accommodating up to 50 children of employees usually staying for a month, either free or at very low cost.

Cinemas

In 1948 there were 470 cinemas in Finland, the attendances at which numbered about 27,000,000. Forty per cent of them are open every night, the remainder are in rural districts, and are only opened on certain days of the week. All are privately owned, but a State Board of Censors scrutinizes every film.

In Great Britain attendances at cinemas number about 1,270,000,000 yearly, and as the population of Great Britain is roughly 12 times that of Finland, it will be seen that the attendances at cinemas in relation to population is about four times as high in Great Britain as in Finland.

Theatres

There are 25 towns in Finland with a population of over 5,000. In 23 of them, and in two rural areas, there is a theatre open for at least ten months in the year. Very few theatres in Finland are working for profit, and these are small and more like music halls than theatres. From the financial point of view, practically all Finnish theatres are conducted on the same basis as the non-profit-distributing repertory theatres in England. They are heavily subsidized, largely from the proceeds of the State lottery. In 1948 the subsidies amounted to £78,610. The estimate of the subsidy for 1949 is considerably higher.

In addition to the theatres named above, a large number of companies consisting of amateurs, who may or may not have a professional or ex-professional paid leader, put on two or three plays a year. The Finnish Association of Theatres sends instructors to help amateurs.

A governing committee was appointed about 25 years ago by the Minister of Education to encourage and assist all branches of art, music, drama and literature.

Public libraries

There are public libraries in all Finnish towns. In rural districts there are central libraries with many branches. 4,718,826 books were lent in 1947. This amounts to a little over one book per inhabitant, as compared with five in Great Britain and Northern Ireland. It must, however, be remembered that a large proportion of working-class people have a number of books of their own. Most of the public libraries are run by the local authorities, with a small subsidy from the State. The number of readers is increasing, and now probably includes about 80 per cent of working-class people. Women read more books than men.

Home industries

Ever since the middle of the eighteenth century home industries have been encouraged by the State. In the first half of the nineteenth century a powerful and influential society did much to develop them. Local organizations were formed, and schools established. At present the National Council of Home Industry Organizations has established a number of instruction centres spread all over the country. It publishes two periodicals, provides brochures, models, and blue prints for home industries, as well as a wide programme of lectures and demonstrations. It encourages people to engage in home industries through competitions and a system of badges of merit. It has a central sales organization, and many localities have sales organizations of their own.

There are three schools for training teachers, and 24 schools for men and 25 for women workers. These have been founded by individuals or local societies. The State pays the teachers' salaries and 60 per cent of the other costs.

Home industries constitute an important source of additional income to small holders, and an effort is being made to draw them all into the home industries field.

Housing

Housing conditions in Finland are not good, though active steps are being taken to improve them. As late as 1937–8 about two-thirds of the houses had only one room and a small kitchen, and only 18 per cent had more than two rooms and a kitchen. I am informed that probably this is still true.

The two wars, in which many houses were destroyed, and the fact that many houses were in the territory annexed by Russia, from which some half a million people fled to Finland, very seriously worsened the situation. Lack of raw materials and of capital, and the fact that so much of the country's wealth has to be paid to Russia in the form of reparations, handicap housing progress, but steady, if slow, advance is being made. Many of the new dwellings compare favourably with those which are being erected in Norway, Sweden and Denmark. In the larger towns they usually take the form of large blocks of flats of four or five storeys.

On page 457 a description is given of houses built right out in the country for the employees of the United Paper Mills. These are of a very high standard, but the Company is a wealthy one with high ideals regarding the welfare of the workers, and timber with which to build the houses is plentiful for the forests are close at hand and land is cheap.

Allotment gardens

The number of allotment gardens in Finland, although not large, has grown rapidly in recent years. There were 1,801 in 1935, 2,275 in 1945, and by 1949 the number had grown to 3,569. These figures are not large, but it must be borne in mind that two-thirds of the people live under rural conditions, and many of them dwell in houses which have gardens attached to them.

As in Norway, Sweden and Denmark, the allotment societies receive subsidies from the local authorities.

Many of the allotment holders have built bungalows on their allotments, in which they spend week-ends in summer. They are attractive in appearance, and bear no resemblance to the untidy shacks which often disfigure allotments in England.

Drinking

The consumption of alcoholic liquors was entirely prohibited from 1919 to 1932 when, in consequence of growing opposition, a plebiscite was taken and the people voted by a large majority for the repeal of the Prohibition Law.

Under the new Alcoholic Beverages Act of 1932, now in force, the manufacture, importation and sale of substances containing more than 2¼ per cent by weight of alcohol is (with certain exceptions) a State monopoly, and sales may only be made through agencies appointed by the State. Most of the profits on sales are divided between the local authorities at the rate of 100 Finnmarks per inhabitant per year, and the Old Age and Disability Insurance Fund; the remaining profits are used for work to promote temperance, and for other social welfare objects.

Finns drink seldom. Not more than 4 per cent of adults drink alcohol regularly, 10 per cent drink it once a week, 17 per cent drink it only occasionally, 20 per cent are teetotal, and 49 per cent drink only on festive occasions. But many people, though they do not drink frequently, drink with the specific object of getting drunk. Frequently persons who can afford it will drink half to three-quarters of a litre (equal to about one to one and a half pints) of brandy at a sitting. The amount of liquor which people are allowed to buy is not rationed but if people drink to excess (which presumably means that they get very drunk very often) their cards entitling them to buy liquor are withdrawn.

In 1948 the sale of hard liquors of various kinds amounted to 17,367,667 litres, that of wines to 2,322,169 litres, and the sale of beer to 3,072,394 litres. This was the equivalent of absolute alcohol amounting to 6,879,349 litres, equal to 1·75 litres per inhabitant, as compared with 3·9 litres in the United Kingdom. Notwithstanding the fact that the consumption per head of pure alcohol in Finland is lower than in Britain, no less than 142,159 people, equal to one in every 29 of the population, were arrested for drunkenness in 1947. Of these, 63,314 were prosecuted. In 1947 the number of persons prosecuted for drunkenness in England and Wales, with a population 12 times that of Finland, was 24,278. The explanation of these extraordinary figures is no doubt that whereas the Finns drink six times as much spirits *per capita* as they do of beer, the British drink 68 times as much beer as they do spirits.

Gambling

This is not a serious evil in Finland. There is very little horse racing, and no bookmakers. On the other hand, a good many people go in for football pools. These are run by a company authorized by the State. The capital has been subscribed by athletic associations in the form of preference shares. All profits go to the State. The amount of money spent in the pools is rising rapidly. In 1948 it amounted to about £1,242,000. Of this sum about £307,000 was paid to the winners, about £354,600 went to the State, and the rest was spent on administration. The money going to the State is used for the furtherance and encouragement of athletics and sports.

There is a State Lottery. The total gross income in 1948 was about £471,700. Of this about £282,650 was distributed to the winners, about £164,350 was given to cultural objects, such as the National Theatre and Opera, and to science and research, and administration expenses amounted to about £24,500.

Communism

The Communist movement in Finland is weaker than it was. There is a close relation between workers and employers. Most of the factories in Finland are small and the managing directors usually know every worker personally.

Communism was illegal before the war. It was declared legal in 1944, when a lot of workers joined the party, but the

Finn is not a natural Communist, and soon after 1944 a number of those who had joined the party dropped out. The circulation of a Communist paper dropped from 70,000 to 20,000 in two years. The proportion of Communists in the Diet is only about 16 per cent, or 19 per cent if the members of the People's Democratic League are included.

At a conference of Finnish trade unions in 1947, attended by 169 Social Democrats and 126 members of the People's Democratic League, a proposition of the trade unions condemning unofficial strikes and unauthorized demonstrations and "market street meetings," was unanimously agreed to by all the members except the F.P.D.L., all of whom voted against it.

APPENDIX I

GOING TO THE DOGS[1]

It was the Dragoman who made me go. "Don't forget your Dragoman," exhorted the advertisement: "The best guide to greyhound racing." The appeal of going to the dogs under Arabic auspices was irresistible. The greyhound fraternity tends to classicism. "Midas" gives tips for a shilling; "Palatinus" is a track correspondent. Nearly all national dailies, including the *Daily Worker*, carry forecasts and at least one morning paper is devoted exclusively to dog racing—the other day it informed its readers that the Exhibition of Royal Pictures is of interest because greyhounds appear in several of the paintings.

The wind cut down the damp street. I had anticipated that the Dragoman and I might be the only sportsmen out on such a night. I soon found I was wrong. Men and women of all sizes and ages were pouring from the railway station and tumbling out of buses to make up a tense, silent, expectant throng. With grim expressions and set shoulders, we marched forward; it was like a scene from a film of the October Revolution.

The track running round the oval stadium is lit with arc lamps. At one end, large illuminated clocks with shillings marked on their dials in the place of minutes reveal the state of the betting on the next race. In the expensive part there is a glass restaurant where you can eat in warmth and watch at the same time. It is all very impressive which, I tell myself, is not surprising when you consider the financial rewards for the organizers of this popular recreation. For instance, the Greyhound Racing Association, Ltd., paid a dividend of 4,250 per cent on its shilling shares in 1944 (double the dividend for 1939).

In the distance a group of tic-tac men are signalling the odds; the lights catch their hands waving and falling. One of them conducts the first eight bars of the Third Brandenburg Concerto while another goes quite a way with the Overture to *The Magic Flute*. Before each

[1] An article by Charles Dimont, published in the *New Statesman and Nation* of the 30th November 1946, and reproduced by permission.

race six white-clad Acolytes in bowler hats lead round the contestants. Occasionally the procession halts while an animal discharges a natural function. Behind walks a seventh Acolyte with a dustpan and brush. To be coprophe r at a dog track! It needs the pen of a Ferdinand Céline or Albert Camus to do the job justice.

A long line of raucous bookmakers shout the odds. In contrast the crowd is silent, jostling and shuffling, staring at the bookies' boards, gazing at the betting clocks, from time to time muttering. White-faced and indistinct, the onlookers tiered in the stygian gloom of the stands behind appear as wraiths. People only come to life for the few seconds the dogs are actually running. Then, as the greyhounds leap from their starting traps, a roar begins on the far side, gathers and is upon us like a hailstorm on a tin roof; it passes, dies and there is silence again.

The programme is scheduled to last nearly two and a half hours; the total time taken by the eight races themselves will be approximately four minutes. So some 146 minutes can be devoted to glum meditation on the betting forecast apparatuses and placing wagers. In a tomb-like vault under the stands, many of the speculators queue morosely before the totalisators, mutter through holes in the wall, grab their tickets, hastily hide them in their pockets or handbags, and slink away. It is important not to let anyone else know what you've backed. It might reduce the odds. Behind me are two well-dressed middle-aged women. From their voices I should have sworn they were mistresses at a Girls' Public School, and their favourite relaxation Miss Dorothy Sayers. They are talking about whether their combinations are going to come off and I am slightly embarrassed until I realize they mean their forecasts for the first and second in the fourth race. They come every week—"It makes a break"—and they instruct me in all the ingenious variations of betting: "two dogs," "three dogs," "backing a trap," "one against the field." These, if successful, pay a far better dividend than going for a simple win or a place. With all the mathematical calculation involved I begin to understand why everyone looks so gloomy: it must be a frightful mental strain.

Nobody ever refers to a dog by name, merely by the number of the trap it starts from. As the greyhounds streak by, the crowd shouts: "Go on, Four," "Catch him, One," "Where are you, Three?" (This is very different from horse-racing, where favourite jockeys and their mounts are given affectionate nicknames.) Leaning on the rails and watching a parade go by, I remark to the girl next to me, "That Captain Charlie looks a nice dog." "What number?" she asks. She and her boy friend don't think much of that number, they've "done" another one (but they don't tell me which it is). Their combined ages aren't more than 45. She works as a waitress, he sells gents' hosiery. Thursdays and Saturdays they go to the dogs; Mondays and Fridays to the cinema; Wednesday is football pool evening; Sundays they dance. Every night they "must have something to do." Greyhounds are their favourite evening because it gives them a thrill and a chance to make money. Sid, the boy, has a system but he's reticent about whether it has made them much so far. They both live at their homes with their parents; between them they earn over £8 a week, but one of the great attractions of betting is that any wins are tax-free. They plan to get married and have a car. The girl leans and rubs the back of her head against her boy's chest; he bends affectionately. Suddenly a bell rings and the dogs come out; they stiffen into impersonality again.

Perce, a burly man in a cap and muffler, echoes their views. He's earning enough at his job but here's a way of spending your excess and getting a profit back which won't be taxed. "Something useful to do, see?" Better than working overtime and getting time-and-a-half, which is taxed. He waves his arm to include all those around us. The syndicate of three boarding-house keepers; the bespectacled city clerk; the fat woman cuddling her sleepy little son ("There's a good boy, come to your Ma. I hope your Dad's got to the tote in time. We'll have a nice kepper when we get home."); the dreary carping married couple ("Oh, leave Mr. Burke out of it, Fred, and let's look at the numbers."); the bus conductors and conductresses (they've been standing all day but seem tireless); the plain women scattered alone among the stands (the lights, the sound of other humans . . . anything is better than a lonely room and the tempting reek of the gas fire). They've all got plenty of ready cash, but there's nothing to spend it on. Such is the peculiar logic of Mammon that they want to make more without owning up to Dr. Dalton.

The attendant said the crowd was "average," on a big race night you couldn't move. In London there is greyhound racing every night of the week bar Sundays; on Thursdays six tracks function simultaneously, on Saturdays eight. There are also numerous tracks in the provinces. Entrance is cheap (the popular price is 2s.), racing takes place in the evenings after working hours, and the tracks are easily reached. A company owning three London stadiums made a profit of £432,500 last year. It is estimated over £318,000 of this will be taken in taxation. Profits, before all taxation, for the year ending April 30th, 1939, were £72,827. The company says: "It is a matter of common knowledge that the popularity of the sport is growing rapidly. . . . The Greyhound Racing Industry had probably been the heaviest contributor in relation to its size of Excess Profits Tax and therefore stands to benefit even more than other industries from the reduced rate of this tax during the present year, and its complete cancellation next year." A deputation from religious bodies is recently reported as having drawn the attention of the Home Secretary to the "extraordinary increase" in betting on dog racing.

I cannot say whether any backer does succeed in making a tax-free fortune but the presence of over 100 bookmakers in the cheapest part of the track I attended leads me to doubt it. Had I taken the trouble to bet, my "Dragoman" would have quadrupled my original stake if I had backed his three selections in each race for a place, but I should have lost an equivalent amount following his first selection alone for a win. On the other hand, Comrade "Grader" of the *Daily Worker* would have doubled my stake on his win selection, but I should have been slightly out of pocket if I had taken his advice for a win and a place. Gambling is a perplexing and worrying business.

Cold and tired, we came away to line up for trains and buses. The bus conductor was cheerful. "Come along, you lucky winners," he called, "hurry along please." But presumably he had been working for the past six hours, not engaging in a recreational industry. Probably, I reflected, I had set up a new record for the stadium; I hadn't had a bet the whole evening. Also I fancy I was the only one who had thoroughly enjoyed himself. Except perhaps for the dogs.

APPENDIX II

SPECIMEN programmes of the Committee for Verse and Prose Recitation (known as "Poetry and Plays in Pubs") for the periods 17th November to 17th December 1948, and 27th May to 30th June 1949.

Date and Artistes	*Performance*	*Place*
November 1948.		
Wednesday, 17*th* John Carthy	*A Poetry Reading*	The King's Head, The Green, Winchmore Hill, N. 21
Sunday, 21*st* Natalie Moya and Gerik Schejelderup	*A Poetry Reading*	The Load of Hay, 94 Haverstock Hill, London, N.W.3
Friday, 26*th* John Carthy and David Pocock	*A Poetry Reading*	The Plough, Norwood Green, Southall, Middx.
Saturday, 27*th* The Taverners	*Doctor Knock* by Jules Romains (translated by Harley Granville-Barker)	St. Saviour's Hall, Alexandra Park, London, N.22.
Tuesday, 30*th* The Taverners	*Doctor Knock*	White Hart Hotel, Collier Row, Romford, Essex.
December 1948.		
Wednesday, 1*st* The Taverners	*Doctor Knock*	The Robin Hood, Longbridge Road, Dagenham, Essex.
Thursday, 2*nd* The Taverners	*Doctor Knock*	The King and Queen, Kimmeridge Road, Mottingham, S.E.9

Date and Artistes	*Performance*	*Place*
December 1948.		
Sunday, 5th The Taverners	*The Rivals* by Richard Brinsley Sheridan	Red Triangle Club, Greengate Street, Plaistow, E.13.
Monday, 6th The Taverners	*Cheezo* Lord Dunsany *An Unwilling Martyr* Anton Chekhov *A Phoenix too Frequent* Christopher Fry	The Olde Maypole, Barkingside, Essex.
Tuesday, 7th The Taverners	*A Dramatic Recital of Poems and Sketches*	The Three Blackbirds, St. John's Road, Boxmoor, Herts.
Wednesday, 8th The Taverners	*Cheezo* *An Unwilling Martyr* *A Phoenix too Frequent*	The Unicorn, Gidea Park, Romford, Essex.
Friday, 10th The Taverners	*Cheezo* *An Unwilling Martyr* *A Phoenix too Frequent*	The Railway Hotel, Hornchurch, Essex.
Monday, 13th The Taverners	*The Rivals*	The Welcome Inn, Well Hall Road, Eltham, S.E.9.
Wednesday, 15th The Taverners	*The Rivals*	The Cross Keys, High Street, Erith, Kent.
Thursday, 16th The Taverners	*Doctor Knock*	The King Alfred, Southend Lane, Catford, S.E.6.
Friday, 17th The Taverners	*Doctor Knock*	The Northover, Whitefoot Lane, Bromley, Kent.
May 1949.		
Friday, 27th John Marsh	*A Poetry Reading*	The Plough, Norwood Green, Middlesex.

Date and Artistes	*Performance*	*Place*
June 1949.		
Tuesday, 14th The Taverners	*Two Gentlemen of Verona* by William Shakespeare	The King Alfred, Southend Lane, Bellingham, S.E.6.
Wednesday, 15th The Taverners	*Two Gentlemen of Verona*	The Unicorn, Gidea Park, Romford, Essex.
Thursday, 16th The Taverners	*Two Gentlemen of Verona*	The Daylight Inn, Petts Wood, Kent.
Friday, 17th The Taverners	*Two Gentlemen of Verona*	The King and Queen, Kimmeridge Road, Mottingham, S.E.9
Monday, 20th The Taverners	*The Tempest* by William Shakespeare	The White Hart, Collier Row, Romford, Essex.
Wednesday, 22nd The Taverners	*The Tempest*	The Welcome Inn, Well Hall Road, Eltham, S.E.9.
Thursday, 23rd The Taverners	*Two Gentlemen of Verona*	The Northcote Arms, Northcote Avenue, Southall Middx.
Friday, 24th The Taverners	*The Tempest*	The Railway Hotel Hornchurch Essex.
Monday, 27th The Taverners	*Two Gentlemen of Verona*	The Olde Maypole, Barkingside, Essex.
Tuesday, 28th The Taverners	*The Tempest*	The Robin Hood, Longbridge Road, Dagenham, Essex.
Wednesday, 29th The Taverners	*The Tempest*	The Manor Hotel, Chingford Hatch, Essex.
Thursday, 30th The Taverners	*The Tempest*	The Northover, Whitefoot Lane, Bromley, Kent.

APPENDIX III

Programme played by Solomon at the one hundredth Tavern Concert on the 21st April 1948.

Prelude and Fugue in A minor	*Bach-Liszt*
Intermezzo in C major	*Brahms*
Rhapsody in G minor	*Brahms*
Carnaval Op. 9	*Schumann*
Prelude in G major	*Rachmaninoff*
Prelude in C minor	*Rachmaninoff*
An Old Musical Box	*de Severac*
Ballade in A flat	*Chopin*
Nocturne in D flat	*Chopin*
Valse in A flat	*Chopin*
Two Etudes	*Chopin*
Polonaise in A flat	*Chopin*

INDEX